Writing Baseball

THE SOUTHERN ILLINOIS UNIVERSITY PRESS SERIES

BREAKING INTO BASEBALL

Breaking *into* Baseball

Women and the
National Pastime

Jean Hastings Ardell
With a Foreword by Ila Borders

Southern Illinois University Press
Carbondale

Cover design: Gary Gore
Author photo: Rachel Hastings

Library of Congress Cataloging-in-Publication Data
Ardell, Jean Hastings, 1943–
    Breaking into baseball : women and the national pastime / Jean Hastings Ardell ; with
a foreword by Ila Borders.
        p. cm. — (Writing baseball)
    Includes bibliographical references and index.
    1. Women baseball players. 2. Baseball fans. 3. Baseball—History. I. Title. II. Series.
    GV880.7.A73 2005
    796.357'082—dc22
    ISBN 0-8093-2626-4 (cloth : alk. paper)
    ISBN 0-8093-2627-2 (pbk. : alk. paper)   2004019010

Printed on recycled paper. ♻

Writing Baseball Series Editor: Richard Peterson

Paperback cover, clockwise from upper left: 1869 women's baseball club at Peterboro, New York. National Baseball Hall of Fame Library, Cooperstown, N.Y.; Virginia Smoot of Columbia Junior High School tagged out by Mabel Harvey of McFarland, 1925. Photo: Library of Congress; the Young Ladies' Base Ball Club No. 1 of the 1890 and 1891 seasons. Photo: National Baseball Hall of Fame Library, Cooperstown, N.Y.; Baseball Annies. Photo: National Baseball Hall of Fame Library, Cooperstown, N.Y.; Jackie Mitchell and Babe Ruth, 1931. Photo: Transcendental Graphics/ruckerarchive.com.; Mary Dunn, owner of the Triple-A Baltimore Orioles. Babe Ruth Birthplace and Museum, Baltimore, Maryland. Photo: Leroy Merrikan; sportswriter Jeane Hofmann, 1942. Courtesy: William C. Greene/ *The Sporting News;* Stephanie Leathers, publisher of *Bleacher Banter,* and friends, Wrigley Field. Photo: Stephanie Leathers; Tina "Sweetbread" Baker, Sonja "Wishbone" Parker, and tally-keeper Eileen Sherwood, townball players, Cooperstown, N.Y. Photo: Author's collection; members of the Colorado Silver Bullets. Photo: Laura Wulf; left-hander Ila Borders. Photo: Dan Wiza—Madison Black Wolf 1996–2000; umpire Pam Postema. Photo: Russell Gates, *Phoenix Gazette,* c. April 1983. Used with permission. Permission does not imply endorsement; Toni Stone of the Indianapolis Clowns of the Negro American League, 1953. Photo: National Baseball Hall of Fame Library, Cooperstown, N.Y.; Brooklyn Dodgers fan Hilda Chester. Photo: National Baseball Hall of Fame Library, Cooperstown, N.Y; Effa Manley, co-owner of the Newark Eagles of the Negro National League. Photo: National Baseball Hall of Fame Library, Cooperstown, N.Y.; umpire Amanda Clement. Photo: National Baseball Hall of Fame Library, Cooperstown, N.Y.

For Dan

Our children

*And our newest
generation of fans:
Amanda and Kaitlyn
Garrett and Trevor
Victoria and Shea*

Contents

List of Illustrations xi
Foreword xiii
     Ila Borders
Preface xvii
Acknowledgments xix

Introduction 1
1. In the Beginning 8
2. In the Stands: Fans 28
3. In the Shadows: Baseball Annies 51
4. For Love of the Game: Amateur Players 79
5. For Love and Money: Professional Players 102
6. Behind the Plate: Umpires 136
7. In the Front Office: Club Owners and Executives 161
8. In the Press Box: Women in the Media 190
Epilogue: Into the Future 216

Chronology 233
Notes 239
Index 263

List of Illustrations

Following page 78
An 1869 women's baseball club, Peterboro, New York
The Young Ladies' Base Ball Club No. 1
Umpire Amanda Clement
Elsie Tydings purchases the first ticket ever sold for a World Series in Washington, D.C.
A girls' junior high school game during a 1925 Field Day
Babe Ruth and adoring women
Jackie Mitchell, Lou Gehrig, and Babe Ruth
Mary Dunn, owner of the Baltimore Orioles
Effa Manley, co-owner of the Newark Eagles
Sportswriter Jeane Hofmann and New York Yankees' manager Joe McCarthy
Brooklyn Dodgers fan Hilda Chester
All-American Girls Baseball League game
Toni Stone, Indianapolis Clowns
Minor league umpire Pam Postema
Julie Croteau, Colorado Silver Bullets
Four team members, Colorado Silver Bullets
Left-hander Ila Borders
Chicago Cubs fan Stephanie Leathers and friends
Linda Alvarado, co-owner of the Colorado Rockies, and Sugar Beet Leagues veteran Victor Duran
Kim Ng, assistant general manager, Los Angeles Dodgers
Renel Brooks-Moon, public-address announcer, San Francisco Giants
Umpires Perry Barber, Theresa Cox, and Brenda Glaze
Town ball players Tina "Sweetbread" Baker, Sonja "Wishbone" Parker, and Eileen Sherwood
Film director Penny Marshall

Foreword

Ila Borders

WHEN I FIRST MET JEAN ARDELL, I was playing freshman baseball for the Southern California College Vanguards in Costa Mesa, California. It was a February afternoon in 1994, a day when my whole world changed. I had just pitched and won my first game in college. Reporters from all over the world were there, and the media attention was extremely intense. Walking away from all the interviews and questions, I only remembered Jean's. They were not your basic, "How does it feel to be a girl playing in a man's game?" As Mindy Rich, the co-owner of the Triple-A Buffalo Bisons, alludes to in Chapter VII of this book, you cannot view yourself as a woman in a man's profession and succeed. Jean understood this. She asked questions that went deep beneath the surface and was knowledgeable about the game and its history. Since that day, I went on to play three more seasons of college ball and three-and-a-half seasons of men's professional baseball, primarily in the unaffiliated Northern League. Along the way, I have had the privilege to become friends with Jean and her family, through whom I not only learned more about the game of baseball away from the diamond, but began to see how baseball reflects our American culture.

In reading this book, I learned about other women's contributions to the game I love and, even more, what made them succeed or fail. Many of these women established building blocks so that others, like me, were able to proceed further in baseball. For example, how far would umpire Pam Postema have gone if it weren't for some of her predecessors—whom some say were unsuccessful? I believe that anyone who works hard, opens people's minds, and makes a positive impact on others is successful. Maybe Pam was supposed to make it, just as I felt I had the chance to— but, if anything, she paved a path for others, like minor-league umpires Ria Cortesio and Shanna Kook, to have a better chance. As long as women keep coming through who have the love for the game and for what they are doing, can withstand brutal criticism and scrutiny and tough physical demands, and can work twice as hard as a man out there, then it is possible to one day have a woman make it to the major leagues as a player or umpire.

Jean also discusses an issue that no one usually does—Baseball Annies. I do not believe that people understand how much Baseball Annies affect the game of baseball and players' families. Jean shows how much of it takes place, how the men view the groupies, and how the Annies view the players. She tells of an incident in which one player reputedly performed poorly after spending the night with one of his Baseball Annies. During my three-and-a-half years in professional baseball, this happened all the time. There were players on my team who said they were playing ball just because of the unlimited amount of sex they could get. Because I kept my mouth shut around their wives, they trusted me and told me stories. One story I could tell is sad, and yet, in a weird, sick sense, funny, too. On road trips, one teammate had a different girl almost every night. He would tell each Baseball Annie that it was his birthday, and she would buy him gifts and birthday cake for the whole team. So after every away game, we would wait and see what kind of gift he got, and what sort of cake we got. I felt bad for the wives and Baseball Annies, but my allegiance was to my teammates.

Baseball is a very tough game for women to break into for many reasons. One that was hard for me to balance was the issue of feminism. Most of the players think that you are out there for woman's rights. They cannot understand why a woman loves the game just as much as they do. The reason I got along so well with the players was because they came to see, day after day, that I was not out there for any reason other than love of the game. On the flip side, some female fans, and women's magazines and organizations were against me. They could not understand why I was not speaking out more for women. Little did they know that you can make a greater positive impact for the present, and for the future, by showing players and managers that you know how to keep your mouth shut. I found it difficult that so many women were against me, as I not only had to prove myself to the men, but also to my own gender. Jean talks about this in the section about Pam Postema. Pam umpired because she loved it and was good at it. After she was released, she had to enter the world of feminism to get what she wanted.

Another issue I faced was how women in baseball look and behave. Jean captures how this issue affects how far we go. As Jean mentions, one of my teammates wanted me to wear a dress. *You have got to be kidding me,*

I thought. Just as pitcher Bob Knepper made his statement about Postema doing a great job but still believed a woman should not dream of umpiring. Jean discusses how certain physical attributes and styles may have held back some women in baseball, while others prospered. Men never have to defend their sexual preference or look a certain way. This was the biggest reason why I never cut my hair short. It would just be one more reason to add fuel to a fire that was pressing on me.

Jean also discusses a topic that I had never heard of before—women in the front office. She shows how women were first given the opportunity there and how those opportunities have changed and why. It always perplexed me why retired players and managers were given the job of general manager when they had no clue as to how to do so. This book gives us great examples of women doing great jobs and getting close to becoming the first female general manager—not because society thinks it is the right thing to do or because of Title IX, but because they are best suited for the job.

The best message that I got from this book is how much women have affected and contributed to the game, and how baseball shows us the evolving history of our nation. We have gone from all white men playing to all minorities, from girls in Little League all the way into women's professional leagues and umpires. This book reflects how women's role in baseball has evolved, how it has changed American culture, and how it reflects the future shape of our society. Our game covers many countries, all ethnicities, genders, and social class. I am proud to be a small part of this book.

Preface

I REMEMBER THE DAY CLEARLY. It was a Saturday morning, early in April, and I was nine years old. I looked out the window of our garden apartment in Queens, New York, over a sliver of old woodland to the green diamond on 78th Street. Some kids were choosing up sides. The pile of leather mitts and wooden bats suggested that a game of baseball was about to be played. Girls were there, too. If I hurried, maybe I could play. I threw on a long-sleeved blue shirt, a white tee shirt over it, and my oldest jeans.

"Don't be gone long," my mother sang out.

"Don't worry," I yelled, as I ran out the door.

But we played all morning, and I arrived home late for lunch.

We played that afternoon, and I was late for dinner.

We played all summer.

For the first time in my life, I was on a team. I also had a crush on the boy who pitched. I tried explaining to my mother the importance of it all, but we never did reach an understanding.

"Don't be gone long," she kept calling.

Sure, Mom. But I've been gone on baseball, and trying to explain why, ever since.

Acknowledgments

THE WRITING OF THIS BOOK would have been impossible but for the help of many people. I am abidingly grateful to the men and women whom I interviewed during the course of my research. Their candor deepened my appreciation of what it takes for a woman to make her way in baseball. Thanks, too, to the members of the Society for American Baseball Research, in particular Evelyn Begley, Dick Beverage, Darryl Brock, Richard Crepeau, Robert H. Davis, Cappy Gagnon, Larry Gerlach, Jim Glennie, Roland Hemond, Skip McAfee, Andy McCue, Dorothy Jane Mills, Yoichi Nagata, Roberta Newman, Anna Newton, John Pastier, Mark Rucker, Jay Sanford, Dan Sullivan, and Jim Tootle. Bill Kirwin's annual Nine Spring Training Conference always offered a collegial gathering place in which to present aspects of my research; Bill and his wife Wendy have my appreciation for their encouragement and hospitality.

For their cordial assistance, I thank the staffs of the Carl A. Kroch Library of Cornell University; the Milton S. Eisenhower Library, the Johns Hopkins University; Tim Wiles, Director of Research, the National Baseball Hall of Fame Library; Raymond Doswell, curator, the Negro Leagues Baseball Museum; Greg Schwalenberg, curator, The Babe Ruth Birthplace and Museum; the Newport Beach Public Library; the New York Public Library; the Northern Indiana Historical Society; and the San Francisco Public Library. Thanks also to Terry Cannon and Larry Goren of the Baseball Reliquary; Jim Haines of the Behavior Research Center; Steve Gietschier, Senior Managing Editor, Research; *The Sporting News;* the News Research Center of the *Cleveland Plain Dealer;* and Jim Arehart and Keith Zirbel of *Referee* magazine. I am also indebted for their research assistance to Luz de Alba, Deborah Silverman, Nancy Cates, Michael D. Sharpe, and Matthew Denton Stevens, and for help with translations from the Japanese by Doreen Criswell and Hikaru Shapiro. Laurie Liss, literary agent and Yankee fan, supplied enthusiasm and wise counsel. I thank the staff of Southern Illinois University Press, particularly Karl and Kathy Kageff and Pete Peterson, whose editorial care and advice helped so very much. Thanks are also due to the ninth-inning readers who helped with the final proofreading: Dan Ardell, Nancy Harrington, Jody Olsen, and Barbara Peckenpaugh.

The support of other writers meant a great deal. Here I thank Thomas Curwen, Shearlean and Bob Duke, George Gmelch, Barbara Goulter, Marjorie Coverly Luesebrink, Noel Riley Fitch, Tammy Lechner, Elinor Nauen (who recommended Southern Illinois University Press), Charlie Vascellaro, and the men and women of Allegores. The inspiration for this book came during my time in the University of Southern California's Master of Professional Writing Program, and appreciation is due to James Ragan and his staff for their encouragement. I owe a particular debt to Gwyneth Kerr Erwin, who never let friendship stand in the way of incisive editorial comment. My family, Jeff and Sonét, Julie, Bob, Matt, and Art and Rachel, understood the importance of the occasional phone call to ask *how's it going?* My husband Dan provided the steady love and patience that enabled me to see the book through. He has all of my gratitude.

BREAKING INTO BASEBALL

Introduction

THERE ARE SEVEN WAYS A WOMAN CAN involve herself in the game of baseball. She can play it. She can umpire. She can own a team or work in some other capacity in the front office. She can root from the stands, as fan. She can marry into it. Failing that, she can sleep with ball players, as Baseball Annies do for a night or a season or two. Or she can make a story about the game, as filmmaker, beat writer, or sportscaster. But baseball has traditionally been a man's game, you say—played by men, officiated by men, run by men, and enjoyed by men. Nevertheless, we periodically hear of women who seek to take part in some way in the manly game of baseball. I was one of them.

I was born into a bifurcated baseball family. On their honeymoon, my father took my mother to see his beloved New York Giants at the Polo Grounds. It was August, during a heat wave, and the Dodgers had come over from Brooklyn for a doubleheader. Beer flowed, tempers frayed on the field and in the stands, and a riot ensued. My mother never returned. As their only child, by default I became my father's baseball companion. One of my earliest memories is that of racketing alongside my father in companionable anticipation on the elevated bound from our home in Queens to the promised land of the Polo Grounds. Dad was a quiet man who sometimes disappeared for days without explanation, but at the ballpark he underwent a transformation. There he relaxed as he reminisced about the Giants' glory years under John J. McGraw during the

1

1920s. With persistence, I could usually elicit a story or two about his adventures back then as a young man-about-Manhattan. "Tell me about the McGraw days," I'd plead, and he would.

The game relieved the tensions in our triangulated family in other ways. Whatever expectations I struggled with at home—*what's this D in math? . . . don't talk back to your mother . . . sit up straight at the table*—fell away at the ballpark, where adding up the hits, runs, and errors was easy with my father's help, where it was OK to question parental sanity (how can you root for *Sal Maglie?*), where there was no etiquette to eating a hot dog.

At age seven, I grieved my father by choosing the New York Yankees as my team. And by age ten, when I ought to have known better, I announced my dream of playing second base in Yankee Stadium. That year, as Marilyn Monroe shimmied across movie screens to the tune of "Diamonds Are a Girl's Best Friend," I was calculating that I'd be ready to take over Billy Martin's job at second when he retired. My father, bless him, never pointed out the lack of women on the field or my utter lack of talent. In those early years, baseball brought me his companionship and acceptance.

The game could not transcend the gulf that opened between us when I became a teenager, however. By then I realized my presence was unwelcome on any field of play, even my neighborhood diamond, and my father seemed discomfited by my new interest in the players as men rather than their batting averages and ERAs. Furthermore, none of my girlfriends considered baseball cool. What *was* cool was the Brooklyn Paramount, where acts like Chuck Berry and the Platters and a new sound called rock 'n' roll were in play. Maybe those early jaunts into Manhattan triggered a yen for travel; for now, with a subway pass and the city before me, I took to cutting class to travel with like-minded friends into the farthest reaches of Brooklyn and the Bronx. I put away childish things, including baseball; or so I thought. In high school, I came up with the idea of becoming a baseball writer. The parental front united. My father informed me that no daughter of his was going into a locker room. According to my mother, I was far too shy to attempt the reporter's job of asking personal questions of strangers. *What was I thinking?*

It took years to understand what I was thinking—that I wanted a piece of the game. And it took more time to understand that this was a reasonable desire. Thanks to my father, I had been imprinted with baseball at an early age; ever after the game informed my life. I raised my sons on baseball. We followed it on television, they began accumulating baseball cards (I swore to them I would never throw out their collections as my mother had mine) and played in the local youth league. I recall summers of perennial carpools, my car filled with boys who smelled like damp puppies, and twilight box suppers in the bleachers at the Community Youth Center. Watching one son struggle through a troubled summer, I confess to sending up a silent prayer: *God, my kid needs a base hit.* God provided: a double down the left field line. Such memories soften the edge of others—of divorce and financial worries and the realization that just because I had turned thirty did not mean I was finished growing up.

In 1979, I met Dan Ardell, who had his cup of coffee with the Angels during their inaugural year, 1961, in Los Angeles. We started out as friends, swapping the stories of our pasts. During college he and his twin brother had played for cross-town rivals, the University of Southern California and the University of California at Los Angeles, where both indulged in the usual locker-room epithets from their respective dugouts. Innocent of irony, Dan confided he would occasionally even question his brother's maternal lineage. This was hilarious. Clearly we both lived in the house of baseball, if in very different rooms. We married two years later and soon after traveled to Cooperstown, where we perused his line of immortality in the Baseball Hall of Fame: *Dan Ardell, 1961, Los Angeles Angels: BA .250, AB 4, H 1, R 1, BB 1, SO 2.* Dan spent four years in the minor leagues, and, of course, his baseball history is far different from mine. In some ways, though, I favor my own memories: I never did challenge Billy Martin, or anyone else, to start at second base, but neither do I awaken in a sweat at three in the morning because I'm digging for first and cannot quite get there.

As I discern the patterns of my life, I see baseball as a unifying thread. The game connects my husband and sons with my father, who died before they were born. When times are uncertain, when communication falters, the language of baseball remains a comfortable litany I share with the people I love. Even my mother, never fluent in the game, chose these words to clarify my father's mysterious absences during my childhood: "Your dad had Pete Rose disease," she explained. "He lived to gamble and couldn't stop. It was a hard thing." My mother had not wanted to tell me this because she feared it would "ruin" my memory of my father, but her words did no such thing. It was time to forgive him his shortcomings, and for dying young, as I hope he forgave me mine: dropping out of college, rooting for the Yankees. During the writing of this book, I also came to appreciate my mother's grace in the matter of baseball. How many mornings did my father and I ignore her as we pored over the sports pages while she sliced grapefruit and brewed coffee? How many hot summer afternoons did we wave her a quick goodbye as we left for the ballpark?

The idea for this book came unbidden on one of those drizzly, late winter afternoons when it seems as if spring and baseball will never arrive. How many other women, I wondered, dreamed as I once had of playing second base or of sportswriting? It was 1992, the "Year of the Woman," and critics were debating the merits of Penny Marshall's forthcoming film *A League of Their Own.* Some wanted to know: *who would pay to see a movie about women playing baseball?*

It turned out that plenty of people did because the film became the best-selling baseball movie in history. Using our frequent-flier air miles (much as I had once used my subway pass to explore the cityscape of New York), I traveled the country, asking strangers the personal questions against which my mother once cautioned me. Beginning at the Hall of Fame Library in Cooperstown, New York, I discovered that women are as closely connected to baseball's origins as the ivy that clings to Wrigley Field's brick walls. At spring training in Arizona's Cactus League, I mentioned the idea for this book to Joe and Audrie Garagiola. Joe responded that former minor league umpire Pam Postema should have made it to the majors. "It's about more than Postema or the All-American Girls Baseball League of the 1940s," I replied. "It's about everyone—women writers, filmmakers, and historians, front-office executives and owners, why female fans are so loyal to the game, and even groupies. The whole story."

Audrie Garagiola looked me in the eye and said, "Write it."

I could not have chosen a better time. The 1990s proved to be the breakthrough decade for women in baseball. When I joined the Society for American Baseball Research (SABR), I learned it had been founded in 1971 by twelve men. (Their wives, it is popularly said, soon organized the Society Against Baseball Research.) At my first SABR national convention in 1992, I walked into a roomful of men. Ten years later that had changed. Claudia Perry, SABR's first female president, presided over the 2002 convention in Boston, Leslie Heaphy chaired the Women in Base-

ball Committee, and Evelyn Begley became the first woman to receive
SABR's highest honor for service, the Bob Davids Award. Begley, who is
active in SABR's Casey Stengel chapter in New York City, says that her
chapter enjoys the support of lots of women, such as Roberta Newman,
who teaches at New York University, and Ernestine Miller, a sports historian "happily sidetracked into baseball," who sits on the Board of Directors of the Babe Ruth Birthplace and Baseball Center. That the men
and women of SABR work together closely and effectively bodes well for
the organization and for baseball research.

I spoke with female umpires from Florida to Arizona. For example, Julie
Zeller Ware discussed her six-night-a-week commitment to Little League
umpiring in the Phoenix area. Ware believes that her son and daughter
learned important lessons through her work on the field. They have seen
their mother stand up for herself, they saw her close study of the rules of
baseball translate into confidence on the field, and they saw her thrive
in a traditionally male role. Veteran minor league umpires Theresa Cox
and Pam Postema frankly shared their experiences in baseball.

Before her death in 1996, I interviewed Toni Stone, who played outfield and second base—*second base!*—for the Indianapolis Clowns and
Kansas City Monarchs during the waning years of the Negro Leagues.
Stone, who grew up a tomboy misfit in Depression-era Minnesota, made
a career of playing professional baseball at a time when opportunities for
black women were severely limited. As she traveled with various ball
clubs, she took to visiting libraries and museums, educating herself on
the history of blacks and, in the process, transforming her sense of what
a black woman could accomplish.

In Bethesda, Maryland, during a rainy Labor Day weekend in 1999,
former players from the Colorado Silver Bullets, high-school girls who
play boys' varsity baseball, and women from as far away as Japan competed in an amateur tournament hosted by the Washington Metropolitan Women's Baseball League. Some women played hurt, some played
pregnant, and all played for plain joy. Their passion for the game recalls
the frequently ignored last words of Jacques Barzun's oft-quoted lines
from *God's Country and Mine:* "Whoever would understand the heart and
mind of America had better learn baseball, *the rules and realities of the
game—and do it by watching some high school or small-town teams* (ital-
ics added). Those who would understand the lot of contemporary American women would do well to study these amateur baseball leagues: the

grit of the athletes and the difficulties they continue to face in playing this perceived man's game.

The variety of women's accomplishments in baseball is much greater than that of player or umpire. Visit any part of the country and you are likely to find a woman working in some capacity once deemed for men only: as agent, announcer, trainer, groundskeeper, or scout; as artist, film-maker, or biographer. Even MLB's Washington, D.C., lobbyist is a woman, Lucy Calautti. When I visited Baltimore's Oriole Park at Camden Yards, I learned that it owes part of its reputation as one of MLB's premier ballparks to Janet Marie Smith, an architect and urban planner. Smith explained, "I'm a fan of cities, and baseball is a fine mirror in which to look at a community. Sometimes, if you change the image of a place, you can change its foundation and its heart." Roland Hemond, the Orioles general manager at the time, said, Smith "did a masterful job. Because of her, there's a lot of the woman's touch in the park. I consider her an absolute genius in her field."

Whatever their area of work in baseball, the women I spoke with around the country were, at the heart of it, fans—many of whom tended to think of themselves as a nut-case minority, as I once had. The truth, I discovered, is quite different. Female fans have always been essential to the game. As the editor of the *Sporting News* declared in 1969, "the women—and baseball can say God bless 'em, stick with the diamond." Since then, as professional hockey, basketball, and football have cut fur-ther into baseball's male fan base, women have continued to "stick with the diamond." Today women make up between 30 and 40 percent of the fans at Major League ballparks and about one third of the game's televi-sion audience. The Minnesota Twins director of corporate marketing told me that some of the team's best fans are young women, well versed in the game, willing to look beyond the won/lost column, and tending to be more loyal. She estimated that 48 percent of Twins fans are female. Such numbers suggest that it is women who bolster whatever claim baseball still has as the national pastime.

It has been said that the basic theme of all literature is this: somebody wants something that is denied them, and they must find a way to get it. That is the theme of this book. The histories of early women in baseball illustrate the barriers they faced in their struggle for inclusion as play-ers, in the front office and press box, and even as fans, as the game took hold in America in the latter half of the nineteenth century. The effects of Baseball Annies upon the game are also explored, for they carry serious, if indirect, ramifications. Baseball historians will note that I came up short in the attempt to be comprehensive, however. Authors before me, among them Gai Ingham Berlage, Barbara Gregorich, and Susan E. Johnson, have published excellent detailed histories of the game's female pioneers, and I direct interested readers to their works. Nor did space permit the inclusion of every compelling story of women's involvement with baseball. Such omissions, it is hoped, will be covered by future writers. The accounts of contemporary female umpires, players, front office executives, and sportswriters demonstrate the barriers that remain and the ways women find to surmount them. These women are aware of their responsibility to instruct and inspire the next generation of girls. For example, Janet Smith once brought two local girls, La'Leta Foster and Phoebe Legg, to Camden Yards for Take Your Daughter to Work Day. "Boys grow up expecting they're going to go to work," Smith explained to *USA Today Baseball Weekly*, "but girls don't always get to see the whole array of opportunities available to them." After Smith's two guests observed the women working in the Orioles front office, La'Leta concluded, "I think there should be more women in baseball, but I want to be a lawyer." Baseball may see her yet.

We know that baseball is a game of tension, between offense and defense, cerebral strategy and bursts of thrilling action. Women experience the additional tension of resistance as they strive to participate in the game they love best. That said, I have come to believe that, at its best, baseball also offers a chance for reconciliation in the ancient wars between the sexes. My field research, correspondence, and interviews show the good that can come when someone—these days it is as likely to be a mother as a father—takes a young girl to her first ball game. This book was written for all fans, men and women, who understand that a doubleheader at the ballpark is the best possible way to spend a Sunday afternoon.

1 In the Beginning

AS THE GLOOM OF THE 1994 players' strike settled over the baseball world, Lil Levant arrived in Cooperstown, New York. She had always been a fan, schooled since infancy by her mother and her grandmother in baseball gospel according to the Chicago Cubs. Distressed over the game's present condition, Levant, a Los Angeles–based sales representative for public television, wanted to get away from the unhappiness for a while. So she made a pilgrimage to the town where Abner Doubleday reputedly invented baseball in 1839. Here, at the home of the National Baseball Hall of Fame and Museum, she hoped to find solace in the game's grand old past. She parked on the outskirts of town and began to walk the shady streets, where cats laze on the porches of early nineteenth-century clapboard houses and church bells toll the hours.

Suddenly the sound of bat on ball cracked the air. "I stopped where I was and burst into tears," Levant recalled. "I'd forgotten about Doubleday Field being there." Following the buzz of the crowd, she discovered a game underway between a team from Japan and some locals and made herself at home in the stands. She later wondered at her reaction, saying, "I don't know why I get so emotional about all this, but baseball is just so beautiful."[1]

Women find the game beautiful for many of the same reasons that men do. After all, testosterone is not required to appreciate the diamond's clean geometry, the tensions between power and pitching, the beauty of a field's freshly mown grass beneath a cloudless June sky, or the mounting drama of Game 7 of the World Series. Fans, male and female, appreciate that baseball is played in natural time, without a running clock. In other ways, however, women experience baseball quite differently than men do. For example, many women prefer baseball to other, more combative sports such as football and hockey. Here is what the Atlanta Braves reported in its 1979 survey of female fans: Singer Toni Tenille said, "I admire the game—there is no intentional violence—not like football or other sports." And Jackie Robinson's widow, Rachel, said, "As a wife and later as a mother, I worried about contact sports—I preferred to see my husband and sons participate in non-contact sports."[2] Another essential gender distinction was noticed by art critic Vanalyne Green when she first entered a ballpark (Yankee Stadium, 1984): heterosexual women appreciate the presence of those marvelous ballplayers on the field in a way that their lesbian sisters and heterosexual brethren do not. Elinor Nauen's anthology *Diamond Are a Girls Best Friend: Women Writers on Baseball* offers numerous testimonials on this point. In her short story of 1912, "A Bush League Hero," Edna Ferber writes, ""when I say that Rudie Schlachweiler was a dream even in his baseball uniform, with a dirty brown streak right up the side of his pants where he had slid for base, you may know that the girls camped on the grounds during the season."[3] In "Why I Love Baseball," Carol Tavris writes, "As a group, baseball players are beautiful to behold. They do not have to be padded or born to the size of the Incredible Hulk; baseball players wear simple, sleek uniforms that reveal the natural physique."[4] And as Bernadette Mayer muses in her ode to Carlton Fisk: "Oh the legs of a catcher!"[5] Women, Nauen suggests, get more out of baseball than men, "who mostly aren't interested in ogling."[6] The fact that the ballpark offers women a safe place from which to eye ballplayers may not be, in these days, a politically correct idea, but it remains a distinguishing factor in women's appreciation of the game. Ballplayers understand this, to the chagrin of some chroniclers of the game. For example, Eliot Asinof, the author of *Eight Men Out*, regrets the penchant that many of today's players show for tight-fitting uniforms. In this, he fears, a player gives up an advantage on close pitches: "The pitch brushes your loose-fitting uniform, and you get first base! Tight pants changed the face of American spectator sports," declared

Asinof. "There is a tailor in the locker room who measures the players' butts and thighs with a micrometer. . . . Every ball player gets fitted so that he can be as appealing as possible to the women in the stands."[7]

Vanalyne Green discovered another gender distinction when she first visited Yankee Stadium. She still remembers her involuntary Oh-my-God sense of astonishment as she looked down at the field. *Why,* she wondered, *had no one told her that it was shaped like a womb?* For Green, entering the ballpark felt "like walking into a body, a closed space, so from the get-go it's gendered female in a sort of deeply unconscious way," she explained. "Then there were all the circles and spheres, and the cyclical nature of baseball. . . . The first time I ever saw all the zeros at the beginning of the season, it was 'Oh, my God' all over again. Rebirth, the idea that you get to try all over again, was another aspect of baseball that was not male."[8] (As we will see shortly, Green was on to something here.) She became so engaged by the game that she spent three years filming the video *A Spy in the House That Ruth Built,* in which she explores the tensions between baseball's elemental femaleness and her sense of being an intruder in a game dominated by men.

Men and women who discover the game at an early age are both prone to serious cases of baseball nostalgia, yet even here gender distinctions apply. "The game of baseball," writes historian Doris Kearns Goodwin, "has always been linked in my mind with the mystic texture of childhood, with the sounds and smells of summer nights and with the memories of my father." In her memoir *Wait till Next Year,* Goodwin examines her 1950s New York childhood through the lens of baseball, recalling that "when I was six, my father gave me a bright-red scorebook that opened my heart to the game of baseball."[9] To be a young fan in that time and place was to believe in certain verities: New York was the center of the baseball universe and your father would always be around for another ball game. But baseball teaches the young fan much about loss. Over time, these youthful certainties come undone. Teams move, heroes fade away, and fathers do not live forever. We hang on to those early days as comfort against the unknowable future.

For women, such memories suggest a further poignancy. There is a golden time between the ages of eight and ten when a girl's self-confidence soars. Unlike boys, whose self-confidence builds through adolescence into adulthood, a girl's tends to peak just before adolescence: "Nature and society conspire to allow a girl to flourish," writes psychologist

Emily Hancock in *The Girl Within.* "Often a tomboy . . . . [h]eady with the power that comes from genuine competence, she brims with initiative. The faster she can run, the higher she can jump, the more she is admired."[10] The young tomboy who dreams of playing second base or of becoming the next Vin Scully foresees no barriers. Introduced to baseball at an early age, she believes she can understand the game as well as any boy and compete on any field. Through baseball, she acquires the ability to more fully take part in American culture. Kimberly Rae Connor was ten years old when the man who later became her stepfather brought her to a Washington Senators game. Connor, who grew up to become a professor of religion, writes:

> My stepfather never once patronized me or assumed I could not appreciate the game the way he did. He gave me a sense of entitlement to baseball—indeed to anything customarily the domain of men, and made me feel like nothing was beyond my ken. His lessons translated into other arenas as well—politics, scholarship, religion. But it was through baseball that I first learned it and came to believe it.[11]

For girls like Connor and Goodwin, the memory of childhood days at the ballpark weaves itself into the fabric of their lives. Yearning for a past retrievable only in memory, however, can be a bittersweet exercise for many young women. Despite inspiring them to dream big and move into other arenas, Organized Baseball's traditional attitude toward women has been ambivalent and even exclusionary. In the game's earliest innings, even female spectators were not always welcome. In recent decades, as women began to move into the press box and the front office, they were often figurative right fielders, out where the action least often occurs. Even the most intrepid groundbreakers have often ended up in court rather than on the diamond. In 1967, Bernice Gera began five years of litigation to win the chance to umpire in the minor leagues. In 1974, lawsuits filed in fifteen states finally prompted Little League Baseball to accept girls; today Little League alumna still face formidable barriers when they seek to continue playing baseball rather than switching to softball in high school. And in 1991, after umpire Pam Postema was fired despite thirteen strong seasons in the minor leagues, she sued Major League Baseball for discrimination. Then she published a memoir entitled *You've Got to Have Balls to Make It in This League,* in which she rails, "The new Postema couldn't care less about baseball and all that

America's pastime shit."[12] Why do women care so for a game that seems to care so little for them? Understandably, those imprinted with the game at a young age persist in their dreams and goals because baseball is so much a part of their personal history. But the reasons go deeper than that. Sport history shows that women enjoy a unique connection to baseball, one sensed by Vanalyne Green, which dates to antiquity.

First, it must be reiterated that Abner Doubleday did not invent the game in Cooperstown in 1839. In recent decades, historians such as Charles Alexander, Harold Peterson, Dorothy and Harold Seymour, and others have shown this account to be a marketing ploy dating to the early twentieth century, promoted by boosters such as Albert G. Spalding, who wanted the game's origins set in an all-American place. Contemporary historians credit Alexander J. Cartwright with adapting the rules of town ball, a nineteenth-century recreational game popular in the Northeast, to develop an early version of today's game. Thus, the first documented game of baseball was not played in a Cooperstown pasture in 1839 but between the New York Knickerbocker Base Ball Club and another New York team at Elysian Fields in Hoboken, New Jersey, on June 19, 1846.[13] Before town ball were English games like cricket and rounders (still played by schoolchildren today), and before that, stoolball, and before that, primitive stick-and-ball games. Baseball's origins have been traced back thousands of years and contain distinctly feminine qualities. A consideration of these origins is not a sentimental stroll through history; it challenges the national pastime's masculine tradition. If baseball is rooted in the feminine, then women have a legitimate claim to full participation.

> *Mohammedans may have their Mecca, but Americans have Cooperstown.*
> —Dorothy and Harold Seymour
> *Baseball: The Early Years*

Cooperstown, despite its discredited myth of origin, remains the best place to begin an examination of baseball's past. Home of Doubleday Field, the National Baseball Hall of Fame and Museum, and the National Baseball Hall of Fame Library, where scholars encamp to sift through yesterday's stories, the town offers up both the game's imagined past and its more complex history. You cannot hurry to Cooperstown. To get there you meander along two-lane roads through the rolling hills of central New York State, past dairy farms, orchards, and hamlets settled by the Dutch in the 1600s. By the time you reach the village on the shores of

Lake Otsego, it is easy to slip back in time. George Washington passed through here during the Revolutionary War, and the town is named for the father of the early American author James Fenimore Cooper, who romanticized the area in his *Leatherstocking Tales*. Generations of prosperous residents have tended the area's heritage fastidiously. During baseball season, baskets of red geraniums adorn the downtown lampposts, and the houses and shops are as trim as a Dutch farmwife's kitchen. A yellow Labrador retriever, glistening from a swim in the lake, ambles her way home. With its single traffic signal, Cooperstown is a remote Eden away from the noisy throb of the cities beyond the hills. A woman alone could get lost here and feel safe. Abner Doubleday did not invent baseball here, but someone should have—Cooperstown is Americana perfected.

The place positively exudes baseball nostalgia. You can see the effects in the eyes of bemused fans as they pose for pictures by the brook bordering Doubleday Field, "the birthplace of baseball," and shop along Main Street at Home Plate (baseball memorabilia), Seventh Inning Stretch (baseball cards), and Third Base (caps, jerseys, and jackets). At the Cooperstown Bat Company, fans are urged to "select a remembrance of your visit to baseball's hometown." Stores like the Cooperstown Baseball Co. sell everything from vintage baseball books to T-shirts of your favorite team. (You want the 1927 Yankees? No problem.) Hungry fans can pause at the Short Stop Restaurant or the Doubleday Café. A fan comes to pay her respects and ends up purchasing shopping bags full of souvenirs.

The success of Penny Marshall's film of 1992, *A League of Their Own*, expanded marketing opportunities here: Mickey's Place sells a replica of the cap worn by the Rockford Peaches of the All-American Girls Baseball League ($19.95). And Pro Image Photo reports a surge of interest from women wishing to be photographed in the full uniform of the Rockford club ($29.95 for an 8 x 10). "We've gone baseball boutique," complained a longtime resident whose heart does not beat to the rhythm of the game: "You can't get away from it."

PRIMAL BASEBALL

In sedate contrast to the kitsch-filled shops, farther down Main Street sits the brick edifice known as the National Baseball Hall of Fame and Museum. The museum does more than house the game's sanctified artifacts; it is dedicated to interpreting baseball's past. The exhibit of the game's origins opens with these words, "In the beginning, shortly after God created heaven and earth, man and woman, there were stones to throw and sticks to swing."[14] The first illustration, showing almond-eyed girls who appear to be playing a ball game, is a reproduction of a drawing found in an Egyptian tomb at Beni Hassan. As sports historian Allen Guttmann writes, "The famous eleventh-dynasty tomb of the Cheti at Beni Hassan contains murals showing girls or women astride the backs of other females and tossing balls back and forth." Guttmann goes on to speculate: "If the young participants also turned their pastimes into contests, as modern boys and girls do, then we have one of the earliest depictions of women's sports."[15] The museum's exhibit also reflects what other historians acknowledge: such games originated not as sport but as religious ritual: "All modern games played with bat and ball descend from one common source: an ancient fertility rite," declares Robert W. Henderson in *Ball, Bat and Bishop.*[16] "Agricultural fecundity was the primary impetus for these prehistoric rites," writes Cordelia Candelaria in *Seeking the Perfect Game.* She calls the rites "primal ur-baseball."[17] "Let's open the door and usher in the darkness of prehistory, the musky, oddly exciting odor . . . of the forgotten fertility rites which cling to this game," enthuses Harold Peterson in *The Man Who Invented Baseball.*[18]

Peterson tells of an Italian scholar who in 1937 encountered a form of baseball being played on a desert plateau in the Berber region of North Africa. The scholar reported that the participants called the runner's base "mother and the game itself *om el mahag,* translated as "the ball of the mother of the pilgrim." Peterson dates this game to the Stone Age, circa 3,000 to 6,000 BC, when women played on the Estonian Island of Runo, and Slavs called the captain of the fielding team "mother, [even] when male." Peterson concludes, "Connections with primitive springtime rites such as egg-carrying were explicit."

Religious ritual, fertility rites, a safe base known as "mother" . . . the national pastime seemed to be rooted in exotic soil. Pursuing the idea that baseball's origins are ancient, I sought out the man then serving as curator of the Hall of Fame Library. Tom Heitz, a studious, sandy-haired man who welcomed inquiries into the past, said this: "Stick and ball games are a sort of anthropologic marker of the human race. Sticks and stones . . . became our tools, hunting devices, defense, agriculture, and food preparation. Every major sport we have is a descendent of sticks and stones games. . . . [They] are ingrained in human behavior, and as familiar as anything we know."[19]

While stick-and-ball games are "as familiar as anything we know," what is often ignored is that their origin as fertility rites rests in the feminine. Guttmann recognizes this point: "that physical training and sports were sometimes associated by the ancients with the woman's role in human reproduction is equally true but much less frequently acknowledged."[20] Indeed, when the ancients prayed for successful crops and harvests, they turned, logically, to female deities. Before we worshipped Allah, Jehovah, or Jesus Christ, there were Ceres and Demeter, the Greek and Roman goddesses of the harvest. Earlier still was Gaea, whom the ancients honored as the mother of the human race. Baseball's very elements come from Gaea's Earth: the grass of the outfield, the chalk of the foul lines, and the red dirt of the infield. In the time when goddesses were revered as powerful and life-giving forces, girls took part in the religious rituals that evolved into sport. Thus, when Annie Savoy professes in the opening scene of the 1988 film *Bull Durham,* "I believe in the church of baseball," her words resonate with more truth than we knew. Despite the contemporary game's masculine tradition, we can reason that in antiquity the "church of baseball" honored the feminine. Each spring the game, rich with individual and collective memory, returns to women and they respond.

As religious ritual evolved into athletic competition, male gods supplanted the earlier goddesses, and girls became less welcome on the field. Even the influence of the memorable goddesses of Greek mythology faded. As Guttmann writes, "Artemis and Atalanta captured the imagination of poets and artists, and they may well have played a part in the fantasies of adolescent girls, but their mythic feats ... were not in accord with the conventional female role. Greek culture—like many others—was always highly ambivalent about women's sports."[21]

In the militant Greek city-state of Sparta, sports were more available to girls, who although they did not play stick-and-ball games participated in other games that moved beyond religious ritual. The reason was pragmatic—an early demonstration of eugenics. As Guttmann points out: "In their athletic competitions, the girls demonstrated their fitness to bear the hardy sons needed to maintain Spartan military hegemony."[22] Ultimately, however, the demands of marriage and family would have ended even the Spartan girls' athleticism. And despite their presumably robust children and legendary beauty—Helen of Troy grew up in Sparta—the Spartan girls' athleticism shocked the cultured Athenians. "They abandon their houses to run around with young men, with naked thighs and open clothes," complained the playwright Euripides in 426 BC. "And if your girls are so trained, is it any wonder that your Spartan women grow up without knowing what chastity is?"[23]

The evolution of stick-and-ball games continued to reveal remnants of the old fertility rites. As early as the fourteenth century, the English game of stoolball was played each spring at Eastertide, with the cries of milkmaids and farmhands ringing out in country churchyards. Three-legged milking stools served as "base," which the batter, stick in hand, defended from the bowler's pitched ball. Stoolball was more than a game, it was an earthy courtship ritual, as shown in this rhyme of 1719: "Down in the vale on a Summer's day, / All the lads and lasses went to be merry, / A match for kisses at Stoolball to play . . ."[24] The game's springtime tradition also leads researchers such as Henderson to conclude that "the Easter stoolball festivities had a direct association with the ancient pagan rites, with connotations of human fertility."[25] Here is another view of stoolball from an unknown poet of the 1700s:

> Set at the goal Pulcheria stand
> And grasp the board with snowy hand!
> She drives the ball with artful force
> Guiding through hostile ranks its course.
> Where does the shame or crime appear
> Of harmless romping once a year?[26]

The closing couplet suggests that by the eighteenth century, some disdain—"shame or crime"—attached to women playing stoolball, an attitude that echoes Euripides' old concern that athletic Spartan women were somewhat lacking in chastity. Slightly less objectionable was younger girls' participation in English children's stick-and-ball games like rounders. The term "base ball" was coming into use, too, and appears in Jane Austen's novel of 1818, *Northanger Abbey*. The following passage is often quoted as evidence that girls, too, participated in this ancestor of the American game. Austen writes, "It was not very wonderful that Catherine . . . should prefer cricket, base ball . . . and running about the country, at the age of fourteen."[27] Austen's wording, "not very wonderful," need not, however, be construed as disapproval of Catherine's preference for base ball. Austen, an early female voice in the English literary canon, was a fan of spirited heroines—and "not very wonderful" can be read as "unsurprising" (not very full of wonder). Catherine is one of ten children, which leaves her mother little time to cultivate in her daughter the more synthetic social graces. To Austen, it is natural that a girl left on her own—particularly one with three older brothers—would delight in "running about the country."[28]

Catherine's behavior, however, was unconventional; in a time when the term was not complimentary, she behaved like a "tomboy." According to the Oxford English Dictionary, the term "tomboy" was in use by the 1550s to denote "a rude, boisterous, or forward boy," and, shortly thereafter, "a bold or immodest woman."[29] Theologians were apt to find the cult of the tomboy suspect: "Of such short-haired Gentlewomen I find not one example either in Scripture or elsewhere," cautions T. Stoughton in 1622. "And what shall I say of . . . Tomboyes?" By Jane Austen's time, English society held a "particular aversion for hoydens and tomboys and women who trespassed against the delicacy of their sex," an attitude that prevailed throughout the nineteenth century.

By the early 1800s, these children's games had crossed the Atlantic and begun a metamorphosis into town ball, which grew in popularity throughout New York and New England. As Bowdoin College student Henry Wadsworth Longfellow observed in 1824, "There is nothing now heard of in our leisure hours but ball, ball, ball."[30] Town ball bats were slim and stick-like, often showing the owner's carvings. The "striker" (batter) was out if "plugged" (hit) by a thrown ball before grasping one of the "stakes" (bases). Happily for the runner, the ball was smaller and softer than today's hardball. To avoid getting plugged, a runner could flee to the nearby woods before attempting to sneak back to the proper stake, an appealing bucolic distinction from the urban game that came later. A gentle, relaxed game of finesse, town ball has been called baseball's "immediate ancestor on the maternal side."[31]

Social conventions had also crossed the ocean, of course; as the Victorian era dawned, town ball was deemed for men only. Families coming to town on market days separated after tending to business. A husband sought a game at a nearby field or pasture, while his wife might barter her needlework at the dry goods store. The Industrial Revolution, however, was stirring women's lives. Since time remembered, women had spent their days spinning and weaving and sewing cloth for the family wardrobe. Now middle-class women could buy ready-made cloth or purchase clothing manufactured by strangers. Industrialization brought change to the daily routines of nineteenth-century women. Soon early feminists were encouraging women to weave new plans for their lives.

Coincidentally, just as the women's emancipation movement was quickening, Alexander Cartwright's "new" game made its appearance in Hoboken, New Jersey. Two hundred miles to the northwest and two years later, in July 1848, the Convention for Women's Rights took place at Seneca Falls, New York. The delegates spoke up for the freedom to be educated, to earn a living on an equal basis with men, to vote, and to maintain a separate identity and existence. The right to enjoy baseball went hand in mitt with those aspirations. Feminist leaders understood that physical fitness exhilarates and empowers a woman and made it a part of their agenda. This more active lifestyle recommended the shedding the restrictive corsets and unwieldy skirts of the day in favor of more comfortable dress—clothing, it has been said, is power, "the human race's next language after speech . . . The bride wears white . . . clothes make the man."[32] Whether it was bicycling or baseball, women who exercised were hampered by their heavy garments. The solution to this dilemma—the bloomer—appeared in 1851, but the sight of women appearing in public in a short skirt over full trousers scandalized traditionalists and delayed widespread acceptance of the bloomer for decades. Not until late in the 1800s do we find accounts of women "baseballists" wearing the controversial costume.

Men suffered no such constraints. In the aftermath of the Civil War, they took up physical fitness with classic American fervor. The fads for exercise and baseball were symbiotic. When the Cincinnati Redstockings barnstormed from Boston to San Francisco in 1869, this first professional ball club won fans at each stop along the way. Baseball soon became "the secular church that reached into every class and region of the nation and bound millions . . . together."[33] This was America's game. As one fan of 1874 claimed, "Among out-door sports, our national game affords a large share of enjoyment to every man and boy of equal timber and healthy frame. Fresh air, good exercise, sharp practice for the eye, and vigorous action for the muscles,—these are the best and cheapest amusements."[34] The brand-new sportswriting profession chimed in, pronouncing baseball clubs to be "missionary organizations preaching the new gospel of health."[35]

Yet beneath the lighthearted view that playing baseball was fun and healthful was the underlying conviction that the game's roots must be masculine and American. Early promoters set about separating it from the children's games played by boys and girls in earlier times. In his guide of 1888, *Base-Ball: How to Become a Player,* the celebrated pitcher and shortstop John Montgomery Ward initially tips his cap to the game's feminine lineage, crediting the invention of the first game of ball to "a certain beautiful lady of Corcyra, Anagalla."[36] Montgomery goes on to state, however, "Base-ball in its mildest form is essentially a robust game, and it would require an elastic imagination to conceive of little girls possessed of physical powers such as its play demands." Montgomery concludes, "But if base-ball is neither sprung from rounders nor taken bodily from another English game, what is its origin? I believe it to be a fruit of the inventive genius of the American boy."[37] If baseball was to become the national pastime, by God and by Doubleday, it must be as a masculine game.

That the game began to flourish in the midst of the Victorian Age (1837–1901) was poor luck for women. "[M]asculine domination of life," writes feminist author Carolyn G. Heilbrun, "was not, of course, unique to the nineteenth century . . . but [p]atriarchy reached its apotheosis in the years of [Queen] Victoria's reign."[38] Consequently, despite the changes portended by the Industrial Revolution and the Women's Suffrage movement, women continued to be discouraged from participating in baseball. In fact, as women demanded more rights, more reasons were devised as to why women should not have them. The cultural norms of the times were translated into medical "truths," according to Kathleen E. McCrone's "The Medical and Scientific Debate on Women's Sports":

> Most physicians sincerely believed that . . . the sexes should occupy separate spheres because women's reproductive functions, absolute physical inferiority and propensity to illness inevitably disqualified them from sharing men's privileges in the . . . sporting arenas. . . . If a woman pursued "unhealthy" modes of life involving too much education and competitive sport, her vital energy would be depleted and she was likely to become sterile or capable of bearing only defective offspring. . . . Excessive exercise masculinised women, unfitting them for their womanly duties by diverting energy from vital areas to the muscular systems.[39]

Such thinkers feared that women who embraced baseball would threaten the natural order by becoming mannish or wanton. (One man's attempt to organize a women's team during the 1880s failed because he was rumored to be recruiting them as prostitutes.)[40] By then, the dictionary definition of the term "tomboy" signified deviant sexuality: "As a rough tomboy of fourteen, she had shown ... a good many uncouth signs of affection." Like the young athletes of ancient Sparta, late nineteenth-century women who aspired to the diamond were sexually suspect. As Dorothy and Harold Seymour write, "Psychologist Richard Krafft-Ebing linked [women's] participation in athletics to lesbianism and declared that preference for playing boys' games was the first symptom of perversion."[41] Implicit in these concerns was the idea that women must be protected from such dangers.

Even so, baseball held a powerful attraction for Victorian-era women. Having learned of the possibilities of gaining suffrage, an education, and equal pay—in short, the right to fully take part in American life—the "weaker sex" would not be dissuaded from the diamond. Vassar College, a pioneer in women's education, opened its doors to students in 1865; by 1866 the girls had organized the Laurel and the Abenakis Base Ball Clubs. In 1869, the Women's Suffrage Base-ball Club posted a 19–16 win in a match game against the Invincibles.[42] Just as it did for men, the national game inspired feminine interest in physical fitness. As one woman of the 1890s claimed, "Base ball taught me how to take care of myself. It was watching those fellows that set me to thinking of physical culture, and I went to work and developed myself from a semi-invalid into a robust woman."[43] Ignoring the conventional wisdom of scientists, doctors, moralists, and the game's patriarchs, women discovered that playing and following baseball undermined neither their health nor their femininity. The game was exhilarating, and many women determined to participate wherever and whenever they could.

TOWN BALL REVISITED

A century later, Tina Baker, Eileen O'Brien, Sonja Parker, and Jessie Ravage give little thought to history as they scamper across a freshly mown field on the edge of Cooperstown. All summer long, local men and women wearing the colors of the Innkeepers, Cardiff Giants, Cat Town Scholars, and Fly Creek Bees vie with one another for bragging rights and postgame beers at the Pit, a tavern beneath the venerable Tunnicliff Inn on nearby Pioneer Street. Under the auspices of the Leatherstocking Base Ball Club, town ball is played on Sunday afternoons behind the Farmers' Museum. The games are a relaxed endeavor, but the rules of the nineteenth century have been carefully researched by its supporters. So it is possible for spectators, who are encouraged to cheer the traditional *huzzah!* to watch Tina "Sweetbread" Baker run barefoot through the grass and, with a satisfying thump, plug a dodging runner with the ball; Sonja "Wishbone" Parker smack the ball into the maple trees near the outfield before dashing for the safety of first "stake" (base); and scoring runners pause at tally-keeper Martha Sherwood's wooden desk a few yards behind home with the polite request to *tally me.*

Tom Heitz is there, too, dressed in an old-fashioned tab-collared work shirt, blue-and-white check flannels, and a top hat. As the local ombudsman of town ball—since 1985, he and his colleagues have dedicated themselves to reviving the game—Heitz wears the uniform with aplomb and appears pleased to explain the nuances to a novice. "Town ball," he says, "is a gentle game, a romp in green grass beneath blue sky and clear air." Indeed, coming upon a summertime game of town ball in Cooperstown brings alive again the rural beauty of this nineteenth-century game. Baseball's very terms still evoke this past: Leaf through a dictionary and you find "infield" defined as "the land or field nearest the farmhouse [or home]" and "outfield" defined as a "distant or outlying farmland, where the sheep grazed", and once known as the "center, left, and right gardens." But where once we spoke of daisy cutters and worm burners, we tend now to speak of hard-hit grounders and sharp rollers, and lose something of the game's poetry.

Heitz calls town ball "social recreation" and laments that this approach toward sport has been overshadowed by the twentieth century's drive toward competition and brute power. Much as baseball veterans of earlier eras decry the Mc-power era of swing-and-stare home runs, Heitz regrets this aspect of town ball's evolution into baseball. To the feminine eye, the town ball game in progress does seem well suited to the female athlete: guile and finesse count as much as sheer strength. The hurler's delivery, aimed at putting the ball into play rather than defeating the "striker" (batter), makes it easy to get a hit (traditionally games ended at one hundred tallies). Might town ball be, as one historian terms it, "baseball's immediate ancestor on the maternal side"? "Men do seem to enjoy games of chase," Heitz avers, "and even town ball has its violent aspects: plugging, the rundown. And men do seem more geared to competition, while women do seem more able to grasp the value of social recreation." Heitz finally shrugs, "Maybe it's the testosterone."

LIFE IN CANDYLAND

After the town ball game, still dressed in her uniform of flannel pants and vest, scarlet work shirt, and floppy bow tie, Tina Baker could be taken for the barkeep of an old-time saloon. Seating herself on one of the low rock walls that mark the countryside, she reflects upon her experiences with town ball. Baker grew up in the nearby village of Fly Creek thinking she knew everyone in Cooperstown. "The local joke goes, 'this is Candyland—it's not the real world,'" she says.[44] She recalls no violent crime here. At night, she sometimes walks home alone without concern. Discovering town ball as a young woman, however, acquainted her with a fuller range of local society, from twelve-year-olds to the elderly, from Jessie "Outlaw" Ravage, a woman then freelancing as a curator at the Hall of Fame Museum, to William Arlt, who dresses for the games in full historic regalia. Town ball has broadened her perspective in other ways, for she has learned that over the course of a summer men can make much fun of a strawberry blonde named "Sweetbread." Sometimes the kidding turns demeaning and sexist, she says. "It's 'Hey you, play over there, outta the way.' Or paying *very special coaching attention* that's embarrassing. Or the usual, 'You throw like a girl,' which I do because I had shoulder surgery. I can't throw at all." Some of the younger Leatherstocking girls take the teasing hard, but Baker says her own sensitivity was tempered by growing up with her brother "Hardtack," a town ball player of repute. Majoring in athletic training and exercise science at Ithaca College also thickened her skin. "I work with football teams, for God's sakes. It's 'roar, roar, grunt, grunt,' with sexist comments all the time. Guys feed on the weak and if you're too sensitive, they don't let up."

Women of Tina Baker's generation are not so willing to give up their tomboy ways as they come of age. Faced with resistance to their participation on the field, they do not call their boyfriend, father, or an attorney—they learn to cope. Baker says, "You play town ball, socialize, pick on each other, then go to the Pit, have a beer, and do some more teasing." Besides, she points out, women have their own brand of locker-room humor, which can be just as crude. Baker admits without remorse that she is one of the worst, returning the jibes until the men lose interest or get embarrassed.

Yet Leatherstocking town ball, even as benign social recreation, has taught her that some men do not enjoy sharing what they consider their territory. Accustomed to contending with their own dreams and insecurities and proving themselves among their own company, some men are uncomfortable sharing the field of play with women. For such men, *taking the field* is a term that speaks of conquest, of ownership. They are not ambivalent about sharing the field with women; they just do not want to do it. The Leatherstocking women have contended with a teammate who considers women players a liability because they cannot hit the ball as hard. "And he won't talk to some of my friends, because he doesn't think they're attractive," complains Baker, "though he likes a couple of us around, because he thinks we're pretty faces, which is equally annoying." Candyland, she has learned, is no haven from gender conflict.

Baker's teammate, Jessie Ravage, agrees. "Some women become frustrated because they get stuck in right field, where the ball never goes."[45] Ravage, whose nicknames of "Jackrabbit" and "Outlaw" allude to her skill at eluding pluggings, grew up playing scrub with her father and brothers. Despite three decades of Title IX–mandated equal opportunity in scholastic athletics, Ravage thinks that too many women still miss out on learning baseball's fundamentals, reducing the ability to compete, even in a sociable game of town ball.

Ravage has moonlighted at Cooperstown High School as the coach of the cross-country team, a co-ed sport. She has seen girls sometimes finish ahead of the boys. She believes that co-ed sports give teenagers a clearer view of their individual abilities. "I think the issue of working out your male or your female identity is better done by sharing the field," she says. "You learn to get along, and over and over I see that's something women and men haven't learned to do. We don't share well." Extending her point, Ravage questions how humanity is to survive in a world of diminishing resources, when such barriers continue to exist. "Women are probably the world's most wasted resource, and the longer I think about that, the more I think it's true, and that it happens by segregation."

THE MUFFINS AND THE GREAT BLACK SWAMP FROGS

Cooperstown's Sunday afternoon town ball games draw many visitors, and Martha Sherwood's tally-keeping desk often serves as information booth for the curious. She says the most frequently asked question is *did women play in the nineteenth century?* While the answer is *no,* Tom Heitz sees no point in trying to exactly duplicate the social mores of those days. He fields teams that include women as well as people of African, Asian, and Native American descent, none of whom were likely to have been invited to play town ball during the 1800s. "These games are just a demonstration," he says. "Whoever shows up plays. There are no dues and the club is not politicized."

Variants of early forms of baseball are played across the country. The Vintage Base Ball Association includes more than fifty clubs that operate under rules dating from 1846 (Cartwright's game) to 1922. When the Ohio Village Muffins, an 1860 club, invited the Leatherstockings to come west for a tournament, they excluded the women players: Women did not play in 1860, the Muffins reasoned, so the Cooperstown women should sit on the sidelines. Tom Heitz took the attitude of "Jeez, let 'em play—it doesn't bother us," but at the time the Muffins were dedicated to a greater degree of authenticity and remained resolute. Rather than watch from the sidelines, the Leatherstocking women stayed home.

When the Great Black Swamp Frogs, another Ohio base ball club, came to Cooperstown, home-turf rules applied. "Sweetbread" Baker, "Moose" O'Brien, "Wishbone" Parker, "Outlaw" Ravage, and Martha Sherwood played, while the Swamp Frog women sat on the sidelines in hoop skirts and parasols. Baker was surprised that the women were agreeable to dressing so in 85-degree heat. "They were so docile—they'd just sit there and cheer them on, using the language of that time." The Ohioans hold a different view. "Part of our mission is to educate the public about clothing and customs of the period," explained James R. Tootle, a baseball historian who plays for the Muffins.[46] (That policy relaxed in 1994, when the Lady Diamonds were organized to interpret what it might have been like for a woman to play ball in 1860. The Diamonds started out playing in tunics and trousers; however, when no documentation could be found for the practice, the women reverted to long skirts, true to the style of the era.)

At the Cooperstown tournament, the Swamp Frog men stayed in the character of the 1860s, professing shock at the presence of the women on the field. When a Leatherstocking woman made a fine play, their opponents feigned surprise, muttering *Oh, scandal! Scandal!* according to Sherwood.[47] "Oh, it was hard to play against them." Tina Baker took to heart the role-playing: "That's just the way it was, and is," she says, "surprise at the idea that a woman can play well." And it is with a sense of competitive satisfaction quite at odds with town ball's ideal of social recreation that the Leatherstocking women still relish their win that day.

COMING HOME

Baseball's mythology, history, and traditions permeate Cooperstown, and the game is likely to work some alchemy upon a woman, whether she is native to the area or a visitor. It happened to Tina Baker in this way: "It's kind of funny," she said. "Growing up in Cooperstown, people expect you to be totally into the whole baseball scene, but a lot of locals are not. Professional sport is about money and power and following it is not of interest to me. I've always preferred playing to watching sports—growing up it was basketball, field hockey, and volleyball—but no baseball." One recent summer, just as the town's annual Induction Week bustle began over the newest admissions to the Hall of Fame, Baker and a friend were out walking and wanted a place to sit and talk. They gravitated to Doubleday Field. With no game underway, they were surprised to find the grandstand half filled. "Workers were mowing the field, and people were watching that—just watching them mow the field," she marvels. "We found a quiet corner and stayed on. And I found it so calming, being a part of that." In her own backyard, Baker had discovered the beauty of a ballpark.

Jessie Ravage came as a stranger both to baseball and Cooperstown. On a rainy March afternoon in 1989, she boarded a bus bound there in order to interview for a graduate program in history and museum studies. "Snow was still on the ground and the trees were all brown," she recalls, "but with each mile I felt like I was getting closer and closer to home." Ravage had always considered herself a loner (for exercise, she favors solitary lake swims), but once settled, she fell into the routine of playing town ball. She soon found herself "sinking deeper and deeper into the community," and by graduation, Cooperstown had become home. All she needed was a job. After a town ball game, she asked Tom Heitz if he knew of any work in her field.

Through Heitz, the Hall of Fame and Museum asked Ravage to collaborate on a gallery of the game's writers and broadcasters. As she sorted through the archives, she uncovered a story that warranted more than a series of photographs with brief biographical notes. "Early writers and broadcasters set the stage for every other kind of sportswriting in this country and, really, the world," she explains. The result of her efforts, "Scribes and Mike Men," captured that history with such wit and style that it was made a permanent exhibit. Ravage then worked on "Ivory

Hunters," which examines the role that early-twentieth-century scouts played, and served as consultant during the design of the Texas Rangers' ballpark in Arlington. Spotting a worrisome drainage flaw in the site plan, she urged that the ballpark's museum be relocated. A Texas-sized storm later flooded the area and would have destroyed the Rangers' memorabilia had her advice gone unheeded.

Ravage says that she was trained to retrieve the past as truthfully as possible and relishes her work at the Hall of Fame: "For all the nostalgia of playing in meadows, baseball is essentially an urban game. But town ball is rural and gives us a chance to rearrange the Abner Doubleday myth, which is so strong." To Ravage, the lens of history is a kaleidoscope, shifting with the times: "The way we record baseball history today will not be the same in forty years. The history I'm doing now at the Hall of Fame—I wonder, will it survive?"

In 1988, the museum officially acknowledged the game's feminine side when it opened the Women in Baseball exhibit. The exhibit started small, with photographs and artifacts from early women's teams, the All-American Girls Baseball League, an early umpire, and the occasional club owner. During the 1990s, it added new images of the Colorado Silver Bullets and pitcher Ila Borders. The exhibit remains small in comparison to others, but its impact can be great. Lingering there one afternoon, I noticed a mother with three young children approach the exhibit. Attracted by the brightly lit uniforms of the AAGBL, her toddler moved toward the glass while her eldest, a boy of about seven, stopped short before the display. "Look, Mom," he said, tugging at her hand. "You could'a played. Mom, you could play baseball, too."

The visitor to Cooperstown, seeking to draw closer to the game she loves best, comes away with more than anticipated. The surrounding countryside, in countless shades of green at midsummer, invites introspection. Here she can close her eyes, imagining the shouts of the Leatherstocking women at a game of town ball to be those of Jane Austen's Catherine, lost in the joy of "base ball," or of English milkmaids, taking a break for a game of stoolball. Here, at the Hall of Fame and Museum, she learns that the fan's modern-day penchant for treating baseball as religion—some call our ballparks green cathedrals—goes back to antiquity, when the feminine in God was honored. She sees that through the ages, young women enjoyed stick-and-ball games despite social and cultural constraints. Now, for the first time in history, an aspiring female ballplayer is free to postpone or reject the rites of marriage and mother-hood, lengthening her playing days. Here, a woman comes to appreciate that it is normal and right and good to be fully a part of baseball. For in the towns and cities beyond these green hills, live women who pursue their interest in and talent for the game, as spectators, players, and um-pires, as front office executives, trainers, and agents, and as sportswrit-ers, novelists, and filmmakers. So it is that in Cooperstown, or anywhere else, the sound of bat on ball may stop a woman in mid-stride.

2 In the Stands

Fans

Take me out to the ball game
Take me out with the crowd
Buy me some peanuts and Cracker Jack
I don't care if I never get back

— Refrain from "Take Me Out to the Ball Game"

LIKE THE GAME IT CELEBRATES, "Take Me Out to the Ball Game" is deceptively simple. Consider the full lyrics, and you find more than escapism; you discover that the song celebrates a young woman in love with baseball. When Jack Norworth wrote the lyrics in 1908, he had not set foot in a ballpark, but he must have known of a young woman who did. Perhaps Norworth was thinking of his wife, Nora, or a girl of their acquaintance when he glanced at the sign—"Ballgame today at the Polo Grounds"—that reputedly inspired him. From its opening lines, "Katie Casey was baseball mad, / Had the fever and had it bad," the song tells of a free-spirited young woman's call for inclusion at a time when her place in the stands was still controversial.[1] When Katie's beau invites her to a show, she turns him down. A tomboy who knows all the players' names and stats, Katie does not want to go on a conventional date; she wants to go to the ballpark. Sung in its entirety, "Take Me Out to the Ball Game" reminds us that women have always have been among the game's most devoted and knowledgeable fans. Yet for many years, Organized Baseball showed a complex ambivalence toward the feminine presence at the ballpark.

The story goes back to the 1840s. As soon as the Knickerbocker Base Ball Club of New York began playing baseball at New Jersey's Elysian Fields, long-skirted women gathered at the fringes of the diamond. Historians Dorothy and Harold Seymour credit the Knickerbockers, baseball's first known organized team, with initiating the custom of special days for female spectators, with club members "requested to invite their wives, daughters, and girlfriends" on the last Thursday of each month. As the game spread in popularity, pavilions were often set up on game days to shield female spectators from the sun's glare. All was well for women when baseball belonged to amateurs who valued civility—it was considered rude to not give the batter a good pitch to hit or to steal a base on the pitcher. Perhaps the early history of female spectators is best summed up by Helen Ward's salutation on her photograph to one of the early game's prominent advocates: "*Avec les amities de à M. [Henry] Chadwick.*"[2]

Even as Chadwick and his friends were toasting their female guests at postgame banquets, a different style of baseball soon captured the interest of average Americans. Promoters began to pay talented players for their services, fenced their fields, and provided seating for paying fans. The game as a gentlemanly exhibition of skill underwent a transformation into a workingman's hard-fought contest. In the stands, crowds of loud, hard-drinking "cranks" (the uncomplimentary term applied to early fans) matched the new competitive intensity of the diamond. After the Civil War ended, women joined in the national enthusiasm for the game—the Seymours note that women were numerous in the crowds drawn to Cincinnati's Great Baseball Tournament of September 1867. That season, a song appeared which supports the idea that women shared the craze for the game that was sweeping the country. "The Base Ball Fever" devotes a stanza to a fad hairstyle involving a ball-shaped bun: "To be in fashion, ladies too . . . way back behind the ears, they wear, / An awful big Base Ball sirs; I shouldn't wonder but 'ere long, / Each Miss, if you'll perceive her, / Will carry Bats all through her hair / 'Cause she too has the fever."[3]

Fever would prove an accurate description of the emotional climate in the stands, for as the game popularized, the "cranks" grew ever more unruly. As one baseball historian put it, "Enclosed ballparks created a special territory that men began to treat as a private club, where they could drink, swear and generally carry on like the male of the species."[4] The presence of women complicated the idea of the ballpark as men's "private club." Victorian-era mores required that women be protected from the rough behavior there. Players who used excessively offensive language were fined, and in the stands, compromises were made for the feminine presence. The New York Giants, for example, closed down a popular beer concession for a while when its patrons became a nuisance to nearby women.[5] Men who found in the ballpark an escape from the pressures of everyday life resented these accommodations. Meanwhile, women who were serious fans chafed at the limits put upon their full participation in the game, not only in the stands, but also in other places where men congregated to talk over baseball. As the *Sporting Life*'s columnist Ella Black complained, "The female enthusiasts are envious of their male friends who, while the clubs are away, can stand around the cigar stores and hotels and get the latest gossip."[6]

Even in these presumably more genteel times, however, the line between good and bad behavior at the ballpark could not be based upon gender. Women of low reputation were advertising themselves at the ballpark as early as 1869, according to the *Cincinnati Commercial*: "Known to the sporting world as 'Maude, the pet blonde' . . . she has attracted glances of admiration from thousands, on the streets, at the theater, or opera, and in the brilliant assemblages of the base ball games."[7] In a time when women were expected to elevate the moral tone of the ballpark, those who carried on there "like the male of the species" were roundly criticized. The *Sporting Life* ran this cautionary account of a fan of the Pittsburgh Alleghenies named Mary Carney: "The sport became so absorbing in its interests for her last summer that she neglected the children at home. At last she got to betting."[8] When Mary Carney spoke of playing for a women's baseball club, her husband decided she had gone too far and filed for divorce.

Even with conventional behavior, women were a distraction at the ballpark because they were considered to be naturally and irredeemably ignorant of baseball fundamentals. The new profession of sportswriting spread the notion that women upset the rhythm of the game. Male fans were distracted when young women chatted of sewing pennants for the home teams and filling their lockets with their favorite players' photos.

This hyperbolic account of 1882 complained that one female spectator's enthusiasms at a New York ball game "filled the grand stand so full of questions and answers (and groans and swear words) that they rolled out into the field and annoyed the players."[9] Women did not have to utter a word, however, to be seen as intrusive. Here is a report of an 1898 Ladies' Day game at Brooklyn's Washington Park: "As the troops of pretty girls and handsome matrons came into the grounds yesterday a few astonished 'rooters' for the New-York team stood by in utter astonishment . . . and watched this army of loveliness pass in without the formality of purchasing tickets."[10]

The problem was, Organized Baseball needed to fill the seats of its ballparks with fans, and many professional teams thought it wise to offer women free admission in hopes of converting them to regular fans as well as consumers of food, drink, and souvenirs.[11] It is uncertain which Major League club hosted the first Ladies' Day—a monograph at Cooperstown's Hall of Fame Library credits the New York Giants with inaugurating the custom on June 16, 1883—but by the mid-1880s, the practice had spread to Baltimore, Cincinnati, Philadelphia, St. Louis, and into the minor leagues. Early in the 1887 season, Abner Powell, the New Orleans (Southern League) Pelicans player-manager, learned the club was in financial trouble and suggested that admitting unescorted women free once a week might turn them into regular paying fans.[12] When the gates of Sportsman's Park opened on April 28, eight hundred women entered, many of them unescorted. Few of the twelve hundred male fans followed the game that day, preferring to scan the grandstand section reserved for women. Powell's experiment succeeded. The women of New Orleans returned often, paying twenty-five cents each, and inspiring a healthy increase in male attendance.

ARDOR IN THE STANDS

Female fans of the nineteenth century complicated life at the ballpark in yet another way, for some clearly were there to view not only the game but also the ballplayers. During Tony Mullane's tenure with the Cincinnati Red Stockings from 1886 to 1893, the feminine presence at the ballpark increased whenever he pitched; consequently the front office made the handsome Irishman the poster boy for the club's advertisements. Columnist Ella Black never forgot the first time she saw Mullane: "It was years ago, when he was with the Toledo club. . . . What a favorite he was then with the ladies! They all used to rave about his good looks."[13] The ardor such players inspired sometimes overwhelmed the game. Here is an incident from the Washington Senators' first Ladies' Day in 1897:

> The front office expected a few dozen curious or adventurous females to turn out and was in no way prepared for the thousand enthusiastic women who stormed the ballpark gates. . . . Most of these women were not there to learn the finer points of the game. They had come to see a charismatic star of the day—the dashing Washington Senators pitcher, George "Winnie" Mercer. And that's where the trouble began.[14]

When Mercer disputed an umpire's call, his ejection from the game caused an uproar among the women in the stands. And when the Senators lost the game, "a horde of women poured onto the field to attack the umpire with parasols. The ump managed to escape into the clubhouse without suffering bodily harm, but the grandstands were left a shambles." It was some years before the nation's capitol saw another Ladies' Day.

Despite such episodes, some in baseball clung to the belief that female fans were the answer to the game's problems. With drunkenness in the stands, brawls on the field, and disputes over calls (known as "kicking") all too common, it was hoped that the presence of women would prop up the game's sagging image. Charles Byrne, the president of the Brooklyn Bridegrooms, was an early advocate of Ladies' Day. Byrne claimed he "would rather have six ladies in my grand stand . . . than twenty policemen. Where there are ladies you will always find that good order will be kept, and that with but little trouble."[15] And as a rather wistful fan of 1908 wrote from North Dakota to *Baseball* magazine: "Wouldn't there be a big turn-out, though, if a lot of pretty girls sat in the grandstand and waved their handkerchiefs when a good play was pulled off? . . . Admission of women would tend to eliminate foul language, and make the game cleaner in every way. I say, let the women in free of charge!"[16] Henry Chadwick, who as sportswriter and editor had promoted the game for so long, however, felt differently. While Americans were singing the hit song, "Take Me Out to the Ball Game," Chadwick was setting down his concerns about women fans in his final essay, "The Sin of Kicking":

> The public school teachers of Brooklyn, as a rule, are very fond of baseball, and I have the pleasure of knowing a few of them, whom I have taught to score the game. But what enthusiastic "fans" these girls are! . . . A few summers ago, I used

to escort a dozen or more of women school teachers to see the games at Washington Park, but of late years, in view of the "kicking" or fault-finding propensities of Brooklyn teams, I discontinued the practice of escorting the women to the grounds.[17]

> *Katie Casey saw all the games,*
> *Knew the players by their first names;*
> *Told the umpire he was wrong,*
> *All along good and strong*
> —Second stanza of "Take Me Out to the Ball Game"

The tensions continued between Organized Baseball's economic need for female fans and its felt obligation to protect them from the game's baser elements. Many women did not share those concerns. Going to the ballpark gave them a place to enjoy fresh air and new freedoms, and they went. By 1908, there were enough real Katie Caseys going out to the ball games to warrant a series on female fans in *Baseball* magazine. In one essay, Ina Eloise Young claimed that in her baseball-mad hometown of Trinidad, Colorado, two-thirds of the spectators were women. She herself took the game seriously, looked askance at women who did not, and despaired of her own mother, who after three years of faithful attendance had yet to grasp the game. Young understood the fundamentals well enough to serve as the club's official scorekeeper, which prompted the old ballplayers she met to often regard her as "something of a freak," she declared. "It doesn't seem strange to me that I should be able to comprehend baseball better than the average man, because I have known the game since I was a small girl."[18]

In other *Baseball* essays, Trixie Cadiz, a Ziegfeld Follies dancer, confessed to arriving late for a performance in Boston as she lingered at the sidelines of a sandlot game, and comic opera singer Lulu Glaser recalled her longing to continue with the game she had played as a girl. Reflecting on a reporter's interest in her love for baseball, Glaser wrote, "I have reason to think that I surprised him with my knowledge of what he called essentially a man's game."[19] At a time when women were still regarded as ignorant of baseball's nuances, knowledgeable fans like Young, Cadiz, and Glaser were rather shocking.

To some extent, the sort of freedom women spectators enjoyed depended upon location and class. In cosmopolitan Manhattan, with the

New York Giants' ballpark at Coogan's Bluff convenient to Broadway's theatre district, actress Stella Hammerstein considered any afternoon to be Ladies' Day at the Polo Grounds. She hurried from rehearsals of George M. Cohan's *Yankee Prince* to attend games and apparently cut it close on show days, too:

> The [stage] manager had sent the call-boy down . . . only to find that Miss Stella Hammerstein was not in. . . . In three minutes her cue would sound. . . . [He] finally sat down in his swivel and let his hands droop limply on the supports. A figure flitted past the door and he straightened up with new life. "Where—where have you been?" he began hotly. "Watching the Giants," she called back over her shoulder, sweetly.[20]

The need for revenue, unsurprisingly, eventually trumped whatever concerns Organized Baseball had over the complex proprieties attending women at the ballpark. Charles H. Ebbets offered free tickets to unescorted women at his Brooklyn ballpark as early as 1910, while other owners realized that trying to maintain the old proprieties was of little effect. When the St. Louis Browns required male escorts for women on Ladies' Days during the 1912 season, the crush of unattached women who gathered outside the gates of Sportsman's Park quickly found escorts among the hopeful men lingering nearby.[21] By 1917, the Browns decided that women did not need an escort for Ladies' Day. Branch Rickey later called the institution of regular Ladies' Days "a very important step forward. Probably no innovation did so much to give baseball respectability, as well as thousands of new fans."[22]

During the 1920s, women won the right to vote, bobbed their hair, shortened their skirts, increasingly took jobs, and continued to show up in the stands. "They had money, independence, and free time. Why shouldn't they be fans?" reasons Richard Ben Cramer in *Joe DiMaggio: The Hero's Life*. According to Cramer, the ballpark became "as smart and stylish for a girl-about-town as smoking (over high-balls!). . . . [E]ven better [the ballpark] was cheaper, for one thing (and you could tell your parents you'd been there)—the kind of place you could go with your girlfriends."[23] Forward-thinking owners capitalized on the new freedoms available to women. One such owner was C. I. Taylor, whose Indianapolis ABCs were a thriving franchise in the Negro National League in the early 1920s. As Paul Debono points out in his history of the ABCs, "A recurring theme in

C. I.'s statements to the press was that women should feel unthreatened at the baseball park, able to enjoy a game and able to maintain decorum by wearing nice clothes—dresses and hats to the game."[24] Taylor's policy helped to set the ABCs at the center of black culture in Indianapolis.

In 1927, Jack Norworth revised his lyrics to celebrate the new sort of American girl emerging out of the freedoms of the 1920s. "Nelly Kelly was sure some fan, / She would root just like any man. / When the score was just two to two, / Nancy Kelly knew what to do, / Just to cheer up the boys she knew, / She made the gang sing this song." When Nelly's beau invites her to Coney Island, she begins to "fret and pout, / And to him I heard her shout . . ." and then the familiar chorus. The new freedoms women claimed during the Jazz Age are evident in Nelly's demand, stronger now than a plea, to go to the ballpark.

All sorts of women were going there. Baseball historian David A. Pietrusza recounts this scene from the first game of the 1924 World Series between the New York Giants and the Washington Senators. The score was tied in the ninth inning at 2–2, with Walter Johnson on the mound for the home team—at which point President Calvin Coolidge, no fan of the game, decided it was time to return to business at the White House and rose to leave.

"Where do you think you're going?" his wife hissed. "You sit down," and Grace Goodhue Coolidge grabbed his coattails.

The president sat.

Bucky Harris, whose managing career spanned four decades, called Grace Coolidge "the most rabid baseball fan I ever knew in the White House." Her interest has been reported as dating to her student days at Vassar College, where she reputedly served as scorer. "Don't believe it," writes Pietrusza. "She attended the University of Vermont."[25] Grace Coolidge apparently turned to baseball after the death of the couple's son, Calvin Jr., in July 1924; perhaps she found respite from her grief at the ballpark. She attended games with the president, often remaining to keep score and chat with the players by the Senators dugout after he left. Her interest in radio play-by-play continued all of her life; in her later years, she frequented Boston's Fenway Park. For decades, she was known as the first lady of baseball. In 1948, when the question of whether there had ever been a triple play in the World Series stumped the speaker at a baseball banquet, Grace Coolidge whispered to him, "Bill Wambsganss, Cleveland infielder in the 1920 World Series."[26]

In Missouri was another future First Lady who had grown up with baseball. As a girl, Bess Truman was an outstanding athlete who played third base on her brothers' sandlot team and was their "champion slugger," according to Bess and Harry's daughter Margaret. Bess Truman once surprised Senator Tom Eagleton with her knowledge of the game, Margaret writes. "'She knew every player in the Kansas City Royals starting lineup and had very strong opinions of the plusses and minuses of each one,' the Senator told me, bafflement in his voice. He did not realize he was dealing with an ex-third-baseman."[27]

Despite the fact that many women fans were as well informed as Grace Coolidge and Bess Truman, they continued to be viewed as curiosities. Those who "knew" baseball were still newsworthy. In "Fair Fans 'Crash' Ball Games, Cheer Plays," sportswriter Harry Shelland reflected on a 1931 Ladies' Day game at the Polo Grounds: "I was struck by the baseball intelligence exhibited by all the fanettes around me. It was a new experience to me and while at first I was inclined to resent the feminine chatter around me as a disturbing factor in my enjoyment of the game, on second thought I concluded the women were no worse in this respect than the men."[28] Luisa Kuhn, the wife of latter-day Baseball Commissioner Bowie Kuhn, remembered well the effect of such attitudes:

> I grew up at a time when baseball was essentially a man's game—that is, male fans felt that the game was exclusively theirs, not just to play, as a few of them might have done, but to reminisce and recriminate about while resurrecting great days and great plays of bygone years. Although distaff enthusiasm for baseball was not specifically discouraged, any girl who expressed an incipient interest was likely to find her questions answered, if at all, with impatient tolerance. Not surprisingly, girls soon tired of this heavy-handed, slightly hostile male attitude and, for many, the impulse to follow baseball died aborning.[29]

Some of the goils wuz no ladies judged by what they shouted at the Giants.
—"Flatbush 'Riot' Turns into Picnic," 1939

Although the tradition of Ladies' Day bolstered the game's image as a wholesome family outing and increased revenue by creating new fans, some women continued to behave in ways that would have left Henry Chadwick aghast. When the Chicago Cubs advertised a Ladies' Day game in 1929, more than thirty thousand women showed up to buy tickets, shoving aside box-seat holders and rushing the gates. The club had to cancel pregame practice and call in the police, after which they sold Ladies' Day tickets by mail. According to sportswriter Dan Daniel, whose career dated to 1909, three of the wildest fans he ever saw were Hilda Chester, the "Brooklyn Foghorn"; Lollie Hopkins, the "Hub's No. 1 Howler"; and Mary Ott, the "St. Louis Screecher."[30] "[T]hey were loud, they were raucous, they were acutely demonstrative," he recalled. Indeed, for more than a generation of Brooklyn fans, Hilda Chester's bronze bell was their call to arms. "That bell is an important part of Hilda's life," claimed the *Sporting News*. "She rings it to signalize every vital turn of Dodger affairs. . . . This spring [1943] it has a joyous, happy ring."[31] Although Daniel had seen male fans just as eccentric—at Yankee Stadium, for example, the Health Bugs liked to sit in the bleachers as naked as the law allowed and bathe their aches and pains in the sun—he perceived gender distinctions among such fans. At the ballpark, men sought an outlet from the pressures of work and henpecking wives, while women like Chester, Hopkins, and Ott represented something loftier. According to Daniel, these women were "devoted to a cause, to a ball club, to baseball."

The truth, however, is probably not so neat. Hilda Chester, for example, had played with the New York Bloomer Girls, married, was widowed, and had a daughter who became a softball player of some talent. Yet Chester saw her regular seat in the center-field bleachers of Ebbets Field as a haven from the disappointments of her life. At the ballpark, surrounded by friends and admirers, the ballplayers on the field before her, she came alive. As Chester once said, "Home was never like this. . . . I never meant anything more in my life. . . . I haven't had a happy life. The Dodgers have been the one bright spot. I do not think I would want to go on without them."[32] Many men surely shared Chester's feelings, but with baseball deemed a man's game and women expected to nurture home and hearth, it was easy for pundits to see Hilda Chester as an anomaly of her gender.

> *Fir mir oys tsu der bolgeym*
> —"Take Me Out to the Ball Game," Yiddish translation

Immigrant women were among those asserting themselves as fans, for the ballpark was a convenient and instructive place in which to assimilate American culture. Franklin Delano Roosevelt once called baseball the great melting pot of America, but unlike men, no woman was going to realize the national dream of coming to bat in the bottom of the ninth with the game on the line. Cheering from the stands was as close as she would get. Sportswriter Red Smith tells of an Englishwoman who lived in Seattle while she undertook the process of becoming a United States citizen. As the paperwork dragged on, she filled her afternoons by attending Pacific Coast League games. After she was sworn in as a citizen, however, she claimed she still did not *feel* American. That changed during a summertime visit to New York City, she said: "This afternoon, I was in Yankee Stadium and I saw Joe DiMaggio hit a home run and now—now I am an American citizen!"[33]

Lil Levant, whose visit to Cooperstown is discussed in chapter 1, is named for her maternal grandmother, Lilyan Solomon. The Solomons emigrated from Prussia in the 1930s and settled in the Rogers Park neighborhood of Chicago. Jack Solomon worked long hours, and Lilyan took to spending afternoons at nearby Wrigley Field. Levant grew up on her grandparents' stories: "Unlike Los Angeles or New York, Chicago did not have a large Jewish community in those days," she said, "and Jews had a hard time in this town."[34] At Wrigley Field, however, her grandmother found a place in which to identify with being an American. In the process, Lilyan began a family tradition of rooting for the Cubs that would extend for three generations of women.

Lilyan Solomon was also a fan of the Detroit Tigers outfielder Hank Greenberg, whose appeal transcended his muscular good looks. As the first great Jewish star, Greenberg embodied the promise of success and acceptance to others of his faith during the 1930s and 1940s, when strong anti-Semitism existed in the United States. Although Lilyan was devoted to the Cubs, she felt no conflict between her loyalties since Chicago and Detroit played in different leagues. The 1945 World Series brought the teams together, however, and Lilyan's moment of crisis came in Game 6. With the score tied and Greenberg up, she broke ranks with the family and the home team to cheer for the great Jewish star. Greenberg had already gone 4-for-4, but this time he struck out. Then, in the twelfth inning, a ball bounced past him for a game-winning double.

After the game, Lilyan waited outside in the parking lot. When her hero appeared, she ran to him, asking for an autograph. Greenberg bore a heavy responsibility to do well. "If you struck out," he once said, "you weren't just a bum, but a Jewish bum."[35] That afternoon, the downcast Greenberg walked right past Lilyan Solomon. "You can understand it," said Lil Levant. "He'd struck out; they'd lost the game; he was in a bad mood; but my grandmother was traumatized by the rejection. From then on, she hated him and never would let go of that."

Throughout World War II, with many men overseas, women helped keep professional baseball going as fans (and, in the Midwest, as players in the All-American Girls Baseball League). When the war ended, however, the independent women working in the nation's factories and offices, personified by Rosie the Riveter, gave way to returning soldiers. With women settling into family life—the baby boom began in 1946—their numbers dwindled at the ballpark. A 1951 joint survey by the New York Yankees and the New York Giants showed fewer than 10 percent of their fans to be women. Six years later, a survey undertaken by the Boston Red Sox determined that 28 percent of the fans at Fenway were female. At home, however, women were becoming a significant part of Major League Baseball's television audience. In August 1962, a Baltimore Orioles survey found that 55 percent of the women of that city followed baseball on TV. The Baltimore study revealed similarities between male and female viewing habits: 56 percent of the women and 61 percent of the men watched twenty or more televised games a season; and 39 percent of the women and 33 percent of the men watched thirty or more games. The report concluded:

> While aware that there are women who watch baseball on television, many advertisers tend to discount this segment of the audience. . . . All too often, it is assumed that women are secondary, captive viewers who happen to be in range of the TV set only because others in the family are watching baseball. This is a highly erroneous assumption that has kept many companies from capitalizing on baseball sponsorship as an effective way to reach—and sell—men and women alike.[36]

Over the next decades, the report's conclusions would be verified, but both Organized Baseball and its advertisers would continue to substantially ignore marketing opportunities to women. In the year that the Baltimore survey appeared, Betty Friedan, a New York housewife and journalist, was completing a book that would challenge the idea that women were universally satisfied with "secondary, captive" roles in any aspect of American society. During a survey undertaken for her Smith College reunion, Friedan learned that many of her classmates, bright and relatively affluent, wanted more from life than they were getting. Friedan dug deeper and published the results of her research in *The Feminine Mystique*. The book appeared in 1963 and helped to launch a social revolution. As the women's movement grew, women became ambitious. Friedan said, "Secretaries went on to law school or to write for the *Wall Street Journal*. They got excited about life's possibilities."[37] Along with these new "possibilities," however, came tighter schedules and greater responsibilities. Women began retreating to the ballpark for the same reason that men always had—to escape pressures at work. As a New Jersey woman explained, "A few hours spent at the ballpark is one of the best ways I know of to relax and enjoy life. When I walk through the turnstile, I leave all my problems and responsibilities on the other side. . . . I can't even be reached by telephone, so I'm in another world."[38]

The 1970s saw great social change. Women were taking their place in the public forum, and those who were fans began using it to speak out about their feelings for baseball. For example, in *A Wife's Guide to Baseball*, Charline Gibson, the wife of the St. Louis Cardinals ace right-hander, Bob Gibson, states that baseball can be enjoyed by the whole family, and that the game now belonged to women, too. Other women claimed that baseball had always been their game: One woman recalled a childhood spent under the influence of Hilda Chester, "where the ring of her bell was as familiar as the voice of Red Barber."[39] "Feminine fans were simply hiding in closets," writes an Oakland A's fan in her weekly newspaper column in 1975. "And why shouldn't we display our devotion. . . . [W]hile we women aren't a part of the playing field—yet—we wouldn't miss sitting in the stands for the world."[40]

A new breed of female fan was now loose, literally, in the ballpark. In 1971, Morganna Roberts, acting on a friend's dare, burst onto the field of Cincinnati's Riverfront Stadium and planted a kiss on Pete Rose. The exotic dancer then took her act to other ballparks, storming the diamond to bestow kisses on the likes of Johnny Bench, George Brett, Steve Garvey, Nolan Ryan, and Cal Ripken Jr. With a cascade of blonde hair and measurements of 60", 24", 39", Roberts made headlines as the "Kissing Bandit" for nearly three decades before retreating from the scene. Her behavior was extreme, but beyond the notoriety, it signified a real shift in women's attitudes. It would have been unthinkable for women of earlier times to trespass onto the field of play or to display their sexuality so blatantly, and for the press to play along with it to the extent it did. Roberts, a woman of the seventies, symbolized the news that women were entering formerly masculine turf and that sexual forwardness was not limited to men.

Major League Baseball tried to keep up with the changing times and the fashions. The idea often seemed to get women to wear as little clothing as possible to the ballpark. For a doubleheader against Kansas City in June 1971, Oakland A's owner Charlie Finley varied the usual Ladies' Day promotions by offering free admission to each woman who showed up in hot pants (tight shorts usually worn with knee-high boots). Eleven thousand women did so, with more than 6,000 of them appearing in the fashion show between games. That August, the Washington Senators hosted Hot Pants Night, and in September, the Kansas City Royals welcomed 4,367 hot-pantsed women to "Beauty in Hot Pants Night." A few years later, at a Cleveland Indians Ladies' Night, women received official club halter tops.

Hot Pants and Halter Nights notwithstanding, the tradition of Ladies' Day was under challenge. In 1970, a man demanded a discounted ticket to a Ladies' Day game at Yankee Stadium, arguing that it was reverse discrimination to economically favor women fans. The New York Human Rights Commission agreed and, in a decision handed down in March 1973, ordered both New York teams, the Yankees and the Mets, to end the sale of free or discounted tickets to women. Feminists agreed, calling the tradition demeaning. If women wanted equal pay in order to make their own way in society, they should pay the same price as men did to see a ball game. It was a reasonable argument, but the unhappy result was that Major League Baseball lost a time-proven marketing tool. "The demise of Ladies' Day was a fatal mistake, because women stopped bringing their kids to the ballpark," reasoned baseball historian Bill Kirwin, who wondered why the tradition could not have been renamed "Family Day." Arguably, the end of Ladies' Day played a role in MLB's loss of young fans to football, basketball, and hockey, which were rising in popularity. (By 2001, baseball's median fan age of forty-seven would be the oldest of the four major sports.)[41]

Yet the social changes that killed off Ladies' Day can be credited with bringing diehard female fans into the game's mainstream. After the passage of Title IX of the Education Acts of 1972 gave American girls the chance to participate in organized sports and to earn athletic scholarships, the perception of women in sports changed. Women began to be more accepted, and to accept themselves, as serious baseball fans. Tilla Vahanian, a New York psychotherapist, noted a difference between earlier generations of female fans, whose parents usually introduced them to sports, and the young women of the 1970s who became fans because they themselves were active in sports. Women were also losing the old fear of appearing odd or unfeminine if they participated in sporting events, according to Vahanian, who predicted that "as society grew to accept the fact that women, too, have a competitive streak, even more women would feel comfortable as fans."[42]

Vahanian was proven correct in this. By 1977, Mike Burke, then president of the New York Yankees, pronounced that the club was drawing more women. Over the next decade, the number of female Yankee fans doubled to 33 percent. And in 1979, Chicago White Sox owner Bill Veeck gained "national attention with his announcement that thirty-six percent of Sox fans are women."[43] In the following decades, women have come to make up between 40 and 50 percent of Major League Baseball's fan base. For a woman, the benefits of fandom go beyond the enjoyment of a game at the ballpark. She returns to work with baseball stories, stats, and observations. For example, Anna Newton, an active member of San Diego's Ted Williams chapter of the Society for American Baseball Research, found that being a knowledgeable fan improved her credibility in the workplace: "Following the game and discussing its issues at work can be a noncompetitive communication for all involved."[44] Vanalyne Green agreed: "Membership in the sports club is a calling card anywhere the language of sport is spoken. Being conversant breaks down sexual boundaries."[45] The game fosters other bonds between men and women. A survey conducted by SportsDating.com found that 41 percent of the women interviewed favored the ballpark for a first-date sporting event. As Joel Benson, a founder of SportsDating.com, explained, "Many of the females responding stated they preferred a sport where they could converse with their date and still follow the action."[46] That would be baseball, which, when we allow it, brings men and women together. The following vignettes demonstrate how richly baseball informs the lives of American women of all ages. While these stories focus on some of the game's most loyal and long-suffering fans—those of the Chicago Cubs—they reflect how baseball colors the lives of women all over the country.

SPRING TRAINING IN ARIZONA'S CACTUS LEAGUE

Through the stands of HoHoKam Field wafted a medley of fragrances that signifies springtime in Arizona's Cactus League: smoke from the grills where Chicago hot dogs sizzle, and the aroma of orange blossoms from a nearby grove of trees mingled with that of the suntan lotion marinating eight thousand fans on a sunny March afternoon. As the Chicago Cubs prepared to play the Colorado Rockies, eight-year-old Brittany Tennyson sat tall beside her father. From her seat behind home plate, she could see the field spread before her in wedge-shaped perfection, the grass impossibly green. Phil Tennyson explained why they were here. "She goes everywhere with me," he said, "but this is her first baseball game."[47] A child of divorce, Brittany saw her father every other weekend and for thirty days each summer. The two hiked Camelback Mountain, and he introduced her with little effect to golf and football. Coming here was her idea. She watched closely as the mayor of Mesa, a red-haired woman in a Cubs-blue business suit, threw a wimpy first pitch, and the fans cheered. Under her father's eye, Brittany studied the program, and soon questions and answers ricocheted between the two—*Why is this guy hitting from the other side of the plate? How come the pitcher only pitched to one batter? Why's that guy spit all the time?*—as she learned the language of base-ball. When the inning ended, Brittany asked for a Cubs cap.

By the fifth inning, Brittany Tennyson had a stomach full of hot dogs and red vines, and wore a bright blue Cubs cap. And when Harry Caray, credited with beginning the seventh-inning stretch tradition of "Take Me Out to the Ball Game" in 1971, leaned perilously out of the announcer's booth to lead the singing, Brittany sang, too, a beat behind as she learned the words. After the game, her father tried to prepare her for endings, explaining that spring training in the Cactus League would soon be over, that the Cubs would then head north. As they left the ballpark, Brittany wanted to know where Chicago was, and when could they go to Wrigley Field, and was it far from home. Many more ball games followed, but when Brittany was a teenager, she became estranged from her father. The two later reconciled, but during the hard times it was Phil Tennyson who hung onto the memories of sunnier days at the ballpark. There he had welcomed his daughter into the world of sports and taught her all he knew of its code of behavior and values.

A RETURNING FAN: SUMMERTIME AT WRIGLEY FIELD

Most often it is fathers (or uncles or grandfathers) who are credited with instilling in a girl a love for baseball. Lil Levant's interest, however, came through her maternal line. As a young girl, Levant lived within walking distance of Wrigley Field in a home filled with baseball tensions, for the family never had an opinion on the game that went unexpressed. Her father, Jerry Levant, who worked twelve-hour days managing a clothing store, liked to root for the Chicago White Sox, either because they played at night when he could watch them on television, or out of sheer contrariness. Lil's schoolteacher mother, Rhoda Levant, edified her three daughters by blasting Cubs games from every radio and television in the house. Lil remembered the arguments: "'How can you like the Cubs?' my father would begin. Then we'd get belligerent about it, with mother leading the call, always. Baseball bonded us and positioned us against our dad. It was all pretty primal."[48]

The family's move to Evanston created a child-care dilemma. Summer vacation for the girls began weeks before their mother finished her teaching duties at James McPherson Elementary School, near Wrigley Field. Rhoda Levant found the ideal solution. During each home stand she drove the girls, aged ten, eight, and six, into Chicago, tuned to the pregame show all the way, and dropped them off at Wrigley Field.

"My parents didn't have a lot of money," said Lil, "but mother always gave us enough: a dollar to get into the bleachers and another dollar or so for a hot dog." The girls would hang around outside for a couple of hours before entering at about 10:30 to watch batting practice. Once in the bleachers, they ignored the tradition of sitting in a regular section and moved around, trying different vantage points. Levant says that in the early 1960s, it was common to see children on the loose in the bleachers. No one looked out for the girls, and she and her sisters did not find their situation in any way peculiar. "In her mind, my mother thought it was the most wonderful thing she could do for us, though now it would probably be considered child neglect to leave a kid on the street from 8:30 until 3:30 with two bucks. We had a hell of a great time by ourselves."

While waiting for her mother one afternoon, Lil suddenly realized she had left her sweater in the bleachers. When she re-entered the park to retrieve her sweater, all the fans had gone. She climbed to the top of the vacant bleachers and looked down. "It was like a shrine," she said. "The greenness, the ivy . . . being there alone, I could almost hear the voices. I still remember the strong feeling of attachment for this park, this game, that came over me then." Levant's sense of attachment carried into adulthood. After years of returning each April for Opening Day, she decided to explore a move back to Chicago. I was in town on the same weekend, and we agreed to meet at the ballpark.

In June, the maples lining the streets leading to Wrigley Field leaf out. Elderly women stand outside their brick walkups, hawking the driveways to their one-car garages as parking spots to cruising fans. At crowded corner pubs, songs like "Margaritaville" play long and loud, and patrons overflow onto the sidewalk. Strangers pause and speak to one another: *the Cubs are back!* Levant was waiting on the corner of Clark and Addison. A businesslike woman in her early forties, she was dismayed by the changes to her old neighborhood. Known now as Wrigleyville, the area had gentrified; when she was growing up on Damen Avenue, the area was simply "the North Side by the Lake." Between innings, she spoke of her feelings for baseball: "It's the same feeling that other people get when they go to church. I spend a lot of time worrying about what is going on in this world, politically, culturally, socio-economically," she said. "Going to the park offers a respite from all that. Come to think of it, nothing else helps. With baseball, you just walk into the park, sit down, and there it is. When I go, I always feel young. I feel like the world's gonna be all right."

THE TEENAGE FAN

About the time that a girl realizes the baseball diamond is in truth closed to her as an athlete, she notices how fine a particular player looks in his uniform. It can be a poignant shift in baseball priorities, the giving up of dreams of glory on the field for fantasies of a different sort. From the safety of the stands, she flits between fan and lover. Lil Levant was fifteen years old when she suddenly discovered Adolpho Phillips: "He played center field, and he had the greatest legs. I didn't know what I was looking at, but I liked what I saw—the whole package." Aviva Kempner, the director of the award-winning documentary film *The Life and Times of Hank Greenberg,* had a teenage crush on Rocky Colavito but said she was too much of a nice Jewish girl to act on it. Kempner added, "These days, when you go up to Yankee Stadium, you see twelve-year-old girls screaming for Derek Jeter."[49]

It is an old story. As early as 1890, Ella Black was writing about the sensation caused when first baseman Paul Hines took the field in "a shirt that fit him like a kid glove . . . and his appearance in that shirt would have brought a blush to the face of many a fair maid."[50] Seventy years later, young women were still presumably blushing. During the Mets' miracle year of 1969, the *New York Times* reported that one twelve-year-old, a fan since "before she could say Ron Swoboda," wore a T-shirt with the legend, "Tom Seaver Is Sexy."[51] Young girls were not alone in their sentiments that frenzied season in Queens. Women of all ages regressed to a teenlike adulation of the Mets, according to the *Times*. "Women like winners," explained a blonde model. "Successful men, whether they're ballplayers or businessmen, are sexy. Right now, the Mets are very successful." The social changes wrought by the 1960s might be expected to have prompted a change in demeanor among female fans. Striving to end their own sexual objectification in business, education, and athletics, why would liberated women treat ball players the same way? At the ballpark, however, eyeing the opposite sex has always worked both ways; and the women's movement only brought the issue out of the closet.

Women grew more outspoken about their appreciation of the ballplayers. During the 1994 players' strike, *Baseball Weekly* surveyed its female readers on the subject: "yes, there have been players who I've thought were attractive," responded a New Yorker, "and it's nice that baseball can offer something to just about everyone, including women who want to ogle good-looking guys!"[52] In October 2000, a new thread of discourse appeared in the online discussion group of the Society for American Baseball Research with a woman's post that announcer Bob Costas was "cute." Debbi Dagavarian, the deputy vice provost of Thomas Edison State College, responded to "the brave female who admitted that she thinks Costas is cute. I agree, and I'm not at all offended. I certainly have had my share of baseball crushes, especially when I was younger, daydreaming about the likes of Art Shamsky, George Brett, and Dave Winfield."[53]

While one of the gender distinctions among fans is heterosexual women's appreciation of a player in his uniform, that pleasure can evolve into something loftier. Watching a favorite star can move a young woman to dream of success in other arenas. Reflecting on the Fernando-mania of Los Angeles in the early 1980s, Alicia Fombona later wrote:

> I was one of the 10,000 extra Latino fans on the days Fernando Valenzuela pitched at Dodger Stadium. I was a young girl living in Watts. Going to the stadium was the highlight of the weekend, even if we were sitting in the cheap seats in the upper deck. Now, 20 years later, I am an engineer working in a nontraditional profession for Latinas. I am very proud of who I am and very comfortable in the

work environments. Valenzuela was a very good role model. . . . I definitely identified with him.[54]

THE ADULT FAN: AUTUMN IN WRIGLEYVILLE

Apropos baseball, Stephanie Leathers did not enjoy a privileged childhood,
attending only one Chicago White Sox game at Comiskey Park. Now a
grandmother, she holds a season ticket to the Wrigley Field bleachers. She
is also the founder and publisher of *Bleacher Banter,* an independent
newsletter sold by subscription to Cubs fans. I joined Leathers, a hearty-
voiced Croatian American, in Wrigley's left-field bleachers on a June afternoon to talk of what it means to fall for baseball in midlife.

We began at the concession stand, where Cecelia (Cece) Esom was
tapping beer with queenly grace. When Leathers stepped to the counter,
Esom drew our beer, urged us to take a sip, and topped it off. Then she
reached beneath the counter for a red scrapbook, filled with photographs
of the regulars. The bleachers are notoriously raucous, but nobody waiting in line behind us complained as Leathers and Esom looked through
the pictures from the last homestand.

Back at our seats, a stream of bleacher regulars visited with Leathers for
gossip, counsel, or a cup of vodka-laced lemonade from her jug of Slug-
gers, while the Ted Butterman Quintet, men in Cubs-blue jackets and hats,
serenaded the fans with tunes like "Peg o' My Heart," the notes from their
horn, banjo, clarinet, and tuba soaring into the breeze off Lake Michigan.
To this outsider, it seemed like a neighborhood had been dropped intact
into the bleachers, and I recalled a comment by Vanalyne Green, who also
discovered baseball as an adult. As she studied the game, Green came to
believe that essential aspects of baseball culture came out of the feminine
tradition of oral history, story telling, and gossip.[55] That afternoon at
Wrigley, Green's thesis came alive as fans came to Stephanie Leathers to
remember, confide, and talk. While men were very much a part of the
milieu, it was Leathers, as editor of the *Banter,* who took the diverse people
and their stories and wove them into something more—community.

Leathers's own baseball story began in 1979. A divorcee with a daughter, she worked downtown as a legal secretary. She also played right field
for a team in the Loop Legal Women's Softball League until a new coach
decided to make her a pitcher, despite her protests that she knew nothing
of the fundamentals. On the day of her debut on the mound, Leathers got

so nervous that a coworker suggested they take the afternoon off to study the pros at Wrigley. The fact that softball is pitched underhand notwithstanding, it was the wrong day to pick up pointers on pitching of any sort. By the end of the first inning, the Philadelphia Phillies were leading 7–6. With the wind blowing up to twenty miles per hour toward the outfield, eleven home runs sailed out that day: Mike Schmidt hit two, Dave Kingman hit three, and Bill Buckner had a grand slam.[56] Pitcher Randy Lerch homered, too. With Philadelphia leading by the score of 23–22, Leathers had to force herself to leave for the softball game. She learned little about the art of pitching that windy afternoon, but she left the bleachers a fan:

> I think it was the correlation between my starting to pitch and what was happening on the field at Wrigley. I felt a connection. Throughout that season, I pestered friends to go with me to Wrigley Field until one, who was really a White Sox fan anyway, said something like, "Hey, going to the ball game alone is OK." And I, who seldom went anywhere alone, thought, *yes, I could do this by myself.*[57]

Although the times no longer permitted the sort of trust that had enabled Lil Levant's mother to leave her daughters at the park, Leathers felt safe enough conversing with the strangers she met at Wrigley Field. Like Cheers, television's idealized neighborhood bar where everybody knows your name, the seats were filled with regulars who had the professional and personal stats of virtually everyone on and off the field. She found the social politics of the bleachers so exotic that she sometimes felt she was entering a cult but reasoned it was simply an elite circle, where you did not let just anyone in. A would-be regular had to prove her worth. Although her affection for the characters in the bleachers kept drawing her back over five seasons, Leathers still felt an outsider. With plenty of time for observation, she saw a community in flux:

> Ticket prices were rising, the fans were aging, and after winning the 1984 National League East Division, the team stunk. In the bleachers, I'd hear *whatever happened to so-and-so? I heard they moved.* There was a network, but it was limited to each section of the bleachers. And I thought it was a shame that there was no way to keep in touch when people couldn't come to the games anymore. I thought, *wouldn't it be nice if people knew when someone was coming back and what was happening?*

When Leathers learned in 1990 that Wilma Fields, a matron she befriended, had been working for the Cubs for thirty-two years, she petitioned the front office to sponsor a Wilma Fields Day. According to Leathers, "Management's response went, 'Gee, if we did this for Wilma we'd have to do it for everybody else who has been here a long time.' They thanked me for letting them know and promised to send Wilma a copy of my letter, but she never saw it." Consequently, Leathers assembled her own one-page tribute to Fields for Opening Day, 1991, and named it *Bleacher Banter*. The *Banter,* she figured, could appear a few times each season to inform the fans of what was happening in everyone's life and to provide news and opinions about the ball club.

The response was underwhelming. The front office denied her requests for a press pass and the usually loquacious regulars were reticent: "They had seen reporters, who usually distort the facts of life in the bleachers, come and go," Leathers explained. "I think they figured *why would Stephanie be any different?* They wanted the facts to be straight but they didn't want to talk with me." Leathers then put out the word that her newsletter was open to everyone; it was not a clique.

The *Banter*'s popularity began to grow through word of mouth and row-by-row circulation, as did its publisher's sense of belonging. When *Baseball Weekly* wanted to know what fans thought of Ryne Sandburg's abrupt mid-season retirement in 1994, it led with Leathers's comments. When the *Chicago Sun-Times* profiled Leathers, six hundred people responded. First baseman Mark Grace (traded to the Arizona Diamondbacks after the 2000 season) used to set out a stack of the latest issue in the clubhouse. By 2001, the *Banter* had developed into a popular grassroots newsletter of eighteen to twenty-four pages, with news and gossip by and about the fans in the bleachers, odes to and critiques of current and ex–Cub players, and musings about the vagaries of Major League Baseball. With the Cubs owned by the *Chicago Tribune,* the *Banter* offered an independent point of view that was frequently critical of the corporation's "little Barney Fife rules and regulations." Thus, when Cece Esom was moved to a distant concession stand, Leathers speculated that management thought Esom overly fan friendly. Leathers also told the front office about Carmella Hartigan. Well on in her nineties, Hartigan rode three buses to get to the ballpark, where she then had to bargain for a ticket. Pointing out the public relations value of one of the few fans alive when the Cubs last won the World Series in 1908, Leathers asked the Cubs to give Hartigan a lifetime pass. She shook her head at the response. "They just said something to the effect *if we did that for Carmella, we'd have to do it for all the others like her.* I mean, how many ninety-something fans do they think are left?" (Leathers later reported that Hartigan did receive a pass for the 2001 season; Hartigan died that December.)

WINTER COMES TO THE WRIGLEYVILLE TAP

Late in October 1999, Leathers and I met at the Wrigleyville Tap, a post-game hangout of the Bleacher Bums filled with old bats, photographs of Cubs dead and gone, and framed World Series ticket stubs from 1945. The Tap had recently lost its lease and was about to close down, and the mood was elegiac. Outside, winter had already nipped at the silver maples, and on Clark Street, Wrigley Field sat vacant against a gray sky. Leathers, who had been staring out at the view, suddenly turned away and said, "I don't like to see the park in winter. The season's over, and it all feels so empty."

A tattooed bleacher bum interrupted her thoughts. He had stopped by for a farewell game of pool, spotted her, and borrowed pen and paper in order to leave his change-of-address for the *Banter.* The two talked over the shortage of affordable apartments near the ballpark for a while, a conversation followed by a right-field regular, attorney Ron Hayden, who stopped by to commiserate on the loss of the Tap. For some years, Hayden has hosted the January Party, a gathering of some 400 Cubs faithful, at the Wrigleyville Tap, and he and Leathers considered where next year's party might take place. Watching her converse, listening to her tales about life in the bleachers, and perusing the *Banter,* I decided that baseball was central to her life. After two decades as a fan, Leathers had learned the ballpark's value as gathering place. Here she found, and then fostered through the *Banter,* what others find at church or synagogue: the warmth of fellowship and the comfort and familiarity of ritual—baseball as community. As we prepared to leave, the cold Chicago sky made the lighthearted days of summer games, of singing "Take Me Out to the Ball Game" with Harry Caray wannabes during seventh-inning stretch, seem far away. But as we left the Tap for the last time, an old Buddy Holly tune was playing: "Every day, it's a-gettin' closer," and behind the bar on a yellow Post-it pad were the words "163 days 'til Opening Day."

3 In the Shadows
Baseball Annies

MICKEY MANTLE. *MICKEY MANTLE.* This attraction to the Mick was surprising and new. Sitting in the bleachers at Yankee Stadium on a chilly April day in 1957, I had suddenly realized that my hero and I were opposites, meant to attract. At age fourteen, this felt like great news. That season, I no longer just went to the ballpark; I made an appearance, which called for thoughtful attention to hair, makeup, and dress. To the discomfort of my father, who kept saying, "He's just a *ballplayer,* for crying out loud," a piece of my heart now belonged to Mickey Mantle.

Other hearts were apparently beating as mine. Songwriter Ruth Roberts had recently written "I Love Mickey," a duet sung by Theresa Brewer and Mantle himself, whose title pretty much sums up the lyrics. Years passed, however, before I realized how many other young women felt as I did: "Once I thought that term cleanup referred only to Mick," writes Roberta Israeloff. "He was the cleanest looking player I'd ever seen. . . . His Oklahoma blondness was as exotic as anything from Odessa."[1]

It seemed wrong to fantasize about Mantle, though I do not remember giving any thought to his wife or his marriage, an early clue that there is little sense of sisterhood among such idol worshipers. Because I lacked the chutzpah to act on my fantasies, Mickey Mantle lived on, innocent of this wannabe groupie. By the time I dated my first ballplayer, I was thirty-six and had learned a few things about ballplayers, groupies, and life. By then, thanks to Jim Bouton's tell-all memoir *Ball Four*, I understood that my old hero's emotional age was probably not much beyond mine when I "discovered" him at age fourteen. Mantle, it turns out, was a team leader in the ballplayers' pastime of "beaver shooting"—the art of finding ways to look under women's skirts from the dugout, the bullpen, and wherever else the opportunity occurred. Of particular interest to players on road trips was the tradition of spying upon female guests from hotel rooftops. The Shoreham Hotel, in Washington, D.C., was prime territory, according to Bouton, who writes, "The Yankees would go up there in squads of fifteen or so, often led by Mickey Mantle himself."[2]

Many a female fan flirts with the idea of romance and sex with a ball-player. Unlike the majority of women who are content with reverie, however, Baseball Annies act on their fantasies. Some women single out a player, hoping to make the cut to bona fide girlfriend or even wife. Others collect one-night stands like baseball cards. Some women sleep only with American League pitchers, or with players from a certain team. Jim Bouton writes of "Chicago Shirley who takes on every club as it gets to town. The first thing she does is call up the rookies for an orientation briefing."[3] Most Baseball Annies are young, between seventeen and twenty-four, and are active for three to four years before they "retire." (An anomaly, however, would be the Milwaukee woman whose career spanned twenty years. She began as a young woman with players; as she grew older, she moved on to coaches and managers.) Other women favor front office personnel, while former minor league umpire Pam Postema maintained that her colleagues enjoyed "a smaller but equally dedicated collection of groupies who reside in just about every major and minor league town. . . . It wasn't uncommon for some of my fellow umpires to have names and numbers of girls who had made the previous crew's stay in town a happy one."[4] Whatever the particulars, a Baseball Annie is willing to trade sexual favors for a more intimate connection to the game.

Early groupies were known as "daisies" and "green flies," and lumped with other "pests," like sportswriters, who also persisted in hanging around the players. Later, the terms "bobby-soxers" and "locals" were used. "Imports" take road trips with their player, while a few women, like Chicago Shirley, warrant a unique moniker. Today, we call them Baseball Annies, a term popularized by the female lead in the 1988 film *Bull Durham*.[5] Susan Sarandon's Annie Savoy is a serial groupie, who each season bestows her sexual favors and her baseball acumen upon a player she culls from the minor league Durham Bulls. "There's never been a ballplayer slept with me who didn't have the best year of his career," Annie claims in her opening soliloquy. "I make them feel confident; they make me feel safe and pretty."[6]

Real-life Baseball Annies, eager for such a trade-off, live in the shadows of Organized Baseball. Attracted by the bright lights of celebrity, they linger in the stands, by the players' entrance to ballparks, in the hotel lobbies where visiting teams stay, and at conveniently located bars like Crackers in Anaheim, Hi-Tops in Chicago, and A.J.'s in St. Louis. For these women and the players they pursue, spring training in Florida's Grapefruit League and Arizona's Cactus League becomes a modern-day incarnation of the game's ancient fertility rites. Baseball Annies are also found in high-school and collegiate baseball and in every minor league town. Wherever one finds them, Baseball Annies form "the vortex where sex and sports collide."[7] And a collision it is, given the inherent risks of divorce and palimony suits, sexually transmitted diseases, and physical assaults. Baseball Annies undermine the game's carefully tended clean-cut image, and they damage and even destroy players' marriages, careers, and reputations. Some Baseball Annies become stalkers and assailants. Their behavior mystifies others: "Women who refuse to give most men the time of day will gladly debauch themselves with a total stranger whose face appears on a bubble gum card," complains Dan Gutman in *Baseball Babylon*.[8] Such behavior usually affects only the participants and, unfortunately, their families. America, we like to say, is a free country, and if grown men and women behave so, that is personal. However, Baseball Annies also had another effect on the game that goes far beyond the individual. They were a key factor in Organized Baseball's lengthy ban on African American ballplayers.

BASEBALL ANNIES AND THE COLOR LINE

To understand why this is so, it is helpful to understand that Baseball Annies did not emanate from the sexual revolution of the 1960s and 1970s. They were eyeing ballplayers from the get-go of Organized Baseball. Recall that in 1869, the year the Cincinnati Red Stockings became the first fully professional ball club, "Maude, the pet blond" was advertising herself to "the brilliant assemblages of the base ball games."[9] By the 1880s, a time when African Americans Moses Fleetwood Walker and his brother Welday were trying (and ultimately failing) to gain acceptance in white professional baseball, women were flocking to the ballpark as spectators—and sportswriters were noting the dynamics between some of these women and the ballplayers. By 1889, Henry Chadwick was ready to declare, "The two great obstacles in the way of the success of the majority of professional ball players are wine and women."[10] In 1890, columnist Ella Black periodically spoke out about the adulation that women were lavishing upon good-looking ballplayers like Paul Hines, Tony Mullane, and John Tener. Black shows that this hero worship could become excessive in an interview with a young Pittsburgh woman who had encountered the members of a local team during their daily run: "One of the men immediately took her fancy, and she could not get his tall, well-shaped figure out of her mind."[11] When the woman's brother discovers her attempts to contact the player, he goes to their father:

> There was quite a scene when he talked to his daughter, and even then she would have persisted in her object only that she learned the player was a married man. However, she still keeps his photo on her dressing stand, and had quite a little weep yesterday while she was telling me the above story. This is one thing there is entirely too much of. Girls are beginning to be as romantic and foolish over ball players as they were formerly over actors.

The early twentieth century was a time of growing racial tensions. The Ku Klux Klan was on the rise again, and eugenicists who saw blacks as inferior were arguing that the races must not mix. By 1913, American League teams were forbidden to barnstorm against black or mixed-race teams.[12] African American ballplayers who hoped for a thaw in such attitudes found their cause badly hurt by the flamboyant black boxer Jack Johnson, who reigned as the world heavyweight champion from 1908 to 1915. Johnson liked to flaunt his sexuality. He also flouted the idea of blacks as subservient or inferior, taunting his white opponents and sometimes humiliating them in the ring. This behavior in itself would have been enough to make those in baseball fear to sign black ballplayers, but Johnson went further. In a time when anti-miscegenation laws forbade marriage between the races in many states, Johnson managed to marry three white women. He was also a womanizer who particularly enjoyed consorting with white prostitutes. (The Mann Act of 1910 attempted to curtail the spread of prostitution by making it illegal to transport a woman across state lines for "immoral purposes," a term that invited various interpretations.) The year 1912 was Johnson's annus horribilis. His first wife, Ella, committed suicide in September; shortly after, he was accused under the Mann Act of "kidnapping" a white woman named Lucille Cameron. (Lucille was Johnson's girlfriend, however, and refused to cooperate in the charges.) In November, a federal grand jury indicted Johnson on eleven counts of Mann Act violations because of his relationship with a white prostitute named Belle Schreiber. The grand jury's presiding judge was Kenesaw Mountain Landis. In *Judge and Jury: The Life and Times of Judge Kenesaw Mountain Landis*, David Pietrusza writes of Landis's reaction to the case:

> Landis demanded $30,000 in bail from Johnson for him to go free but refused to accept Johnson's money for this purpose. "I will not accept a cash bond in this case," said Landis. "There is a human cry in this case that cannot be overlooked in consideration of a bond." After the heavyweight champion spent four days in prison, Landis consented to accept $32,000 in property from Johnson's mother as bail.[13]

Johnson was found guilty. Facing a thousand-dollar fine and a year and a day in prison, he fled to Canada with Lucille, who was by now his wife. He returned seven years later to serve out his sentence but never did untangle his romantic life—he was linked at various times with the likes of Mae West and Mata Hari. Johnson wanted his full measure of freedom: "I want to say that I am not a slave and that I have the right to choose who my mate shall be without the dictation of any man."[14]

Scholars of sports history have since examined the results of Jack Johnson's notoriety. "Because of Johnson's arrogance and love for white women, many whites considered him a serious threat to racial order. Many blacks were lynched as a result of the actions of Johnson," writes R. Reese in the *Journal of African American Men.*[15] Johnson's behavior affected the next generation of African American athletes. When boxer Joe Louis appeared on the scene in 1934, his advisers warned, "The white man hasn't forgotten that fool nigger [Johnson] with his white women. . . . [A]bove all you never have your picture taken with a white woman."[16] Landis's familiarity with the Johnson case surely influenced his attitude toward integration when he became the first commissioner of baseball in 1920. Clearly, Landis was not the only man responsible for the lengthy ban on blacks. As Pietrusza has pointed out, with owners like Tom Yawkey and his cohorts in the Red Sox front office, whose racism is now well documented, there was a climate throughout the game that precluded integration for several reasons: among them the fears of race riots, losing to blacks, and alienating white fans. For such men, the idea of white female fans fawning over black players was bad enough, but the thought of Baseball Annies "mixing" with black players was intolerable. It was only after Landis's death in 1944 that Branch Rickey felt the latitude to sign Jackie Robinson.

Why Robinson from among the wealth of talent in the Negro Leagues? Sam Lacy, the well-regarded black sportswriter who had lobbied for integration, explained it this way: "Robinson was educated, was accustomed to interracial competition at UCLA, was religious, was fearless and, equally important, was engaged [to a black woman]. You have to understand that all the white establishment was fearful of bringing a black man into a white situation. They feared they would chase white women."[17] Actually, the "white establishment" running baseball knew very well that white Baseball Annies were likely to do much of the chasing. Jackie Robinson knew this firsthand; and after his retirement from baseball, it bothered him that the truth had not been told. In *The Boys of Summer,* Robinson tells sportswriter Roger Kahn, "And then there's a point about women. When I was at UCLA, more white women wanted to go to bed with me than I wanted to go to bed with white women."

"Congratulations," said Kahn.

"Everybody thinks it's all the other way," Robinson went on. "All the black guys are panting to get into bed with white women. Well, a lot of white guys are just dying to get hold of black women. I'm not kidding. I've seen it. And for me, with white girls, like I said, I didn't have to make much of a move."[18]

Even after the integration of MLB, the issue continued to affect black players. Home-run king Henry Aaron recalled going for a drive with a friend and two white women in the mid-1950s in Covington, Kentucky, where they were suddenly stopped by a police officer. "He asked me if I was married to the white girl sitting next to me, and I said no.... [H]e made me get out of the car right then. He said, 'Boy, you get out of town. We don't have that kind of thing around here.'"[19] Scouts and front-office men remained wary of black players who consorted with white women. Roger Kahn claims that in the 1950s, George Weiss, then the general manager of the New York Yankees, "unloaded an outstanding black Puerto Rican prospect, Victor Pellot Power, informing people at the *Times* and the *Herald Tribune*, 'Maybe he can play, but not for us. He's impudent and he goes for white women.'"[20] Baseball Annies were not the only reason segregation endured for so long in Organized Baseball, but they clearly contributed to the ban, providing Judge Landis and the white men who ran the game with one more excuse to maintain the status quo.

A CODE OF SILENCE

For much of baseball history, sportswriters were reluctant to discuss Baseball Annies and their effects upon the national pastime. While news occasionally appeared about the springtime free-for-alls in Arizona and Florida, or when a woman cried *rape*, the file on "Groupies" in the Baseball Hall of Fame Library is thin. Ignoring the subject was beneficial all around. Because such women undermined the game's all-American image, Organized Baseball certainly did not want the subject explored in the press. Sportswriters (some of whom enjoyed their own cadre of groupies) cooperated, taking the position that their job was to cover what happened on the diamond, not after hours. Besides, sportswriters were reliant upon the cooperation of the front office and field personnel. Write the full truth of what you saw, and your sources were likely to fall silent. Consequently, a 1929 article by Al Demarce, a National League pitcher from 1912 through 1919, sheds rare light on the subject:

> Sometimes a girl who has an eye for the bright lights is known as the "fifth pitcher" of the club, because she takes the hurlers of the visiting club out for a round of the cabarets at night, and they are not as effective as usual in the game the next day. Certain pitchers never win in certain towns because of these "baseball daisies," as Wilbert Robinson used to call them. "There's always a baseball daisy," he maintained. "Every town has one."[21]

Periodically, an image-conscious manager or a front-office executive tried to curtail a valued player's excesses. When second baseman Jimmie Reese joined the New York Yankees in 1931, the front office assigned him as Babe Ruth's roommate in hopes that the clean-living rookie would temper the Babe's notorious late-night adventures. The plan failed because Ruth would arrive at the hotel, pick up a stack of phone messages, and disappear. Reese never tired of telling reporters that he did not room with Babe Ruth, he roomed with his luggage.[22] Most ballplayers, however, were understandably reticent on the subject, until Jim Bouton broke the code of silence in 1970. Other ballplayers followed with their confessionals: In Bo Belinsky's *Bo: Pitching and Wooing* (1973) and Joe Pepitone's *Joe, You Coulda Made Us Proud* (1975), you can read all about Baseball Annies from the male point of view. Meanwhile, players' wives, including Jim Bouton's ex-wife Bobbie, began to tell the truth of their marriages. Ironically, Baseball Annies, though initially drawn to players' celebrity, seldom publicize their sexual exploits unless they feel they have been done a grievous wrong. It is mostly in fiction and in films like *Bull Durham* and *The Natural* that Baseball Annies step out of the shadows. The following story portrays a real-life woman who was willing to speak of how she went from fan to the sometime girlfriend of a married World Series–winning pitcher. She requested anonymity, and I call her "Betty."

Betty was in her thirties when we met and had begun to examine some of the connections in her life. Baseball, she realized, was the thread that tied her life together. "I've abandoned a lot in my life, but not baseball," she said. "It's the one link I still have to my childhood." When Betty was six years old, her mother bought her a small gold-colored aluminum bat so she could play ball with her sisters and the neighborhood kids in the backyard:

> Home plate was the worn-out spot in the lawn where the birdbath had once been; the cement gutter at the side of our house was first base; another worn-out spot (slightly deeper than home plate) was second, the clothesline pole was third. If the ball hit the roof, it was foul; if it hit the dirt driveway, it was an automatic homer; and if it hit a window both teams evacuated to the left-field bushes![23]

As Betty played, she could hear the crowd cheering at the nearby ballpark and pretended the cheers were for her. By the time the boys her age began Little League play, however, she realized that her athletic talents were limited. Her father died when she was young, but a brother-in-law introduced her to the role of fan, buying her junk food at the ballpark and showing her off to his friends in the stands. Growing up, Betty noticed that whenever the homegrown big leaguer returned, he was mobbed. Despite his average statistics, the townspeople saw him as a hero who connected them to their own baseball dreams, "proof that a kid from our small town could make the big time."

Over the years, Betty's old golden bat oxidized to a dull gray, the result of sitting out in the rain too many summer nights, but baseball continued to inform her life. Chafing at her parochial high school's strict rules, she took refuge in the bleachers, away from the scrutiny of school officials. "I bubbled with excitement each March. What a pleasure it was to sit in the bleachers in the warm sun, even if the only action on the field was baseball practice," she recalled. "The opening of the season signaled that summer, with all of its lazy fun, was just around the corner. To me, baseball always meant freedom and relaxation."

During her junior year, Betty and a friend lobbied to become the first batgirls in the school's history, promising "the soft-hearted coach we'd be good girls and that he'd never know we were there." Being good meant keeping quiet and staying in the background. Betty was proud of her role. She had lost the desire to play years ago but still craved closeness to the game. As batgirl, she was on the field, and some glory attached to that; she became the team manager, earning a varsity letter. After graduation, other girls lined up to take her place.

By then, Betty had lost two important men in her life to sudden death: a brother, in the Vietnam War, and the brother-in-law who had introduced her to baseball, of a heart attack. Following Major League Baseball on television offered some respite from her grief. From her living room, she was soon following the players as much as the game. The 1973 World Series between the New York Mets and the Oakland A's stands out in her memory, its appeal a confusion of sport and sex. In college, Betty met her first serious boyfriend through baseball when she saw him standing in the hallway, looking at baseball cards with friends. Her knowledge of the game prompted a conversation, and the two started dating. After graduating with a degree in journalism, she passed up a promising job interview to join him in Florida.

Spring training is a six-week-long tryout for Baseball Annies to make the big leagues. Young women plan their vacations around it. "We followed them down here," a woman from Connecticut told a reporter. "We've got some of their autographs. We're dying to get to know them better."[24] Decorative in short tight dresses and rhinestone jewelry, some of the women "are diehard fans who want nothing more than to watch the game, meet some players, and get some sun," the reporter observed. "Others have a little more in mind." Betty, now living with her boyfriend in Florida, was not at all clear as to what she had in mind when she went with a girlfriend to an exhibition game. But out in the bleachers, surrounded by fans, was a player she had always admired. Even so, her friend had to push her into the line for autographs. It was, Betty explained, "a low time in my life, when I was very self-conscious. As they later said in—what movie was it? *Bill and Ted's Excellent Adventure?*—I didn't 'feel worthy.'"

Her friend's camera caught the encounter on film, the moment when Betty moved from fan to something else. She still keeps the photograph, showing her radiant smile as she looks up at the player's frankly approving face. After the picture was taken, he asked her out for a drink, and she blurted, "Your place or mine?" The memory still made her blush. "I don't know where that came from—I'd never talked that way." By the time they arrived at his motel room, she had second thoughts, and told him, "This doesn't feel right. I've got a boyfriend at home."

"Great," he replied. "I'm married and you're not, but you've got a problem with the ethics? Something's screwy here." He was years older, experienced in the ways these things go, and said, "Call me if you ever change your mind."

Over that season and into winter, Betty grew increasingly unhappy with her boyfriend's behavior toward her. By spring, they had broken up, but her team, "her guy," had won the World Series and was back in Florida. Under the guise of writing a story about him, she showed up at spring training. He remembered, and invited her out for pizza. Their relationship boosted her confidence. She was an insider now, and she liked it. "[Some of the other women] I would classify as 'B' groupies," Betty explained. "They got second-string players. I was more of an 'A' groupie. Hard to explain—like, the higher caliber players went for higher caliber women. Minor league and major league." Despite the excitement of the relationship, Betty was not proud of using her credentials as a writer to meet a man she had a crush on. Women in the media who sleep with athletes are disdained. (When Rebecka Mendenhall, a Cable News Network assignment editor, filed a paternity suit against Steve Garvey, alleging that he reneged on an agreement to marry her, she was roundly criticized for getting involved with a celebrity.) Betty did not want other baseball people to know of the affair, either, although she suspected that at least one man knew—the elderly gatekeeper she befriended. Members of the security staff are part of the perennial chain that channels the "pink notes" written by women to the players. "The public relations guys know who the girls are, too," Betty said. "We were called 'locals', no matter where we were from."

Caught up in the reflected glamour of the Show, a Baseball Annie learns to accommodate her player's schedule. She stays home because he might call. She may take a lower-paying job that offers flexible hours or neglect her career. According to Betty, one woman's obsession led her to follow several players from town to town, working her entire life around their schedules. As a freelance writer, however, Betty's own career began to thrive. Through her new contacts, she obtained a press pass, giving her access to the field and to previously unavailable players: "As a reporter, it was thrilling to do those interviews—there were writers from all over the country competing for them. It gave a boost to my career."

NEW MEANING TO "A CUP OF COFFEE" IN THE SHOW

The idea of having sex with a ballplayer is likely to be more romantic than the actual experience. A man pursued by countless willing women is not likely to concern himself with the art of lovemaking. "Baseball players are not, by and large, the best dates," admits Jim Bouton in *Ball Four*. "We prefer *wham, bam*, thank-you-ma'am affairs."[25] In bed, Betty's idol liked to do push-ups over her. They had sex, but little intimacy. Nights out on the town were rare. The two usually met at her place or his. After one rough night of sex, she bloodied the sheets. With his wife due in town the following afternoon, he panicked, and Betty recalled the rush to wash the linens. When she went to the doctor for treatment, he did not accompany her or offer to pay the bill, although she said he knew she was financially strapped. During their last year together, Betty and her ballplayer happened to be in the same city during the All-Star break, and he suggested they meet for coffee at the stadium. Betty recalled:

> The thing was I really thought we were just going to have coffee. I couldn't imagine anything else happening. Like where? Well, I found out where when he led me into a men's room on an empty level. At the time I thought that was very thrilling, but afterward, I felt disappointed that we hadn't just had coffee and talked. On the one hand, I enjoyed feeling attractive (that low self-esteem thing again), but on the other hand, I was starting to feel used.

The following spring, Betty questioned the relationship even more. At one party, she watched her guy parade around nude with a beer bottle stuck up his behind. On another night, he disappeared into his bedroom four times with different women. When the party was over, he wanted her. "No way," she said. "I'm not going near those sheets." That evening

Betty did not feel safe or pretty. Seeing her role taken up by other women made her wonder *is that how it is for me? No self-respect?* Over three seasons, she had seen women go through an entire team, and teenagers go with any player who would take them. At spring training, she remembered her disdain when a woman past the age of thirty made a fool of herself over a young player. Betty was turning twenty-five, and by now she understood that next year, and every year, a fresh supply of young women would arrive at spring training with the goal of bedding as many ballplayers as possible. One night, Betty dreamt that Lou Gehrig had transformed into her deceased brother. In the dream, she asked, *Are you alive again, and is it me who's dead? It looks like a little bit of both,* her brother responded. The dream awakened her. She was tired of being with someone important so that she might feel more important. Her future, she decided, was not best served by living in the shadows, waiting for her guy to phone. She decided to make a video, an eight-minute postscript to her three seasons as a Baseball Annie. She entitled it *After the Game;* when our interview ended, she played it for me.

To the tune of Carly Simon's "Anticipation," Betty's video-cam scans the diamond as the groundskeepers tend the field. Outside the chain-link fence, a postgame crowd awaits its big-league heroes. The camera's eye lingers by the gate, where young women preen and wait, their eyes revealing a sense of expectancy that increases with each moment. At a nearby telephone booth, a girl of about fourteen waits as her friend calls home to say, "Mom, we're going to be home late, but don't worry. We're fine."

The tune changes to "These Are the Good Old Days" as the players, freshly showered, clothes trim, begin to stream out of the stadium. A future Hall of Famer appears, a jumbo cup of soda pop clenched in his teeth as he stops to sign autographs for the fans clustered around him. As a writer, Betty had observed closely the odd details of those years. She hit the "Pause" button, and pointed out another player walking by with soft drink cans clasped in both hands. "That's an old trick, to have your hands full," she explained, "so you can't sign autographs."[26] Then, as quickly as they appeared, the players slip into their cars and drive away. The fans, and the autograph seekers, and the hopeful women and girls disappear in the dusk, the camera returns to the field, where the groundskeepers continue to groom the field, and fades out.

Betty does not judge that world harshly. "It's so easy for the players to find a woman, they don't even have to go looking," she said. "You can't blame them." It took her years to accept that being in the stands was enough. She thinks that her time as a Baseball Annie was tied to low self-esteem. "You have to attach to someone important, so that you feel more important. But you can't love and respect yourself and go screwing some guy you don't even know." She sees that time as a youthful rite of passage, inspired by the one ballplayer who sparked her passion. Her embarrassment over what happened—she has not shown the video publicly—is mixed with a defiant pride that for a while she was an insider. Being a "veteran," she still checks out the possibilities. To this day, she does not like stadiums that isolate the players from the fans. Dodger Stadium, for example, makes it difficult to connect with a player. Suddenly her eyes glow. "To be there! Spring training was one big party. The joy of it is the kiss and tell—the *I* slept with *him.*"

Like *Bull Durham*'s Annie Savoy, young women like Betty persuade themselves that trading sex for a closer connection to the game is a fair exchange. Yet as Savoy points out, the confidence she instills lasts her men a lifetime, while she gets to feel "safe and pretty" for a mere 142 games. "Sometimes, it seems like a bad trade," she philosophizes, "but bad trades are part of baseball. Who can forget Frank Robinson for Milt Pappas, for god sakes!"[27] Betty was fortunate that her tradeoff ended privately on friendly terms. The affair never made front-page headlines, she did not end up in court over real or perceived injustices, and she did not get pregnant or come down with a sexually transmitted disease. Even so, she ultimately decided she had made a bad trade.

Women have settled for bad trades for a long time. The problem dates to antiquity, when pantheistic religions, which included female deities, gave way to monotheistic, patriarchal religions. With God now seen as male, the feminine lost whatever spiritual authority it had possessed. Woman moved from inspirer to temptress. The result, as author Carolyn G. Heilbrun suggests, was that woman became man's "plaything, their slave, dowered only with physical beauty, and with a slave's tricks and blandishments."[28] Women who grow up as Betty did may try to develop their sense of autonomy and identity as the "plaything" of someone powerful, like a ballplayer. Baseball Annies also adopt the role of temptress when other roles are denied them. A librarian once spoke of her frustration at being excluded from her dream career in baseball. As a girl in 1950s Brooklyn, she was enamored of the graceful commentary by the young broadcaster of the Dodgers' games. "When I was growing up, my ambition was to be a baseball announcer, just like Vin Scully," she recalled. "I remember how angry I was when I found out I couldn't." A few years later, she had the opportunity to be with an athlete, and she took it. "You take an awful ribbing, but you're so proud to have this connection with a winner. You're a part of it, even though you can't go out on the field."[29]

The idea that women can achieve recognition on their own has yet to be fully realized, which is why in 1992, feminist Gloria Steinem organized Take Our Daughters to Work Day. "[S]ociety trains girls to live vicariously through men because they have few other job mentors or role models," said Steinem, "and fall in love [or lust] with powerful men as an expression of female powerlessness."[30] A Baseball Annie epitomizes this behavior. Competing sexually, she will win a ball player, if only for a night, a home stand, or a season. It is a carnal Olympics, where a young woman can compete.

The trading of sexual favors for a connection to baseball's power and celebrity works as long as both sides understand that this is a one-night stand or a casual arrangement. "I know the deal," said a sometime girlfriend of a Montreal Expos player. "Any girl knows it's only seasonal. I didn't mind."[31] Some of these relationships do not end neatly, however, because the territory where sport and sex meet is notorious for its blurred foul lines and changeable rules of play. Trouble comes when a woman misunderstands the deal, learns that her ballplayer has changed the deal, or tries to change the deal herself. During the mid-1980s, a California mortgage banker named Margo Adams, dressed in a hot pink mini-dress, walked into Crackers, a popular bar near the Anaheim Angels' ballpark. When she saw the Boston Red Sox third baseman Wade Boggs, she told a friend, "Bring him."[32] Adams quickly became an "import," ultimately joining Boggs, who was married, on sixty-four road trips. Her banking career became secondary. But when Adams learned that Boggs was also seeing other women, she said she retaliated by spending the weekend with another ballplayer, the unfortunate-in-love Steve Garvey. Then Adams began to press Boggs to honor his reputed oral agreement to reimburse her for wages lost during their time together. He refused; she threatened to go public with the details of their affair; he considered that extortion and went to a friend who worked for the FBI; and she filed a $1.5 million lawsuit. Margo Adams fared poorly in the ensuing media circus. Her own grandmother chastised her for interfering with Boggs's career; *Pent-*

house magazine ran her story as a titillating tale of baseball mores; and the *Los Angeles Times* mocked her: "On the Road Again: Wade Boggs' Former Traveling Companion, Margo Adams, Crisscrosses Country 'Telling All.'" Concluded one reporter, "Don't spend a lot of sympathy on Margo Adams. She knew what she was getting into. She was as much the hunter as the hunted."[33]

"Anything can happen between players and groupies," said a retired first baseman, "because neither knows who they're dealing with. Many groupies are regulars, and word gets passed around among the guys, who could care less about a relationship. They want to get laid as quickly as they can, for the least amount of cash." One evening stands out in this player's memory: In a Class-D baseball town, two teammates met a couple of women and brought them back to their motel. After the first round of sex in the darkened room, the men decided it would be fun to switch beds and see if the women noticed the difference. After a while, one woman did, expressed her outrage, and left. "Some of the girls are aggressive, wanting only another notch on their belts. In the days when I played, alcohol was almost always involved, and the majority of meetings took place at bars." According to Jim Bouton, "It is permissible, in the scheme of things, to promise a Baseball Annie dinner and a show in return for certain quick services for a pair of roommates," he writes. "And it is just as permissible, in the morality of the locker room, to refuse to pay off. The girls don't seem to mind very much when this happens. Indeed, they seem to expect it."[34]

A woman who lets herself be used in these ways, however, may awaken the next morning feeling like a fool. Sometimes she decides to fight back. During spring training in 1991, a woman on vacation met three New York Mets players at Jox, a bar in Jupiter, Florida, and accompanied them to their home. She later claimed they sexually assaulted her, although the charges were eventually dropped. The following year, two women alleged that another Mets ballplayer lured them into the bullpen and masturbated before them. "[Ballplayers] consider women sex servants, sex objects, and they want you totally under their control," complained one of the coplaintiffs. "They hate being turned down."[35] The women then filed an $8.1 million civil suit, adding the charge of slander because the pitchers had called them groupies. Each season, similar charges of sexual misconduct are filed and reported. Only the players and women involved know what really happened; thus, the evidence to support the charges is often lacking, and the charges are often dropped. However, to a woman with an uncertain sense of herself it can seem less painful to seek out a sympathetic attorney than to face up to her part in the situation.

LEGAL TROUBLE

Throughout Organized Baseball, from Rookie League to the Major Leagues, it is popularly thought that the age and desirability of Baseball Annies increases with each level. For example, Betty, just out of college, considered herself an A-type because she was with a Major League star. After *Bull Durham* appeared in 1988, the press interviewed a number of ballplayers as to the film's plausibility. "Yeah, we've got baseball group-ies," said Pete Palermo, then playing Double-A ball in the Baltimore Orioles organization. "They just get a little more attractive as you go to each higher level. Most of them are a lot younger than Annie [Savoy]. In A-ball, they're a little older, so you'd at least think about going out with them."[36]

In truth, teenage girls who have yet to reach the age of consent make themselves available at every level of the game, from high-school and college ball to the majors. If they cannot pass the ID test at a bar, they find other ways to meet ballplayers. Betty had seen two sixteen-year-olds—city girls, she called them, streetwise and sophisticated—repeat-edly hopping into the cars of ballplayers after games. During the 1989 season, a fifteen-year-old Milwaukee girl frequented Brewers games at County Stadium. After one night game, she met outfielder Luis Polonia, then of the New York Yankees, by the team bus in the stadium parking lot. She agreed to meet him at the Pfister Hotel, where the two went to his room and had sex. Meanwhile, the girl's mother, who may have fielded too many "Mom-I'll-be-home-late-but-don't-worry" phone calls, tracked her daughter down and telephoned Polonia's room to warn him that he was with a minor. (In Wisconsin, the age of consent is sixteen.) After that conversation, Polonia and the girl had sex again. When the police arrived and found the girl still in Polonia's room, he was arrested, and the story hit the papers.

Polonia argued that the girl's friends told him she was nineteen, and that she told him she was sixteen. Faced with a possible nine-month jail term and a $10,000 fine, however, he made a public apology, pleaded no contest, and was convicted. The court ordered him to pay a $5,000 fine and to make a $10,000 contribution to the Sinai Samaritan Medical

Center's sexual assault treatment center in Milwaukee. Polonia spent twenty-seven days at the Milwaukee County House of Corrections before returning to the Dominican Republic, where he completed ninety hours of community service with youth groups. The following spring, he told the *New York Times,* "I know what can happen to you at the bars and at the ball park. I try to stay out of trouble."[37]

Polonia's troubles did not end, however. Grandstand chants of "jail-bait" followed him wherever he played. After the Yankees traded him to the California Angels in 1990, Polonia was threatened with a lawsuit for assault when he reportedly slapped a spectator who repeatedly taunted him. The jeers continued into the 1991 season, when the Milwaukee teenager, now seventeen, filed a civil lawsuit, citing "significant physical and emotional damages." Polonia later told a reporter that he had learned from the experience and that he had grown careful of his off-hours conduct. He now demanded that the women he dated show two pieces of identification proving they were of age. By 1992, however, Polonia had fathered and was supporting three children by three different women.

STDS

In *Ball Four,* Jim Bouton reports that the Seattle Pilots front office once circulated a questionnaire among the ballplayers. The publicity department wanted to know: "What's the most difficult thing about playing major-league baseball?" And one player responded, "Explaining to your wife why *she* needs a penicillin shot for *your* kidney infection."[38]

The response was a flip reference to the sexually transmitted diseases (STDs) swapped between ballplayers and Baseball Annies. Yet STDs have affected, and even shortened, the careers of a number of ball players. After Babe Ruth collapsed at a train station in April of 1925, his mysterious ailment was widely reported as an over-indulgence in "hot dogs, peanuts, and soda pop."[39] In truth, Ruth had a whopping case of gonorrhea and/or syphilis. It is unknown just how many timeouts on the Disabled List are prompted by bouts of STDs. Gonorrhea and syphilis are now at least treatable. Betty's main concern as a Baseball Annie of the mid-1980s was herpes simplex, which is incurable, though not fatal. Like most people, she had heard of AIDS but considered it a disease of gay men. That commonly held perception soon changed. A few years later, during one of her sixty-four road trips with Wade Boggs, Margo Adams learned in Seattle that five of his teammates had hired a couple of prostitutes. Adams later detailed her response for *Penthouse* magazine: "I said, 'You're kidding me. Do you know that I just read that 22 percent of the hookers in this area carry the AIDS virus? Are they using condoms?' Boggs looked at me with a smile and said, 'Ooh, they could be in trouble.'"[40] Athletes have a tendency to live in denial of the realities of time: the waning of their skills, the aging of their bodies. Like retirement, AIDS happens to other people, not to them. "It's hard to stop," reflected Luis Polonia in 1992. "I think to myself, ain't no way I can live without a woman. I like women the same way I like baseball. Ain't no way I can quit. If [AIDS] happens, it happens, but it will be with me being careful."[41] Due to the publicity attending AIDS, other players changed their habits. Near the end of the 1987 season, sportswriter Susan Fornoff sat in a Chicago bar with a married pitcher who reminded her that he had once unsuccessfully offered her his room key. That season, however, for the first time ever, he had not strayed once. Fornoff wondered at the change in behavior. "'Fear of AIDS,' he replied, somewhat sadly."[42]

MUTUAL COMFORT

Part of the attraction between Baseball Annies and ballplayers has to do with their mutual insecurities. Life on the road gets lonely, and a professional baseball player can live in perpetual anxiety about his performance on the field. Subject to daily criticism by the press, the fans, and the field management, he quickly learns that uncritical acceptance is just an embrace away from any number of women, many beset by their own self-doubts.[43] Sometimes it even works out well, particularly at the lower levels of the minor leagues, as George Gmelch points out in *Inside Pitch*:

> One ameliorating factor in many players' adjustment is the companionship offered by the young local women who befriend them. Most are roughly the same age as the players and are often just looking for excitement and something to do during the lazy, hot summers. The players' initial interest in these girls—who they collectively label as "groupies"—is usually sexual, but friendships often ensue. . . . As surrogate girlfriends, they fill voids created by the absence of the players' female friends back home. Occasionally they become real girlfriends. Either way, they offer a pleasant and much-needed diversion from baseball.[44]

Margo Adams claimed that Wade Boggs's batting average was .341 when he was with her and about .221 when he was with his wife. She ministered to his whims, donning "a sexy little outfit, a little apron and garter and stockings," to serve their favorite, double-anchovy pizza. Adams felt a sense of rivalry with his wife. She sat near Debbie Boggs at Fenway Park and came to believe that Wade Boggs was trying to get his wife to look more like her. "I was the one who took him to each of those playoff games in '86, not his wife," she claimed. "It was the way he wanted it."[45]

FOUL PLAY

For a ballplayer, however, such liaisons can lead to a Peter Pan–like existence, in which ordinary standards need not apply. Baseball Annies treat ballplayers as sex objects, and the players return the favor. When women ask nothing more of a ballplayer than a one-night stand or in-town-for-a-series sleepovers, they confuse his understanding of appropriate behavior towards all women. Phyllis Goldfarb, a professor of law who has studied domestic violence among athletes, said that the culture of sports celebrity sends the message that women exist primarily as rewards for athletic achievement. "Groupies simply accept this understanding of themselves (a sign of their own emotional impoverishment)—that they believe their best chances for happiness are in exploitative relationships with rich super athletes."[46] The problem is they put not only themselves at risk for poor treatment, but also the ballplayers' girlfriends and wives.

Because a wife is likely to make greater emotional demands of her husband than a Baseball Annie would, she may spark feelings of resistance, frustration, and even anger in a man accustomed to expecting pleasure without responsibility from the women who make themselves available to him. He may then turn physical: domestic violence is the leading cause of arrests of professional athletes, according to Goldfarb. "A celebrity athlete may simply be taught by the culture that he is superior to his wife, that she can ask nothing of him that he doesn't want to give, that if she persists in doing so, she deserves mistreatment, and moreover, is expendable, as there are countless women out there for him."

Although charges of domestic violence against ballplayers are made each year, as late as 1997, Major League Baseball had no set policy regarding such cases. Because the Players' Association is protective of its members and because club policies are inconsistent, the message players receive about the issue is confusing. And because wives are often fearful about ruining their husband's career and hurting their own economic welfare, they often elect to drop the charges. The damage done to an athlete's reputation and his family's financial well-being, even when the charges are dropped, is real, however—advertisers balk at paying millions of dollars in endorsement contracts to a ballplayer who hits the headlines as an alleged wife-beater. Less quantifiable is the emotional damage done to the player's wife and children. Goldfarb has called for a reassessment by MLB of its policy. She would like to see crisis intervention and a twenty-four-hour hotline; a counseling network, player education, and player discipline, with a renegotiation of the guidelines with the Players' Association.

DIVORCE, BASEBALL STYLE

The crux of the triangle formed by Baseball Annies, married ballplayers, and their wives is that of trust and fidelity. Baseball wives have always known that women are easily available to their husbands and fight back as best they can. During the 1929 season, pitcher Otis (Doc) Crandall was enduring a disastrous outing on the mound, when in the stands Crandall's wife overheard a nearby woman brag, "How can Doc expect to pitch today? He was out with me all night. We were in a saloon together until four o'clock this morning."[47] Mrs. Crandall smacked the woman over the head with her umbrella.

Because contemporary players inexplicably give their tickets to the family section to both spouse and girlfriend, a suspicious wife scans for unfamiliar women seated nearby. She may also run a jewelry check, as players have been known to present both their wife and their girlfriend with matching baubles—a sort of two-for-one special. When a wife spots a match, anything can happen. In *Baseball Babylon,* Dan Gutman reports that when Pete Rose's first wife spotted a woman wearing a duplicate diamond pendant a few rows back, she hit her. The recipient of the attack later became the second Mrs. Pete Rose.[48]

Baseball Annies have undone many a baseball marriage. In 1971, sportswriter Dick Young told of a pitcher who was holding out for a better contract from his ball club. In a letter that contained the club's third offer, the general manager added a note:

> Unless the pitcher signed this contract, his wife would be informed about his activities on the road with a certain young lady. It named the young lady. The pitcher's wife opened the envelope to see the latest offer. . . . The pitcher and his wife have been divorced, and any day now he'll probably be traded. Why would a general manager put something like that in writing? Why do wives open up their husband's mail?[49]

A wife opens her husband's mail, listens in on telephone calls, and keeps a watchful eye on unidentified women in the players' family section at the ballpark when she faces the reality of Baseball Annies. In *Home Games: Two Baseball Wives Speak Out,* Bobbie Bouton and Nancy Marshall maintain that a baseball wife goes through three stages of awareness. Stage one is "denial"—other players are involved with groupies, but not her husband. Stage two comes when the evidence accumulates to suggest otherwise, when "those lies start to eat at you like cancer. . . . And it doesn't take long before you doubt everything that is told to you, including 'I love you.'" Many wives are able to move on to stage three, as they "realize that their husband's flings on the road are no reflection on them. They see it for what it is. Entertainment."[50]

For a ballplayer and his family, the entertainment can be costly. In the spring of 1997, Karin and Chipper Jones were the toast of Atlanta and trying to start a family, when the Atlanta Braves third baseman met a waitress in West Palm Beach, Florida. She was not the only woman he was dating. As his star rose, Jones admittedly lost perspective. "I was going to go out and do what I wanted to," he later said. "The only thing that mattered was self-satisfaction." Then the waitress told him she was pregnant. Knowing he could hide an affair, but not a baby, Jones told his wife. The news shattered her. As Karin Jones later said, "You live out the dream that you always wanted. This was my whole life, as well, and now it's gone. And when you fall, it hurts so bad, because we were so high up."[51]

The United States leads the world in the rate of divorce.[52] A marriage taking place in 2002 had a 50 percent likelihood of ending in divorce, and the likelihood has fluctuated between 40 and 50 percent over the past fifteen years.[53] It has been even higher among professional athletes, particularly those who are newly retired, according to Tom House, a former Major League pitcher who went on to earn a PhD in psychology. In *The Jock's Itch: The Fast-Track Private World of the Professional Ballplayer,* House details the pressures brought to bear upon players' marriages, including his own. "There have been some statistics cited recently indicating that the rate of divorce and separation among newly retired athletes is close to 80 percent," House claims. "I heard one ex-player comment on that figure by smirking, 'It'd be even higher, but how many ex-players can afford a divorce?'"[54] Tom House's marriage survived; however, the first marriages of Betty's boyfriend, Jim Bouton, Steve Garvey, Chipper Jones, Mike Marshall, and Pete Rose all ended in divorce.

Baseball Annies may not only undermine and destroy players' marriages but also make it seem acceptable to a ballplayer to have sex with any woman whenever he pleases. Athletes commit date rape at more than four times the rate of non-athletes, according to the *Los Angeles Times*.[55] "They don't have a thermostat for empathy," Tom House explained to the *Times*. "Athletes are expected to understand two things: anger and aggression. Those are the only emotions they are really capable of dealing with." Each year, charges of date rape and sexual assault by baseball players hit the newspapers; however, most are dropped before the cases go to trial. (In an article entitled "In Sexual Assault Cases, Athletes Usually Walk," *USA Today* reported the results of 168 allegations of sexual assault by athletes: twenty-two cases went to trial, and six resulted in convictions. In forty-six other cases, a plea agreement was made.[56]) The following account illustrates the power a baseball player holds over young women who are uncertain as to how to set appropriate boundaries. In 1995, a ballplayer of some promise met a twenty-year-old woman on a blind date arranged by Luis Polonia. After three drinks at a suburban bar and an exchange of telephone numbers, the woman accompanied the ballplayer to the hotel where the ball club was staying and went to his room. She later filed charges of rape and sodomy. "I know what he probably wanted," she said, "but I didn't want to go into his room in the first place. I felt I had no choice. I felt once I told him 'no' it would be the end of it."[57] What truly happened there is known only to her and the player, but the charges were eventually dropped.

Cultural differences further confuse the encounters between ballplayers and Baseball Annies. On Opening Day in 2003, more than a quarter (230) of the 827 Major League players were listed as born outside of the continental United States. Such players often sign as teenagers for a little money up front and the hope of fame, wealth, and all that goes with it. Each spring, beset by linguistic and cultural differences, they enter the bewildering world of spring training. In the spring of 1998, an up-and-coming minor leaguer in the New York Mets organization, Vicente Rosario, became acquainted with a seventeen-year-old high-school girl by a hotel pool in Port St. Lucie, Florida. Rosario's English was limited and the girl did not understand Spanish, but the two managed to communicate to the extent that she agreed to accompany him to a hotel room. "She trusted him," a police spokesman said later. "She said she actually liked Rosario and may have had sex with him until the others got involved."[58] The "others" were Ruddi De La Cruz, Milton Gonzalez, Natividad Tavarez, and Jose Brea Tousent, all eighteen to nineteen years old, fresh from the Dominican Republic, and non-English-speaking. According to later reports, when she and Rosario arrived at room number 304, he and Tavarez begin removing her clothes. Tavarez was the first to have sexual intercourse with her as Rosario kissed her. (Later, she said Rosario was the first one to have sex with her.) Tousent and De La Cruz then entered the room, and forced her to perform oral sex on them before they and Rosario had sexual intercourse with her. De La Cruz said Rosario told him, "Come on, come on, go on her. Do it, do it."[59]

According to police reports, the girl never said "no" loud and clear. She stayed because she was too afraid to go. She did say, "don't", and "I have to go . . . I don't wanna be here," several times. "I didn't really kiss back or anything. . . . I tried to push [Rosario] away and I tried to move myself to get away, but I couldn't. They were stronger than me."[60]

The arrest of the five players made national headlines. Because the Mets policy precluded legal or financial assistance to players under criminal investigation, the club suspended the five with minimum pay. "They have to bear the legal consequences if this is criminal. Even if it's not criminal, this is so low on human behavior that it's tantamount to criminal," said Mets co-owner Fred Wilpon. Gonzalez, Tavarez, and Tousent were not wealthy (Tousent's father, a factory worker in the Dominican Republic, borrowed the money for his son's bail bond)—and requested a public defender. De La Cruz agreed to testify, and the charges against him were dropped. Rosario, the alleged ringleader of the gang rape, borrowed money from his mother-in-law to hire an attorney, Anthony Suarez, who stated:

> Here's a groupie taking down a baseball player. This is not the spoiled baseball player with a lot of money who's raping and pillaging Florida, but rather kids who are young . . . and they don't realize they could be the target of groupies even though they're warned. I think that from a male point of view, we're . . . so vulnerable, man, to this s—. Any girl can suggest at anytime today, "he raped me." This women's lib movement has us up against the wall. And I feel awful for this kid.[61]

The verdict on Rosario was "not guilty," but Gonzalez, Tavarez, and Tousent were sentenced to two years in prison and two years probation. The attorney, Suarez, was elected to the Florida legislature. Nothing further is known of the young woman.

At the time of the gang rape, Gonzalez, Tavarez, and Tousent had been in the United States less than two weeks. One wonders what sort of preparation they had for what they encountered here. Major League Baseball does offer a Rookie Development program, an eight-day retreat in which players learn about the challenges of life in Organized Baseball, but after that it is up to each club to determine the level of ongoing support. The Mets offer a spring training program that schools its international players in English and in social situations, particularly those involving women. "That's where the Mets' responsibility ends," said the team's general manager at the time, Steve Phillips. "What it boils down to is every player, like every citizen, is taking responsibility for their own actions."

In the wake of the sexual assault charges that made headlines during the 1990s, many ballplayers have grown wary of making a connection with Baseball Annies and instead favor strip joints, where the women are more likely to know the score. Yet any woman who accompanies a player she has just met to his hotel room puts herself at risk, not only for STD and sexual violence but also for the aftermath of emotional damage and notoriety. She is seldom seen sympathetically. In the scandal involving Vicente Rosario and the others, the press referred to the girl as "the alleged victim." During such trials, the defense attorney is likely to claim the woman is a predator. Rosario's attorney, Tony Suarez, publicly warned "the alleged victim": "[I]f she goes to trial I'm going to tear a new a———— in her. It's going to be very embarrassing for her."

When things go wrong between a Baseball Annie and her ballplayer, both sides lose. He can see his career affected or destroyed. After a public relations disaster, the front office may trade or release him. Ruddi De La Cruz, Milton Gonzalez, Luis Polonia, Vicente Rosario, Natividad Tavarez, and Jose Tousent are all out of Organized Baseball. First baseman Steve Garvey maintained a squeaky-clean image during his eighteen-year career with the Los Angeles Dodgers and the San Diego Padres. He spoke of entering politics some day. That hope ended with Garvey's acrimonious divorce from his wife Cyndy and later publicity during his annus horribilis, during which he fathered two children out of wedlock while engaged to another woman and ultimately married yet another. Outfielder Darryl Strawberry's excesses with drugs and alcohol were well known; less known was his trouble with Baseball Annies. After he had lost his career, he mused in an interview, "Women, you know, not one, not two, but you know, women, women, women, and I just couldn't get myself away from it. I was addicted to the women. I know everything about hitting, but nothing about living."[62]

There are other ways to bring down a ballplayer. When a woman's passion for him becomes unbearable, it can drive her from sexual obsession into violence. Shortstop Bill Jurges was one such victim. As a ballplayer, Jurges welcomed a good brawl. Early in his career, in June 1932, his fist-fight with Mickey Finn sparked a memorable battle between the Chicago Cubs and the Brooklyn Dodgers. Three weeks later, Jurges encountered violence of a different sort in a Chicago hotel room when Violet Valli, a despondent cabaret girl, shot him in the side and hand "because life without Billy isn't worth living ... and why should I leave this earth alone?"[63] She then turned the gun on herself, but both she and Jurges survived. Valli's notoriety earned her bookings in burlesque as "The Girl Who Shot Bill Jurges," while Jurges spent fifteen more years in the National League, where chants of "bang-bang" greeted his appearances on the diamond.

Ruth Ann Steinhagen's attack on Eddie Waitkus on June 14, 1949, was more chilling. Waitkus was unaware that Steinhagen, a shy nineteen-year-old, existed. Her interest in the Chicago Cubs first baseman burst into her troubled consciousness during a game at Wrigley Field on April 27, 1947, when a nearby woman in the stands shouted, "Hey, funny face," at Waitkus. Ruth Ann took a closer look, and became fixated on him. She frequented the ballpark to watch him play, trembling outside the gates when he walked by. She made a shrine of his press clippings and slept with his picture beneath her pillow. The twenty-seventh of the month became her "anniversary." One November day, without explanation she left the offices of the Continental Casualty Insurance Company, where she worked as a typist, to wander the city in hopes of spotting him.

Steinhagen cried when the Cubs traded Waitkus to the Philadelphia Phillies in 1948, saying that she could not live if he left town. The following spring, she spoke of traveling to Boston, Waitkus's hometown, to become his girlfriend. That June, with the Phillies due in town for a series with the Cubs, she went to a pawnshop and purchased a .22-caliber rifle. On the night of June 14, she rented a room at the Edgewater Beach Hotel, where the players stayed, downed two whiskey sours and a Cuba libre, and paid five dollars to a bellhop to deliver a note to her idol. When Waitkus came to her room, he was abrupt. "What do you want to see me about?" he asked. Steinhagen went to the closet and retrieved her rifle.

"For two years you have been bothering me, and now you are going to die," she said. Then she shot him. During the ensuing psychiatric examination and court hearings, Steinhagen offered several explanations:

"I guess I got the idea to shoot him because he reminded me of my father."[64]

"I always wanted to be in the limelight and this is it."[65]

"As time went on I just became nuttier and nuttier about the guy and I knew I would never get to know him in a normal way, so I kept thinking I will never get him and if I can't have him nobody else can."[66]

Steinhagen's attack on Waitkus was front-page news. According to one flight attendant, every newspaper that passengers brought on her plane, from Kansas City to New York, carried the story. "I don't think she should have been given so much publicity," said the attendant. "I think that girl . . . got just what she wanted—headlines."[67] Indeed, the newspapers that had reported the daily feats of Waitkus now recounted Steinhagen's. In this way, she and Eddie became an ersatz couple, if only in the media. In the years ahead, their names would always be linked. The Waitkus-Steinhagen story informs the opening section of Malamud's novel *The Natural:* After the mysterious Harriet Bird stalks Roy Hobbs, she invites him to her room and asks, "Roy, will you be the best there ever was in the game?"[68] "That's right," he replies; and Bird shoots him. Then, Bird commits suicide, as Steinhagen had planned before changing her mind at the last moment.

During her trial for attempted murder, Steinhagen said, "I think if he had walked into the room a little decently," she said, "I would have told him to call the police. However, he was too confident. He swaggered."[69] Her comment helps to explain the sense of rage felt by a woman of conflicted sexuality toward a ballplayer whom she perceives as arrogant in his power. The court's psychiatric diagnosis was "schizophrenia in an immature individual." Judged insane, Steinhagen was sent to the Kankakee (Illinois) State Hospital.[70] Waitkus survived four operations and played in the 1950 World Series. His marriage to one of the nurses who had tended him in the hospital ended in divorce. After Waitkus died young, at age fifty-three, a former teammate, Richie Ashburn, told reporters, "Eddie survived but he was never the same ball player after that and it was then when he started his heavy drinking. He didn't survive that."[71] Little was known of Ruth Steinhagen's later life until John Theodore published in 2002 *Baseball's Natural: The Story of Eddie Waitkus.* Theodore discovered that Steinhagen spent thirty-three months in the state mental hospital before returning to live with her parents and her sister Rita on the Northwest Side of Chicago. After their parents died, the sisters continued to live in the family home. Steinhagen, who apparently never married, has minimal contact with the outside world, according to the neighbors Theodore interviewed. She avoids reporters and refuses to speak publicly about the attack on Waitkus. Theodore concludes: "For more than five decades, Ruth Ann Steinhagen has lived a shadowy existence, trying to keep her past from reappearing. The garage door that faces the alley carries the faint stain of graffiti, and the tall oak gate leading to the property is secured with a steel padlock."[72]

Sex is no longer the taboo subject it was in 1846, when the New York Knickerbockers set out to play at Elysian Fields. Through the ensuing years, the game has informed our changing attitudes about sex. The very language of baseball is found in the vernacular of our sexual encounters—*I pitched her (or him) a line, I couldn't get to first base, we went all the way, I scored.* In 1999, the television documentary *Playing the Field: Sports and Sex in America* examined the issue. "The question for the twenty-first century," it concludes, "is whether we can free ourselves from the narrow and damaging ways that sports and sex mix, so that all athletes and spectators can revel in the pure sensual joy of watching beautiful bodies doing miraculous things."[73]

It is doubtful. It is true that Major League Baseball and the Players' Association could work together more effectively to develop a comprehensive and effective policy toward instances of sexual misconduct, a policy less oriented to managing public relations disasters and more toward helping the players and their families understand the costly aftereffects. Such a policy, however, would only help the players and their families cope better with the provocations of Baseball Annies. Such programs are likely to have little effect upon the behavior of the women themselves, influenced as they are by a culture that both encourages and condemns women who trade on their sexuality. Some young women with an uncertain sense of who they are will continue to choose the groupie's path. Some teenaged girls will continue to attempt to demonstrate their personal worth through their sexuality. As in Betty's case, the loss of important men early in their life will prompt some to try to recoup their sense of loss through the game of their childhood and a liaison with a baseball player. Beset by their own uncertainties, some women will always be content to bask in the reflected light of celebrity, grateful for a temporary connection to an equally insecure winner. Despite the risk of STDS, sexual assault, and plain disrespect, Baseball Annies will continue in the game's shadows, outside the lines of fair play. Like Betty, some of them will grow up and beyond the experience, while others will wonder at the speed with which their self-respect has rusted away, like a child's discarded baseball bat left out too many nights in the summer rain.

This depiction of an 1869 women's baseball club at Peterboro, New York, shows male spectators on the sidelines and women intent at play, a reversal of the usual scenario.
Photo: National Baseball Hall of Fame Library, Cooperstown, N.Y.

The Young Ladies' Base Ball Club No. 1 of the 1890 and 1891 seasons. It took "attitude" for women of the late nineteenth century to play hardball.
Photo: National Baseball Hall of Fame Library, Cooperstown, N.Y.

Umpire Amanda Clement won renown on the semi-pro circuit throughout the Upper Midwest from 1904 to 1908. Photo: National Baseball Hall of Fame Library, Cooperstown, N.Y.

Elsie Tydings proudly stands at the head of the line to purchase the first ticket ever sold for a World Series in Washington, D.C., 1924. Photo: Library of Congress.

Virginia Smoot of Columbia Junior High School is tagged out at third by Mabel Harvey of McFarland during a Field Day baseball game, May 1925. Photo: Library of Congress.

Baseball Annies adored the legendary Babe Ruth, and he returned the favor.
Photo: National Baseball Hall of Fame Library, Cooperstown, N.Y.

Jackie Mitchell demonstrates her form to Lou Gehrig and Babe Ruth, 1931. Photo: Transcendental Graphics/ruckerarchive.com.

When Mary Dunn inherited the Triple-A Baltimore Orioles in 1936, she made her presence known in both the front office and the grandstand of Oriole Park.
Photo: Babe Ruth Birthplace and Museum, Baltimore, Maryland. Photo by: Leroy Merrikan.

To Effa Manley, the co-owner of the Newark Eagles of the Negro National League, the ballpark was home, the players like family.
Photo: National Baseball Hall of Fame Library, Cooperstown, N.Y.

Sportswriter Jeane Hofmann interviews the New York Yankees' manager Joe McCarthy at spring training, 1942. Courtesy: William C. Greene/*The Sporting News*.

The ebullient fan Hilda Chester led the cheering for the Brooklyn Dodgers for decades.
Photo: National Baseball Hall of Fame Library, Cooperstown, N.Y.

The South Bend Blue Sox' Marie Mahoney is safe at first in this All-American Girls Professional Baseball League game of 1947. Photo: Transcendental Graphics/ruckerarchive.com.

Toni Stone, shown here in a publicity shot for the Indianapolis Clowns of the Negro American League, 1953, earned her living playing baseball.

Photo: National Baseball Hall of Fame Library, Cooperstown, N.Y.

Umpire Pam Postema takes charge behind the plate, 1983.
Courtesy: Russell Gates, *Phoenix Gazette*.

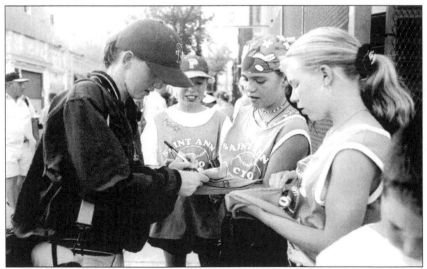

Julie Croteau's battle for the right to play men's baseball at the high school and collegiate levels inspired the next generation of female athletes. Photo: Laura Wulf.

The Colorado Silver Bullets enjoyed the camaraderie of an all-women's team as they barnstormed the country during the mid-1990s playing men's collegiate, semi-pro, and minor-league teams. Photo: Laura Wulf.

Left-hander Ila Borders pitched for the Madison Black Wolf of the Northern League in 1999 and 2000. Photo: Dan Wiza—Madison Black Wolf 1996–2000.

Stephanie Leathers, Chicago Cubs fan and the publisher of *Bleacher Banter* (center), and friends celebrate an afternoon in the sun in the left-field bleachers of Wrigley Field. Photo: Stephanie Leathers.

During a pre-game ceremony in 1999 at Coors Field in honor of Colorado Hispanics in Baseball, Linda Alvarado, one of the owners of the Colorado Rockies, autographs a bat for Victor Duran, a veteran of the Sugar Beet Leagues. Photo: Reproduced by permission of Linda Alvarado (Alvarado Construction Inc.)

Kim Ng, the assistant general manager of the Los Angeles Dodgers, 2003, is often touted as the most likely to be named the first female general manager in history.
Photo by Larry Goren.

Renel Brooks-Moon, the San Francisco Giants' public-address announcer, greets the crowd at Opening Day ceremonies, 2003. Photo: © 2004 S.F. Giants.

Umpires Perry Barber, Theresa Cox, and Brenda Glaze relax after calling a fantasy camp game in Fort Myers, Florida. Photo: Theresa Cox.

Town ball, baseball's "immediate ancestor on the maternal side," is still played in Cooperstown, where Tina "Sweetbread" Baker, Sonja "Wishbone" Parker, and tally-keeper Eileen Sherwood pause after a Sunday afternoon game. Photo: Author's collection.

Film director Penny Marshall on the set of *A League of Their Own.* Courtesy: Photofest.

4 For Love of the Game
Amateur Players

IT IS FRIDAY OF LABOR DAY WEEKEND, 1999, and more than a hundred women have driven from New England, New Jersey, and Pennsylvania, or flown from Chicago, Cleveland, Detroit, Florida, and South Bend, Indiana, for four days and nights of hardball. Hosted by the Washington Metropolitan Women's Baseball League, the amateur tournament is a celebration of the league's tenth anniversary. Part of the excitement involves the venue, for women's amateur baseball is seldom played in such fine surroundings as this brand new community ballpark. Shirley Povich Field—named for the late *Washington Post* sportswriter—has clubhouses, dugouts, a concession and ticket building, and comfortable seating.[1]

The tournament rosters of the eight teams offer an exotic alphabet of players: Amundson, Ballantine, Chin, Deutsch, Garcia, Levine, Ng, Provenzano, Strozynski, Wallace, and Yamamoto. The players range from fresh-faced teenagers to a sinewy forty-four-year-old pitcher. Mamie "Peanut" Johnson, who played for the Indianapolis Clowns of the American Negro League during the 1950s, is coaching first base for the Michigan Stars. Two women from Japan are here, having spent the past three months with the Ocala (Florida) Lightning to improve their skills. One of the Michigan Stars is a few weeks pregnant. "Show me the doctor's OK," demands Jim Glennie, the Stars coach, who knows well that his players will play despite being pregnant, ill, or injured.[2] A slogan seen on one of the many T-shirts captures the prevailing spirit of the weekend: "Chicks Were Born to Play Softball, Real Women Play Baseball." The players are, indeed, real women—attorneys, physicians, firefighters, engineers, students, and mothers—and getting to Bethesda on the eve of a holiday weekend by game time has been difficult.

As the game between the Chicago Storm and the Ocala Lightning gets underway, the cool September air is so still that the dust from a slide into second base takes minutes to dissipate into the grove of evergreens beyond the outfield. Out of the grove, the cries of a thousand protesting crickets and frogs carry across the diamond into the stands. There, oblivious to the night sounds, a fortyish woman leans forward in her seat. Jeri Baldwin is the co-owner of the Ocala Lightning, an amateur women's baseball team from north-central Florida. For more than five years, Baldwin has financially supported the Lightning. For this tournament, she paid for the team's turquoise and purple uniforms and its travel costs to Maryland. Baldwin appears to be getting her money's worth. Since play began this evening, her drawl has been evident. Now, with runners on base against her pitcher, Tike Gardner, Baldwin uncorks a fount of encouragement:

> Oh, my Lord, have mercy, you gotta be kiddin', ump. That's OK, Tike. Plenty o' room out there. . . . Good job, Kari. . . . Reach down deep, find your hummer, Tike. . . . Oh my heav'nly day. Safe? Is that the only word you know? Ump, you need to increase your vocabulary. Lord, have mercy.[3]

Thanks to Tike's pitching and a nice diving catch by the left fielder, Ocala carries an 8–1 lead into the eighth inning, when manager Terry Sparks decides to bring in a fresh arm. Renee Basho is a teenager, though an infant in baseball experience, as she grew up playing softball. As Basho warms up, two Florida latecomers converse behind the backstop: "Good Lord, what's he thinking? Renee's never played baseball 'til six weeks ago. This is the first time she's ever *pitched* in a game."

"Well, you have to start her sometime," philosophizes her teammate.

"Still, it's tough. It's a hell of a long way, those sixty feet. After playing softball, I couldn't get used to it, and the ball's comin' so fast." The two return their attention to the game, snapping their chewing gum as the team's lead evaporates. The Ocala shortstop, who suited up immediately upon her arrival from Fort Lauderdale (no time to warm up), drops a grounder, does it again, and makes a low throw to first. Renee Basho cannot find the plate, ultimately giving up four bases on balls and walking in the tying run. She leaves the game with an ERA of infinity. Chicago eventually gets the go-ahead run and the win. After the game, Basho hangs her head as she walks with her parents to their car in the darkened parking lot.

Welcome to the world of women's amateur baseball, where there is no money and little glory, only the joy of play. The stars of the Major Leagues make the game appear effortlessness, but the effort it demands of jet-lagged, weekend players reveals the true difficulty of well-executed fundamentals. This is eat-dirt-and-die-in-the-grass baseball. Amateur baseball is also the outback of women's sports, because it offers talented female athletes none of the glamour, recognition, and athletic scholarships available in basketball, soccer, softball, swimming, and tennis. There are several reasons why the ranks of women who play baseball are thin, and why, historically, the female side of the national pastime has not prospered.

We know that baseball evolved from nineteenth-century stick-and-ball games. While girls enjoyed such games, too, unlike boys, they were expected to abandon them when they approached adulthood. As baseball was capturing the national imagination after the Civil War, however, privileged students at the new women's colleges took up the game, despite parents' and administrators' concerns over propriety and safety. Historians Dorothy and Harold Seymour credit baseball as "the first active team sport for college women [beginning in] the 1860s with students sometimes playing scrub and interclass games."[4] By 1875, Vassar College had three baseball clubs, the Sure-Pops, the Daisy Clippers, and the Royals. At women's colleges, baseball was played well into the twentieth century.

With the professional game bent upon establishing itself as a male endeavor, however, most young women were left to play baseball wherever they could. A few even managed to play on co-ed teams. In 1903, for example, the *Boston Herald* announced a "novel ball game" to be played between the Hickey and the Clover clubs, who fielded five women and four men.[5] Amanda Clement was another who shared the field with boys and, later, with men. Clement grew up playing baseball with her brother and cousin at the town ballpark in Hudson, South Dakota. In a time when fierce rivalries among the prairie towns were fought on the diamond, Clement was good enough to play first base for the Hudson men's team and eventually parlayed her knowledge of the game into a celebrated five-season umpiring career. The passion and the talent to play baseball may have existed among young women, but even talented ones like Amanda Clement were, at best, tolerated. As one sportswriter said of Clement, "By the age of twelve or thirteen, it would not have mattered how good she was or how much she wanted to play. What mattered was whether enough young men showed up to play."[6]

Meanwhile, another game was evolving that stunted the growth of girls' and women's baseball. Softball developed from games known as kitten ball, mush ball, and playground ball. By 1908, the National Amateur Playground Association of the United States was codifying the rules of softball.[7] A softball is, of course, softer than a hardball. At 60 feet apart, regulation softball bases are 30 feet closer to one another than baseball bases, and the distance between the mound and the plate in softball, 40 feet, is 20 feet, 6 inches shorter than that distance in baseball. In fast-pitch softball, the pitcher throws underhand, which is less strenuous on the arm, and the game runs seven innings. Those who viewed baseball as a man's game believed that these qualities made softball a physically easier game, ideal for the perceived "weaker sex." The problem was, nobody thought to ask the girls which game they wanted to play. Some did not want to play a derivative of mush ball and kitten ball. In her memoir *An American Childhood,* Annie Dillard remembers the "dumb softball" she had to play as a schoolgirl:

> A baseball weighted your hand just so, and fit it. Its red stitches, its good leather and hardness like skin over bone, seemed to call forth a skill both easy and precise. . . . [Y]ou could snag a baseball in your mitt, where it stayed, snap, like a mouse locked in its trap, not like some pumpkin of a softball you merely batted, with a terrible sound, like a splat.[8]

Yet another barrier to girls' access to baseball was arising. Near Doubleday Field in Cooperstown stands the bronze statue, "The Sandlot Kid." Bat cocked, the barefoot boy evokes an earlier time when unsupervised children organized their own games in fields and vacant lots. As the twentieth century wore on, that freedom gave way to adult-run youth leagues. With adults making the rules, the idea that baseball is for boys and softball is for girls became the standard. The founding of the National Amateur Baseball Federation in 1914 for boys only under the age of nineteen was a portent of what was to come. Eleven years later, when American Legion Baseball was organized for middle-teen ballplayers, it did not even occur to the founders to exclude girls. Thus, in 1928, fourteen-year-old Margaret Gisolo was able to slip by on a technicality to play for the Blanford (Indiana) American Legion team. Her twelfth-inning single won the county championship against Clinton, she scored the winning run against Terre Haute for the district title, and she pitched in a sectional victory against Evansville, in which she won the tournament's sportsmanship trophy. She had four hits and a walk as Blanford won the state championship. In Blanford's first round loss in the nationals, Gisolo singled, walked, and sacrificed in four at-bats. In seven tournament games, she batted .429 and fielded without error at first base.

Clinton had protested her presence on the diamond, and the complaint went through the American Legion hierarchy before it was referred to Kenesaw Mountain Landis, then serving as the commissioner of Major League Baseball. Landis ruled Gisolo eligible to play because American Legion Baseball had no specific rule forbidding it. When the season ended, the organization acted to change that. The American Legion's revised rulebook of 1929 stated that "competition will be open only to boys who are amateurs."[9] "Baseball is a 'He-Boys' Sport," asserts a Legion handbook of 1931. "Every red blooded boy prefers the 'crack' of the bat against a baseball to the 'punk' of a softball."[10] For nearly fifty years, American Legion Baseball remained a game for boys only.

LITTLE LEAGUE'S EXCLUSION OF GIRLS

When Little League, incorporated in 1939 in Williamsport, Pennsylvania, became the dominant organization for youth baseball, it undoubtedly improved the quality of play and the teaching of fundamentals. Some of the plain joy of the game was lost, however, as parental control and organizational hierarchy supplanted the native democracy of the sandlot. The decade or so after World War II was a low point for girls who wanted to play baseball. Little League's federal charter called for instilling the values of citizenship, sportsmanship, and manhood. The message was clear: Girls need not apply.

Thus, despite the fact that nine-year-old Donna de Varona could hit the ball farther than some of her brother's twelve-year-old friends, her application to play Little League baseball in 1956 was rejected. In order to play, some girls were even encouraged to conceal their gender: In 1958, a Little League all-star team traveled to Puerto Rico to play the sons of the personnel stationed there at the U.S. naval base. The "skinny pitcher" for the home team struck out the side in the first inning and in the top of the second fanned a fourth batter "on a pitch that got by him so fast he couldn't have hit it with a paddle," the *New York Post* recounted.[11] Having proved her point, the pitcher removed her cap, revealing by her long hair that she was a girl. "The crowd laughed. The batter complained to the umpire. The umpire looked to the sky for help," continued the *Post*. Amid the laughter, Donna Terry, the skinny pitcher, proceeded to win the ball game, but her days of baseball were done: "When it was over, a lot of young boys and old coaches on the Island thought about it and said, 'What the hell are we laughing at? She beat us all year.' Which, in what was then a socially retarded international Little League structure, is how Donna Terry got barred from playing baseball with the boys in Puerto Rico." Terry switched to softball, eventually coaching the game at the University of California, Berkeley, while de Varona became an Olympic gold medalist in swimming. Their experiences show why girls' baseball was unable to develop a wider pool of talent: talented female athletes usually switched to more accessible sports that offered greater opportunities.

The cultural sea change of the 1960s challenged these limitations, and feminists took the lead in speaking up. Writing in 1964, Carolyn G. Heilbrun illustrates the "rigidity with which human beings have been divided, not by talent, inclination, or attribute, but by gender," in this account of a girl who had managed to join a Little League team:

> The ensuing ruckus might have been justified had someone been caught practicing medicine without training or license, though the response where this does happen is less hysterical. The girl was thrown off the team together with the manager who had been unpolitical enough to let her play. There followed long discussions about the weakness and physical vulnerability of girls, the wisdom of their partaking in sports, and so forth. But the obvious points were nowhere mentioned: she had qualified for the team by being able to play better than any available boy, and whatever physical disabilities her sex may be thought to have endowed her with, so wide is the extent of individual variation that she was clearly better able to cope with the rigors of competitive contact sports than many boys. What she had outraged were preconceived ideas of the "feminine" role and the "masculine" rights to certain activities.[12]

By then, baseball had become an entrenched American institution, and even at the Little League level was proving slow to change. While it was true that some enlightened Little League coaches were open to fielding girls, they continued to want to conceal the fact. Ten-year-old Dot Richardson was playing catch when a Little League coach noticed her strong arm and invited her to play on his team. Richardson was delighted with the offer until he added, "We'll just cut your hair short and call you Bob."[13] Richardson stuck with softball and became a four-time All-American and an Olympic champion. More common was the experience of psychologist Michele McCormick, who grew up during the late 1960s playing baseball in the lot behind her home in Dallas, Texas. In that time and place, McCormick said girls were expected to go to beauty school early on to learn how to walk, apply makeup, and dress properly to get that competitive edge. A Dallas mother's highest aspiration for her girls was that of beauty queen. So her mother believed her daughter was on track when Michele was named the local Little League princess in seventh grade. McCormick was less enthusiastic:

> She fixed my hair for the team picture, and I put on this great dress. The ceremony was at Ridgewood Park, and I stood there, at the center of my universe, surrounded by the boys in blue caps. But underneath my dress, my knees were scabbed over I was just a tomboy at heart and never did fit those traditional feminine roles. Although I loved the attention at the park that day, I felt like I should have been standing there with my baseball glove.[14]

As the boys entered formal sports, McCormick found few outlets for her athletic interests. She played slow pitch softball for her church team and swam competitively in high school. "I set city and state records and was team captain, but for girls in those days there was nowhere to go with it—no athletic scholarships. Senior year, I gave up swimming when I made cheerleader."

By the 1970s, girls around the country were clamoring to play Little League baseball, and many parents were increasingly supportive of the idea. Lawsuits charging that Little League discriminated against girls were filed in fifteen states, and the league spent nearly $2 million to keep the girls out. With the story making headlines across the country, Yogi Berra was quoted as saying, "Why don't the girls play softball and shut up?" But girls who wanted to play baseball would not "shut up." Ultimately, Little League was named in twenty-two class-action suits, and in March 1974, the Appellate Division of the New Jersey Superior Court ruled that girls were entitled to play Little League baseball.

It was big news that spring when a freckle-faced nine-year-old named Elizabeth Osder became the first girl to play under the New Jersey ruling. Osder's father had been at Ebbets Field to see the Brooklyn Dodgers' Jackie Robinson cross Major League Baseball's color line in 1947. "Twenty-seven years later, Mr. Osder was a guest of honor at the opening day ceremonies of the Englewood [New Jersey] Little League season, where he watched Elizabeth break another baseball barrier as a second baseman—Robinson's position—for the Englewood Orioles."[15] That day, not even the latest reports on the Patty Hearst kidnapping bumped the image of the first "legal" female Little Leaguer from page one. Beneath the headlines about the Hearst case was a photograph of Elizabeth Osder.

Caught amid the media's spotlight, a sympathetic political climate and judicial system, and the clamor of countless American girls and their parents, Little League officials asked Congress to amend their federal charter. On December 16, 1974, President Gerald Ford signed the bill that eliminated its mention of gender. The term "boys" was replaced with "young people," and the league's stated purpose was amended to instill only "citizenship and sportsmanship."

American Legion Baseball, to avoid the sort of lawsuits and controversy that had confronted Little League, changed its rules to accept girls in 1975. Yet if the doors to youth baseball were now open to girls, great numbers did not flock to the game. There were two reasons: Little League promptly organized Bobby Sox Softball, which siphoned many girls into that game. Besides, trying out for Little League was only the first hurdle; making the team and sticking with it still offered formidable challenges. Coaches, managers, and other parents had plenty of subtle and not-so-subtle ways of making a girl feel unwanted in Little League Baseball.

TITLE IX: A SEA CHANGE IN WOMEN'S SPORTS

If it was gratifying for a young girl to now be permitted to sign up for Little League and American Legion Baseball, it proved absolutely transforming for her to be recognized and accepted as a competitive athlete in scholastic sports. Prior to the mid-1970s, most schools offered few girls' teams. In 1971, for example, only 294,015 high school girls (approximately one in twenty-seven) played varsity sports, according to the Women's Sports Foundation. Nineteenth-century thinking was still evident in this 1971 ruling by a Connecticut judge. "Athletic competition builds character in our boys," he argued. "We do not need that kind of character in our girls."[16]

A challenge to that attitude arose out of the confluence of the Civil Rights legislation of 1964, which addressed inequities of race, and the women's movement, which raised concerns about educational and career inequities of gender.[17] It began with a former schoolteacher, congresswoman Edith Starrett Green (Democrat-Oregon), who held the first hearings in the House of Representatives on gender equity in education. Other legislators soon joined in, and the issue became a political cause *du jour*. The legislation ultimately enacted, the Education Amendments of 1972, included a section that became known as Title IX. Its preamble states, "No person in the United States shall, on the basis of sex, be excluded from participation in, be denied the benefits of, or be subject to discrimination under any educational programs or activity receiving federal financial assistance." Few pieces of legislation have had such far-reaching effects.

For the first time in American history, the same education from kindergarten through the university was made available to girls and boys, women and men. Writing on the twenty-fifth anniversary of its passage, then U.S. Secretary of Education, Richard W. Riley said, "What strikes me most about the progress that has been achieved since Title IX was passed in 1972 is that there has been a sea change in our expectations of what women can achieve."[18]

Title IX opened up opportunities to women in all fields of endeavor, from the law, to business, to academia, but it became best known for its effect upon girls' and women's sports. By 2003, 39 percent of high school athletes were female, and the number of women participating in college sports had increased five-fold since 1971–72.[19] From the beginning, however, Title IX's broad sweep and vague language wrought confusion and discord. Athletic departments resented the idea of cutting funds for established men's sports, particularly revenue producers, in order to support women's sports—despite the fact that athletically gifted co-eds had to pay their way through college, or drop out, because sports scholarships were seldom available to them. Charlene Wright, a pitcher for the amateur women's baseball team the New Jersey Nemesis, recalled what conditions were like before Title IX took effect. For Wright, playing softball for UCLA in 1972 meant living on hamburgers, staying in Motel Sixes, and using castoff uniforms from the track team. The team received no money for out-of-state travel or scholarships until the athletic department began sponsoring women's intercollegiate athletics in 1974.

For years, Title IX was tested in the courts, revised, and slowly strengthened. When the U.S. Supreme Court ruled in 1992 that monetary damages could be awarded to plaintiffs, hundreds of gender discrimination lawsuits and civil rights complaints were filed under Title IX and state Equal Rights Amendments. Many of the suits were resolved in favor of women's sports, resulting in the reinstatement of women's teams scheduled to be cut, the upgrading of women's club sports to varsity status, and more equitable pay for women coaches. The California chapter of the National Organization for Women (NOW), for example, sued the entire twenty-campus California State University system. One of the schools in that system, Fresno State University, had spent more than $15 million on men's athletic facilities and only $300,000 on women's. Under legal pressure, the university agreed to build an $8 million women's softball stadium. The oft-used argument that women's sports do not draw well was put down when the team played its traditional rival. The stadium's seating for twenty-five hundred required the addition of bleachers to accommodate the crowd of five thousand. Playing conditions have improved, too. When the UCLA women's softball team won its first NCAA national championship in 1978, home turf was the intramural field. In 1994, the team moved to Easton Field, which has a clubhouse, locker room, lounge area, coach's office, and storage area. UCLA's athletic department now funds softball scholarships and travel to the team's opponents. The hard-won freedom to learn a sport's fundamentals and to develop one's talent in organized play from youth into adulthood has produced collegiate and Olympic champions in women's softball, soccer, and basketball. As Cheryl Miller, a 1984 Olympic gold medalist in women's basketball, said, "Without Title IX, I'd be nowhere."[20]

Title IX may have enhanced opportunities for girls in softball, as well as in basketball, soccer, and swimming, but not in baseball. When a girl outgrows Little League, she is still caught in a perpetual rundown—she has aspirations to advance but nowhere to go. The problem, again, is softball. Although Title IX permits girls to try out for boys' sports when no girls' counterpart is available, baseball and softball are considered equivalent sports. Consequently, high school is the crossroads, where female athletes must decide whether to continue the battle to play baseball or switch to softball. First baseman Julie Croteau was among the first to challenge the rule of equivalency by going to court in 1987 after she was cut from her high school varsity baseball team, the Osborn Park Yellow Jackets. She lost the case. Attorney Sue Lukasik, an advocate of women's baseball, looked into the matter and found that sometime during the 1970s, softball and baseball had been deemed equivalent sports; thus individual schools were within their rights in denying girls baseball when softball was available. But Lukasik argued:

> The law needs to be adjudicated because the two are *not* the same—baseball has leadoffs, pickoffs, stealing, balks. If you ask, every woman baseball player will say *no, they are not the same!* We have the evidence to take it to court, but it'll take five to ten years. Women's baseball needs this court case because there's still the notion that women don't play. It's time to do it. We have to bend the culture.[21]

In the midst of the changes embodied by youth baseball's admission of girls and Title IX's mandate for gender equity in education, a girl was born in Downey, California, who would grow up to "bend the culture" of baseball. Ila Jane Borders, born in February 1975, would challenge the expectations and perceptions of what a girl could accomplish on a baseball diamond. Her father, Phil, had played professionally and taught his firstborn all he knew of the game. From her earliest years, she could be found at the local park, working out with her father, while her mother fielded fly balls. Ila caught the dream of making it to the Major Leagues. When she was ten years old and a veteran star of Bobby Sox softball, she told her parents that she wanted to switch to baseball. In her first Little League at bat, hair flying, she ripped a double off the center-field fence. Ila's power prompted an opposing coach to assume she was a boy and ask, "Okay, so who's the hippie who hit that double?" Over her three-year career in Little League, Borders dazzled at the plate and on the mound. At age twelve, she enjoyed a magical season, hitting eighteen home runs and pitching for an all-star team that went to the Western Regionals. Joe Moschetti, Borders's all-star coach, ran the sports program for the City of South Gate for twenty years and coached youth baseball, football, and basketball in his spare time. Moschetti remembers Ila Borders with admiration:

> At twelve, her fundamentals were just so good. Nobody could touch her; she was dominant. I always felt that when Ila pitched, we were going to win. She pitched in five games in [one] tournament and gave up two earned runs. . . . This girl could hit the ball farther than most boys, including one home run that I figure went close to 300 feet. She was by far in the best shape of anyone on the team. I used to see her running in the park—this was before regular practice—and I didn't see the other guys or my son, Mike, doing that, and he was a pretty good athlete.[22]

The fact that Ila Borders could compete with athletes like Mike Moschetti (who grew up to become the Oakland A's second-round draft pick in 1993 before switching to football and starting at quarterback for the University of Colorado) did not mean she had an easy time of it in Little League. Some of her toughest opponents were not on the field but in the stands, that convenient bully pulpit for parental ambitions for a son's baseball career and their own prejudices. Despite her unquestionable ability, and also because of it—many parents hated seeing their sons lose to a girl—Borders's days were shadowed by a textbook case of Little League bad attitude in the stands. "Once I showed I could play, the guys were, 'OK, let's get her on our team,'" she said. The parents were a whole other matter. "Little League mothers were the toughest—obviously, they didn't like the idea. There was only one other girl playing. The mothers went to my parents and said, 'How can you let your daughter play a boy's sport?'"[23] Some of the milder comments Ila heard included, "Go back to [your] Barbie dolls. Stick with your tea party."[24] One man in the stands confronted Phil Borders to demand, "'What do we do? Put our sons in dresses and send them off to school?'"

No matter how well a girl plays baseball, by age thirteen or fourteen, most boys will begin to surpass her in strength and speed. Borders had always been tall for her age, but the boys were now catching up. Even after an all-star summer of two perfect games and three no-hitters, her critics questioned how far she could progress in middle school. "Ila was looking ahead," said Joe Moschetti. "She knew she would have to make sacrifices, not unlike Jackie Robinson, to get ahead." Getting ahead meant running four miles when the boys ran three, and increasing her weight training. It was also time to look beyond her family for moral support. She found it in Rolland Esslinger, the baseball coach at Whittier Christian Junior High School. Given that nearly sixty boys were competing to make the team, Borders feared it would be easy for the coach to say no. She still remembers his response when she approached him about tryouts. "I saw no hesitation. He was completely at ease and OK with everything. I was just blown away by that."

As a seventh grader, Ila posted a .571 batting average and a .44 ERA and threw 37 strikeouts in 16 innings. For her role in leading the Crusaders to an unbeaten season, she was named co-winner of the Most Valuable Player award. Borders was lucky in playing for Esslinger because coaches willing to serve as a girl's advocate were not easily found; moreover, other educators posed a problem. After her MVP season in seventh grade, the Christian School League of Southern California held a meeting. Ila was the first girl in league history to play on a boys' team. She was allowed to play because there was no rule that said she could not. After her great year, no one could argue that she could not keep up with boys, but did that mean girls should be allowed to play boys' football and basketball, too? Where should we draw the line? After much debate, the league decided that baseball would be its only crossover sport.

The following year, with the winning streak on the line, Esslinger relied upon her as the team's pitching ace and batted her third. "I kept her in the lineup every day," he said, "because she was an excellent defensive player along with her ability to go with the pitch."[25] Borders led the team to another unbeaten season, pitching shutout ball for six innings and fanning twelve batters in the championship game. She later called this her golden time. "In junior high, it was still cool to be an athletic female," she said. "And my teammates gave me absolutely no crud at all. At a public school, it might've been different, but the guys here were pretty respectful. It was the time in my life when I felt most like part of a team."

Before entering high school in 1989, Ila spent the summer playing baseball with her father's semi-pro team. Phil Borders wanted his daughter to understand the challenges that lay ahead, in the dugout and the locker room, and reasoned that playing with adults would be an effective reality test. Could she adapt to adult baseball culture? Would she want to? The league was competitive, and Ila, outmanned physically, learned to pitch smarter. She was also learning how to get along with her teammates, men in their twenties and thirties. She grew up fast that summer. She found herself in the midst of players' brawls and chased by an opponent's knife-wielding girlfriend after she struck him out. "You saw a bigger world," she said. "I learned to look over my shoulder; I got more heads-up—I felt like a kid from New York City. To this day, you drop me off somewhere alone, I'm gonna survive."

That summer toughened Borders's drive to continue in baseball; however, the administration of the local public high school rebuffed her interest in pitching for the team. Under Title IX, the school was within its rights, given that it fielded a girls' softball team. Instead Borders's parents enrolled her at Whittier Christian High School, a private school amenable to her trying out for boys' baseball. Borders made the team, pitching well enough as a freshman to jump to junior varsity and, for the playoffs, to varsity. The statistics for her sophomore year (5–2, 57 strikeouts in 45 innings, 2.07 ERA, and a no-hitter) and her junior year (3–4, 39 strikeouts in 35 ⅔ innings, 3.25 ERA, and four complete games) proved she could hold her own at this level. During her senior year, coach Steven Randall started Borders in a tournament game against tough competition. Ila got into trouble during the sixth inning and loaded the bases, then struck out the side. "We won, 5–3," said Randall, "and the way she walked off the mound, I knew then she was something special." Borders graduated in June 1993 with academic honors, the co-winner of the National Army Reserve Scholar/Athlete award, and winner of the baseball team's MVP award.

The honors came with a cost. Ila knew as soon as she entered high school that her golden time was over. As with Little League, her fiercest opponents were on the sidelines. "Girlfriends and mothers of opposing players are the worst," reported the *Los Angeles Times*. "They're the ones who've threatened her life, told her she'd better watch her back. Forced her to seek a kind and willing soul after the game to help her get to the car safely."[26] She also sensed that many of the girls at school no longer found it "cool" that she played baseball with the boys. Randall saw what she experienced. "Some girls really encouraged her, while some said, 'What're you doing in a man's game? Or is it the publicity?' They questioned her motives, just as a lot of other coaches questioned my integrity: was I playing her for the publicity?"[27] Borders's summer on the semipro men's team had sensitized her to the cares of the adult world; she had seen one teammate through his wife's difficult pregnancy. By comparison, her classmates' adolescent interests in popularity, dating, and looks seemed shallow. An outsider to both the girls' preoccupation with fitting in and the boys' camaraderie on the field, Borders struggled to find her place. "I'm more of an introvert," she explained, "and didn't mind being on my own. Still, it bothered me, not fitting in socially." Through the rest of her teenage years, baseball would increasingly isolate her.

Borders had received letters of interest from several colleges during her senior year in high school. Southern California College (now Vanguard University) seemed a good prospect. Situated in a leafy byway of Costa Mesa, thirty miles from home, the Christian college of nine hundred students seemed to offer a safe and quiet venue in which to pursue her baseball dream. As a member of the Golden State Conference of the NAIA, SCC valued high standards of sportsmanship. Its stated code read, "Opponents are our guests," umpires' "honesty and integrity are never questioned," and "an outstanding play deserves a hand—regardless of who made it." Besides, SCC's baseball coach, Charlie Phillips, a former left-handed pitcher himself, was a fan of hers. "I'm going to sign that kid someday," he had told his wife. "She's something special."[28] Ila Borders was by no means the first woman to play college baseball—in 1985, Susan Perabo had pitched in one game for Webster College (NCAA, Division III); in 1989, Julie Croteau played first base for the men's baseball team at St. Mary's College (NCAA, Division III), lasting for three seasons before dropping out to reflect on the issues her presence on the field had raised; and in 1990, Jodi Haller pitched 5 ⅓ innings for St. Vincent's College (NAIA). Yet neither Borders nor Phillips was prepared for the criticism and media attention they received when Borders became the first woman granted a baseball scholarship. Phillips, on the defensive, said, "I don't sign anybody who cannot pitch. I'm not in the game for publicity. If she can get outs, who cares if she's male or female?"[29]

Lots of people cared when, on a sunny February afternoon in 1994, Borders made her collegiate debut against Claremont-Mudd College. More than five hundred spectators overflowed the bleachers behind first base. Representatives from FOX, ABC, NBC, CBS-TV, the Japanese media, the *Sporting News*, and *Sports Illustrated* were there to record the event. Even the construction workers completing the new dormitory building beyond third base paused to watch as the Vanguards came alive with inspired hitting and fielding behind Borders's five-hit complete game for a 12–1 victory. The cameras flashed; the postgame interview took place by second base to accommodate the crush of reporters. The small campus had never seen anything like it. The local press called it "Ila-mania."

The diamond of SCC proved to be no haven for Borders, however. When the first batter flied out, he angrily spiked his bat, hitting his teammate in the on-deck circle. His demeanor would prove typical of the responses her presence triggered in the Golden State Conference, its high standards of sportsmanship notwithstanding. (After Borders threw 109 pitches in a 4–3 loss in March, SCC athletic director Pat Guillen complained of the opposing team, "Their players were very abusive. They were calling Ila names and using profanities throughout the game."[30]) Phillips was taking flak, too. "Before games, opposing coaches would corner Phillips and whisper, 'you're not throwing Ila today, are you?' Privately, not a single coach or player could stomach losing to a woman pitcher."[31]

Some of Borders's teammates resented the attention she received. After all, none of them had received a congratulatory letter for "courage and determination" from Dusty Baker, then managing the San Francisco Giants, and inviting them as his guest to Candlestick Park.[32] During workouts, she was often plugged in the back by hard-thrown balls. Returning to her dorm room after practice one afternoon, her roommate noticed the welts on her back, and questioned *Why are you doing this?* Borders just shrugged. Professional baseball was her dream, and to keep it alive she would do whatever it took. To relax, she developed the habit of returning to the playing field late in the evening. She would gravitate to the pitcher's mound, lie back, and look up at the stars. It was her way of maintaining her closeness to the game, until the evening that four young men jumped her. She recognized only one of them—a teammate, she said, who made no attempt to hide his identity. As they shoved her and tugged at her clothing, Borders thought *Oh, my God, I'm at a Christian college and I'm going to get raped.* Then she went into a rage. Kicking, yelling, and punching back, she made enough of a ruckus to break free, and fled to her room, scratched and bruised, her clothes torn. Fearing that it would cause a scandal if she spoke up about what happened, and that someone would be kicked off the team—probably her for raising a fuss— Borders kept silent about the attack, but from then on she grew more watchful of her safety. "That night was a big turning point in my life. I realized I wasn't just playing for fun now or because I loved the game; I was playing for all women in sports, and pitching became a role, a duty."

That spring, the campus became a media circus, with reporters calling her and showing up at her dorm at all hours of the day and night. Her grades slipped, and she began ducking interviews. Still, she would not quit, and she would not complain. Ila Borders's story was big news in Japan, and the summer after her freshman year, she was honored there at the annual World Children's Baseball Fair, and invited to throw out the first pitch at a Japanese-U.S. all-star game. On the scene were Sadaharu Oh and Joe DiMaggio. Borders told the young women of Japan that they must keep their passion for baseball, even though female players there could not yet play in official games.[33] She returned to play two more seasons of varsity baseball for Southern California College, before leaving to play in Canada the summer after her junior year. Scouts had expressed their concern that Borders could not take care of herself on the road. To prove that she could, and to continue working on her pitching skills, she played in the Saskatchewan Major Baseball League. Traveling the open stretches of prairie and living in the basement of her host family's home in Swift Current (population 14,815), Borders came to terms with just how lonely the baseball life can be. When she returned, she learned that Charlie Phillips had been replaced by a coach who did not want her on the team. Borders transferred to Whittier College, where she graduated with a bachelor's degree in kinesiology in 1997.[34] After graduation, she awaited the call that would let her take the next step into professional baseball.

Few young women followed Ila Borders into high school and collegiate baseball. During the 1990s, fast-pitch softball grew 73 percent at the high-school level and 41 percent at the college level. A softball player can develop her skills unimpeded, through Bobby Sox softball, the junior leagues for ages thirteen to fifteen, and on high school teams. For elite players, softball scholarships can pay their way through college, and after that comes the promise of Olympic competition. Meanwhile, girls' baseball has continued to languish. Given the barriers—the *wish you weren't here* messages from coaches, the scarcity of competitive league play after the age of twelve, and the dominance of softball, it is not surprising that so few young women followed in Borders's footsteps.

Part of the problem remains the conviction that softball is the feminine counterpart of baseball, an idea ingrained in American sports culture. It is still difficult to persuade people that women can and do play hardball. In 1999, I presented a paper about the career of Ila Borders at the national convention of the Society for American Baseball Research. After listening for twenty minutes about what it is like to be the only woman on the field, one man in the audience wondered aloud, "Why not just play fast-pitch softball?"

Julie Barela, who limped into the conference on crutches (she had torn the ACL in one of her knees playing center field for a local women's amateur baseball team), responded with passion about having to play softball when the game you love is baseball. "We need to stop with the mentality that softball's the only game for women."[35]

"But what about the difficulties women face in baseball?" the man persisted.

"You just don't get it," Barela answered. "I don't want to play fast-pitch softball. We play it when baseball is no longer available to us. But they are not the same game."

RAINED OUT IN BETHESDA

During the 1999 WMBL tournament in Bethesda, the first rainstorm in six months washed out a day of play. Some players saw it as a fitting analogy to the status of women's amateur baseball. The diehards who refuse to opt out for softball must go to great lengths to play the game they love and often find themselves rained out in some metaphorical way. In this case, however, the rains had a salutary effect. The players and organizers gathered in a hotel conference room to discuss the difficulties they faced. Breadth of ability was a common problem they found, with teams tending to a fragmented collection of former pros from the Colorado Silver Bullets, aging softball players, teenagers just out of Little League, and recreational wannabes. If you had earned money and celebrity as a Silver Bullet and now contended with third-rate fields, a lack of uniforms, and spotty competition that felt like a step back. Justine Siegal, the coach of the brand-new Cleveland Bears and the organizer of the Women's Baseball League, Inc., said that if you are a start-up team, it is not much fun to get thrashed 22–0 week after week. Siegal said she sometimes wonders *why bother?* "Then I think *it's not for me, it's for my daughter Jasmine.*"[36]

Stories circulated about coaches who were still intolerant of girls on their youth baseball teams—sixteen-year-old Jessica Nardone, there with the New England Clippers, for example. Nardone (whose great-grandfather Rip Wade, played for the Washington Senators in 1923), began T-ball at age six; at age ten she was drafted to the Major Division of Little League; at eleven and twelve she was a home-run hitting all-star. When Jessica moved up to the Babe Ruth League the following year, however, the manager made clear his displeasure at having a girl on his team. "There were so many walls up against her—not among the players, but among the managers and the politics of the league," said Jessica's mother, Denise. "Jessica gave up baseball at thirteen because there was no future in it. As for college, she'll go for a softball scholarship." Only in women's amateur leagues and in tournaments like this one in Bethesda does Jessica get a chance to play the game she loves best, which is when her mother sees the light in her daughter's eyes again. "Funny," said Denise Nardone, "I always hoped she'd play for the Boston Red Sox some day."[37]

Jim Glennie, the coach of the Michigan Stars, has been serving as an ombudsman for women's baseball for more than a decade. Glennie, an assistant attorney general for the state of Michigan, had been away from baseball for decades when his daughters brought him back. Witnessing the obstacles they faced frustrated him. "Having the girls showed me what lousy coaching was out there," he says. "My daughters appreciated my game so much and wanted to learn so badly. I thought they deserved a chance."[38] Glennie was coaching the Little League team of his elder daughter, Kristen, in Lansing during the summer of 1988 when he happened across an article about Darlene Mehrer's American Women's Baseball Association, which was in the Chicago area. He telephoned Mehrer to say, "You guys are really playing baseball? Send me some information."

Mehrer told Glennie about Philip Wrigley's All-American Girls Baseball League of the 1940s and 1950s. Glennie used that bit of history as publicity when he founded the American Women's Baseball League (AWBL) in 1992. It was a humble beginning, he said, with six people involved. Glennie often filled in by serving as catcher or pitcher because he lacked enough trained players. "I felt it was important for them to begin playing as a team, and this would be one way to both model and to get them playing. Of course, as soon as I had players with sufficient pitching and catching skills, I turned it over to them."[39] In 1993, Glennie struggled to field two traveling teams after the league lost access to its fields due to a scheduling lapse by the city of Lansing. "That was tough—getting them to travel," Glennie said, "because the women had to give up their entire weekends, traveling as much as three or four hours away. And because these were first experiences in baseball for many of the women, they had not developed a deep commitment to the team—a sense of the soul of baseball—that some later would have. There were still loyalties to softball teams and that style of recreational play." Glennie also bought the uniforms, rented the fields, paid for the insurance. Along the way, he fell again for the game of his youth.

THE MONEY HUNT

When Darlene Mehrer was organizing her league in 1988, she contacted Baseball Commissioner Peter Ueberroth to seek financial support. She received this reply from Robert W. Brown, the president of the American League:

> We are very interested in your projected plans for a women's baseball program. Virtually all of our funds that are directed toward amateur baseball are sent to

organizations involving the younger age groups. Our basic aims are to develop both interest and skill in baseball in our young people as they mature into early adulthood. Your plans probably involve older age groups but we are interested, and will be anxious to monitor your progress.[40]

Jim Glennie met similar responses during his struggles to develop women's amateur baseball: tepid interest and little money. He quit counting his own out-of-pocket expenditures at $50,000. "Legitimate sponsorship would have allowed more women to play who could not afford entry fees or equipment costs," he said. "Travel would have been easier. Sponsorship also provides publicity and awareness in the community." Glennie saw scrapping for sponsors to be a chicken-and-egg dilemma: "Sponsors want to see the interest before they fork over money. Well, give me a little money, and I'll make the interest happen."[41]

Even grass roots fund-raisers like garage sales were problematic when Glennie was fielding his traveling team because the players lived in diverse areas of the state—from Detroit, Grand Rapids, and Mio (170 miles north of Lansing) to Toronto, Canada. While local teams were more successful at raising money, he saw that it was hard enough for women who worked all week or were raising a family to carve time out for practice and games, let alone time-consuming fund-raising events. Unless a team had a benevolent owner like the Ocala Lightning's Jeri Baldwin, the cost could wipe players and teams out of the lineup.

Glennie tirelessly promoted the cause of women's baseball throughout the 1990s. He traveled to Cooperstown, where his Michigan Stars and the Philadelphia Strikers played Doubleday Field's first complete women's baseball game. In 1995, he organized a regional league, the Great Lakes Women's Baseball League, with teams in Lansing, Chicago, Battle Creek, South Bend, and Fort Wayne. Pursuing his goal of greater national exposure, he teamed in 1996 with an Arizona woman, Lexie Emaneth, to establish an umbrella organization named the National Women's Baseball Association. The two organized a few tournaments in Phoenix before Glennie decided that the partnership would not work. "I think they wanted to make a living from this. Capitalism's great, but at this point it's got to be a labor of love."

By 1999, Glennie was close to burn out in the cause of women's baseball, and after Justine Siegal organized the Women's Baseball League, he joined its board of directors. Siegal began an electronic newsletter, a me-

dium that has proven enormously helpful in connecting interested players and spreading information about both the WBL and girls' and women's
baseball in general. In 2002, Siegal was interviewed on Major League Baseball Radio, and she began talks with the Amateur Athletic Union, eventually winning their agreement to accept women's baseball on a probation-
ary basis. By 2003, visitors to her web site at www.baseballglory.com could
find the following opportunities:

- March: The WBL hosts their third Annual Leadership & Women's
  Baseball Conference in Toronto.
- May: The WBL hosts an instructional baseball clinic for boys and
  girls, ages five and up.
- June: Colorado Women's Baseball League hosts a five-team women's
  tournament in Denver.
- July: WBL Sparks travel to Cooperstown Dreams Park for a tour-
  nament. The AAU West Coast Women's Baseball Classic is played in
  San Diego. Women's Team Canada 2003 hosts a summer baseball
  camp. An instructional clinic and tryouts are held for national and
  international players in Tacoma, Washington.
- August: Team Québec Baseball Féminin hosts an eight-team women's
  tournament in St. Jerome. Eastern Women's Baseball Conference
  conducts clinic and national tryouts.
- September: Team Canada enters the Women's World Series, Ouzu
  City, Japan.
- November: Team Canada loses to the Chicago Storm in the semi-
  finals of the AAU tournament in Fort Myers, Florida.
- December: Due to popular demand, the WBL announces plans to
  include fifteen-year-old girls on its forthcoming Baseball Exchange
  trip to the Dominican Republic.

To Siegal, the early 2000s are critical for women's amateur baseball.
Although the number of leagues and teams has somewhat diminished
since the heyday of the Silver Bullets—she estimated that in 2003, there
were thirty-five women's teams in the United States—she has seen pockets of activity on the West Coast, and in Arizona, the Chicago area, and
metropolitan Washington, D.C. And Pawtucket, Rhode Island, has had
a viable young women's baseball team since 1973. Ironically, for female
players, the game that is so much a part of America's heritage thrives more

outside of the United States, particularly in Australia and Canada. In 1994, when Australia's Victorian Baseball Association solicited players for a women's league, more than forty teams registered. Australia now has tiers of participation for elite and recreational women players and in December of 2002, hosted the International Women's Baseball Tournament in Geelong. The country's weak link is youth baseball, because up to the age of twelve, Australian girls must play on boys' teams. Canada, by contrast, has the best girls' program in the world, but nowhere to go after age seventeen, according to Siegal. Toronto, where she now lives, is the exception—the ideal "whole package." The Central Ontario Girls Baseball League enables girls to play competitive baseball without interruption, from Peewee to Bantam to Junior baseball, in leagues for twelve to eighteen year-old girls, and then on women's teams. Even in the United States, Siegal found cause for optimism despite the fact that the country is top heavy with adult leagues:

> The growth is behind the scenes. . . . Girls' baseball is growing tremendously, but you have to be in the know to find it. For girls' baseball to thrive, however, we need more volunteers nationally—women who're willing to take off their cleats and get it going. But after you've waited your whole life to put your cleats on, it's hard to justify taking time out to help. Perhaps in a few years, when this generation of players retires from playing, they'll be willing to make the time.[42]

Siegal has sensed a change in the public's attitude toward girls' baseball. "The question of whether girls play softball or baseball isn't so relevant anymore—that's where the growth has happened." According to Jim Glennie, such growth was prompted by three events of the 1990s: the success in 1992 of the film *A League of Their Own* about the All-American Girls Baseball League of the 1940s and 1950s captured the national imagination; the announcement in 1993 of Ila Borders's college baseball scholarship made national news; and the Colorado Silver Bullets, the first women's pro team in fifty years, reminded people yet again in 1994 that women, too, play hardball.

It is one thing to agree that girls and women can play baseball. Less agreeable is the idea of girls and boys competing on the same field. Twenty-five years after Little League admitted girls, ads targeted only to the parents of sons were still appearing in *USA Today Baseball Weekly:* "Give your son 90+ mph bat speed. . . . Is your son an all-star this year? The personal pitcher will give him the edge!" "How Hard is Your Son

Throwing? The RADARWATCH is only $69!" "Is Your Son Making These Pitching Mistakes?" None of these advertisers thought to address the parents of daughters.

The minority of girls and women who persevere in baseball demonstrates that gender distinctions are not so neatly drawn on the diamond. As Chad Callahan, one of Ila Borders's high-school teammates, said of playing with her, "At first it was like, 'Oh my gosh—it's a girl. . . . But once you see what she can do, you know she is as good as anybody out there. She's just like one of the guys."[43] Jim Glennie put it this way: "When men see that women play baseball well, barriers go down."[44] Furthermore, in a time when baseball scholars find themselves spending about as much time dissecting MLB's business and financial aspects as on what happens on the field, women's amateur baseball offers a refreshing grassroots alternative. For an afternoon, or a weekend, women play for sheer love of the game. In the twenty-first century, women's amateur baseball recalls the modern game's nineteenth-century origins as joyful, amateur exercise.

5 For Love and Money
Professional Players

ON THE AFTERNOON OF SEPTEMBER 22 IN 1883, the autumn sun that turns the New York landscape golden was shining upon the Manhattan Athletic Club Grounds, where a new kind of baseball game was about to be played. Spectators debarking at the Eighty-first Street elevated train station encountered a neighborhood where change was in the very air. The area's saloons and shanties, where goats and ducks foraged in scrubby yards, were giving way to middle-class row houses on the side streets that dead-ended at Central Park, just beginning to fulfill its promise as the city's communal playground. Doubtless, few of the patrons headed for the ball game thought much about such things, given the novelty about to occur on the diamond that day: two teams of women had been hired to play baseball.

The game had been heavily promoted. "Coming! Coming! The Great and Only Young Ladies' Base Ball Club," heralded one advertisement.[1] Admission was only twenty-five cents, with "no extra charge for ladies on Grand-stand." On the day of the game, yellow handbills explained the ball club's raison d'être, reaching back to antiquity to claim, "Open-air gymnastics were very popular among the women of the ancient Greeks—likewise the ancient Romans."[2] Fifteen hundred people paid to see the game, though to call them more than curiosity seekers would be inac-

102

curate—serious fans would have continued uptown to the Polo Grounds, home of the New York Giants. Those attracted to the Manhattan Athletic Club were primarily idlers out for a Saturday diversion, and, of course, reporters, one of whom described the crowd as "[y]oung men, profuse of jewelry that made up in quantity what it lacked in quality," a cigar-smoking Irishman, who repeatedly murmured, "Well, if this ain't fun," matrons with a group of young girls in tow, and a swarm of small boys, who kept up a steady buzz of vulgarities at the sight of women playing a man's game. From the stands came a "stentorian voice," urging the young man serving as umpire to put on a dress.

The promoters had promised the "sensation of the day," nine blonde and nine brunette "baseballists." The recruits, however, were more entertainers than athletes. As the fine print in one advertisement for players stated, "Wanted: two extra young ladies with experience, or those who can play fife or drum preferred. Good salary and expenses." Musical talent was helpful for the pregame parades that publicized the ball club. In truth, the "Great and Only Ladies Base Ball Club" managed to field only eight players per team. The Blondes could not effectively field, and by the end of the first inning the Brunettes led 16–3. Nevertheless, the crowd good-naturedly cheered a fine play and showered endearments upon the best-looking players, who began the game in immaculate dresses of red or blue over trousers gathered at the knee and with their hair done up. By the end of the fifth inning, the autumn sun had sunk beneath the board fence of the Manhattan Athletic Club Grounds, and by the time the "show" (one reporter refused to call it a "game") was called on account of darkness, the Brunettes led 54–22. The next morning, the *New York Times* reported that the women played "in a very sad and sorrowful sort of way, as if the vagaries of the ball had been too great for their struggling intellects . . . [and] like an unsubstantial pageant faded."[3]

The Ladies' Base Ball Club did not fade away, however. They played again two days later, then moved on to other cities before the money ran out in Chicago. Nor was the club the first and only of its kind. After the first men's professional club, the Cincinnati Red Stockings, barnstormed across the country in 1869, women's teams were not far behind. On September 11, 1875, the first known game that women played for money took place between two teams, also known as the Blondes and the Brunettes, in Springfield, Illinois. That year also saw the Dolly Vardens, a black women's team, who played in "calico dresses shorter than propriety allowed for."[4]

THE "SCANDAL" OF WOMEN PLAYING BASEBALL

These early women's teams were professional in the sense that they were paid to play, for the games were more spectacle than sport. The exhibitions proved that people would pay to see such a show but did little to persuade fans that women could master the game. Most of the players were unschooled in baseball fundamentals, making recruitment in sufficient numbers difficult, and prompting negative press coverage of the games. When two players quit in New Orleans, a local girl filled in at center field. As the *New Orleans Daily Picayune* reported, "It was evidently the first time she had ever seen a baseball outside of a shop window, and she has not exactly acquired the art of handling it yet."[5] The very diamond had to be altered (in the 1883 game, the distance between bases was reduced to forty feet), prompting charges that women were "prostituting the game."[6] The *Sporting Life* felt moved to editorialize that "no reputable base ball club should degrade itself and the game by renting these female ball players and their manager their ball park to play in. . . . [A]ll should imitate the example of President Byrne, of the Brooklyn Club, who refused to lease his ground for such a disgusting exhibition *at any price whatever.*"[7]

The players were viewed not only as threatening to the purity of the game but also as morally suspect themselves. Although owners took care to advertise their clubs as above reproach—the members of the Young Ladies' Base Ball Club of 1883 were advertised as primarily Sunday-school graduates—the idea of women traveling about the country to play a man's game was, at the least, risqué. When Harry H. Freeman attempted to organize such a team, he was suspected of recruiting the players for prostitution, and proper Georgia ladies refused to ride on the same train with such women. This sense of moral outrage is clear in the following clippings from the *Sporting Life* of 1886: *May 12:* "Freeman's Female Base Ball club is in New Orleans. During an alleged game recently, a young man ran out of the crowd, caught one of the girls by the neck and began dragging her out of the grounds. He was arrested, but on proving that the girl was his sister he was released. He took her home." *July 7:* "The Freeman's Female Base Ball Club turned up in Nashville, Tenn. The Nashville Club wisely refused to let their ground to the disreputable party." *September 8:* "The female base ball club seems to have extinguished itself. The only decent public connection women can have with the game is as spectators."

Just before the turn of the century, a young woman challenged the question of whether a woman could effectively play competitive baseball. On July 5, 1898, Lizzie Arlington became the first woman in history to sign a minor league contract, thanks to Edward Grant Barrow, the owner of the Atlantic League's Reading franchise. Barrow declared that Arlington "could really pitch . . . with plenty of stuff and control."[8] But it was clear why she was on the mound. The thousand spectators who watched Arlington pitch a scoreless ninth inning did not meet Barrow's expectations of a big turnout, and he released her. Her experience set the pattern for the elite female player over the next century: no matter how well she could play, she could expect to be used as a curiosity to draw paying spectators. For Arlington, like other talented female ball players, the best chance of playing baseball consistently was with women's traveling teams, which by 1900 had been barnstorming the Midwest and the East Coast for more than a decade. Arlington herself played for years for such clubs. Lacking enough female opponents, they sometimes played sandlot, semi-pro, and minor league men's teams. The fielding of inexperienced players continued to cast the games as more show than sport, hurting the cause of talented women who were serious about advancing in baseball. During one ten-day period in the summer of 1900, the Chicago Bloomer Girls lost 5–2 before a crowd of twelve hundred in Covington, Ohio, 10–3 before a crowd of five hundred in Maysville, Ohio, and 14–0 before a crowd of three thousand in Delphos, Ohio. To make their teams more competitive, women's teams often used a male battery, a shortstop, or, at any position, a man in drag known as a "topper." As a teenager in 1912, future Hall of Famer Rogers Hornsby served as the Boston Bloomer Girls' topper.

A whiff of the carnival attended these teams. Living on the fringes of the national pastime, traveling women's teams, as the Negro Leagues later did, played to the crowd in order to survive—sometimes to ill effect. In 1903, a Brooklyn club wound up in the Fort Worth, Texas, jailhouse, where they "sang up-to-date topical songs, roasted the jail officials and male prisoners, turned handsprings . . . and other startling performances."[9] Serious players, however, sought to separate themselves from that image. As this published notice about pitcher Maud Nelson and the Star Bloomer Girls states, "The management wishes it understood that the Bloomer Girls do not travel with the intention of drawing crowds, just through the novelty of ladies playing ball, but through their ability to play an interesting and scientific game of ball."[10]

These teams, however, represented more than the pleasures of novel entertainment—they were a portent of the future awaiting American women in the new century. Organized Baseball, already socially conservative to its core, resisted such change. Even as they lay claim as the national game—the first World Series was held in 1903, and the Mills Commission adopted the Abner Doubleday creation myth in 1907—baseball's promoters sought to exclude half the citizenry from enjoying the pleasures of playing the game professionally. Reach's *American League Guide* of 1911 called the idea "positively repugnant." Despite such criticism, the Bloomer Girls played on, crisscrossing the country. In doing so, these clubs demonstrated that American culture would not cave in because women were playing a "man's" game. The ballplayers also influenced the trend away from the cumbersome clothing and hairdos of the 1800s. Earlier female ballplayers tended to pin up their hair as best they could and don the bloomer, a bifurcated, full skirt. Lizzie Murphy, for example, had started out on the semi-pro circuit in 1909 in bloomers, with her strawberry blonde hair long; by the time she signed with Ed Carr's Traveling All-Stars in 1918, her braided hair was tucked beneath her cap, and she wore the same uniform as the men. The Bloomer Girls also upended the notion that women were inherently weak, and not up to the physical challenges of life on the road. Maud Nelson's career as player, scout, and manager lasted forty years, while Lizzie Murphy played for nearly thirty years with the Bloomer Girls. Murphy, a Rhode Islander who worked in the off-season as a mill hand and on riverboats, boasted, "[P]laying ball every day, long bus rides, sometimes only a few hours sleep and living out of a suitcase never knocked me out."[11] By the time women gained the vote in 1920 and embarked upon a decade of new independence, numerous female baseball teams had been on the road for more than thirty years.

> *Dozo arrigato Koodai Bonzi!*
> —From the Philadelphia Bobbies team song, in Japanese, 1925

Those horizons expanded internationally in 1925. On the morning of September 23, fourteen women, accompanied by chaperones, the promoter, and a male battery comprised of pitcher Earl Hamilton and catcher Eddie Ainsmith, boarded a westbound train. Known as the Philadelphia Bobbies (after the popular new hairstyle), the team barnstormed through the Northwest before embarking for Japan. Nettie Gans Spangler, one of the players, kept a diary of the venture. Her notes suggest what the trip meant to a young woman who grew up in the Odd Fellows Orphanage, as well as something of the team's personality:

> *September 28th, White Fish, Montana:* This town, as a number of other towns, reminds me of the places you see in Western movies. . . . We went sightseeing this afternoon and played a Ball Game. In the evening, we went to a Barn Dance. They danced very "odd." No doubt Diary, they thought our steps were odd also when we did the Charleston and the Collegiate. Mary made a speech. *October 4th, Tacoma, Washington:* Slim pitched. She is from Illinois. She is six feet tall and sixteen years of age, with a wonderful pitching arm. *October 5th:* We played the Seattle team. I was spiked, kicked in the mouth, and bruised two fingers. We got our new white suits today.[12]

After arriving in Japan on October 19, the Bobbies played in Tokyo, Osaka, Kyoto, and Kobe against men's teams comprised of university and vocational-school students, newspapermen, and actors. Although the Bobbies won sixty percent of their games, the Japanese saw the enterprise more as entertainment than sport. The players may have felt the same way, as Spangler's account of later games tails off in favor of tales of transport in *jinrikishas,* dinner with local royalty, and a Japanese actress with diamond studded teeth. There were "bouquets galore and banners," she wrote. "They are spoiling us!"[13]

As with other female traveling teams, however, funds ran short; and the venture ended before the team could continue to Formosa. A landowner from India named Mr. Mody paid for the Bobbies' return voyage. As the freighter neared the West Coast, Spangler mused in her diary, "*November 30th:* Tonight is our last night on the ship and the girls seem to be restless. They don't want to go to sleep." Small wonder—their baseball travels had awakened them to a world seen by few Americans of the time. The Bobbies had danced with royalty, dined on exotic food, and encountered the customs of the Asian world, and the women were forever changed. The spirit that led Spangler to write a song celebrating the ball club—"Baseball, Baseball, Oh we sure do love it / Nothing goes above it, yah!"—was shared by her teammates. Some of them kept baseball at the center of their world for most of their lives. For example, thirteen-year-old shortstop Edith Houghton was the youngest player on the Bobbies. At age ninety-one, Houghton could recall few details of the club's tour of Japan but still remembered the sense of adventure she felt. For Houghton, the trip was just another chance to play ball. She had been at it since the age of six, when she had spied a game in progress in the park across the street from the family home in Philadelphia. By nine, she was working out with the Bobbies. "I was into baseball so much by age thirteen that my parents didn't think to not let me go to Japan," said Houghton.[14] She went on to play baseball for the New York Bloomer Girls, for the Passaic (New Jersey) Girls, and on men's semi-pro teams. During the Depression, although she preferred baseball, she switched to softball because it was easier to find games, playing twice a week for pay at Madison Square Garden in New York City. During World War II, as a Wave stationed in Washington, D.C., she was recruited to play for a men's navy team. She was also involved with the navy's women's softball teams, organized as a way to give the servicewomen, many of whom were far from home for the first time, a sense of community. When she left the service in 1946, she contacted the Philadelphia Phillies and offered to scout for them. She brought along her baseball scrapbook for the interview with manager Bob Carpenter, who said yes.[15] Houghton continued playing softball as she scouted high-school and college players for about five seasons throughout Ohio and Pennsylvania. A back operation ended her playing days, but not her love for baseball. "It's the only game I ever knew. I didn't have a lot of help—you just went out and worked hard at it—you were on your own. Baseball has meant everything to me."

Baseball has become Japan's favorite sport. Much of that popularity can be attributed to Babe Ruth's visit of 1934 and tours by other major leaguers. The Philadelphia Bobbies had a somewhat different effect. In modeling the freedoms of the 1920s, they served as ambassadors to Japan of feminine modernity. Spangler and her teammates had fretted over two young Japanese girls who had entertained them at a dinner. "Some of these girls are sold by their Fathers to the house to pay off a debt, we were told," she confided to her diary. In another entry, she observed, "Men always come first in Japan (how silly)!" Late in her life, Spangler's request that the Bobbies be included in the National Baseball Hall of Fame and Museum was denied; her diary, however, is archived nearby in the Hall of Fame Library. When Spangler appeared at the museum's 1998 celebration of women in baseball, she tap-danced down the front steps. Time had not dimmed her spirits.

The years of the Great Depression saw softball take hold as the culturally acceptable game for female ballplayers. In addition, Organized Baseball's growing farm system was drawing fans from touring women's teams, and they began to fade away. During these hard times, only a few individuals managed to break into men's baseball, and their sojourns were brief. In the spring of 1931, pitcher Jackie Mitchell signed a contract with the Chattanooga (Southern Association) Lookouts. Pitching an exhibition game against the New York Yankees, Mitchell struck out Ruth and Gehrig back to back, whereupon the question was raised as to whether the two stars had conspired in a gentleman's agreement to make Mitchell look good. Mitchell never got the chance to prove her performance was not a fluke because Commissioner Landis (who a few years earlier had ruled that Margaret Gisolo could play American Legion ball), moved quickly to void Mitchell's contract as the "baseball life was too strenuous for a woman."[16] Mildred "Babe" Didrikson could have challenged Landis on that issue. Baseball was her first love; as a girl, her prodigious hitting earned her the nickname "Babe," after baseball's premier slugger. For several seasons, Didrikson pitched for a House of David traveling team. Didrikson earned about $1,000 a month—excellent pay during the Depression—but she could find few other opportunities to play baseball. Too competitive to live on the game's fringes, Didrikson turned to the sports of track and field, setting American, Olympic, and world records in five events; basketball, winning all-America honors; and golf, winning eighty-two tournaments. In her brief life she died of cancer at age forty-five—Didrikson was often referred to as the world's greatest woman athlete. What a loss that baseball had no room for an athlete of her caliber.

The only way a woman was going to appear on a Major League diamond was by fluke. It happened on a July night in 1935 at Crosley Field. Cincinnati Reds fan Kitty Burke heckled the St. Louis Cardinals left fielder Joe "Ducky" Medwick until he retorted, "Yah, you can't hit anything yourself."[17] Burke, a nightclub entertainer, seized the moment, entered the field, and at the on-deck circle, demanded Babe Herman's bat. Amazingly, the umpire responded with, "Play ball." Burke, described in the press as "a pretty young blond in red," did so, grounding out to the pitcher, Paul "Daffy" Dean. The Cardinals wanted the out to count, but the umpire rightfully refused. Herman then doubled home a run; and the Reds, to Burke's satisfaction, won, 4–3.

SEEKING THE HEART OF BLACK BASEBALL

Second baseman Toni Stone also got a break with a House of David ball club and went on to a lengthy professional career that culminated with the Negro American League. Her story is notable on several counts: Unlike earlier female ballplayers, Stone played alongside men virtually all of her life. Enduring the vicissitudes of injuries, low pay, lengthy road trips, and teammates' and opponents' harassment, she proved once again that the baseball life is not too strenuous for a woman. Stone also earned a living at it at a time when opportunities for black women were severely limited. Stone was not the first woman to play in the Negro Leagues—in 1933, Isabel Baxter played one game at second base for the Cleveland Giants (committing one error in five fielding opportunities)—but she lasted the longest.

Born Marcenia Lyle in 1921, she grew up in St. Paul, Minnesota, a tomboy misfit in a staunch Roman Catholic family. "My mamma, all of them, loved education. That's what they tried to bury into our minds," said Stone. "But I was always wanting to find out who I was."[18] Stone's schooling, however, gave her a limited understanding of her heritage—all she knew, she said, was the story of John Smith and Pocahontas, and her ancestors picking cotton in the South. Her parents had high aspirations, telling Stone that, with an education, she could be of value to society. But hers was not an academic mind. One of her teachers, a Miss Egan, suggested to her restless student that her hands would be her fortune and put Stone in touch with Gabby Street, a retired American League catcher, who ran a local baseball school. Stone attended for a number of years.

Like many children of the Depression, Stone padded the soles of her worn shoes with cardboard and went to sleep listening to her parents' worries over the bills. To help out, she sold newspapers for five cents a copy; three cents went to her mother. Stone read what she was selling, and in the black press she began to learn, and to dream, of a life beyond St. Paul. "Now these newspapers [the *Chicago Defender* and the *Pittsburgh Courier*] told me many things about who I was. That made me feel good; I didn't feel inferior. I got a chance to travel." For Stone, travel was part of baseball's attraction. She started out as a young teen with the House of David, shagging balls for a bit of cash, but soon graduated to playing second base and the outfield. On Sundays, after attending early Mass with the family, she traveled with the team to Kenosha, Wisconsin. "I took a little job there—they wanted me 'cause I could play a little basketball. My mother wanted me closer to her, but I told her it was a way to make a little extra money. It was so little—two or three dollars—but it would help. I hadn't hit my fifteenth birthday."

Stone also played for a time with the Twin City Giants, a semi-pro club, whose managers, George White and Scobie Wright, taught her the game's fundamentals. Wright counseled her to try softball, but Stone found the game too slow. During World War II, she made her way to San Francisco, arriving hungry, with fifty-three cents, and no job. To Stone, wartime San Francisco was filled with worldly views and opportunities. She worked a series of jobs, as a salad girl at Foster's Cafeteria, a truck driver, and a forklift operator in the South San Francisco shipyards. One summer, as she walked by Kezar Stadium in Golden Gate Park, she heard the familiar sounds of a ball game. "The fellows was working out, getting ready for the season. And I thought *it's in my mind to be wandering.*" In 1947, Stone joined a traveling black club, the San Francisco Sea Lions. The pay was minimal—they passed the hat around to spectators to make expenses—but Stone was back in baseball. After suffering a severely broken ankle that season, she was expected to quit but returned the following year. Stone jumped to the Black Pelicans of the Negro Minor Leagues, for more money, and then to the New Orleans Creoles for the 1948, 1949, and 1950 seasons. In 1949, as a .265 hitter, she was earning $300 a month, enough to send money home to her mother.

Life in black baseball was hard whether you were man or woman. When it rained, the players burned the field with kerosene, as was the custom in baseball's outback. When Stone was injured in New Orleans, she went to the Sisters of the Poor, a charity hospital, got patched up, and managed to hitch a ride to the ballpark on a policeman's horse. Like many retired ball players, she found the old times more satisfactory. "You hear of ballplayers getting hurt now and they carry them to the doctor, right? Say his arm gets out of whack—well in the Negro Leagues, they'd just slide over and swap positions when they got hurt. They'd throw out that soreness in their arm. We had no doctors—shoot, we hardly had enough uniforms to go around."

By 1953, the Negro Leagues, once a center of black culture and pride in towns from Newark to Kansas City, were in decline. After the integration of MLB in 1947, black fans' increasing abandonment of the Negro Leagues pressured the club owners into all sorts of marketing ploys to attract customers. Syd Pollock, the owner of the classy Indianapolis Clowns, had always fostered a particularly successful style of ball. As James A. Riley writes, "[T]he Clowns were one of the better-known teams in the Negro Leagues, and, as the forerunners of the Harlem Globetrotters, always provided the crowds with a blend of baseball and showbiz."[19] Mindful of the gate, Pollock had wanted a woman, namely Stone, on his team since 1951. She eventually agreed to play the 1953 season for $12,000, twice the amount the typical Major League rookie received that year.

On the field, she was first treated as if she were invisible. "I understood that," she said. "They felt you should be home, that this was a man's game." She tried to stay out of their way, spending her nights in private homes and changing in the umpire's room. She usually played the first three innings at second base and was then replaced by Ray Neil, one of the team's strongest hitters. Coming to the plate before the advent of batting helmets was an exercise in fear, Stone admitted. "That curve ball gave me a fit, the fastball scared me to death." Her fears were well founded. When she entered the league, some opposing owners wanted their pitchers to throw nothing but fastballs to (or, perhaps, at) Stone. The pitchers declined, but that did not mean special privileges applied to her. At second base, she was taken out on double plays; at bat, she was brushed back. When one opposing pitcher repeatedly buzzed fastballs by her head, Stone got angry, went up to him, and said, "Now you let me play." That day, she played nine innings. "At the big [white] ballpark in Kansas City, they wouldn't let me play," Stone recalled. "I had no problem with any of it until you told me what I couldn't do, where I could eat."

Pollock wanted Stone to play in shorts, in similar fashion as the women of the All-American Girls Baseball League. Determined to look like the rest of the players on the field, Stone refused. The black press, however, seemed more interested in what a female ballplayer looked like, trying to reconcile her oversize (42) shirt, worn "to accommodate her 36 [inch] bust," with the fact that she "thinks, talks and plays like a man." Away from the field, Stone posed for photos in a dress; and it was reported that, "In street clothes, Toni looks like any other girl, but during the season prefers to wear slacks."[20] In 1953, she appeared in fifty games, hitting .243. If she was there primarily to draw fans, no one would publicly admit it. "She was signed, not to add more turmoil to the already disconcerted diamond opponents of the clowning Clowns," claimed *Our Sports,* "but because of her proven ability as a ballplayer."[21] Her popularity with fans and her perseverance on the field opened the way for two more women to play during the final year of the Negro Leagues. In 1954, Stone moved to the Kansas City Monarchs; to replace her at second, the Clowns signed two women: Connie Morgan, a nineteen-year-old whiz from Philadelphia, and Mamie "Peanut" Johnson as a utility fielder/pitcher.

Baseball served Toni Stone as more than a vocation. Through it she acquired what her family valued—an education, if a nontraditional one. She used her travel with different clubs to discover her African American heritage. "I was so happy to visit the black colleges, like the one where Franklin D. Roosevelt contributed so many of his books. Hampton University in Virginia—that was the most beautiful of all," she recalled. "I found out that in black southern colleges they had many fine things." There Stone encountered black athletes in baseball and football programs, and black students who went on to become school administrators, attorneys, and doctors. With a church and a school, a black community had hope, she decided. Visiting the colleges and libraries encouraged her, she said. "It boosted my ego. Then I didn't have to say, 'Well, the only thing my people ever did was pick cotton.'"

Stone continued playing recreational ball near her Oakland home into her sixties. During her later years, as the story of her baseball career circulated, she spoke to schoolchildren about her experiences in baseball and the value of education. In a time when racial segregation was the norm in American society, Toni Stone fulfilled her dream. For her, the heart of the game was playing second base in the twilight of the black Show. She lived to see her career recognized by Cooperstown's National Baseball Library and Museum, five years before her death in 1996 in an Alameda, California, nursing home.

A DARN GOOD BRAND OF BASEBALL

Part of Stone's career overlapped the All-American Girls Baseball League (the AAGBL). Stone claimed she contacted the league's Chicago Colleens to request a tryout in 1948 but never heard back. The year before, Jackie Robinson's arrival in Brooklyn had begun Major League Baseball's integration of blacks, but the AAGBL did not follow suit. Given one novelty—women playing baseball—perhaps the thought of blacks and whites playing together was deemed too much. The closest the league came to integration was the signing of a few light-skinned Cuban ballplayers. Darker-skinned, homegrown talents like Stone, Johnson, and Morgan were ignored.[22]

Most fans are familiar with the AAGBL story, which was reprised in the late 1980s in a television special, in a number of subsequent books and articles, and in the film *A League of Their Own*. War was the catalyst for the league. With many minor and major leaguers fighting World War

II, Philip K. Wrigley, then the owner of the Chicago Cubs, assigned a task force led by Ken Sells, the club's assistant general manager, to organize a women's league to help lift the morale of the workers in the war effort at home and to sustain fan interest in baseball. The AAGBL brand of baseball began, as one writer noted, as a "miniature model of men's professional baseball adjusted to meet the strength, endurance, and speed of girls."[23]

The league actually opened the 1943 season as the All-American Girls' Softball League; by mid-season it was known as the All-American Girls Baseball League; and by the end of the season as the All-American Girls Professional Ball League.[24] The nuances of the league's form of baseball changed about as often as its name did. In 1943, the mound was forty feet from home plate, the bases were sixty-five feet apart, and pitchers threw the twelve-inch regulation softball underhand. Pitching soon shifted to sidearm and later to overhand. By 1948, pitchers were throwing a modified 10 ⅜" hardball from a mound fifty feet from home, and the bases were seventy-two feet apart; and by 1954, the league's last year, the ball was the same 9 ¼" used in the majors. As its players gained experience, they played a spirited brand of hardball, highlighted by stolen bases, squeeze plays, and deft fielding. Their games dispelled, once again, the Landis canard that women could not withstand the physical demands of baseball. The Fort Wayne Daisies star pitcher, Dorothy Collins, pitched into her sixth month of pregnancy. The Racine Belles second baseman, Sophie Kurys, won the 1946 Player of the Year award, with 201 steals in 203 attempts, while the Belles ace right-hander Joanne Winter tied as the league's leading pitcher with a record of 33–10. At the end of that season, in the Shaughnessy Playoffs, the league's equivalent to the World Series, Kurys and Winter starred in an extra-innings thriller that Max Carey, the league president, called one of the best games of baseball he had ever seen: Carolyn Morris pitched nine innings of no-hit ball before leaving in the twelfth, while Winter was giving up thirteen hits—only inspired fielding kept the game scoreless. In the bottom of the fourteenth inning, Kurys singled, stole second, and was on her way to stealing third, when shortstop Betty Trezza singled to right. Kurys made her final slide of the season, touching home just under the tag.

PLAY BALL LIKE A MAN, LOOK LIKE A WOMAN

Philip K. Wrigley was a chewing gum magnate who had succeeded on his company's image of wholesomeness. He was also cognizant of the negative images attached to earlier women's teams. "Wrigley, a stolid moralist, was after something different" than the women's barnstorming teams with names like Barney Ross' Adorables and Slapsie Maxie's Curvaceous Cuties, claimed writer Ron Berler. "He envisioned a league of all-star Gidgets—hard-nosed ballplayers who dressed and acted like his Double-mint Gum twins."[25] To achieve his goal, Wrigley established a strict code of appearance and behavior. Players' social engagements had to be approved, as did their living quarters and even the restaurants they visited. Public smoking and drinking were forbidden. Players with cars were not allowed to drive beyond the city limits of their home club. Moreover, the team uniforms were designed to be appealingly feminine: tailored tunics that ended above the knee, worn with satin shorts and knee socks. Before games, players were taught to scratch a bar of soap to avoid dirty fingernails. Number One in the AAGBL's "Rules of Conduct for Players" was the command: "ALWAYS appear in feminine attire when not actively engaged in practice or playing ball." Consequently, the wearing of comfortable slacks or shorts was prohibited. With the players back in skirts, it is tempting to see the league as a Victorian throwback. Wrigley, however, had a product to promote and believed that its feminine image was key to winning the greatest degree of community acceptance in the conservative Midwest. The reception to the league proved him correct in this.

Wrigley sold out after the first season, but management carried on the campaign to maintain the league's feminine image throughout its existence. At the start of the 1950 season, Don H. Black, the owner of the Racine Belles, urged the team to remember that they were selling both baseball and femininity. Black's March 1950 newsletter to the Belles reveals his preoccupation with the issue: "You'd be surprised at the importance [femininity] holds with the average fan. Nobody is especially surprised or impressed if a rough, tough mannish looking babe shows some ability at sports. But to realize that a truly feminine creature can reach the top . . . is refreshing and pleasing."[26] Warming to his role as fashion adviser, Black told the Belles to "avoid the mannish touches in jackets and shirts. Keep the little feminine frills and fancies where you can. We all love 'em! I've got a special personal feeling about shoes. I know it isn't so comfy to wear high heels after bouncing around in spikes for a few hours but there is nothing like a neat, feminine shoe . . . to set off womanly charms." In his next newsletter, Black advised, "Your hair-do is especially important—it can be feminine and still kept under control so that you can avoid the 'Wild Man from Borneo' look."[27] Players for the most part complied. Pitcher Joanne Winter said she liked the standards:

> It was a wonderful thing that the league seemed to be geared to higher standards of conduct in that they emphasized the fact that we were women, and the skirts lent to that effect, even though we didn't like them that well, and I always felt very sorry for Sophie [Kurys] sliding on her bare skin, others, too. There was a high degree of professionalism . . . of conduct. I appreciated that—probably more in retrospect.[28]

The enforcement of these standards fell to that nineteenth-century throwback, the chaperone. Chaperones served a number of purposes. They reassured parents of the players, many of whom were understandably reluctant to see their teenaged daughters leave home for the first time on an unorthodox enterprise in the company of strangers. Moe Trezza's mother refused to let her daughter play until she was assured she would be chaperoned. Chaperones served as counselor, surrogate parent, disciplinarian, friend, and trainer, according to Helen Hannah Campbell, who began a five-season stint as a league chaperone in 1947 with the Muskegon Lassies. Chaperones assigned and monitored housing, enforced curfews and dress codes, arranged for bus drivers and transportation, and nursed the players' minor injuries. Chaperones were also reassuring to the league's financial backers, who wanted the league's image upheld to the press and the fans. "We worked twenty-four hours a day on the road and in their home cities," said Campbell. "It was necessary that these girls presented the right public image at all times. . . . There was a deliberate attempt to counteract the tomboy image of most female ball players."[29]

THE "L" WORD

Ken Sells, as president of the league, believed the code accomplished an important purpose because "women didn't have to sacrifice their femininity to be standouts in a man's world."[30] That was true for some players. For others, however, obeying the code meant that they sacrificed something of their very identity, for the hidden reality was that many in the AAGBL were lesbians. The owners always knew that among their ranks of players were an appreciable number of such women, many of whom preferred short, uncomplicated hair styles, no makeup, and trousers to skirts. For these women, a display of traditional femininity was innately false. In *When Women Played Hardball,* one of the few histories of the league to address this issue in any depth, author Susan E. Johnson calls sexual orientation "the [league's] most potentially divisive issue." Johnson points out that the code of silence meant that many young rookies had no idea what a lesbian was, while gay players went to great pains to conceal their orientation. "To this day no player wants to talk openly about the existence or impact of lesbians in the League," concludes Johnson, who "heard estimates running all the way from 'eighty percent of the girls on my team' to 'no one on my team.'"[31] Josephine "Jojo" D'Angelo, who came into the league in 1943 with the South Bend Blue Sox, learned the cost of going against the code. In a televised interview, D'Angelo said she understood that the league was selling "good old-fashioned [hetero] sex appeal." But in her second season, when she returned to the club from the hair salon, her manager said, "'I have a ticket for you to go back to Chicago. We're terminating you.'" D'Angelo wondered why. "He just said, 'Your hair is too short, and those are the rules, and you knew it when you came in.' It always hurt me a lot because I was just a kid, so inexperienced. . . . I didn't go in there wanting to come out like a man." The result of such examples was that lesbians in the league grew even more "careful and guarded."[32]

The quality of play in the AAGBL improved as its players gained experience, and talk naturally turned to whether the best of the women could compete among men. In 1948, the Fort Lauderdale franchise of the Florida International League expressed interest in the Rockford Peaches all-star first baseman, Dottie Kamenshek. The AAGBL refused to sell her contract, and Kamenshek herself declared that she preferred to finish out her career as a Peach. Dottie Schroeder, who played shortstop for four league teams, was thought by Connie Mack to be another who might make it. Charlie Grimm, then managing the Chicago Cubs, observed, "If she was a boy I'd give $50,000 for her."[33] Such comments made for good reading in the sports pages, but one of Schroeder's opposing pitchers said, "I always thought [Connie Mack] was kidding. . . . Dottie could throw and field real well, but she had trouble hitting *me.*"[34] The ability to hit for power would have been a drawback to any of the women breaking into MLB—the most home runs ever hit by a player in a season in the women's leagues was sixteen—but the good will built up by the league over the years gave its best athletes the chance of the century to break into Organized Baseball, one that was, unfortunately, passed up.

By 1950, the opportunities afforded women during the war years were fading, and women were expected to return to more traditional roles. That was fine with MLB, but if you were a minor league club struggling to survive, the idea of fielding a woman was worth considering. The Harrisburg (Inter-State, Class-B) Senators of 1952 were just such a team—that season, they would finish 42 ½ games out of first place and average 440 fans per home game. So on June 21, they offered a contract to Eleanor Engle, a twenty-six-year-old stenographer and softball player. The following day, Engle suited up and took some batting and fielding practice. Ed Barrow, who a half century ago had signed Lizzie Arlington, stated, "The sensible thing, I would think, is to accept or reject a player on merit alone. I admit that I signed Lizzie strictly as a stunt. But I'm not so sure she couldn't win a spot somewhere in organized ball if she were in her prime today."[35] Barrow's opinion did not prevail, however. George M. Trautman, the president-treasurer of the National Association of Professional Baseball Leagues, quickly circulated a bulletin that settled the matter.

> Subject: SIGNING OF WOMEN PLAYERS. . . . So as to remove any possible doubt as to the attitude of the National Association office toward any such contract, I am notifying all Minor League clubs that no such contract will be approved and that any club which undertakes to enter into such a contract . . . will be subject to severe disciplinary action. I have consulted Commissioner Frick on this matter and he has asked me to express his concurrence in the view that it just is not in the best interest of professional baseball that such travesties be tolerated.[36]

Two years later, the AAGBL closed down, a casualty of changing times and its own lack of firm leadership. Diehards, like Dottie Schroeder, continued to tour with Bill Allington's All-Stars for a few years, but the glory days of women's professional baseball were over. "I put that part of my life in the background," Dottie Collins later said. "Women have other things to do in this world, like raising children."[37] Decades passed before she understood what the league had meant to her. "When we were playing, we didn't realize what we had. We were just a bunch of young kids doing what we liked best. But most of us recognize now that those were the most meaningful days of our lives."[38]

The AAGBL was not the only women's league to emerge from World War II. In November 1949, Shinichi Sekiura had just returned home to Tokyo from detention in Siberia when he overheard the radio relay of a baseball game between a Japanese team and the San Francisco Seals. Sekiura spotted an old friend in the crowd gathered around the radio, who told him that he had just organized the Blue Birds, a women's baseball team. Sekiura got involved, organizing a tryout for a second team, the Red Sox, which drew two hundred prospects. One was Shigeko Kono, an actress who "found some common fascinating factors both in baseball and Takarazuka Theater."

For a young woman like Kono, playing baseball for pay in 1950 was a three-star opportunity. First, in postwar Japan, food and money were terribly scarce. Female office workers averaged two thousand yen a year, while the average female ballplayer earned three thousand and stars made as much as seven thousand. Second, the entertaining games helped to lift the spirits of the war-torn nation. And third, playing a "man's game" enabled the women to challenge traditional Japanese gender roles. Other clubs, such as the Nissan Pearls and the Tokyo Stars, soon organized but were unable to maintain continuity. Teams withdrew from play, went amateur, or changed sponsors, with some teams becoming primarily sales tools for their companies' products. After a few years, women's professional baseball in Japan faded away. Much like the women of the AAGBL, the women of Japan's postwar teams enjoyed their moment of fame while it lasted. "I was very happy," Shigeko Kono later said. "I even wish to go back to those days. Baseball was not only an entertainment or women's liberation; it was also the players' love."[39]

PRETTY FAILURES

Over the next few decades, few individuals challenged Organized Baseball's gender barrier. Some women's challenges were simply awkward, one-day statements that times were changing: When the federal bill against job discrimination on the basis of race, color, gender, or national origin became law in 1965, the *Chicago American* sent reporter Barbara Tiritilli to check out these new possibilities for women.[40] Tiritilli requested an "audition" with the Chicago White Sox, who reluctantly complied. Donning the smallest uniform available (that of second baseman Al Weis), she headed for the mound. "It was a little clumsy carrying a bat, a glove, a brand-new ball—and my handbag—out to the mound," she writes, "but

I set the handbag down and assumed something of what I thought might resemble a Juan Pizarro stance and threw the ball." A photograph of her moment on the mound appeared in the paper the following day, and that was the end of Tiritilli's "tryout."

"This is a lifelong dream," claimed Jackie Jackson on the eve of her minor league tryout in August 1971. "I grew up with a bat in my hand. My mother was always telling me to put it down. I always wanted to be a major league player. I just didn't know didn't know how to go about it before," said the twenty-three-year-old cost analyst. Whatever her ability, Jackson lacked the years of competitive experience that men had, and was quickly deemed "a pretty failure."[41]

For nearly a century, American tomboys like Jackson had grown up dreaming of playing Organized Baseball. The social changes of the 1970s, the women's movement, and federal legislation mandating gender equity, made that dream appear achievable. In 1977, commenting on the rise in college athletic scholarships for women fostered by Title IX, C. C. Johnson Spink, the publisher of the *Sporting News,* predicted, "If women eventually invade the domain of pro sports, the pioneers will come in baseball. Henry Aaron feels the same way." Aaron, then a vice president with the Atlanta Braves, was quoted as saying, "Girls excel at basketball, golf and tennis and there is no logical reason why they shouldn't play baseball. It's not that tough. Baseball is not a game of strength; hitting is not strength. The game needs a special kind of talent, thinking and timing. Some women, as well as some men, qualify in that respect. . . . People can't be put in categories."[42]

Such statements suggest that at least some in MLB's front offices had grown sympathetic to the idea of women playing professionally. The sympathizers were of two camps: men like Aaron, who felt women had the physical capability to play competitive baseball, and men like Bill Veeck, who also saw the promotional benefits of fielding a woman. Bob Hope (no relation to the comedian, but a former public relations and marketing director for the Atlanta Braves) was of the latter persuasion. In 1984, Hope announced plans to field an entire women's team known as the Sun Sox, underwritten by his brother-in-law, real estate developer Major Hope; and it was reported that the Class-A Florida State League had promised them a franchise. Their problem was the old one: finding enough women—nineteen would do—who could compete at the Class-A level. Covering Hope's two-day camp at Georgia Tech was sportswriter

Furman Bisher, who wrote, "[T]he bases are too far apart. The pitcher's mound isn't close enough to the plate. . . . The women's long-ball range was just over the infielders' heads."[43] From among the forty aspirants, Bisher found a single "natural": twenty-year-old Kimberly Hawkins. A shortstop on her softball team and a delivery truck driver, Hawkins could do it all—throw, run, and hit, but she was "a thoroughbred in a field of mules." By contrast, players like Rosie Grubbs hustled but barely made it around the bases. "They won't be seeing Rosie in the Florida State League," Bisher concluded, "if they see the Sun Sox at all. First comes finding a roster of girls who can stand the gaff and play the men at their own game." Bob Hope soon understood that there were too many Rosies and not enough Kimberlys out there; reverting to the practice of earlier times, he attempted to field a gender-integrated team but ultimately failed in winning a franchise in the Florida State League.

Bob Hope did not give up on the idea of an all-female professional team, and young women continued to dream of the chance to play. A movie brought them together. The popularity of the hit film of 1992, *A League of Their Own*, enabled Hope to persuade the Coors Brewing Company, of Golden, Colorado, to sponsor his idea. In December 1993, Hope announced his all-women baseball club would be based in the Northern League, which operated independently from Organized Baseball. The team would not have a home field but would travel from ballpark to ballpark. Named the Colorado Silver Bullets, after the Coors brand of light beer, the company committed $2.6 million annually. For the first time in forty years, women's baseball had a substantial backer. For their work, the players would be paid $20,000 plus expenses for a forty-five game season.

More than a thousand women dropped what they were doing to seek a spot on the twenty-four player roster. Debbie Rodgers, of Olympia, Washington, left her children and her career as a fire fighter. Gina Satriano, of Malibu, California, put her job as deputy district attorney on hold. Julie Croteau, who a few years earlier had fought to play high school and collegiate baseball, left her job as assistant baseball coach at Western New England College to try out, saying, "By getting a chance to play here, I feel like justice has been done."[44]

"Justice" meant the chance to play hardball. Although baseball was their first love, excepting Croteau and Satriano, the members of the Silver Bullets were primarily softball players. Phil Niekro, the former knuckleball pitcher hired as the manager of the club, explained the consequent problem. "They're used to swinging 25-, 26-ounce aluminum bats, and now they're swinging 30-, 31-, 32-ounce bats," he said. "They're just not conditioned physically or mentally to get into this wooden bat. It's hard to throw something away you've done all your life."[45]

Supporters of women's baseball felt ambiguous toward the Silver Bullets. On one hand, men who had been involved with professional baseball appreciated the Silver Bullets' attitude toward the game. Tommy Jones had kicked around the majors and minors as a player and coach for twenty years. In 1994, a season soured and shortened in MLB by its players strike, Jones volunteered to help with tryouts. Jones said, "I came as a non-believer. . . . But I quickly became intrigued . . . with the energy level and the purity of wanting to play baseball for the love of the game. I realized that everything that had disappeared from the game I was involved in . . . was present with these women. There were no agents, no guaranteed contracts, everything so screwy with major league baseball."[46] While it was gratifying to see major corporate support and media exposure attending the club, Hope's vision for the Silver Bullets defied logic. Hope had once envisioned his Sun Sox competing against Class-A players barely out of high school and college. Now he wanted to start the Silver Bullets against the teams of the Northern League, whose experience ranged from seasoned minor leaguers to former major leaguers. After barely two months of practice, the Silver Bullets opened against the Northern League All-Stars on Mother's Day, 1994. In a nationally televised game, the women lost 19–0. The club's schedule was quickly amended to include men's amateur and semi-pro teams, but the club continued to lose. In three and a half months, the Silver Bullets traveled twenty-five thousand miles across the United States and Canada, ending the season at 6–38, and enduring thirteen shutouts. No batting average was above .220, and no ERA was below 4.50. "You want to keep the level of play competitive, not only for us but for the men's team," observed the Bullets general manager, Shereen Samonds. "It's a no-win situation for them to blow us out, 22–0. The crowd's 100 percent behind the women."[47] The uneven contests made the Silver Bullets games more spectacle than sport, a throwback to the women's teams of a century ago. Furthermore, in taking on men's teams superior in experience and fundamentals, the Silver Bullets reinforced the idea that in the power era of Barry Bonds, Mark McGwire, and Sammy Sosa, the possibility of a woman in the Show was dim. (In the spring of 1995, two Silver Bullets, pitcher Ann

Williams and infielder Shannon Mitchem, were among the fifty-three hopefuls trying out with the New York Mets. Mitchem played second base, singled, and struck out twice in a six-inning simulated game. She made the first cut, but neither she nor Williams were one of the eight the Mets ultimately selected.) In retrospect, it would have been more beneficial for the long-term prospects of women's professional baseball had Bob Hope and Coors tried the format of an all-women's league.

To some observers, however, not even a new league of their own could resolve the essential dilemma facing women who want to play professional baseball. Leslie Petty, for example, called the Silver Bullets a "war between the sexes" and the idea of a women's only league "A Lose/Lose Battle of Clichés."[48] Petty initially hoped that the Silver Bullets would offer a way for women to "assert their athletic ability and challenge masculine dominance in the sports world." That hope waned as she considered the "already in-place structure of professional baseball." Petty decided that Organized Baseball's patriarchal nature would never permit women to thrive in the game; indeed, the very nature of the way professional baseball is played is the core problem. Petty accepted that the physiologies of men and women differ. Given that American sports were based upon masculine standards of strength and sensibilities, the Silver Bullets' uneven match-ups simply perpetuated traditional prejudices about gender differences. Worse, in Petty's eyes, the club lost a golden chance to effect a grassroots change in American sport. She noted that much was made in the press of having to teach the Silver Bullets "baseball etiquette. . . . Left fielders needn't to run over to congratulate second basemen after each good play. It is unnecessary to yell, 'I'm sorry' after every error. Don't jump into a coach's arms [to celebrate] under any circumstances." *Why not?* asked Petty, In calling for an entirely new set of assumptions about how women's baseball should be played: ignore masculine biases; play the game our own way. Petty concluded, "Perhaps the real revolutionaries are those who refused to join the Colorado Silver Bullets and continued to stay and play on all-women softball teams." One need not look to softball for that sort of revolution, however, because women's amateur baseball offers much the same qualities. And while Petty's ideas may sound revolutionary, her new construct is reminiscent of nineteenth-century town ball, "baseball's immediate ancestor on the maternal side," where winning was not everything, opponents were not demonized, and the joy of play was sufficient.[49]

THE "L" WORD REVISITED

The Silver Bullets often heard people say *you play baseball? You must be gay.* The club gives us the opportunity to reexamine the old prejudices over female ballplayers' sexual orientation. After all, times were changing. Gays and lesbians were coming out of the closets of America to claim a fuller measure of their civil rights. (When Coors signed on as sponsor of the Silver Bullets, gay and lesbian rights activists were closing in on the twentieth anniversary of their boycott of the company over its alleged anti-gay policies.) The Silver Bullets did include lesbian players, who tended to keep quiet about it, as well as a transsexual, Geri Lisa Fitz, who as a man had played shortstop for the Kentucky Bourbons. And while it was true that the Silver Bullets appeared in the same uniform as men, some felt that the selection of its players resembled that of the AAGBL of the 1940s and 1950s: the more feminine you looked and acted, the better your chances of wearing the uniform.

Moreover, female baseball players must still contend not only with the questioning of their own sexual preference but also with Organized Baseball's strain of general homophobia. From Tony Mullane to Babe Ruth to Mickey Mantle, male professional baseball players have been commonly marketed and perceived as innately red-blooded heterosexuals. The truth is quite different. Privately, baseball researchers mention the handful of gay players in the Hall of Fame, as well as gay coaches and managers. Major League umpire Dave Pallone, who declared his homosexuality only after his release from Organized Baseball in 1988, knew who some of the gay ballplayers of his time were. One can only speculate as to the current number of gay major leaguers because those who are stay deep in the closet. The unwritten rule among those in the know is, you do not "out" a player because it could ruin his career. Even the editor-in-chief of *Out* magazine, Brendan Lemon, did not name names when he wrote in May 2001 about his year-and-a-half long affair with a well-known major leaguer on an East Coast team. Lemon honored his lover's desire for anonymity, saying that it was "a concealment that has been awkward at times but nothing in comparison to the maneuverings that my ballplayer has had to make. I have spent many nights, awakened by a 3 a.m. phone call after a West Coast game, talking with this guy about his homosexuality and the way it affects his behavior toward his teammates, and I have concluded that coming out would, on balance, lessen his psychic burden."[50]

People close to the game thought Lemon naive. "This might be 2001," wrote Jim Caple of ESPN.com, "but many clubhouse calendars are stuck firmly in 1957. Sports often are at the leading edge of societal change, but trust me, not on the issue of homosexuality. . . . Playing in the majors is difficult enough, it will be grueling for a player who endures the constant ugly jeers from fans, the hate mail, the physical threats, the animosity from teammates and the resentment of management."[51] Only two baseball players have publicly acknowledged their homosexuality, Glenn Burke and Billy Bean (no relation to the Oakland A's general manager, Billy Beane). Both waited until their playing days were over before emerging from the locker room closet. As Bean said, coming out during one's baseball career would have been "professional suicide." Imagine, then, what women, straight and gay, who aspire to play professional baseball must contend with.

In 1995, Bob Hope announced plans to launch a six-team women's Mediterranean Baseball League in France, Italy, and Spain to develop players for the Silver Bullets, but the idea went nowhere. The club began to improve—in its third season, its record was above .500— but fan attendance was dwindling. When the season ended, Coors withdrew its sponsorship. In retrospect, it is surprising how little had changed for women's professional baseball over the years. The neighborhood surrounding the Manhattan Athletic Club of 1883 had by now transformed into the Upper West Side, but a physical landscape can change more swiftly than social prejudices. The issues that once surrounded the Young Ladies' Baseball Club of 1883 still existed for the Colorado Silver Bullets of the 1990s. The question remained: what kind of woman wanted a career in baseball anyway? Still problematic were the lack of committed long-term sponsors willing to spend sufficient capital along with the baseball establishment's resolve that the game belongs to men, and the media's sensationalized coverage of women's baseball as novel spectacle. As in the nineteenth century, the viability of women's professional baseball revolves around issues of money, power, and sex. Even those sympathetic to the cause of women's baseball criticized the handling of the club. "By having the Silver Bullets play only men's teams, Hope unknowingly doomed them to failure," decided author Gai Ingham Berlage.[52] Sportswriter Dave Kindred acknowledged the obstacles the team faced in "achieving competence on a male-dominated playing field" and wondered where that left women who want to stay in the game. Kindred concluded, "On their best nights, the Silver Bullets may have been the match for a men's junior college team. Someday, maybe a day in the near future, a woman will pitch in the minor leagues."[53]

CROSSING PROFESSIONAL BASEBALL'S GENDER LINE

While the Silver Bullets barnstormed across the country, Ila Borders was aiming to live out Dave Kindred's prediction. As she prepared for her college graduation in the spring of 1997, she worried that her chance to play in the minor leagues was slipping away. Despite the shortage of pitching talent due to MLB's recent expansion, none of the scouts who followed her collegiate career recommended that a Major League club sign her. Some asked *why not play with the Silver Bullets?* Borders said she received a letter from someone prominent in the women's movement who criticized her desire to continue playing hardball with the men: If Borders succeeded she would undermine women's sports (i.e., the Silver Bullets); if she failed, she would set back the cause of women's sports ten years. Borders shrugged off such damned-if-you-do, damned-if-you-don't reasoning. If you dreamed of a Major League career, as she did, you had to live among and prove yourself against the other contenders, not with a women's team. She also knew that the Chicago White Sox had drafted a woman—Carey Schueler (like Borders, a left-handed pitcher)—in the forty-third round of the 1993 First Year Player Draft, but Schueler, who had last played baseball as a high school sophomore on the junior varsity team, happened to be the daughter of Ron Schueler, the general manager of the White Sox. With Schueler in mind, Phil Borders went to a friend who scouted for the National League and asked, "Then why not Ila?" "Oh, that was just a publicity stunt," he was told. "But Ila's for real—what if she makes it?"[54]

The argument against Borders was her pitching speed. She had developed a good repertoire of pitches, including a curve with a variety of breaks, a changeup that worked like a screwball, and a sinker, and she was working on a slider. Her self-described strengths were "great control, a lot of movement on the ball, and pitching smart."[55] Her perceived weakness was the fastball, which, in college, averaged in the low 70s. The fastest she had been clocked was 83 mph. Borders has always maintained that pitching speed is overemphasized. "When you hear about somebody's 90-plus mph fastball, it's usually a closer, like Troy Percival, they're clocking. Unless you're Randy Johnson, lots of pitchers just don't have that speed."[56] Pitchers lacking that speed, however, must justify their existence.

Borders's stature was another problem. It is true that MLB made room for the occasional undersized player—two such stars of the 1950s were Bobby Shantz, the Philadelphia Athletics pitching ace, 5'6", 139 pounds, and Phil Rizzuto, the New York Yankees' "Scooter" at shortstop, 5'6", 150 pounds. By Borders's time, however, size was favored at all positions and in pitchers in particular. (Right-hander Pedro Martinez's slender stature, 5'11", 150 pounds, influenced the Los Angeles Dodgers to let him go, to the enduring gratitude of the Boston Red Sox.) At 5'10" and a few pounds less than her official 150 pounds, Borders was close to Martinez in stature, but she was not throwing 93-mile-an-hour fastballs. So Borders had two strikes against her.

Size and velocity were quantifiable, however, unlike the question of whether a woman even belonged in Organized Baseball. The 1952 prohibition against the signing of women was no longer in MLB's rulebook, and by the 1990s, it was no longer good form to publicly ridicule the idea. Even so, the thought of a woman on their team was enough to raise the hair on the necks of many players, managers, and owners. It was not The Way Things Are Done. For a chance to play, Borders needed an unorthodox baseball man.

Mike Veeck was just such a man, having grown up under the influence of the promotional schemes of his legendary father, William L. "Bill" Veeck Jr. During the latter's tenure as owner of the Chicago White Sox, the two had attended a company picnic and watched as a woman from the accounting department socked a home run during a softball game. The Veecks looked at one another with the same thought: *Somewhere out there lived a woman capable of playing professional baseball, and someday they would find her.* By 1997, Mike Veeck co-owned, with the actor Bill Murray, the St. Paul Saints of the Northern League, which operates independently of MLB's minor league system. With clubs from Sioux Falls to Whiskey Bay in the Upper Midwest, the league is one of professional baseball's last outposts of chance, where players go to reinvent or hang on to their baseball dreams. The troubled outfielder Darryl Strawberry began one of his comebacks here, thanks to Veeck's appreciation for second and third chances. In the spring of 1997, the fifty-six-year-old author Pat Jordan, a once-promising minor league pitcher who wanted to try a comeback, had contacted Veeck. Jordan thought they had a deal and was waiting to hear back.

Barry Moss, the Saints hitting and outfield coach, was also in touch with Veeck. Moss lived in Southern California, had seen Borders pitch, and called his boss with the news that she might be The One. Moss vouched for her good attitude and work ethic, and her abilities to get outs consistently and field credibly. Veeck was agreeable. Ila bought a ticket and was on a plane to Minneapolis before he could change his mind. Arriving at Midway Stadium, she noticed a lone man in a raincoat standing outside. It was Veeck, who later said of their meeting:

> I'd been through the first female sports announcer, the first blind sports an-
> nouncer, and I was presumptuous enough to take her for a walk in the stadium
> parking lot to warn her about what she faced. She tolerated me for three-and-a-
> half, maybe four, minutes, before she looked me in the eye and said, 'Mr. Veeck,
> I've been almost run over, spat upon, and called things you can't believe. I can
> take care of myself.' I loved her for being so direct; and I felt reduced, as most
> men should, I would think.[57]

It frustrated Borders whenever her desire to play professional baseball was seen as a gimmick. The Saints already had a sellout season, and both she and Veeck hoped this would quell speculation that her tryout was designed to draw paying customers. It did not, of course. A sportscaster quipped, "Last year the Saints bring in a guy with no legs [Dave Stevens]. This year a woman. What's next? Dennis Rodman?"[58] Meanwhile Pat Jordan realized that Borders was the reason for Veeck's lack of response to his own request for a tryout. "So that was it," he muses in *A Nice Tuesday*. "Mike didn't have the heart to tell me he couldn't have two novelties on his team at the same time. An old man and a broad. Too much even for the son of Bill Veeck."[59]

Veeck cheerfully admitted to exploiting Ila, and pointed out that she was doing the same with him, since nobody was standing in line behind him to sign her. Still, he maintained that he saw her primarily as a ballplayer, one with some of the purest pitching mechanics he had ever seen, and left the decision on whether she made the team to his manager, Marty Scott. Borders knew this could be her only chance. After the first practice, she wrote in her diary: "God, I am scared to death right now. . . . Why did I get myself into this? I love it so much, but then the pressure is so great that I wonder sometimes if it's worth it. Every time I pitch, I feel I lose a part of my soul to someone out there, maybe a fan. Why do I feel this way? Why can't I just be an asshole? It would be a lot easier."[60]

When she made the team, the traditionalists of the Northern League responded. Doug Cimunic, the manager of the Fargo-Moorhead Redhawks, threatened to pull his team from the field if Borders appeared on the mound. Ed Nottle, the manager of the Sioux City Explorers, referred to her as "that *thing*." Some of her teammates and male fans asked her out. She declined, knowing how that would look in the press. Gay women wanted to date her, too. And "even people of intellect wanted to know . . . was Ila straight," according to author Neal Karlen, who covered the Northern League that season.[61] During one road trip, she opened the door to her hotel room and found two strangers—Baseball Andies—who greeted her with, "Hey, let's party."

Borders was fairly accustomed to all of this. What surprised her, even shocked her at times, was the affection pouring from the stands, where chants of "Ila, Ila, Ila," greeted her every appearance on the mound, good, bad, or mediocre. Borders wrote in her diary, "I hate to say it, but after being hassled for so long, it gives me chicken skin to hear the PA in every city play Roy Orbison's 'Pretty Woman' or the Doors' 'Love Her Madly' every time I run out of the bullpen to pitch."[62] Mike Veeck felt the Borders effect at home, too. His own three-year-old, Rebecca, did not yet read, but regularly tore apart the sports section of the morning paper. "What're you looking for," Veeck finally asked his daughter.

"Looking for pictures of Ila," came the response.

By late June, the Saints were in the midst of a pennant race, and Borders had pitched only 6 innings, with 11 hits, 8 runs (5 earned), 4 walks and 5 strikeouts, for a 7.50 ERA. Veeck felt that Borders would gain more experience and face less notoriety with a team more remote from the pennant race and the media scrutiny of the metropolis. On June 25, he traded her to the last-place Duluth-Superior Dukes. Ila was hurt, scared, and uncertain. Awaiting her flight to Duluth, she wrote to her best friend (her diary), "They didn't want me anymore, but I guess someone else did. What's in store for me? God, I don't even know myself."[63]

Duluth proved beneficial for Borders. She took a room in a house owned by a woman who prepared fresh blueberry pancakes for her breakfast. The front porch faced the Dukes' Wade Stadium, a gem of a ballpark built by the W.P.A. in 1941. When Borders was due to pitch for the Dukes, attendance soared. A fan club was organized. When she struggled on the mound, the empathetic fans booed not her, but the manager for leaving her in. Such attentions worried her, as she feared that her teammates and opponents, trying to hang on to their own careers, would resent her. Ila pitched 8 ⅓ innings for the Dukes, striking out 6, and giving up 5 walks, 13 hits, and 9 runs (7 earned). By the end of the season, her fastball was clocked at 78 mph; that winter she continued working out, and got it up to 80.

When the Dukes invited Borders back in 1998, her 7.56 ERA prompted some in the Northern League to question whether she would have lasted were it not for her draw at the gate. Doug Cimunic complained that Borders could "taint the quality of the league" because of her high ERA (The Northern League's average ERA in 1997 was 5.08, however, Borders by no means had the highest ERA, even on the Dukes.) She got rocked in her first appearance, leaving after one inning, but the next time she faced Cimunic's Redhawks she pitched six scoreless innings. To make things worse for the Redhawks, Mike Wallace, of CBS-TV's *Sixty Minutes,* was there to do a profile on Borders. Chris Coste, the Redhawks all-star catcher, told Wallace what it was like to face a woman on the mound:

> The only thing that was going through my mind was how I'm gonna see myself on *Sixty Minutes* striking out. I can't even tell you how many pointers guys were giving everybody. I mean, stay back, be patient, take it to right field, stride late, take a pitch. . . . And—and, you know, you're on your way up to the plate, and you're actually thinking of this stuff. . . . It's almost unexplainable, the feeling you get when you look up at her and she's coming for her wind-up, her hair's flying around.[64]

In her next appearance, Borders scattered three hits over six more scoreless innings against the Sioux Falls Canaries. Her 3–1 win that day, July 24, 1998, made her the first woman in history to win a professional men's baseball game. Her string of twelve scoreless innings did not silence her critics, however. Larry See, the player-coach of the Thunder Bay Whiskey Jacks, complained that the league's umpires gave her a wide strike zone. "Coming up against her is a no-win situation. I mean if you get a base hit, you're expected to off a woman. And if you don't . . . well, you look like a fool."

By the end of July, Borders had lowered her ERA to 4.88. One night, after going out for pizza with some teammates, she fell violently ill. In a few days' span, she dropped fifteen pounds, weight she could ill afford to lose. She kept to herself and worried. "If I went DL they'd release me. [Besides], if you're hurting you never go to anyone at the club—you handle it yourself." So Borders tried to pitch too soon and was hit hard. She ended the season 1–4, with an 8.66 ERA over 43.2 innings in 14 games, 65 hits, 45 runs (42 earned), 14 walks, and 14 strikeouts. She returned home bone weary and thin.

Playing men's baseball had turned Borders into an introvert who felt most accepted among other minorities, people who understood what it was like to be unwanted. She relied for friendship on David Glick, a Jewish pitcher who went on to play for the Houston Astros; Bob Owens, an African American football coach; and a closeted gay man. Borders understood that her presence affected the male camaraderie of the locker room, the dugout, and the team bus. She did not shower or change in the clubhouse (she did that at home or in her motel room), and knocked first, calling out "housekeeping." Borders had grown to be a loner, perhaps by temperament, but surely by circumstance. Given the day-to-day uncertainty of life in the Northern League, she started out there hesitant about forming attachments. Nor did she want trouble from her teammates' wives, who sometimes looked askance at a woman sharing the intimacies of the baseball life with their husbands. And when she was friendly, some players misunderstood her interest and asked her out.

During her second season with the Dukes, Borders grew somewhat freer about joining in for postgame beers and pizza. She became close friends with pitchers Chris DeWitt and David Glick, "guys who believed in me when I had stopped." If baseball had caused her to lead a solitary life, it was one that allowed her time for deep study of the game. Some pitchers grew to respect her knowledge of the game, and those who were not too proud came to her for pitching advice. As Mike Veeck observed, "The guys she reaches, she teaches so beautifully. I'll tell you something— the moment Ila retires, I'd hire her as a pitching coach." Borders, who bore the scars of others' judgmental attitudes, avoided passing judgment on the off-field behavior of her teammates. A listener more than a talker, she did not repeat confidences, and some players talked with her in ways they would not do with men, serious talk about her views toward Baseball Annies or cheating on a wife. As a reliever, she spent hours in the bullpen, where sex is a favored topic of conversation, and where Borders was sometimes enlisted to scan the stands for female prospects. She wondered at the free and easy sex the players had, and cautioned them about playing around, saying, "Don't you guys ever worry about getting a disease?"

On the field, Borders wanted to be treated the same as anyone else, but off the field, she could see the players did not treat her as they did their wives and girlfriends. Rick Wagner, a pitcher with the Dukes, thought that could change if Borders tried to look more feminine—*why not wear a dress sometimes?* Ila still kept her wavy hair long, but her postgame uniform was a baseball cap and nondescript warm-ups. And having witnessed the frenetic interaction between Baseball Annies and players as the team traveled from town to town, Borders did not want to draw unwanted attentions to herself. "Wear a dress on a bus with twenty-five ballplayers?" she reasoned. "I don't think so."

Established major leaguers can go blonde, like Mike Piazza, or wear diamond earring studs, like pitcher Arthur Rhodes, but for those scraping for their break into the Show, wisdom suggests just blending in. As the only woman in the Northern League, Borders was wise to choose camouflage. Besides, warm-ups were cheap. Borders had not received a signing bonus; nor was she affiliated with a Major League organization—she could be gone tomorrow—so sponsors were unwilling to sign her up for lucrative endorsements. Her $1,100 per month salary left little cash to buy clothes.

Borders returned in 1999 for her third season to a different regime in Duluth. The new Dukes pitching coach was Steve Shirley, whose own daughter had played competitive softball and who seemed to wish Borders had chosen the same, less arduous path. Asked if Ila had what it took to make it, Shirley replied, "She's got the stuff . . . but I played ball in Japan, and they have a term there, *genki.* It means to have good feelings about yourself. I don't think Ila's had *genki* for some time."[65] It was the first time I heard someone question Borders's resolve. The new manager of the Dukes was Larry See, who liked to remind the team of two homers he hit off Borders in 1998. (Ila dared not retaliate by reminding See of his two strikeouts against her.) Early on, See had warned all of his pitchers: two bad outings and you're gone. And after looking good in spring training, Borders had already turned in two poor performances. On a chilly evening early in June, See put her in to pitch the ninth inning of a game already out of reach, when suddenly the stadium lights behind first base went dark for twenty minutes. When the lights came on, Borders proceeded to give up 6 hits, 6 runs (3 earned), a walk, a hit batsman, and a wild pitch. The fielding behind her was, to put it charitably, passive; at times, the infielders seemed frozen in place.

The next day, the Dukes put Borders on revocable waivers. She had appeared in 3 games, pitched 2.1 innings, and given up 10 hits, 11 runs (8 earned), 4 walks, and 1 strikeout. Her ERA was a swollen 30.56. Then the Madison Black Wolf called to tell her they had picked her up. She was to pitch for them the following evening. During the drive through the Wisconsin countryside, Ila considered the vagaries of baseball. She wondered where the "good bully," the confident, outgoing girl of her elementary school days had gone. There was the matter of her faith, too. She had grown up believing that God had called her to play this game. If that was true, why was the baseball world so resistant? She preferred the attitudes of Christian ballplayers to those of the partiers but could not accept the critical attitudes that often went with born-again spokesmen. She herself was uncomfortable being a poster girl for Jesus, being well aware of her imperfections. "When I'm on the field, I swear—a lot," she confessed. She was not proud of it, but there it was—and how would that look in the press if she publicized her faith?

Although her career was groundbreaking for women, Borders would not declare for feminism. She had grown, in truth, mistrustful of her own gender. As with the Little League mothers and girlfriends of her opponents in high school and college, she continued to find women, even those in the media, to be her severest critics. "My personal opinion about it is that we're taught to be victims. You can see it in women's magazines. When women see another woman out there being successful, they're threatened. Whereas I think many men, like my boyfriend, like to see a strong woman."

When Borders arrived at her motel in Madison, the receptionist handed her the key, singing out, "Room [555] is across the parking lot." Ila's response was sharp and immediate: "Rule number one on the road: never let anyone know what room I'm in." So there was that too, the fear of rape. That summer, Borders turned her season around. She liked the buzz of the college town, where she had some friends from home and could hang out like any other twenty-four-year-old young woman. Her pitching improved dramatically: she picked up another win and led the Black Wolf staff with a 1.67 ERA in 15 games and 32.1 innings. She gave up 33 hits and 10 walks, but only 7 runs (6 earned). When she returned home to California, she declared that her love for baseball was back. Later that year, *Sports Illustrated* named her one of the hundred top female athletes of all time.

Borders returned to Madison for the 2000 season, where she pitched an exhibition game on May 19. The 25-degree weather, however, underscored the chilly reception to her in the clubhouse. In June, she moved on to Utah, and the Zion (Western Baseball League) Pioneerzz. It was a step down from the Northern League, but the club guaranteed her a spot on the roster for the remainder of the season. A postcard from Ila arrived from St. George, Utah. She wrote, "I am doing OK. Things look like they are going well, but things are very tough here." On June 29, she gave up 5 hits, and 3 runs in a 10–6 loss. By then she had pitched 8 ⅔ innings over 5 games, with 17 hits, 10 runs (9 earned), two walks, two strikeouts. Her ERA was 9.35. The following day, she met with Zion's manager, Mike Littlewood, after which he told reporters of Borders's retirement from baseball. "She came to me after the game and said she thought she had her best stuff and still got hit hard. . . . She said she wanted to go in another direction."[66]

We do not choose our passions; they come to us unbidden. Borders's was to play Major League Baseball. She did not make it, just as ninety-eight percent of those who sign minor league contracts do not. In *Take Time for Paradise,* A. Bartlett Giamatti writes, "Much of what we love later in a sport is what it recalls to us about ourselves at our earliest. . . . They are memories of our best hopes. . . . One hoped not so much to be the best who ever played as simply to stay in the game and ride it wherever it would go, culling its rhythms and realizing its promises."[67] For seventeen seasons, Borders followed the game wherever it would take her, around the United States and to Canada and Japan. This is all any ballplayer can ask.

Borders initially struggled to adjust to the world outside of baseball. She expressed a desire to coach—the game was still in her blood—and sent out her resume. There were no takers. She considered a master's degree so she could coach at the college level but worried about surviving graduate school—though after what she had endured in baseball, what terrors could graduate school hold? She spoke of the Toronto Blue Jays, known for their favorable attitude toward women, and going back for a tryout next spring. The stress lines around her eyes began to soften, and she lost that haunted, preoccupied look. A few weeks before September 11, she entered a training program to become a fire-fighter.

It took Borders time to begin to comprehend the value of her accomplishments: the first woman in history to earn a collegiate scholarship in baseball, win a men's collegiate baseball game, pitch and win a men's professional baseball game, and play three-plus seasons of men's professional baseball. She answered a number of questions about a woman's place on the diamond. Her years in the Northern League demonstrate beyond doubt that a woman can handle the days and nights of lengthy bus rides, late night games, dugout and bullpen hazing, and media scrutiny. Fans accepted her, as did many of her teammates. Borders also proved that women can play competitively with men and gain their respect. Mike Littlewood, her final manager, called her "one of the most courageous people I've ever met or seen play the game." Her ultimate contribution is perhaps more subtle. Ila Borders supplies the missing image of the female baseball player. Ever since the Blondes took on the Brunettes, it had been said that women did not *look* like professional baseball players. The women of the AAGBL, despite the league's popularity, perpetuated this image by having to wear inappropriate clothing— try sliding into second in a short skirt. And while the Silver Bullets represented the good-natured camaraderie integral to the tradition of women's baseball, no star player emerged to capture the media's and the nation's imagination. From her Little League years through her professional days, however, Borders's image appeared repeatedly across the country in newspapers, magazines, and on television, to be seen by girls like Mike Veeck's daughter. Premier photographer Annie Leibovitz captured the essential image of Borders. During a photo shoot at Whittier College, Leibovitz caught Borders, eyes focused, jaw set, arm cocked to throw. The shot is the centerfold in Leibovitz's and Susan Sontag's photographical essay, *Women*.[68] The picture has also appeared in a traveling exhibit of the photographer's work through the Smithsonian, and on the cover of Colette Dowling's *The Frailty Myth*. For every girl who dreams of playing professional baseball, Ila Borders's image inspires and instructs.

6 Behind the Plate
Umpires

IF BASEBALL IS OUR NATIONAL RELIGION and ballparks our green cathedrals, the umpire serves as parish priest. From Little League to the World Series, umpires rule on each pitch, each play, and, when necessary, restore the participants to order. They regularly see players, managers, coaches, and fans close up in full tantrum but are themselves expected to maintain the highest degree of composure.[1] Watch a vintage baseball game, played under rules of the 1800s, in which the umpire dresses in top hat, coat and tails, and his presence is downright majestic. Contemporary umpires, however, tend to fade into the background, their clothing muted, their calls blending into the cadence of the game. It is even possible to forget our need for an arbiter until a critical play, when fans and players breathe as one as the umpire signals: *Safe* or *Out. Fair* or *Foul. Ball four* or *Strike three.*

The work is unforgiving. A player who goes 3-for-5 enjoys a good game, but an umpire is expected to approach perfection. One or two bad calls out of the three hundred or so a plate umpire makes in a game can change the outcome. Little glory attaches to the job. For years, the pay of professional umpires was low, the living and travel conditions poor. The working conditions have always been harsh: The hours of standing and crouching in spring and autumn chill and summer heat, and the seasons on the road wear upon an umpire's back, legs, and feet. The work entails other difficulties, too. Umpires are routinely harassed in creatively framed profanity; at times, the abuse turns physical.

The competition is surprisingly fierce to live such a difficult life, to become one of the sixty-eight umpires who call Major League games. It begins each winter in Florida, at the Harry Wendelstedt School for Umpires and the Jim Evans Academy of Professional Umpiring, Major League Baseball's two accredited training schools. Each year, fewer than one in ten graduates of these five-week courses are invited into the Evaluation Course, after which the cream of each class is assigned to work in a rookie league. The 225 umpires in the minor league system can expect to spend seven to ten years (twice the amount of time the average player spends in the minors) earning between $1,800 and $3,400 a month, before they get a chance at one of the rare openings in the majors.

Organized Baseball has seen only a few female umpires. Pam Postema, whose thirteen seasons in the minor leagues brought her the farthest of any female umpire until her abrupt release in 1989, filled a book with the daily battles she endured: In *You've Got to Have Balls to Make It in This League,* Postema argues that the barriers she faced went far beyond those confronted by her male colleagues. Umpiring is an area of the game where the door has slammed hard on women. To succeed, a woman must:

- Handle gracefully the media's intense scrutiny, for few who cover baseball can resist examining the novelty of a female umpire.
- Prove she can withstand the job's physical and emotional demands.
- Demonstrate the necessary aura of control to oversee the events that unfold, and sometimes unravel, on the field—a quality women have been thought to innately lack.
- Defend her sexual identity. Because she dresses in a man's uniform to serve in a traditionally masculine role, a female umpire's hetero-sexuality has often been questioned by the orthodox thinkers who run the game.
- Find a way to fit into a close-knit, yet often fractious and competitive, fraternity.
- Transcend the notion that female umpires undermine the manly image of the role. What do you even call her—Lady Ump, Lady Blue, Umpress?

Few women have tested Organized Baseball's willingness to share with them the power embodied in the role of umpire. The first known female umpire goes back to the mid-1800s. In those days, umpires were simply recruited from one of the ball clubs and given the responsibility for enforcing a mere twenty rudes. When the Knickerbocker Base Ball Club of New York finished their games, the umpire customarily signed the game card, which showed players' names, runs scored, and "hands out" (times at bat). Under "Remarks" the umpire noted any fines levied upon misbehaving gentlemen—a typical entry being "improper language . . . Paid."[2] Among the relics of this era is a game card from 1846 with a scrawled signature that some read as "Dolly Freres," which would make her the first female umpire. An alternative reading, however, suggests "Jolly Freres" or "Jolly Brothers," befitting the club's camaraderie.

A later Knickerbockers game card, however, clearly shows the umpire's signature as Mrs. Doolittle. The game of June 8, 1847, was apparently uneventful, there being no entries under "Remarks," and we know nothing else of Mrs. Doolittle's venture. Baseball historian Mark Alvarez suggests she may have been "the first of those mothers or sisters or aunts who have been pressed into duty over the years when all the boys wanted to get into the game, or, more likely . . . a barmaid from one of the taverns adjacent to the Elysian Fields."[3] Whatever Mrs. Doolittle's particulars, nearly sixty years passed before the next known female umpire appeared.[4]

"QUEEN OF THE DIAMOND"

In July 1905, a heat wave swept through the town of Hudson, South Dakota, bringing worries of drought and outbreaks of hog cholera. For respite, local citizens enjoyed the pleasures of box socials, gooseberry pies, and baseball. The game instilled a sense of community in the Dakotas settlements, and the competition among teams from neighboring towns could grow as fiery as the sun that baked the dirt of their diamonds to a harsh crust.

Out of the prairie's shimmering heat that summer came this startling news: a young woman was umpiring. "She is just 17 years old, good looking, strong and healthy," reported the *Denver Post*.[5] Amanda Clement, Hudson's native daughter, had called an important semi-pro game the previous year after the hired umpire failed to show. Her appearance that day started out as something of a joke to the spectators, but Clement took the assignment seriously and turned it into a success. "I know base ball," she declared, "and made good because I would not stand for the beefing that day."[6]

Clement had grown up tagging along after her brother Hank and her cousin Cy Parkin, to Hudson Park's baseball field, just across the street from the family home. Prairie towns like Hudson were fertile producers of gifted ballplayers (Hank and Cy were two), yet Amanda was talented enough to play first base for the local men's team. She was also asked to call games, and it was her mastery of the rules that enabled her to continue on the field into her teenage years, given the demand for umpires who could effectively control the local rivalries. The self-assured teenager ran a firm game. A devout Congregationalist, she tolerated no swearing, would not work on Sundays, and once tossed six players from a game. As news of Clement's ability spread, she became a preferred umpire for games of consequence. For five summers, she traveled the semi-pro circuit throughout the Dakotas, Nebraska, Iowa, and Minnesota.

At the turn of the century, the benefits of physical activity for women were still under debate; however Clement disproved the notion that her gender was inherently frail. As the sole umpire, Clement stood behind the pitcher, calling balls and strikes as well as plays at the plate and in the field. Her stamina, a job requirement, was evident when she called a seventeen-inning game in hundred-degree heat. "It certainly is healthful, and many a woman in poor physical condition would be benefited immensely if she could spend a summer out in the sun umpiring," she told a reporter. "There's a good deal of exercise about the work, if it's done right." When he wondered whether umpiring was a suitable job for a woman, she replied, "There is no reason why a young woman cannot make a business of umpiring and be a perfect lady."[7]

Clement's demeanor made her opinions palatable, for she possessed that quality shared by the best umpires, calm assurance. Piling her dark hair beneath a peaked cap, she was also attractive, with dark eyes and gentle features. Her physical stature was another advantage. At 5'10", she carried herself well. In her long, full skirt, a white blouse with UMPS lettered across the front, she was a compelling figure on the field. She may have been doing a man's job, but unlike later women who wore men's umpiring suits, Amanda Clement's appearance was unambiguously feminine. Will Chamberlain's poem of 1905, "Queen of the Diamond," celebrates her as "Hudson's belle" and "Dakota's handsome daughter."[8]

There is no record that she encountered the harsh treatment suffered by male umpires of the time. "They always treat me well, possibly because I am a woman," Clement reasoned, "but they are satisfied with my decisions or they would howl. Not many teams would stand for the loss of a game because of a woman umpire."[9] In 1906, inquiries for her services came from the East, and she entertained the idea of moving up to the minor leagues. Although she did not follow through, Clement felt strongly about the idea. "Can you suggest a single reason why all the baseball umpires should not be women?" she challenged a reporter.[10] The veteran of Hudson's scrappy diamond knew that fines could not prevent unruly players and spectators from battling umpires, who at that time in professional baseball often carried blackjacks and other tools of self-defense and were sometimes escorted under guard from the field after a controversial call resulted in a home-team loss. Just as some in the game believed that encouraging women as fans might alleviate the notorious rowdiness of the grandstand, Clement expected that the social taboo against insulting or abusing women in public would permit female umpires to serve as a beneficial influence on the diamond.

The press treated her kindly. The *Hudsonite* praised her in the best hometown tradition, and if metropolitan papers treated her as a novelty, they were benign about it. Yet she retired without testing her ability to be accepted at higher levels of the game. Circumstance made her an umpire, and talent made her a success, but she showed no interest in taking up the cause of gender equity. Perhaps she sensed that the pleasures of calling balls and strikes on prairie diamonds might not survive in the minor leagues. Clement's income from umpiring helped to pay for her studies at Yankton College and the University of Nebraska, after which she coached and taught physical education. (Still an innovator, she taught dance to the football team of the University of Wyoming in order to improve the players' agility.) As a justice of the peace and police matron, she continued to serve as an enforcer of the rules before embarking upon a lengthy career in social work. Clement, who never married, maintained a lifelong affinity for the Chicago White Sox and attended minor league games throughout the Upper Middle West. She died at eighty-three in 1971 and is buried in Hudson's Eden Cemetery.

After Amanda Clement called her last game, fifty years passed before another "opportunity" arose for a female umpire, and then it was clearly a ruse to sell tickets. In August 1960, Max Hess Jr., owner of the Allentown (Eastern League, Class-AA) Red Sox, invited Maureen Galvin, a talented local softball pitcher, to work behind the plate in a game against the Binghamton Triplets. Galvin was agreeable; however, the two clubs were contending for a playoff berth, and Binghamton promptly protested to the New York Yankees, its parent club. The Yankees then brought the proposal to the attention of Baseball Commissioner Ford Frick. "Woman-Ump Gimmick Given Fast Heave-Ho," announced the *Sporting News* of Frick's veto, and Max Hess moved on to plans for a Water Follies aquacade promotion at the ballpark.[11]

NO LADY OOMPHIRES NEED APPLY

In 1966, a thirty-five-year-old housewife awakened from a dream early one morning at her home in Jackson Heights, New York. Bernice Gera got up, brewed some coffee, and told her husband Steven that he was looking at a future Major League umpire. His surprise was momentary; he had always known that his wife bore an extraordinary passion for baseball that went back to her childhood days on the sandlots of Pennsylvania's mining country. Gera's parents had abandoned their five children when Bernice was two. "I stayed with whoever would take me," she later said. "I think basically that's where it came in, the love of baseball, because there you joined in with kids, you belonged."[12]

The longing to join in informed her adult years. At the time of her dream, Gera was working as a secretary, but evenings she coached neighborhood children in the game's fundamentals. When she could afford to, she took them to games at Shea or Yankee Stadiums. By 1966, she had written without success to every Major League club, seeking a job in their front office. Then, Gera spotted an advertisement for an umpiring school in the *Sporting News.* If the front office was closed to her, perhaps the climate was right to umpire. She applied to the Al Somers School for Umpiring in West Palm Beach, Florida, and was accepted as "Bernie" Gera (her error was, perhaps, deliberate) until the day she telephoned with a question. When Somers realized "Bernie's" true gender, he withdrew his acceptance. Gera persevered, and finally gained admittance to an unaccredited school, Jim Finley's National Sports Academy.

Nineteen-sixty-seven is remembered as the "Summer of Love"; it was also a year when the subject of women's rights was under debate, and Gera quickly found herself in a firestorm of speculation. For example, the *Columbus Citizen-Journal* wondered whether Gera would "burst into

tears" when she was booed, postpone a game "when a drizzle threatened
a new hairdo," or prolong an inning "by extravagant exercise of a woman's
right to change her mind? Baseball might survive," concluded the editorial. "But it would no longer be recognizable."[13] Journalist Charles
McCabe argued that an umpire is a father figure, that "righteous old brute
who won't let you have things your way."[14] Deep Oedipal feelings are
worked out upon him. Only that blue suit of authority and a "fairly natural reluctance not to do their old man in," restrain fan and player from
violence. Since Gera could never be a father figure, McCabe concluded
that she was unfit to umpire.

Such responses were typical in a time when women were moving into
traditional men's roles, but Gera's case was exacerbated by the fact that
in her blue men's suit, she was, in effect, cross-dressing. The media coverage during her weeks at umpiring school shows the anxiety over just
what sort of woman would want to umpire. Jim Finley reassured the
press, "I had expected a tomboy . . . but Bernice is every bit a girl."[15] Journalists evaluated her measurements of 36-25-36, and Gera played along,
kidding about her difficulties with the flat chest protectors that did not
fit her figure. Much was made of the fact that Gera was married and feminine in demeanor—a regular gal beneath that masculine suit of authority. The coded message was *relax, Gera is not a lesbian.* (Few writers, however, discussed Gera's most significant personal statistics: at 5'2" and 130
pounds, she was far smaller than Organized Baseball's regulation minimum of 5'10", 170 pounds for umpires.) At the time, Gera laughed off
the scrutiny but later described her weeks at umpiring school as a "hor-
rible, lonely experience . . . they all thought there was something wrong
with me."[16] At night, beer cans and bottles crashed against her bedroom
door. On the field, players hazed her, spat tobacco juice on her shoes, and
cursed her. Yet when she graduated with honors on July 17, 1967, Finley
said, "I don't think they will be able to deny her a job because of her sex,"
and promised to see that she got to do "some form of umpiring."[17]

Gera's diploma did not guarantee a job, however, and "some form of
umpiring" turned out to be calling an occasional game at places like the
National Baseball Congress in Wichita, Kansas. She filled her time officiating in youth baseball until Vincent M. McNamara offered to hire her
in the Class-A New York–Pennsylvania League for the 1968 season. When
Philip Piton, the president of the National Association of Baseball
Leagues (NABL), rescinded the contract, saying that she was too old and

too short to umpire, Gera went to court.[18] As her suit became a cause, the story moved from the sports pages to the op-ed and news sections of the nation's papers, thanks in part to her attorney, Bronx congressman Mario Biaggi. Congressman Samuel S. Stratton (Democrat–New York) joined the debate, questioning whether federal civil rights law against discrimination by race, creed, national origin, or sex applied to all Americans save those running Organized Baseball.[19] The NABL hired Wall Street lawyer George S. Leisure Jr., who argued that Gera was "over conscious of publicity, an undesirable trait in an umpire."[20] This was a curious defense, given both Gera's preference for working without notoriety and Organized Baseball's own history of manipulating the flow of public information to its best interests. Bernice Gera, however, disrupted everything. Leisure likened the NABL's need for male umpires to that of a French restaurant's need for a French chef or a religious organization's preference for salesmen of its own creed. The New York State Human Rights Commission, however, took a more liberal view, pointing out that many currently employed umpires did not meet the height and weight requirements. Three times the commission ordered that Bernice Gera be hired, and each time the NABL appealed. Gera filed another lawsuit, seeking damages of $25 million. That figure had teeth in it. After five years as Organized Baseball's pariah, Gera again received an assignment in the New York–Penn League. She was to report for work in Geneva, New York, in June 1972.

The battle had been costly to Gera. Patches of her hair fell out due to stress, and her face bore a haggard look. The legal bills left the Geras broke, yet she happily abandoned a potentially lucrative lawsuit in favor of $400 a month, plus expenses, to umpire. To prepare for her debut, she traveled to Miami to study the rulebook with Don Chappell, an old umpiring friend, and she also began an exercise regimen.

Gera drove to Geneva with borrowed expense money and arrived smiling. On Saturday, the 24th of June, the town was like a carnival. The sun shone, a band played, and girls in the grandstand waved sheets that read, "Right on, Bernice!" The manager of the Geneva Rangers made a welcoming speech. One hundred and twenty-six years after modern baseball was born, a woman was about to umpire a professional game. She did not last long. Assigned to work the bases, Gera blew a basic call on a force-out at second during the fourth inning. Realizing her error, she reversed the call. The manager of the Auburn Phillies, Nolan Campbell, charged onto the field, yelling that Gera had made two mistakes. "The first was you put on that uniform and came out here as an umpire. Your second mistake was you left the kitchen. You should be home peeling potatoes."[21] Gera ejected Campbell and continued the game. Slated to work the second half of the doubleheader, she abruptly announced her resignation when the first game ended, fled to a waiting car, and left town. Citing fatigue, she refused to talk with reporters. The press mocked her as a quick theatrical flop: "Bernice Is a Woman—and Too Tired to Talk?" "Woman Umpire Returns to Plates at Home."[22]

Gera was roundly criticized for walking off the job. Most people assumed she caved in to the pressure on the field and quit spontaneously; but in an interview later that year with Nora Ephron for *Esquire* magazine, Gera explained that her bags were already packed before the game started. Her decision to quit had been made the day before during a five-hour league umpire meeting, where her colleagues made it clear she was unwelcome. "You're supposed to work your signals out with your partner. . . . You're a team," she said. "But my partner [Doug Hartmayer, who had publicly termed her changed call a cardinal sin] wouldn't talk to me. . . . If they won't work with you, you can't make it." "[This] was not the way it was supposed to happen," Ephron wrote, "she was supposed to have been tougher and stronger and better than any umpire in baseball and end up a grim stone bust in the Cooperstown Hall of Fame. Bernice Gera turned out to be only human, after all, which is not a luxury pioneers are allowed."[23]

Ephron speculated that Gera might have survived had the women's movement rallied to her cause during her five-year battle. Pioneers like Gera, however, tend to be too focused on their quest to join in a community of women—or to wear their labels. Upon her legal victory in 1972, Gera had declared, "Goodness knows, I'm no women's libber."[24] So feminists sat this battle out. Unfortunately, Gera's rejection of feminism isolated her from those who could have supported her. Three weeks after her retirement, however, Gera apparently had an awakening. At a meeting of the National Organization for Women, Gera spoke with the new convert's passion of the "calculated harassment by the sexist operators who control baseball."[25]

After turning in her blue suit, Gera became a minor celebrity, signing autographs as "First Lady Umpire," officiating at media softball games, and coaching the Atlanta Braves' wives in an exhibition game. In 1974, she took a job with the New York Mets, handling the Lady Met Club and other promotions, for which she often appeared in a team uniform. Her final dream of founding a children's athletic facility foundered after her diagnosis of kidney cancer. She died in Pembroke Pines, Florida, on September 23, 1992.

Gera once claimed that she should have been born a man, but there are other reasons why her career faltered. The fact that she was married may have allayed Organized Baseball's concerns over her sexual orientation, but the incessant publicity, the lack of support by her coworkers, and her age and size made questionable the prospect of an extended career in umpiring. More than anything, Gera symbolized a tentative beginning. As one reporter observed, "We're in an evolutionary period—both men and women—and there are new guidelines. . . . Thanks to people like Bernice, we know that women can function in sports."[26]

Gera's abortive career affected other women, even those on the fringes of the game. By the early 1970s, the formerly splendid Indianapolis Clowns of the American Negro League had become a ragtag barnstorming ball club of black and white has-beens and wannabes. During the 1971 and 1972 seasons, in hopes of selling more tickets, the Clowns employed Nancy Miller, a blonde from Chicago, to call the last two innings. The work was rough—Miller broke a finger on her first tour and had to leave the field within the protection of a flying wedge of players after a racial incident in Jamestown, New York—but she was certainly enthusiastic. As Bill Heward writes in his memoir *Some Are Called Clowns*, "The fans [in Newport News, Virginia] were upset . . . when Nancy, the lady ump, goosed one of their ballplayers while he was in the batter's box."[27] Miller managed to keep her job, however, until Gera quit. As the Clowns general manager, Ed Hamman, said, "The day Bernice Gera walked off the field last year was the day it became a losing proposition for us to have Nancy. . . . Up till then, though, I think she helped put some people in the stands. You could always get her picture in the paper, too."[28]

The specter of Gera's quitting clung like a bad dream to a young woman named Christine Wren, who was set on becoming a professional umpire. Like Gera, Wren grew up a loner in a fragmented family but found her niche in sports. After playing softball in Spokane, Washington, she called prep basketball and softball games, where she grew exasperated at the poor quality of officiating she saw. She decided she could make a difference and with the door open to her, thanks to Gera, entered in 1975 the Bill Kinnamon Specialized Umpiring Training Course, in Mission Hills, California. Wren stood 5' 7 ½" and weighed 130 pounds but was fine-boned; and school officials, fearing she would get hurt, declared playing baseball and the pitching machine off-limits for her. Wren, who had already lost four teeth working a high school game, responded, "I'm here to learn. Let me do it or give my money back."[29] The lone woman in Kinnamon's school, she graduated in the top 10 percent of her class. With a contract with the Class-A Northwest League in her pocket, and looking a bit like a female Huck Finn, with her freckles and a ponytail that bounced in the breeze, Christine loaded her Chevy van with a cooler, hibachi, fishing pole, and dog named Mack and took to the road.

With the memory of Gera's walk-off retirement still fresh, the press scrutinized this newcomer. Wren tried to distance herself from her predecessor's housewifely image, however, pointing out that she didn't own a home, was unmarried, and had no job to return to. To her it was simple—she wanted a career that combined her love for baseball with her respect for good officiating—but reporters wanting more story than that hounded the switchboard operators at the motels housing the umpiring crews. Wren came to believe that most of the reporters she met were biased and full of inane questions. "They treat me as a freak," she told *Referee* magazine. "[O]ften their demands are humanly impossible."[30] She cited a typical exchange:

"What's a girl doing in baseball?"
"Calling balls and strikes."
"Are you a libber?"
"No."

Wren was able to enter umpiring school and get a job in the minor leagues in large part because of advances made by the women's movement, but like Bernice Gera, she spurned the feminist label. Given the pressures upon her, Wren, too, could have used the support of such women. She handled the critiques of her performance—early on, she was called hesitant, easily rattled, and often out of position on the bases—by working harder on the fundamentals. Yet what response could she make to the taunts of the elderly Oregon fan, who called her umpiring partner, Gary Lieberman, "Lieber-person"; or to the evaluation by Portland Mavericks manager Frank Peters that "She's a good umpire if you judge her only by an umpire's qualifications;"[31] or to the comment by

Mavericks' pitcher Jim Emery: "She's like a mother hen. Everything has to be just so, shirttails in, no smoking in the dugout. She'll do stuff like call two straight strikes on a guy, then you'll throw another one right down the pipe and it's a ball because she feels sorry for him. Just like a woman. And what makes the whole thing even worse is that she isn't bad looking."[32]

The physical demands of umpiring wore upon Christine Wren. In the Northwest League, the longest trip between ballparks required an overnight drive of more than a thousand miles. Her knees, injured during her softball days, throbbed from the constant squatting. Other injuries accumulated: a broken collarbone, a separated sternum, and a burst fluid sac in her elbow from 90-mile-an-hour pitches she claimed some catchers purposely avoided. "It's a dirty business," she told a sportswriter, who described her eyes as between fury and tears. At the end of her second season, Christine walked into a Seattle hair salon and said, "Mister, cut my hair and make me beautiful." Hopeful that her short hair would cut down on flack from the grandstand, she said, "I think my sex is not as noticeable now."[33]

The system of promoting umpires is a mysterious one, and the subjects live in anxiety as to where they stand. Wren was relieved when an assignment came through in 1977 to the Class-A Midwest League. There, travel was less wearing, with the longest drive between ballparks only 370 miles. Even so, she grew ever more frustrated by the continuing glare of media attention and the sense of isolation. During the 1970s, as women fought for acceptance based upon their performance rather than gender in fields once exclusive to men, they could try persuasion and appeals to reason. Should those fail, however, they could turn to the new federal laws requiring that women have an equal chance at a job. Things were different for women in baseball. Wren felt that to complain of harassment and bias would only hurt her cause. Although she maintained she had not given up on becoming a Major League umpire, her optimism was obviously fading after her third season. "I get to the point where I think baseball is so traditional that they're just not going to allow it," she said. "I know that I've been put in a position where I have to be better than a lot of young male officials at this point."[34]

Wren spent the winter wondering if the call for a fourth season would come. After one spring training assignment fell through because there were no facilities for women, she received a three weeks' notice to report

again to the Midwest League. Instead, convinced that Organized Baseball did not want women to umpire, she took a leave of absence that
became permanent. Wren left quietly, saying that she did not stand for
any causes. For those who would follow her, she advised, "[M]ake damn
sure that's what you want to do first. Second, make sure you're good
enough to do it."[35]

FEMALE UMPIRES ENTER YOUTH AND AMATEUR BASEBALL

In 1979, *Referee* magazine published the results of its two-year study on
female officials. "It seems to be the view of most male officials that women
just cannot do the job—especially under the more strained conditions,"
stated Roy L. Askins.[36] Many of the people interviewed for the study felt
that tradition precluded the idea of female officials. Many fans considered it their right to hassle officials; yet American culture did not sanc-
tion such behavior toward women. To justify their behavior, some fans
resorted to challenging a female official's femininity. Some of those interviewed doubted that women could or should withstand such verbal
assaults and profanity. And many male officials felt that introducing
women into the profession undercut the manly nature of umpiring. "It's
hardly surprising," Askins concluded, "that men are reluctant to give up
this privileged position, especially when admittance of women is seen as
lowering the prestige of that activity."

With a welcome like that, it was understandable that women were not
flocking to follow Wren into the "privileged position" of minor league
umpiring. Due to the proliferation of youth sports and the consequent
shortage of qualified male officials, however, female umpires were on the
increase at the Little League, collegiate, and semi-pro levels of baseball.
Julie Zeller Ware was out walking in her Fountain Hills, Arizona, neighborhood when the president of her son's Little League drove by and said,
"How about it, Julie, would you umpire for us?"[37] Ware discovered she
had an affinity for the task, although success did not come easily. A self-
described perfectionist, Ware became a student of officiating, traveling
to the Little League umpiring school in San Bernardino, California, and
working closely with a local umpire-in-chief who "critiqued, critiqued,
and critiqued." Ware ended up working five and six nights a week at Little
League games throughout the Valley of the Sun and came to believe that
women can make a unique contribution to the profession. Like any good
umpire, she took control of the game but tried also to send the message

that *I don't have to cut your throat to get what we need here.* She had seen many men come onto the Little League fields wanting to be "the ruler." Ware did not believe she had to emulate that behavior to be effective:

> This goes back a long time, doesn't it? Men have been the decision makers, the rulers, and the power—and umpiring is considered a power position. So any of us who break out of the mold, whether we're a female running for the Senate, a policewoman, or an umpire, we all deal with the same thing: Those preconceived ideas about who belongs out there, who makes and can best enforce the rules. They want us to be teachers and nurturers, but I've never understood that. I'm just not a spectator; I've always been a participant. I can be aggressive and competent—and nurture.

Perry Barber is another woman who has succeeded in making a career of umpiring. A self-described "trivia nut" and fan of the television game show *Jeopardy,* Barber was in her midtwenties when she decided to study up on baseball in order to beat a friend at their trivia contests. She fell in love first with baseball history and then the game itself; and when the strike of 1981 left her without Major League baseball, she filled the void by volunteering to call Little League games in Indio, California. She was untrained and, she admitted, terrible at the job. She was also hooked. "I knew about the game as history, but not as a competition, and once I began to experience that, it affected me profoundly. I'd always been a leader and realizing I was really bad at [umpiring] somehow infused in me this desire to become a stronger person, as a woman, as a human being."[38]

Barber attended Harry Wendelstedt's umpiring school four times. Seeking experience, she called whatever games came along: Little League, high school, college, and semi-pro. Barber, the trivia buff, had joined the Society for American Baseball Research, and soon a SABR member in Japan was publishing articles about her officiating. That brought her in 1989 to Japan, where she appeared in uniform in a series of commercials and umpired. "I was treated like a goddess there; it was amazing," Barber recalled. "The Japanese hadn't seen many women in positions of authority, but things were changing and they seemed to be fascinated by my work as an umpire." While Barber is not exactly treated like a goddess when she umpires in the United States, she has made her peace with the flak. "So many players$ coaches, and umpires let their testosterone do their thinking. I see this as their problem, not mine. I'm managing the game; I'm not there to prove I'm manlier than anyone else."

Being able to work at something she loves more than makes up for the groans and looks of surprise over her gender, she said. For more than twenty years, in fact, Barber has made a career of umpiring. In addition to calling games for the independent Atlantic League, she was appointed the league's Director of Umpiring, in charge of assigning other umpires to games. She was the first woman in history to umpire in the venerable Cape Cod League, a summer league stocked with elite college players, and she has worked for the New York Mets in both their spring training and fantasy baseball camps. Recently, she ran into a former Mets coach she had not seen in a while. Barber recalled their conversation: "'Hey, Blue, whatcha doing?' he said. And I asked him the same. 'Retired,' he said. 'Lost my joy in it.' But for me—I'm fifty years old now—I haven't lost the joy." Consider Perry Barber's calendar for 2003:

> January: college scrimmages, tournaments and Major League fantasy camps in Florida; February and March: Major League intra-squad games for such teams as the Boston Red Sox, New York Mets, New York Yankees, and Philadelphia Phillies at spring training in Florida. April: high-school, college, and amateur league games in New York. Summer: the Cape Cod League. November: the Roy Hobbs amateur tournament in Florida. December was fairly quiet.

Theresa Cox was told she had the talent to get to the Show, but for the timing—she was early. Instead, she became mentor and counselor to the next generation of female aspirants to the Show. In 1979, at age nineteen, Cox was calling slow pitch softball games in Houston, Texas, when Major League umpire John McSherry noticed her work. He introduced himself and asked if she had considered baseball. "A switch went [on] in my head—I realized I loved the game," Cox said. "I used to yell at the umps at baseball games, thinking I could do better."[39]

Cox began with high-school games; even at that, the path was not easy. Texas high schools circulated a "scratch list" of umpires they did not want to use. Cox's name was universal: out of one hundred high schools, none wanted her. Cox persuaded a couple of men in the umpire's association to give her a chance, earning her way game by game. She ended up the preferred umpire of Ray Knoblauch, the well-known coach of Houston's Bellaire High School (and major leaguer Chuck Knoblauch's father). She went on to call college ball throughout Alabama, women's amateur baseball, and whatever other games came along. Cox took the jobs other umpires refused—for example, a semi-pro game between a white team and a black team that ended when one player drew a gun. She attended both Joe Brinkman's and Harry Wendelstedt's schools, hopeful of breaking into the ranks of minor league umpires. "I hated what I was told there," she said. "No one wanted to be the one to bring in a woman." She recalls an instructor telling her that he wanted her to make it, but worried that his employers would lower his salary, reasoning that if a woman could umpire, the work must be easier than everyone thought.

Cox eventually persuaded Jimmy Bragan, the president of the Double-A Southern League, to give her a chance. She became the league's first woman in history to umpire in 1988, working there periodically until 1992. Under the auspices of the Professional Umpire Development Program, she worked two seasons in the Arizona Fall League (1989–90.) That year, because she thought it important, she agreed to participate in umpire Pam Postema's gender discrimination suit against Organized Baseball, which effectively ended her progress. When Cox moved to Florida in 1997, she discovered a fresh bonanza of umpiring opportunities. At the Major League spring training camps, there are intersquad, exhibition, and fantasy baseball games, and at Disney's Baseball Quadraplex in Orlando, visiting youth teams to Double-A minor league clubs play the year round. Cox has called them all, working hundreds of games a year at $45 to $125 per. She finds the work gratifying, on and off the field. "When you put on your uniform, you represent the game, the history of it and its future, and women are a part of that future." She counsels the next generation on the pitfalls earlier umpires encountered—handling the media, physical confrontations on the field, after-hours protocols. "For me, starting out as an umpire at age nineteen gave me a chance to help other women in so many ways."

ONE STEP FROM THE SHOW

If it took large amounts of perseverance and resilience for women such as Julie Zeller Ware, Perry Barber, and Theresa Cox to succeed as umpires in the lower echelons of baseball, what was it going to take for a woman to make it to the Major Leagues? Growing up a tomboy in rural Ohio, Pam Postema was raised on competitive sports and the conviction to go after whatever she wanted to do, and do it well. As a teenager, she was something of a softball phenomenon, but by 1977, she was adrift, working as a wait-ress in Florida, when her mother alerted her to a story about Christine Wren. Postema was interested. For six months, she cajoled Al Somers, the man who had turned down "Bernie" Gera a decade earlier, until he agreed to admit her to his school. More so than Gera and Wren, Postema had the presence of an umpire. She had grown up doing farm work and at 5'8", 175 pounds, felt confident about her ability to survive the punish-ing schedule of a professional umpire. Postema also boasted an outgo-ing manner and a raffish sense of humor suited to the give-and-take of the diamond. Besides, life on the road was attractive to her, a self-de-scribed partier. If she had a shortcoming as a pioneering umpire, it was perhaps her ebullience. In her autobiography, she writes of her weeks at Somers's school: "I wanted zero publicity; I got almost a full-page story in *The Sporting News.* I should have kept my mouth shut. . . . Instead, I bdabbered happily away. . . . I had become, against my own wishes, a ce-lebrity. And it was partly my fault."[40]

Postema graduated lower than she would have liked—seventeenth in a class of 130—but high enough to become one of the chosen few offered a job in the minor leagues. She began in the Gulf Coast League by mak-ing typical rookie mistakes; even so, one manager, Carlos Alfonso, rated her as one of the top two plate umpires. Postema was confident behind the plate; her weakness was working the bases, where she sometimes struggled to get into position—a criticism that would stick like a burr throughout her career.

Postema moved up to the Class-A Florida State League in 1979. That season, some of the feedback was positive: "She did a better job than I thought she would," said left-hander Brent Strom. "That was the best-called game we've had this year," said catcher Kevin Ruffler. "Pam's a hard worker and that's important," said her umpiring partner Tim Welke.[41] In 1980, she was one of sixteen umpires promoted to Double-A baseball, and spent the next two seasons in the Texas League. And by 1983, Postema had won the plum of minor league umpiring: a call to the Triple-A Pa-cific Coast League. She endured a rough first year there. Walking onto the field for a game, she found a frying pan at home plate, and the mes-sage, "Go home, where you belong." In another game, Portland catcher Mike Diaz yelled profanities from the bullpen, spit in her face, and hollered "dyke" until she finally restrained him.

By 1986, Postema was a veteran. She had proven herself physically able to withstand the rigors of an umpire's life on the road and on the field. She had learned to shrug off the sexual innuendoes and to keep her eyes shut when arguing with tobacco-chewing players. She had also learned to handle the media, joking with sportswriters that she would prefer to slip up to the Major Leagues quietly. She knew, however, they would not let that happen. As for the issue of profanity, A. Bartlett Giamatti, then the president of the National League and a former professor of English, reasonably said, "The modern world has absorbed a level of coarse language, I'm sorry to say. I don't feel a need to protect women from the English language."[42] If any woman did not require protection it was Postema, who gave as good as she got. Postema's autobiography, for example, includes her diary entries of 1986 about her encounters with the Las Vegas Stars excitable rookie manager, Larry Bowa:

> April 17: [H]e's spitting all over my face and yelling, "You're a fucking liar! You're fucking horseshit!" He says that shit four or five times before I dump him.
>
> May 22: I awarded Howell first base, and a few moments later, Bowa ran out of the dugout and started ranting and raving. "That's the second time you've changed your decision on me!" he yelled. . . . The guy wouldn't even give me a chance to explain. Finally, I had to scream right back. "Now wait a minute! There's fucking baseball seams on his arm. I can't do anything but give him first base."
>
> May 27: I called a strike on Vegas' Ed Rodriguez for a count of 1–1. That's when Bowa yelled. "You stink!" I turned around and yelled back. "You're gone!"[43]

Postema may have had the last word with the man she thought of as "the little weasel," and although the league backed her up against Bowa, there remained concern over her record of numerous ejections. Diffusing and controlling the behavior and language that can lead to a player's or manager's ejection is one of the toughest aspects of an umpire's job. "Dumping" them disrupts the game and must be used as a last resort. Postema, however, was unrepentant. "If they're hassling me from the bench," she said, "I pick out a face I know and dump him."[44]

On July 27, 1987, Postema was invited to work behind the plate for the forty-fourth annual Hall of Fame game in Cooperstown. In the stands were Baseball Commissioner Peter Ueberroth and the American and National League presidents, Bobby Brown and Bart Giamatti. The assignment was an honor, and speculation grew as to whether she was about to be called up to the Major Leagues. Giamatti said, "Obviously, we are considering her seriously or we wouldn't have had her work this game."

Said Dick Butler, the American League supervisor of umpires, "Her progress has been good. I'd like to take a look at her this season."[45]

The 1988 season was crucial for Postema; everyone knew she was one of seven candidates for two openings in the National League. With twelve years' experience, six in Triple-A, it was time to move up or make room for younger prospects. That spring, however, a serpent appeared in Postema's field of dreams. On March 14, she called an exhibition game in which Bob Knepper pitched for the Houston Astros. Afterwards, Knepper, a born-again Christian, praised her work but criticized her presence to the press:

> A woman's a woman, and they shouldn't have to compete with men in certain jobs. That goes for sportswriting, too. It's not that woman is inferior, but I don't believe women should be in a leadership role. I believe God has ordained that there are some things women should do and some things they should not do. I think umpiring is one of them.[46]

The *New York Times*'s Ira Berkow found it easy to understand why Knepper might look for a scapegoat, as he was coming off an 8–17 season with a 5.27 ERA, yet Berkow argued that such diatribes led to "stereotyping, discrimination and worse. . . . Sometimes," he concluded, "a woman wants only the rights and opportunities accorded to a man."[47] Meanwhile, the *Los Angeles Times*'s Mike Downey suggested that the Astros trade the chauvinistic Knepper to the San Diego Padres, then owned by a woman, Joan Kroc. Downey, a Roman Catholic, warmed to the controversy: "As God is my witness, I maintain an honest confusion as to why a woman should not be permitted to be a priest, and I have absolutely no idea why the Holy Redeemer would not want a woman to be a baseball umpire."[48]

So near her goal of reaching the majors and relieved to see journalists scrutinizing Knepper rather than herself, Postema did not fire back at him. Wanting to appear above it all, she kept aloof, even from sympathetic supporters—when National League umpire Dave Pallone invited her to dinner, she did not respond. Yet Knepper's comments had deeply affected her. "It was amazing to me that I could call a great game for him and still not be accepted," she later said. "And I thought *what hope is there? I'm dead meat—I'll never make it in Major League Baseball*."[49]

Postema's fears were confirmed on December 14, 1989, when she was released. The reasons given were that she ejected too many people and her attitude had worsened toward the end of the 1988 season. At first, Postema just felt numb—she had come so close—but then she decided to fight back. Postema had always maintained she was not a feminist, but now she hired attorney Gloria Allred, known for championing women's causes. Allred filed a sexual discrimination suit with the U.S. Equal Employment and Opportunity Commission (EEOC) charging the American and National Leagues, the Triple-A Alliance (TAA), and the Baseball Umpire Development Program with "a longstanding prejudice against women," and "conspiracy" to keep females from becoming Major League umpires. Postema also began her autobiography. "I never had this deep desire to write the book," she said, but she changed her mind after a number of writers convinced her she had a story worth telling. She chose Gene Wojciechowski as coauthor because she liked his style and they got along well. The book that resulted was an unflinching look at her years in baseball—the nightly battles with managers and players and fans, the internecine politics of the Baseball Umpire Development Program, and the tireless probing by the media. "I just wrote my story," Postema later said. "Even though I didn't feel I was mad at baseball, others seemed to think I was. . . . Still, I agree it was a hard-edged book—swearing is the language of baseball—and I did love the swearing."

"I told [Gene] everything—I wanted it to be honest. He embellished the alcohol, but he left out the controversial stuff." The unpublished "controversial stuff" is what she believes really derailed her promotion to the Major Leagues. Others who saw her work vouch it was not for lack of ability. "Pam Postema, now there's an umpire could've made it," said announcer Joe Garagiola. "All that talk about the language—that was B.S.—that wasn't it. I'll tell you, when the game started, you couldn't tell there was a woman out there. She ran the game."[50] *Referee* polled its editorial board as to whether it was Postema's gender that stopped her: fifty-nine percent replied "maybe" and twenty-seven percent replied "yes."[51] One sports editor blamed her dismissal on "politics behind closed doors."[52] And a noted sports historian, who requested anonymity, said this: "I've always suspected that Organized Baseball did some 'purifying' that season."[53]

The "purifying" began with umpire Dave Pallone, the author of Postema's ignored invitation to dinner. Late in 1988, Pallone was linked in several newspapers to a homosexual sex scandal in Saratoga Springs, New York. Although he was never charged with any crime, Pallone lost his contract and left the game under a cloud. In *Behind the Mask: My Double Life in Baseball,* Pallone declared his homosexuality, saying that in Major League Baseball that is crime enough: "They believed I was gay and therefore guilty of everything—and that's why they wouldn't hire me back."[54]

For Postema, the timing of Pallone's release was disastrous. Organized Baseball, ever conscious of its image, harbored a long-standing discomfort over homosexuality in its ranks, and any woman aspiring to a career on the diamond could expect to have her sexual orientation questioned. Postema said that by 1988, that question may have hardened into certainty among some of the men who held her career in their hands. "The bottom line is that they thought I was dating women, and Ed Vargo didn't want that at all. He was great to me one year; he may have heard rumors the next year, and his attitude changed. I'd say they might have let a straight woman in, but when they found out I might not be—that's when they really pulled back." Postema said she dated both men and women on the road, but tried to keep it quiet, knowing that to go public would have been career suicide.

Pam Postema walked away from Organized Baseball and did not look back. In 1995, she was living happily in San Clemente, California, when "everything fell through." She lost her job at Federal Express and the love of the woman she thought she would be with for the rest of her life. By then, her lawsuit against MLB was resolved (as part of the settlement, she agreed to keep the details private). With no ties to California, she returned to Ohio to care for her mother, who no longer could drive a car, and her father, who had Alzheimer's disease. When we spoke by phone, Postema was at his home, his voice sounding in the background. "It's not some wonderful thing I'm doing—it's what you do. I just want to [be able] to say that I didn't miss anything when they die." Caretaking along with her advocacy of the adoption of former racing greyhounds take up her days. She kept in touch with Theresa Cox in Florida, and out of friendship for her, came out of retirement to umpire a couple of games. As to her contribution to baseball, Postema seemed nonchalant. "When I first got here, friends asked where all my umpire stuff was, but I don't have a thing out—it's all up in the attic, sitting," she said. "I didn't really do that much—I missed my goal to get to the majors, so I don't think it's such a great thing I did."

It is true that Postema's goal eluded her and that few women followed in her path. Melvin Driskoll, of Jim Evans's Academy of Professional

Umpiring, said they have a hard time attracting women. Between 1977 and 2002, thirteen women attended Harry Wendelstedt's school, with only Postema and Theresa Cox making it into the minor leagues. Yet Postema's legacy involves more than numbers. In recognition of her historic career in baseball, the members of the Baseball Reliquary, the West Coast populist version of the Hall of Fame, voted her into its Shrine of the Eternals in 2000. At the ceremony, the Reliquary's archivist/historian, Albert Kilchesty, said this:

> Baseball is a mirror of American life, but it reflects more frequently all that is wrong with America, not what is right. America's struggle with issues of "difference"—race, class, gender, sexual orientation—are all reflected glaringly in the great American pastime. While one could cite any number of instances in which baseball has responded to perceived "threats" to its purity by blackballing alleged "offenders," the case of Pam Postema, an umpire, is especially appalling.[55]

The years after Postema left the game in 1989 saw Organized Baseball revamp its program for umpires. In her time, umpires were underpaid, subsisted on bad food in second-rate hotels, and tended to be out of shape. The fatal heart attack suffered by veteran umpire John McSherry on Opening Day in 1996 in Cincinnati, however, prompted a set of new standards. McSherry weighed 328 pounds, and ESPN estimated that almost half of his colleagues were also overweight. The commissioner's office of MLB mandated more intensive physical examinations and initiated a health-care program for the umpires. The tired blue suits gave way to trim taupe golf shirts and black trousers and jackets. The Umpire Development Program, in operation since 1964, having undergone an overhaul during the late 1980s, now saw further changes. Pay and benefits were increased, and the cronyism attached to the advancement of umpires gave way to more impartial evaluations. Swearing also went out of vogue for umpires. "You would not use any language that would cause the ump to eject a player," explained former umpire Jim Evans. "This has been evolutionary as baseball sought to market to families. 'Audible to the stands,' is the key. Cleaning up the language is a way to start gaining respect."[56]

THE NEXT GENERATION

In 1993, after floods washed out the Quad Cities (Midwest League) ballpark, fans had to drive over to Eldridge, Iowa, to see the River Bandits play. High-school student Ria Cortesio was one of those fans. Admission at the substitute ballpark was only a couple of dollars, and the players were more accessible, as were the umpires. One afternoon, Cortesio noticed the umpiring crew in the parking lot and approached them. "Being the kids we were, we just started talking to them," she said. "I made it a habit. Scott Higgins [who by 2002 had moved up to the Pacific Coast League] told me all about the umpire process, and to check out the accredited schools."[57] Intrigued by the role of officiating, she followed his advice, and at age nineteen was accepted to Jim Evans's school. "I had a blast. I still have friends from all over the world. I was always treated as an equal there. Male, female, black, white—every student received the same instruction."

As a teenager, Cortesio had made the acquaintance of George Spelius, the president of the Midwest League. Counseling her on the life of professional umpiring, Spelius suggested that she attend college. Cortesio graduated from Rice University in 1998 with a degree in sports management. (Her semester as an intern in the Houston Astros front office left her amazed at the amount of behind-the-scenes work and the large number of people required to put on a ball game. The internship also confirmed her interest in being on the field rather than behind a desk.) During her college years, Cortesio umpired in amateur ball virtually the year round, from Select Little League play (Roger Clemens's son played on one team), high school, Connie Mack and American Legion leagues to intersquad college games, adult men's baseball, and Men's Senior Baseball League games. She even got a taste of what earlier women faced because she never could break into the College Association. "They offered lame excuse after lame excuse—they were not impressed with the fact that I was a woman. Officially, they said it was because I was a student at Rice, but other students—male—were officiating."

Cortesio returned to Evans's school for more training in 1999 and then attended the week-long Professional Baseball Umpires Course. The course ended on a Friday, and by Monday she was in Ogden, Utah, to begin working in the Pioneer (Advanced Rookie) League. "That first season, I expected something, but no one ever openly questioned my gender preference. It was a hundred percent different than what Gera and Postema went through. It was remarkably quiet." She attributed the friendlier reception to two things: first, she was working in a league where most of the players, aged seventeen to twenty-three, were her contemporaries and trying just as hard as she was to make the cut. "If they're worried about what the umpire looks like while they're trying to make it in baseball, they're going to have a problem," Cortesio said. "And a handful of cases tried to hit on me, but I took care of that real fast." Secondly, she felt that perceptions had changed for those, like her, who grew up in the post–Title IX era. "In my generation, a woman involved in sports isn't defective, or a bull dyke. Today women can be authority figures—it's not like twenty years ago."

For her third year in the minors, Cortesio moved up to the Florida State League, where she began to understand that her gender meant a certain degree of isolation and disadvantage. "A lot of umps do have senior umps that mentor them, but that's something I pretty much know I'll never have," she reflected. "If some Triple-A ump were to take me under his wing, word's gonna get around real fast that we're 'sleeping together.' It's not right, but there it is." That season, the 5'10", 150 pound Cortesio also felt the physical toll that umpiring exacts. She could no longer arch her back and her feet had grown a full size. She came to terms with the constant challenges that umpiring entails, pitch after pitch, night after night. "You have to be one step ahead of everyone else on the field, particularly with just two umpires. . . . You're always working to find the perfect position and the perfect angle for every play, and to be in the right position to see every pitch and get every pitch right."

Cortesio was chagrined to find herself interviewed as to the novelty she presented on the field of play. She considered the "whole 'woman thing' a non-issue. . . . The only people who care are the media, and moron fans, or stadium personnel. I'm constantly amazed (and irritated) by the local media's insistence that I'm a 'story.' No, I'm not a story. There are 225-ish minor league umpires, and I'm just one of them." It is clear that she is less intimidated and defensive than her predecessors had been about challenging this male institution. When we first spoke by cell phone, Cortesio was relaxing in the umpires' locker room after calling a Major League spring training game in Arizona. She spoke as if women had always taken phone calls in the locker room. "All I'm doing," she later e-mailed, "is making a living according to my interests & abilities, a right guaranteed by the U.S. Constitution."[58]

For all that has changed in the umpiring profession and for American women, Organized Baseball's prejudices and perceptions die slowly. Pam Postema's memoir documents the perils for a woman in blue as she moves through the ranks. At each level, the stakes for all umpires rise. In the spring of 2003, Cortesio moved up to the Double-A Southern League. One night in May after making a call that went against a team, she heard this from its dugout: "Title IX sucks!" The comment gave her pause, then rolled off her back. After all, Cortesio, in her fifth season now, was on track in her advancement. She had the encouragement of Theresa Cox, who suggested she apply as an instructor to Jim Evans's umpiring school. There Cortesio met a female student, Shanna Kook. By now, Ria Cortesio was coming to terms with her place in the game. "I know I'm not doing anything different from any other umpire out here," she told a reporter in search of a novelty story. "Because there haven't been many women before me, maybe it means a little something. . . . Society has all sorts of implicit, subtle messages that tend to be real negative toward girls. . . . There's got to be something to counteract that message. . . . I would love to have a positive impact in that direction."[59]

In June 2003, the ranks of female minor league umpires doubled when Shanna Kook received her first assignment to the Pioneer League.

7 In the Front Office
Club Owners and Executives

A FEW WEEKS AFTER THE ANAHEIM ANGELS WON their first World Series championship in October 2002, I visited Edison Field. The temporary press box was still standing, though the stands were now empty and silent. I wondered how the front-office staff had responded to the club's emotional gallop through the playoffs. Was it hard to concentrate on work, given the heroics happening just beyond the stucco wall that separates the front office from the bleachers? Nancy Mazmanian, Manager of Media Services, replied that there was little time to react or enjoy it, given the responsibilities that descended upon the employees as soon as the Angels won the American League wild card. Mazmanian pulled out a thick white three-ring binder. "This is the Post Season Manual, and it covers everything from hospitality, parking, and hotels to adding space for visiting press," she said, adding that initially she worried about the myriad details. "I was really anxious. For a front office, the World Series is a media event, and Major League Baseball puts a lot of emphasis on servicing the media."[1] She remembered thinking *so much of the world's attention is focused on us right now—this is a big deal.*

The operation of a baseball club is a big deal. And if you are an owner, it is also a big thrill, which is partly why hard-eyed businesspeople have been so willing to open their wallets for the privilege of sitting in the owner's suite. (The thrill of owning a ball club is akin to playing the game of Monopoly, and buying up Park Place and Boardwalk, with hotels.) Organized Baseball clings to its image as game—it is the perennial argument used to justify Major League Baseball's Antitrust Exemption, upheld in 1922 by the U.S. Supreme Court. It is here in the front office, however, that this manicured image of game collides with the practicalities of running a baseball club. By definition, the concern of the front office is "the business and financial side of a baseball club; the realm of a club's general manager and his staff."[2] It is a serious business, fraught with byzantine economic, political, and social issues, and a consuming one—not just at World Series time for the franchises fortunate to make it that far, but for every club throughout the calendar year.

The front office is also where women have made the greatest advances in baseball. In 2003, women were working for the Boston Red Sox, the Los Angeles Dodgers, and the New York Yankees as assistant general managers; for the San Diego Padres as Director of Minor League Operations; for the Chicago White Sox as Director of Minor League Administration; and for many other Major League and minor league franchises as the heads of public relations, ticket sales, and media relations departments. Other women, such as Katy Feeney and Phyllis Merhige, have worked for years in various executive capacities at Major League Baseball headquarters on Manhattan's Park Avenue. As for ownership, women have held, at one time or another, controlling interests in minor league and Negro League franchises as well as the Boston Red Sox, Brooklyn Dodgers, California Angels, Cincinnati Reds, Milwaukee Brewers, New York Giants, New York Mets, New York Yankees, Pittsburgh Pirates, St. Louis Cardinals, and San Diego Padres.

This lengthy list can be deceiving, however, because throughout baseball history, women have had to struggle for their place in the front office. Traditionally, those who found work here usually did so through nepotism and cronyism, while women who became owners almost always did so through inheritance. For example, the first female owner of a Major League ball club, Helene Hathaway Robison Britton, was born into a prominent baseball family. Her father, Frank deHaas Robison, owned the National League's Cleveland Spiders, and her uncle, M. Stanley Robison, owned the St. Louis Cardinals.[3] "My father and uncles talked baseball ever since I can remember," she once reminisced. "My father early insisted that I should keep score and he didn't have to use any coercion.

. . . I grew up, as I say, in a very atmosphere of baseball. I even played it when a girl."[4] When Uncle Stanley died in March 1911, Helene inherited a 75 percent interest in the Cardinals. (The remaining 25 percent went to her mother.) Despite her acknowledgement that she was in a man's game, Britton got involved, attending every home game and sitting in on the previously all-male National League owners' meetings with the likes of William F. Baker of the Philadelphia Phillies, Barney Dreyfuss of the Pittsburgh Pirates, and Charles H. Ebbets of the Brooklyn Dodgers. She signed manager Roger Bresnahan to a five-year contract at the end of the 1911 season, but after enduring a season of his profanity-laced diatribes, she consulted her attorneys about releasing him. Despite their warning that she was inviting a lawsuit, she made a private settlement with Bresnahan and released him at the end of the 1912 season. Britton then gave an ex-ballplayer named Miller Huggins his first opportunity to manage. (Huggins later piloted the New York Yankees' rise to dominance during the 1920s.) By 1913, Britton was embroiled in a larger matter—the incursion by the Federal League into cities with Major League franchises. The Federal League began signing players from existing clubs and cutting into attendance at the St. Louis Cardinals' Robison Field. The outbreak of World War I in 1914 further affected the gate. Talking over the matter with her husband, Helene reasoned, "You know that even if the team is playing only .500 ball the men will turn out in large numbers if they know the women are there." To draw more women to the ballpark, the Brittons offered live music between innings. It is unknown whether the singer they hired ever crooned "Take Me Out to the Ball Game," to the crowd at Robison Field, but the plan worked, according to one contemporary sportswriter:

> More women have patronized the Cardinals' games this season than ever before, and don't overlook the fact that the presence of so many fair daughters of the Mound City at the games surely influenced a lot of men in turning their attention from golf, autoing, tennis and card games to base ball.[5]

Photographs of Helene Britton reveal a woman with a clear gaze and a firm jaw. Those attributes served her well in 1916, when the National League engineered a truce with the Federal League. Believing that "a woman has no business in baseball," one of the terms of the agreement was that Britton would sell the Cardinals to the upstart league for a fraction of the club's worth "for the good of the game." Britton seemed amenable until the National League owners tried to force her hand at a league meeting. "I have not sold the Cardinals and I'm not going to sell the Cardinals," she announced.[6] In truth, she did want out, but on her own terms. In February 1917, she sold the ball club to a group of St. Louis businessmen. Britton passed away in 1928 and is buried in Cleveland's Lake View Cemetery in the company of the remains of such baseball players as Ed Delahanty, Luke Easter, Charles "Red" Ruffing, and Bill Wambsganss.

Milwaukee's Agnes Malley Havenor became the first female owner of a minor league ball club when she inherited the American Association's Milwaukee Brewers in 1910 upon her husband's death. When the Brewers won their first pennant in 1913, *Baseball* magazine announced the amazing news that the Minneapolis Millers' "little pennant monopoly has been broken up—and by a woman at that" and credited Havenor with being the first female owner of a ball club to win a pennant.[7] She married Al Timme, who then named himself president and ushered her out of the game.

In the 1920s, the Indianapolis Indians, a popular Triple-A farm team of the Cleveland Indians, shared their field, Washington Park, with the Indianapolis ABCs, a charter member of the National Negro League—despite a virulent local strain of racism supported by the Ku Klux Klan. Charles Isham (C. I.) Taylor, who in 1916 bought a half interest in the club, made the ABCs a source of inspiration to local blacks. As the vice president of the newly organized Negro National League, Taylor (who, like his wife, Olivia, was African American) emerged as a respected community leader. In February 1922, however, after traveling in bad weather to the league meeting in Chicago, he was felled by pneumonia.[8] On his deathbed, Taylor promised 75 percent of the club to his wife, Olivia, and 25 percent to his brother Ben. That spring, Olivia took over the business aspects of the club, while Ben oversaw the field operations. The ABCs started the season well but soon slumped, a decline echoed by the growing acrimony between Olivia and Ben.

The ABCs front-office troubles apparently did not affect Olivia's relations with the Negro National League—she had been touted to take her husband's place as league vice president but declined and accepted instead a board position. As Paul Debono writes in *The Indianapolis ABCs*, "No published account hints at any uncomfortableness whatsoever about a female owner," and at least two black civic leaders endorsed her policies.[9] According to Debono, however, Olivia Taylor faced other obstacles. Her star, Oscar Charleston, was reputed to be moving to another club, but Taylor offered him more money and managed to keep him for the 1923 season. Charleston could not save the club from another poor season, and Olivia Taylor went to Chicago for the postseason league meeting seeking help for the beleaguered ABCs. "Some fans might have expected Olivia Taylor to sell or transfer ownership duties, but she would not consider that," Debono notes. "Taylor once again went into smoke filled board rooms to haggle with the baseball magnates."[10]

Raids (led by Ben Taylor who had moved to Washington, D.C., and involved himself with the Potomacs of the newly organized Eastern Colored League) resulted in the losses of all but two of the ABCs regulars for the 1924 season. With the team no longer competitive, the NNL decided to drop it from the league. Olivia Taylor protested without success, and after two and a half seasons, she was out of baseball. She maintained her presence in Indianapolis, however, winning election as president of the local chapter of the NAACP in 1925. Despite her brief ownership, Paul Debono argues for Olivia Taylor's significance to baseball history:

> [She] demonstrated something important about the Negro leagues. Negro league baseball did not place a premium on exclusivity, but on inclusivity. Women, Latinos, Native Americans and whites had dignified roles in Negro league baseball. This ideal eventually constituted the mirror held to the face of major league baseball. . . . She was the first black female owner in the Negro leagues. Her drive was very similar to C. I. Taylor's and Rube Foster's. She faced her formidable challenge with enthusiasm.[11]

Throughout much of the first part of the twentieth century, the Dunn family was synonymous with baseball in Baltimore, Maryland. Jack and Mary Dunn met in high school, where he was a star pitcher and she his devoted fan. After their marriage, Jack pitched in the minor leagues and for the New York Giants before embarking upon a managing career. In 1908, he led Baltimore to a pennant-winning season and eventually acquired the ball club. He was said to never forget a player or a play and was known for signing Babe Ruth to his first contract. Between 1919 and 1925, his popular Orioles, a Triple-A farm team in the Eastern and later the International League, won seven straight pennants, a record that still stands. When Dunn died suddenly in 1928, Mary inherited both the ball club and Oriole Park. Working with the couple's attorney and George Weiss (later the general manager of the New York Yankees), she was a presence in the front office and in 1936 became the president of the organization. Dressed in black and wearing spectacular hats, Dunn was a regular in her box seat behind the home-team dugout, where players frequently paused to visit with her. Bill Ellis, a longtime Baltimore fan, remembered her well: "When it comes to women in professional baseball, the majestic presence of Mrs. Jack Dunn will never be forgotten here and elsewhere. . . . No one that saw her ever forgot her and believe me, a generation of Baltimore fans saw her."[12] Wanting to keep the Orioles in the family, she refused all offers to buy the club over the years. When she died in 1943, ownership passed to her grandson, Jack Dunn III, who stayed on as vice president when the club was taken into the American League. "She was as much a part of that park as the home-plate," Ellis claimed. "[She] was a team symbol to end all team symbols."

In 1929, the *New York Times* announced that "women are in the ascendancy as owners of ball clubs." That made for an intriguing headline, but in truth, women remained a small minority in Organized Baseball's ownership. Increasing numbers of women had entered the business world during the 1920s, however, and were finding work in various front-office jobs, typically starting out as secretaries. Some went on to careers distinguished by longevity and loyalty. William L. Veeck hired Margaret Donahue in 1919 as a stenographer; by 1926, she had become Major League Baseball's first ever female corporate secretary.[13] Two years later, Donahue instituted the sale of season tickets and the promotion of Ladies' Day at Wrigley Field. In 1930, family connections opened the way for Frances Levy to get a job with the Cincinnati Reds as club secretary—her brother-in-law, Sidney Weil, owned the club. Working for the Reds for thirty-five years was more than a just a job for Levy, a passionate fan who seldom missed a home game and counted as one of the thrills of her lifetime Johnny Vander Meer's pair of no-hitters in June 1938. For thirty-one years, Mary Murphy worked for the St. Louis Cardinals, where she attended every contract signing of Stan Musial and served as secretary to such notables as Branch Rickey and August A. Busch Jr. until her retirement in 1962. Murphy's sister Margaret worked in baseball, too, for the St. Louis Browns.

During the Great Depression, women found work with minor league clubs. When Eleanor Rike joined the Chattanooga (Southern Association, Class-A) Lookouts as a temporary secretary in 1931, she could not have known the job would define her life. She stayed for thirty-seven years, married the team trainer and road secretary, Davis (Sandy) Sandlin, and literally reared their three children at the ballpark, putting them to work at clubhouse chores.[14] Such was her reputation for honesty that when baseball commissioner Kenesaw Mountain Landis refereed an issue between a player and the club, he accepted as truth her claim that mice had eaten a letter crucial to the dispute.

EFFA MANLEY AND THE GOLDEN AGE OF THE NEGRO LEAGUES

Few women in baseball have understood how a front office's mosaic of politics, power, money, and sport fits together like Effa Manley did. Effa's mother was white and her father was reputed to be a wealthy white Philadelphian; however, her siblings were mulatto, and she grew up in a black neighborhood and always identified with blacks. After her marriage to Abe Manley, an African American some fourteen years her senior, Effa exerted a profound effect upon Negro League baseball from the Depression through the years following World War II.

Abe Manley had made his money in real estate and by running numbers. As baseball historians Lawrence Hogan and James Overmeyer point out, "numbers bankers could be respectable if they didn't get into more nefarious rackets and plowed some of their profits back into black society."[15] Abe did so. After failing with a Brooklyn team that could not compete with the popular Dodgers, the Manleys moved to Newark, New Jersey. In 1933, with a reorganized league and a new stadium, their ownership of the Newark Eagles quickly made them local celebrities. Abe liked to scout talent, play cards, and drink beer with his players, while Effa preferred the civic and social occasions she attended through her advocacies of the National Association for the Advancement of Colored People, the Urban League, and the Newark Student Camp Fund. Their styles may have differed, but the Manleys shared a passion for black baseball and aimed to see it run properly.

Effa was born to the role. Without children of her own, she treated the Eagles players as family. She found off-season work for them, loaned money to Monte Irvin, and served as godmother to Larry Doby. Although she fought for recognition of her players' talent, she was not shy about standing up for her rights, suing pitcher Satchel Paige over a contract dispute. She wanted her players to represent their race properly and held them to high standards: they were to dress well, pay their bills, and live respectably—a code of behavior akin to Philip K. Wrigley's for the All-American Girls Baseball League. Effa's call for propriety was more direct: "Don't wear your hog-killing clothes on the boulevard."[16] The code worked. As the Eagles star Max Manning stated with pride, "The Eagles were to [black] Newark what the Dodgers were to Brooklyn."[17]

Gifted at public relations—no easy feat, given white journalists' shunning of the Negro Leagues—Manley reached out to the white community, attracting celebrities such as Lowell Thomas and Fiorello La Guardia to Eagles games. Yet she was not afraid to fight what she saw as white dominance of the Negro Leagues. At an owners' meeting in 1940, Effa lost her temper over booking agent Ed Gottlieb's share of the league's profits. (Like other white sports promoters, Gottlieb supplemented his income through his involvement with black baseball.) Manley criticized what most of her colleagues simply accepted: white agents monopolized the best stadiums and controlled the schedules. During their years in baseball, the Manleys fought such practices, but their only significant progress was to ensure that a quarter of the booking fees went into the Negro Leagues' treasury. Even so, the white agents retaliated by cutting the Eagles out of more lucrative dates and venues: for two years, the Eagles did not play in Yankee Stadium.

The onset of World War II offered further opportunities for Effa's activism. When wartime segregation became a hot issue in the black press, Manley did her part by inviting the all-black, twenty-five-hundred-member 372nd Infantry Regiment of nearby Fort Dix to Opening Day in 1941; Newark's mayor declared the occasion official "372nd Day." Two years later, she invited the black members of the Free French forces at Fort Dix to Ruppert Stadium. In a postscript to the post commander, she added that white members were also welcome, if there was room. With black war industry workers flocking to northern cities such as Newark and gasoline rationing ensuring a captive audience at local ball games, the Negro Leagues were thriving. When the Eagles beat the Kansas City Monarchs in the 1946 World Series, they could look back on a season of record-breaking attendance.

That spring, Jackie Robinson crossed Organized Baseball's color line when he stepped onto a Florida diamond for the Montreal Royals, the Dodgers' Triple-A farm team. The irony that Robinson's breakthrough sounded the death knell for the Negro Leagues has been well recorded by sports historians. Black fans abandoned their teams to follow the saga unfolding in Brooklyn. The Eagles began 1947 as one of the best draws in the leagues; they ended the season in decline. Although Effa supported the integration of Major League baseball, she had always feared it would mean the end of the Negro Leagues. She fought unsuccessfully to let the Negro Leagues carry on as part of Organized Baseball's farm system and argued unsuccessfully for compensation when Branch Rickey signed Eagles pitcher Don Newcombe. "She stood up to Jackie Robinson when he denounced the bus rides and seedy hotels of the black leagues by saying they're not our fault," pointed out SABR member John Holway.[18] Later, Manley wondered whether Jackie Robinson was "used" by white-run Organized Baseball.

In the winter of 1948, the Negro National League shut down, and the remaining league absorbed the surviving clubs. Abe and Effa soon retired. After his death, she moved to the West Coast, where she died in 1981. Few landmarks remain to mark the golden age of Abe and Effa Manley and the Newark Eagles. Gone are Ruppert Stadium, the club's storefront office on Montgomery Street, and the Grand Hotel, the team's favorite hangout; only the Manley's residence on Crawford Street remains.

Effa Manley's story, however, endures through the work of baseball historians and authors. Holway argued that Manley belongs in the Hall of Fame. "I once proposed to Joe [Reichler, longtime writer and aide to Bowie Kuhn, who was the self-styled chairman of the first Negro League vets committee] that Manley be added to the almost all-white vets committee," he wrote. "Joe, already hunkered down in a defensive crouch against any more black old-timers, cried out, 'A WOMAN!'" Her story is, however, a part of the Women in Baseball exhibit in the National Baseball Hall of Fame and Museum. Further traces of Manley's influence can be found in the memoir of Amiri Baraka, who wrote of the Eagles games of his childhood as "those bright lost summers." To Baraka, the Eagles represented "legitimate black heroes. And we were intimate with them in a way and they were extensions of all of us, there, in a way that the [white] Yankees and Dodgers and what not could never be."[19] Black entertainers like Stepin Fetchit, however, "were clowns—funny, but obviously used against us for some reason. . . . [But] we was NOT clowns and the Newark Eagles laid that out clear for anyone to see!"[20]

For much of the first half of the twentieth century, New York City laid claim as the center of the baseball universe, with three successful franchises: the Brooklyn Dodgers, New York Giants, and New York Yankees. In 1939, women controlled the ownership of all three, a novelty noted by the press. In truth, these women came to their ownership in the usual way, by inheritance from the men in their lives. Jacob Ruppert bequeathed his stately Yankees to his nieces, Mrs. Joseph Holleran and Mrs. J. Basil Maguire, and to his friend, Helen Winthrop Weyant. Across the Harlem River, Mrs. Charles A. Stoneham and her children, Mary and Horace, had become co-owners of the Giants upon her husband's death. In Brooklyn, Marie McKeever Melvey held substantial stock in the Dodgers. While these women made for intriguing headlines, they tended to be passive owners who left the operations to men. They probably had little choice, as few baseball men would have wanted to take orders from a woman.[21]

Opportunities for front-office work continued to open up in the minors, where smaller markets and payrolls made for more flexible thinking. Women had long made up an appreciable percentage of fans, and it made sense to market to them. For baseball's ersatz centennial in 1939, the American Association inaugurated what it termed "a new department to be devoted exclusively to women . . . to interest more of the fair sex in baseball and to aid those who are already fans to gain a better understanding of the sport."[22] The association named Ohio newspaperwoman Florence Walden as Director of Women's Activities. Her duties included running contests and recruiting speakers for club and organization meetings.

Into the post–World War II years, the occasional woman continued to demonstrate that she could work effectively alongside men in baseball's front offices. The *Detroit Free-Press* described the Detroit Tigers as a team that is "always talking about stability," yet "change general managers about as often as they change pitchers."[23] Only one person in the organization remained "as firm and unshakable as the Rock of Gibraltar": Alice Sloane, the club's executive secretary, who outlasted ten general mangers. During Sloane's eighteen-year career, she saw the club change from a one-man show to a sophisticated operation. Sloan recalled that when she began in 1948, "there was no such thing as a farm department or a publicity office. If Mr. Evans [the general manager] wanted to announce something, he just told me to call the newspapers."

KEEPING THE GIANTS AND DODGERS IN NEW YORK

The center of the baseball universe was shaken in 1957 by the news that the Dodgers and Giants were moving to California. Had two women prevailed, that might have been prevented. Dorothy Johnson Killam had been a Dodgers fan since the 1940s, often entertaining guests at her Ebbets Field box seats with buffets served by uniformed servants. The death of her husband, a Canadian financier, left her one of the world's wealthiest women, and when she learned of the planned move, she tried to buy the Brooklyn Dodgers for six million dollars. When her offer was rejected, Killam joined Branch Rickey's attempt to set up a reorganized Continental League as a third major league, investing in the New York franchise of the proposed league. She died in 1965, an aspiring owner whose wealth could not gain her that distinction. In Manhattan, Joan Whitney Payson, who had owned 9 percent of the New York Giants since 1946, tried to keep that club from moving to San Francisco but failed to persuade the majority owners. (A few years later, Payson invested in the city's new franchise, the Mets.)

Men were still running the front-office show in the minor leagues. Neal Ridley presided over the Knoxville (South Atlantic, Class-AA) Smokies, while his wife, Bonnie, as the club's business manager, was in charge of preparing player contracts, keeping the books on program and fence advertising, and managing the club's correspondence and public relations. During the season, she also sold tickets, answered phones, and visited with fans. "Everybody looks to me for the answers," Neal Ridley told a reporter in 1963, "but Bonnie does most of the work."[24] That decade, however, would see other women, many of whom who had paid their dues as secretaries, begin moving up into executive roles: in 1968, for example, Betty McCoun was named business manager of the Louisville (International League, Class-AAA) Colonels, and Juanita Faye Smith was promoted to general manager of the Greenville (Western Carolina League, Class-A) Red Sox.

By the 1970s, the opportunities opening up for women in other industries were beginning to carry over into Major League Baseball's front offices. Many women started out in public relations or ticket sales. Millie Johnson, of the Chicago White Sox, became MLB's first woman ticket manager, Marea Mannion was named the Chicago Cubs promotions manager, and Fran Moulden was appointed assistant public relations director for the Baltimore Orioles, assigned to concentrate on projects to interest women. These opportunities, however, were on the business side of front-office operations. The perception remained that women did not play professional baseball, and so were unsuitable in jobs related to baseball operations, which still relied upon cronyism. Retired ballplayers who knew how to get along were usually able to find a comfortable front-office role. As one female baseball executive said of this time, "People thought a guy could just stick a cigar in his mouth, open the gates and people would flock to the games."[25] (The guy with the cigar was almost always white. As Charline Gibson, the wife of Bob Gibson, the St. Louis Cardinals' pitcher, observed in 1970, "unlike whites, [blacks] have no opportunity to . . . have a significant front office job. There are some black players who are eminently qualified for such positions, yet there has never been any suggestion that when their playing days were over they would be able to work within and for the game they love."[26]) Gibson did not point out that women of any color were also largely shut out of baseball operations, but others did. A female shareholder in the Baltimore Orioles questioned why the club's nine-member board of directors was all male. Female fans had supported the team for years, so why not a woman on the board? Jerry Hoffberger, the chairman of the board, demurred: by-laws, amendments, and further meetings were necessary before such a thing could happen. Apparently it was all right to have women in supportive positions, but not in baseball decision-making roles.

During these years, Organized Baseball was undergoing tumultuous changes that would affect the old ways of thinking. The modern era of expansion begun in 1961 continued to see changes in the number and alignment of teams. The Major League Players' Association, revived under Marvin Miller in 1966, saw salaries, pension benefits, and working conditions begin to improve.[27] Increased competition by professional football and basketball were challenging MLB's marketing practices. In response, postseason playoffs were begun, the American League adopted the designated hitter rule, and more night games (during prime television time) were scheduled. The ownership of MLB clubs was evolving, too. The old baseball men, like Tom Yawkey, who had bought the Boston Red Sox for $1.5 million in 1933, were dying off. With ball clubs becoming ever more expensive to buy and operate, family money was not enough. Corporations and syndicates increasingly bought into the game. When the New York Yankees were sold in 1973 for $8.8 million to a sixteen-member partnership headed by George Steinbrenner, the *New York Times* ran a critical editorial. One of the new owners responded, denying that she was a "heartless new absentee owner." Charlotte Lazarus Witkind declared, "This limited partner is in it for pure, joyous sentimentality."[28] Witkind recalled twenty-five years of summer evenings with her ear "glued to a static-filled radio." Her partnership was no mere investment, she argued. "Those sacred acres in the South Bronx are my spiritual home ... and the men in pinstripes are among my dearest kin.'Ich bin ein Yankee.'" But Witkind was in the minority, by gender and by sentiment. In 1982, she sold her financial interest in the club.

During the 1970s and 1980s, three women came into ownership of Major League clubs who could have done a great deal to improve front-office opportunities for minorities, including women. Karen Paul, who had worked her way from bookkeeper to executive management with the El Paso Diablos of the Texas League, called on the trio for help. "I think it will take a woman owner to hire a woman to manage the front office," Paul said. "Maybe at this point, those three owners assume the people with expertise are men, but I know there's women who could come in and do the promotions, the sales, anything."[29] None of the three, however, were among the new breed of corporate owner who might be likelier to hire the most competent person available, regardless of race or gender, rather than an old baseball pal.

Tom Yawkey's death in 1976 resulted in a protracted struggle for ownership of the Boston Red Sox. Yawkey's widow, Jean, was a private person averse to publicity. As the battle for control wore on, however, Baseball Commissioner Bowie Kuhn, in one of those for-the-good-of-the-game decisions, decided that the venerable franchise should still carry the Yawkey name. So Jean agreed to participate in the syndicate, which included the club's former trainer Buddy LeRoux and Boston executive Haywood Sullivan, that purchased the Red Sox for $20.5 million in May 1978. Yawkey turned out to be no figurehead. She fired general manager Dick O'Connell, fought off a take-over attempt by Sullivan, and began to involve herself in the club's daily operations. She became the first woman to join the Board of Directors of the National Baseball Hall of Fame and had the satisfaction of seeing the Red Sox win three AL East Division titles. Carl Yastrzemski remembered her as a "firm [but] gracious, down-to-earth leader who had a smile for employees, from players to vendors."[30] Yet opening the way for minorities of any sort was not a priority for Yawkey, according to *Boston Herald* sportswriter Howard Bryant. (In *Shut Out: A Story of Race and Baseball in Boston*, Bryant documents why, under Tom Yawkey, the Red Sox were the last Major League club to sign a black player, having earlier

passed, God help them, on Willie Mays and Jackie Robinson. Bryant argues that racism—rather than the sale of Babe Ruth to the New York
Yankees in 1919—was the true root of the curse on Boston's lengthy quest
of a World Series championship.) As for Jean Yawkey, Bryant writes:

> As an owner, she followed very much in the footsteps of her husband by doing
> little to change the Sox culture or even move into the new era of free agency. The
> most damning sin under her watch was the club's refusal to sign black free agents.
> They did not sign one until after she died. This, of course, does not make her
> the sole mastermind behind a racist organization, but, like her husband, some-
> thing of a disinterested party to the greater, defining forces around her.[31]

Joan Kroc came to ownership of the San Diego Padres when her husband,
Ray, died in 1984. Prior to that, she had stumbled into some of the club's
management issues. In 1981, the Padres had traded future Hall of Famer
shortstop Ozzie Smith after a salary dispute during which Joan Kroc was
quoted as saying that "Ozzie could be her gardener if he needed some extra cash."[32] Initially, she wanted to sell the team but quickly changed her
mind. "I don't want to sound melodramatic," she explained to the *Sporting News,* "but the people who work in the Padres' office were so visibly
emotional that it touched me. . . . For the first time I realized the emotional investment and the love that people have for the Padres in this city.
. . . There is no way in this world that I would ever sell San Diego out."[33]

Like Jean Yawkey, Joan Kroc did not push for more women or minorities in the front office, but her acts of charity were notable. She established the Padres Employee Assistance Program to help players and staff
with alcohol and chemical dependency. In 1989, she attempted to donate
the team, along with a $100 million endowment, to the city of San Di-
ego. Kroc's idea might have transformed Organized Baseball. With the
city running the Padres, local fans would have a direct voice in the running of a Major League ball club. Given that city, county, and state gov-
ernments were now expected to fund the costs of the new stadiums so
coveted by MLB owners, this was reasonable and democratic. The plan
was voted down, however, by MLB's owners committee, who were quoted
as saying they "were more comfortable with keeping the teams in the
hands of smaller groups." As writer Tom Gallagher pointed out, "This was
probably less a statement of class solidarity than a reaction to the fact that
municipal ownership would bring public access to the game's books,

possibly cramping the style of some poor-mouthing owners."[34] In 1990, Joan Kroc sold out to an entity more agreeable to the owners committee, a group of Southern California businessmen.

> *Marge Schott is not a bigot—she just hates everyone.*
> —Pete Rose

Marge Unnewehr Schott was ideally situated to open doors for women in baseball. Instead, she threw away the chance of the century to demonstrate that a female owner could both effectively run a Major League franchise and erase some of the long-standing taint of racial discrimination that still attached to the game's front offices. Schott liked to say she became a businesswoman by necessity when her husband, Charles, died. In truth, the sixth-generation Cincinnati native had grown up with an interest in her father's dealings, eventually dropping out of college to work for him. By the time her hard-drinking husband made her a widow in 1968, she had the background and the moxie to take charge of an empire that included an auto agency; cement, trucking, and brick companies; and real estate. She added holdings of her own, including a share in the high-flying Cincinnati Reds (who won more games between 1970 and 1981 than any other club). When the club went up for sale in 1984, Schott hesitantly mentioned an interest in buying the majority stake. She then negotiated a $10 million loan from a local bank. (She made a great buy—two years later, the New York Mets sold for $100 million.) Her stated plan was to stick with womanly tradition and stay in the background. "She assured me she would have no active role in the management of the Reds," claimed George Strike, one of the Reds minority investors, in Rick Bass's biography, *Marge Schott: Unleashed.*[35]

Schott's attitude changed once she was installed as president and chief executive officer of professional baseball's oldest franchise. She became an active, not a passive, owner. During her tenure, Schott kept ticket prices among the lowest in the Major Leagues and promoted season ticket sales to new team highs. (The Reds drew more than fourteen million fans to Riverfront Stadium during her first seven years.) After the Reds' 1990 World Series championship, she led the victory parade through downtown and joined the players at the White House. She made goodwill visits to Japan and presented the Pope with a Reds jacket during a visit to the Vatican. *Savvy* magazine recognized her as the head of one of the forty largest woman-owned businesses in the country.

Schott was also mercurial. She could be generous, donating millions of dollars to charitable causes; she could also be tight-fisted, "selling day-old doughnuts to fans standing in line to buy Opening Day tickets," according to the *Cincinnati Enquirer's* Paul Daugherty.[36] The *Sporting News* criticized her "twisted logic" in gutting the fine Reds scouting staff to save money and in her dealings with field manager Lou Piniella and general manager Bob Quinn, both respected baseball men, and observed, "Schott has always been brutal on her general managers."[37] She was hard on other employees, too. In 1992, the former Reds controller Tim Sabo filed a lawsuit against her. But it was Schott's own words in a December 6, 1991, deposition to MLB that undermined her position as owner of the Reds. Her remarks, later leaked to the press, revealed a strain of bigotry that made news beyond the sports pages:

Q: Do you have any prejudice against Jews?
A: No. They are not smarter than us, just sharper.
Q: Do you have a swastika armband that you keep as a memorabilia of anything?
A: At my home. In a drawer. . . . I don't think [a Jew] would be offended by seeing the armband.[38]

Organized Baseball, despite its checkered history toward minorities, had become sensitized about such statements. (Schott was not the first to get into trouble. During a television interview in 1987, Al Campanis, a longtime Dodgers executive, had commented that African Americans innately lacked management skills. The controversy prompted people in baseball and the press to speak out on the inequities in management.) When MLB's executive council faced the issue of Schott's comments at its December 1992 meeting, she explained that her use of words like "kike" and "nigger" around the front office and her possession of a swastika armband were not meant to offend. "I want to make it clear to everyone and especially to your young people that prejudice and bigotry are hurtful, hateful, unacceptable and demeaning to all people."[39] It was too late for damage control, however, and Schott was suspended for a year and banned from her owner's box.

Schott's comments did not shock everyone. A native Ohioan said that while she did not like Schott's sentiments, she understood them. "Cincinnatians don't travel well. They don't do well out of that little pocket of culture," she said. "For minorities, there's an abiding sense of fair play but no love lost. One on one, Cincinnatians are absolutely isolationist within their own pockets of ethnicity."[40] As for Organized Baseball's true attitudes toward minorities, the Afracan American outfielder Reggie Jackson estimated that 75 to 80 percent of baseball owners felt as Schott did. Some saw her as simply foolish. "There is no IQ test before they let you be rich and powerful," reflected Dave Kindred of the *Sporting News*. "Marge Schott's ignorance is breath-taking." She had also become an embarrassment, doting on her dogs and giving them the run of the playing field. After umpire John McSherry's fatal heart attack at home plate in 1996, Schott offended everyone by trying to continue the game. Some observers surmised that her fondness for vodka undermined her judgment. Financially, Schott came out well, selling most of her shares in the Reds in 1999 for $67 million. She also left baseball as the only female owner wearing a World Series ring.

Ironically, the comments and attitudes that led to Schott's exit from baseball may have been her finest contribution. By stating publicly what others only thought or spoke of privately, Marge Schott ensured that the issue of the game's racial inequities was debated, discussed, and addressed. In response, Major League Baseball retained Dr. Harry Edwards to develop a pool of black and Hispanic applicants for management jobs. Baseball Commissioner Peter Ueberroth then hired Alexander and Associates, a Washington, D.C., consulting firm to catalog jobs by race and gender on a team-by-team basis. "Baseball has made some progress with regard to the hiring of women and minorities, but we're still disappointed with the pace and consistency of the progress," said Clifford Alexander, the firm's president. Others took a jaundiced view of the prospects for change.[41] "Their past record doesn't speak well for them," cautioned Robin Monsky, who was banned from the Atlanta Braves clubhouse and team bus during her time with the club as director of public relations. "The resistance to a woman lessens the farther she is away from the game, but the closer her job gets to the actual baseball side of things, the more obstacles she faces."[42]

A BLACK OWNER IN SAVANNAH

Shortly after Marge Schott acquired the Reds, another history-making purchase took place in Savannah, Georgia. During the winter of 1985, a twenty-four-year-old African American named Tracy Lewis was working at a New Orleans radio station owned by her father's firm, Inter-

Urban Industries, when he telephoned with the news. Thomas Lewis had just purchased the Savannah Cardinals of the South Atlantic (Class-AA) League. He wanted his daughter to act as president, a role he foresaw as "a stepping-stone for other blacks."[43] Tracy Lewis's doubts arose early, at a meeting of baseball executives. "I was the only black there, and Marge Schott was the only other woman," she told a reporter. "It was clear the people were recruiting from their own peer group, boys who hung around the locker room for 30 years. When I got up to speak, one gentleman said, 'Well, Tracy, I know you're new and . . .' I cut him off right there."

The Lewises were new. Inter-Urban was the first black owner of an Organized Baseball team since the demise of the Negro National League in 1954, and Tracy Lewis was new to baseball. Although she had grown up in Chicago just a few blocks from Comiskey Park, she declared that the piano and shopping, not baseball, had been her childhood interests. Now she was expected to oversee the Cardinals in addition to her responsibilities at Inter-Urban, commuting between New Orleans, St. Louis, and Savannah. As her days grew more frenetic, Lewis discovered a haven in the Cardinals' Grayson Stadium. "It's deserted and it's so peaceful," she said. "I just sit in the stands and look at it. It's a beautiful ball park."[44]

Grayson Stadium had seen a lot of history since opening in 1926. On April 14, 1953, four black players—among them Hank Aaron—had broken the South Atlantic League's color line. Segregation in the stands, however, remained the rule into the 1960s. In protest, the NAACP organized a picket outside the stadium early in 1962. Racial tensions increased to the extent that in mid-August, the Savannah club decided to move to Lynchburg, Virginia, for its final eight games, a move formalized at the league's winter meeting that year. Baseball returned to Savannah in 1968, where in 1983, Tommie Aaron, Hank's younger brother, made history as the first black manager in Double-A baseball, indeed, the first black manager of any minor league club in the Deep South.[45] Lewis, with her big-city, northern background, must have been surprised at what she encountered at Grayson Stadium in 1986. After a white security guard allegedly told a white girl holding hands in the stands with a black boy that if he were her parent, he would "beat the daylights out of her," Lewis fired the guard.[46] She noticed that some of the black old-timers still congregated in the former colored section behind third base and that the building that once housed the colored-only bathroom remained in the left-field picnic area. "Segregation," she realized, "wasn't that long ago."

Marcus Holland, then a sportswriter for the *Savannah Morning News* and who served as the Cardinals official scorer during Lewis's tenure, could have told her a lot about current local mores. "The fans really didn't like the idea that a black family owned the ball club," he said. "That's changed now—we have a black mayor—but then it was a problem."[47] There were other problems, too. Lewis was young and inexperienced. "I'm not sure Tracy was that interested in baseball—certainly, she was gone a lot and left others in charge." According to Holland, the Lewises brought in more family members and other blacks who also lacked backgrounds in baseball. To make things worse, Savannah had always been a marginal baseball market, and earlier franchises had periodically foundered. In 1986, with a poor team on the field and poor oversight in the front office, attendance declined again. "I just showed up and kept score," Holland said. "They never failed to pay me. But in the end, they didn't pay all their bills." On November 4, 1987, the St. Louis Cardinals acquired the ball club from the Lewises.

Tracy Lewis was one of many children whose parents installed them in a position their experience did not warrant. As a longtime baseball executive who requested anonymity said, "Some of the Major League club owners—and I can't blame them for this—involve their kids. But they haven't paid their dues and don't yet have the background. They're better off starting in the minors, where you have to do everything for yourself and you learn greater respect for everyone involved: the groundskeepers, scouts, and vendors." (Even offspring weaned on baseball can run amok—Mike Veeck's Disco Demolition Night at Comiskey Field in 1979 culminated in a game-ending riot, damaging the standing in Organized Baseball of both himself and his father, Bill.) Given Tracy Lewis's lack of baseball background, her other responsibilities with Inter-Urban, a poor team on the field and in the front office, and Savannah's racial attitudes at the time, it is not surprising that she failed in her father's mission to serve as a stepping stone for other blacks.

By the 1980s, cronyism became another baseball tradition affected by changing times. For years, former players and others associated with the game, many of whom were short on formal education but had a wealth of baseball experience, had moved into the front office when their playing days were over. If you did your job well and got along with people, you could bounce from position to position, from club to club, for the rest of your life. (The lucky ones stay with one club: Tommy Lasorda parlayed his two years as a pitcher with the Brooklyn Dodgers into a life's career, moving to Los Angeles with the team as coach, and longtime manager, and ultimately as the club's Senior Vice President, Enthusiasm.) But baseball's share of the sports market was shrinking while corporate ownership, which had a stronger tendency to see baseball in entertainment and financial terms, was rising. To survive in this changing climate, franchises at all levels needed fresh ideas, with the result that the old-timers often found themselves working alongside young college graduates, some of them females, with degrees in sports management or business.

Although women filled only about a dozen of the approximately 250 jobs of executive rank in MLB by 1987, they were being hired in greater numbers and were ambitious about moving up. It still helped to be born into a baseball family. Katy Feeney, for example, the daughter of former the National League president Chub Feeney, has worked as Director of Media and Public Affairs and as Vice President of Club Relations and Scheduling at MLB headquarters in Manhattan. But she still had to get results. In this tougher environment, women with strong baseball credentials foresaw opportunity. Patty Palmer Cox Hampton had worked her way up the old fashioned way—a club, a league, at a time. Hampton had been tutored in the game by her grandmother, a fan of the Kansas City Blues, and after majoring in psychology and social work (good fields of study, come to think of it, for a career in baseball), she raised four children before founding the Cox Advertising Agency in 1970. The Oklahoma City (American Association, Class-AAA) 89ers were one of her accounts. When the team's owner, Harry Valentine, sought a new general manager in 1977, he looked to Hampton, his "dynamic and innovative account executive."[48] For the 1978 season, Hampton launched an energetic sales campaign, increasing attendance by 53 percent and earning the Rawlings award for National Association Woman Executive of the year. "I came into baseball with an expertise in marketing at a time when most front-office jobs were staffed by field people or frustrated male athletes," she later reflected. "Baseball has changed since then; it's opened up a new industry not just to women, but to astute business people."[49] When Dallas Green became the president of the Chicago Cubs in 1985, he asced Hampton and her husband to serve as vice presidents during the organization's restructuring. Although she said Green gave her free rein, other male executives were not as receptive. Hampton noticed that despite her credentials and her executive status, when it came down to meeting with bankers, some Cubs executives preferred to invite other men rather than her. By the time Hampton retired in 1989, her career included the "first woman ever" titles of minor league general manager and active female vice president of a Major League club. Hampton, however, warned the women coming into the front office after her that the life of a baseball executive was especially hard for women with families. "This just isn't a 9–5 job. Your life has to revolve around it." The women whose stories follow understand that to succeed in any business is no nine-to-five job. Five-tool executives, bringing their education, a driving work ethic, an ability to get along with male colleagues, creative thinking, and the resilience that promotes success in any field, are the face of the future in Organized Baseball's front offices.

Buffalo, New York, is home of one of the most successful minor league franchises in history. The Bisons (International League, Class-AAA) routinely draw more than a million fans—more than some Major League teams—and Pilot Field, the first of the neonostalgic ballparks, has sparked a downtown renaissance. On a drizzly June afternoon, Mindy Rich, the Bisons co-owner, ran a hand through her short brown hair. Whatever makeup she might have put on that morning was gone. "My office is a mess," Rich observed without guilt, before explaining that baseball is in her blood, a legacy of her Cincinnati childhood. "Yeah, it's definitely an old story: I grew up playing sports in a neighborhood of all boys, so I was a typical tomboy. But it wasn't my aspiration to work in baseball. I never thought *I want to work in baseball as a career.*"[50] Since marrying Robert E. Rich Jr., however, that is what she has done: When they returned from their honeymoon, he asked her to draw up the proposal that won him the rights to the Buffalo franchise.

Rich may have come to her involvement with the Bisons the old-fashioned way, through marriage, but her dedication to the club's success has earned her the respect of the people who work for her. "Mindy Rich is unbelievable," said a young man in the Bisons front office. "She's always asking, 'Who had the hits? How did Wichita do?'" With women making up 45 percent of the Bisons fan base, Rich sought to cater to that market, from the food served to safety in the parking lot. She found nothing unusual in her work with the Bisons. "I'm just a woman in baseball, though I don't even think of myself as that," she said. "It's like having brown eyes—I am what I am." Despite her gratitude toward those who made women's rights their cause, she believes she would not be able to do what she does, nor even be as comfortable, if she had to worry about focusing on being a woman. And she considers her best contribution to the women's cause to be doing what she does best. Her involvement is so intense that she is unaware of her uniqueness. Rich recalled attending a heated meeting of 250 minor league owners and general managers, when her husband suddenly tapped her on the shoulder and said, "Do you realize you're the only woman in this room?" She had not noticed. Although both the club attorney and its assistant general manager are women, Mindy Rich maintained that the club does not go out of its way to hire women into the front office. "It's not a cause with us," she said. "We just hire the best people for the position, and there are a lot of good professional women who have just happened to end up working for the Bisons."

A HISPANIC WOMAN BUYS INTO DENVER'S NEW FRANCHISE

Amid the cheering crowd, the attractive dark-haired woman in purple T-shirt and shorts, moccasins, and straw hat looked much like many other fans. Linda Alvarado is, indeed, a longtime baseball fan, but she also owns a substantial interest in the Colorado Rockies. In 1991, Alvarado was invited to a breakfast meeting with the governor of Colorado. She brought along her checkbook because she had never attended a "free" breakfast for a politician, but the subject of the morning turned out to be baseball, not politics. Major League Baseball was entertaining bids from various cities for two new National League expansion teams. Bill White, an African American on the selection committee, had made it clear that successful bidders would have ethnic diversity among their investors. "We wanted to 'wow' Major League Baseball with a powerful group," explained Denver attorney Paul Q. Jacobs.[51] Linda Alvarado was ideal. As the founder and owner of Alvarado Construction Inc., one of the fastest growing commercial general contracting firms in the country, she had both the money and the reputation of getting along well in a man's field; her community involvement and charitable giving were well known; and as a Latina, she was a minority twice over.

To participate in the proposed ownership group, she eventually wrote a check that had a lot more zeros in it than she was accustomed to. The pro forma concerned her, too: win or lose, the consortium's money would belong to the National League. "Many gamblers would not have bet on us winning the franchise," Alvarado conceded, "but as an entrepreneur, I often take risks."[52] She wrote the check for several reasons: a Major League franchise in baseball-loving Denver, with an outlying market throughout the West, seemed like a good investment over time and could prove positive for business development and marketing. The invitation to become a big-league owner was a once-in-a-lifetime opportunity. It offered her a niche in baseball history on two counts: first, she would be MLB's first Hispanic owner, and second, earlier female owners—even Marge Schott and Joan Payson, who were invited into ownership—had done so primarily with inherited money. Alvarado was a self-made woman who had earned the capital she was being asked to invest.

Sentiment was involved, too. Alvarado, the only girl amid five brothers, had grown up following baseball with her family in Albuquerque, New Mexico. At age five, she was dusting off home plate between innings at the local recreational league in which her father played. As the children tended to their chores, they listened to baseball on the radio. "We took pride in hearing names and following the careers of Latino players like Alou, Clemente, and Marichal. As a Hispanic, that meant something to me—that this was a sport in which Hispanics excelled." Alvarado was also aware that although more than twenty-five percent of the current Major League ballplayers were of Hispanic descent, those numbers did not carry over into baseball ownership or MLB's front offices.[53] As a Hispanic owner, she might be able to influence change.

Her financial stake as one of seven owners of the Colorado Rockies changed her life. When the Rockies took the field at Mile High Stadium on Opening Day in 1993, Alvarado felt a rush of adrenalin at the capacity crowd. She saw her partners smiling in the sunlight with tears running down their faces as they acknowledged the ovation. Driving to work, she now found herself listening to the baseball talk radio shows, rather than the business news. Because of her experience as a commercial general contractor, Alvarado was involved in the feasibility study and cost analysis for Coors Field, which was built in a formerly rundown warehouse district near downtown. With preparations underway to open the new ballpark and fan interest high throughout Colorado and even neighboring states, the Rockies ownership team knew they could reap a cash bonanza on the inaugural Opening Day through the sales of advance and season tickets. Alvarado, fearing this would cut out many fans with time or financial constraints, argued that five thousand tickets be held back for sale the day of the game. "Ultimately they agreed . . . and as owners we decided to cap annual season ticket sales and reserve five thousand tickets . . . for every home game. As it turned out, the Colorado Rockies sold out every home game anyway. It was a home run for everyone." Alvarado was getting acquainted with others in Organized Baseball. One day, Manny Mota telephoned to invite her to lunch to talk about baseball and his involvement with inner-city youth. She has used her position as owner to advocate diversity and academic excellence among the youth of Denver. "Through baseball, I encourage kids to excel not just in sports but also in academics and in pursuing a career." Alvarado's ability to communicate in Spanish helped her to reach out to the club's players, too, who often feel uncomfortable in the United States:

> For example, there is no R.S.V.P. in our culture. When I invited the Galarragas for dinner, one just knew that you may also get his mother, in-laws, cousins, and second cousins as well. As Hispanics, this is something we all do and value. The dinner menus can be complex, because the Venezuelans don't eat what the Dominicans do. The socialization develops a network and a level of comfort for the players, as I try to provide a common link through our heritage. Although this is not required of an owner, I can assist in ways that others cannot.

Alvarado respects, however, the line between management and players. "A good owner lets baseball personnel manage baseball, but as with any enterprise, employees (or in this case, players) want to be recognized as individuals. That recognition quality is not a gender trait, it's just good business." Over the years, she has found the level of media interest in her surprising. "As the first Hispanic owner (male or female) of a Major League baseball club, I have even been on Mexico's Telemundo. I do numerous public speaking events, and frequently I am asked to sign autographs now, none of which I realized would happen when I entered baseball." Some would call Linda Alvarado lucky at the business of baseball. "Women have niche opportunities, but it is not luck. In business, you work hard to position yourself. Then, when the opportunity comes, you must take action not to miss it." Alvarado's readiness to take part in the leadership of the Colorado Rockies has inspired other women. After the Rockies' inaugural game in 1993, Alvarado received a letter from a Hispanic woman, who spoke of the pride she felt in seeing Alvarado stand with the other owners on the field. Alvarado finds satisfaction in knowing that she has inspired other women to reach new heights. "If my experience encourages women to say to themselves, 'If she can do it, so can I,' then we all can win."

By the 1990s, the number of women in MLB's front-office senior executive positions was increasing—from Sharon Pannozzo, Director of Media Relations for the Chicago Cubs, to Christine Hurley, the chief financial officer for the Los Angeles Dodgers, to Pam Gardner, President of Business Operations for the Houston Astros. In January 1990, the Boston Red Sox made history when they hired MLB's first female African American assistant general manager. Elaine Weddington Steward grew up in a household that did not recognize limitations of gender or race. She received the Jackie Robinson Foundation Sports Management scholarship and graduated with honors from St. John's University in 1984 with a BS in athletic administration. By then, she had worked for several summers during college in the New York Mets public relations department. "Working at the ballpark gave me a wonderful opportunity to meet and get to know the executives of that Ballclub," she recollected.[54] The experience proved to inform her choice of career.

Steward, an attorney, was later named the Red Sox vice president and club counsel. Her hours on the job fluctuate, running longer when the team is at home. As the mother of three, however, she said she tries "not to get home too late." She keeps at it because, as she put it, "Working in baseball allows you to experience a refreshing 'new beginning' each year. I can't help but be excited at the possibility of a new season, and the ever present hope of the Red Sox participating in post season play." Her proudest achievement is being named the first female assistant general manager in MLB. "There are many qualified females working in the sport, and it felt great to have that door opened to females."

In 1990, Kim Ng was enjoying her senior year at the University of Chicago playing varsity softball—she won MVP—and researching her senior thesis on Title IX. When she graduated with a BA in public policy, however, she could not find a job in the financial industry. "Thank goodness," she later said. "A coach told me about an internship with the Chicago White Sox. It paid $750 a month. I was thrilled."[55]

Dan Evans, then the White Sox assistant general manger, assigned Ng to gather information for the upcoming players' arbitration. When she presented him with an eight-inch stack of research, Evans knew he had someone special. "It was apparent to me that she was more than an intern," he said. "She was trying to find out not the why, but the *why* why."[56] She was promoted in 1991 to Special Projects Analyst and in 1995 to Assistant Director of Baseball Operations. She was involved in all facets of daily operations, including contract negotiations, trades and free agent signings, and the tracking of Major League player movement. Her years with the White Sox probably gained her the equivalent of a graduate degree in the running of a Major League ball club. She also gained a mentor in Dan Evans.

In January 1997, Ng moved to the offices of the American League, where she worked as Director of Waivers and Player Records. She approved all player transactions and contracts and worked closely with the league's general managers to help them understand and interpret and apply both the Major League rules and the Basic Agreement. Her exposure to the highest levels of MLB in New York gave her valuable background, exposure, and contacts. She said of her time there that she learned this: "if people like you and you have a good reputation then things may happen for you but I just try not to get too ahead of myself."[57]

In the spring of 1998, the New York Yankees hired Ng at the age of twenty-nine as the youngest ever assistant general manager in MLB. She was the only woman under consideration. By then, Dan Evans was cheerleading: "This is absolutely a brilliant hire by Brian," Evans told the press. "She has a chance to be one of the true leaders in the game. She has unlimited potential."[58] Ng's own response was more measured. "As a woman you are sort of a novelty and people will look at you a little bit differently. You just have to work a little bit harder to have people understand that you can do the job," she told a reporter.[59] On the occasion of her promotion to vice president, George Steinbrenner boasted, "A lot of teams appoint ladies because they think it's the thing to do. . . . [Ng] deserves every bit of it."[60]

She was involved in the trade of David Wells for Roger Clemens, and the acquisition of David Justice. Ng spent four seasons with the Yankees, during which they won four pennants and three World Series championships. But the nature of an operation owned by Steinbrenner can be complex. In the *Sporting News,* Michael Krisley details Steinbrenner's response to losing arbitration cases to Derek Jeter and Mariano Rivera in 1999. "[H]e did what any iron-willed, sore-loser competitor would do. He said, 'Wait 'til next year,' and he found some new hired guns to make the club's cases for Y2K."[61] Krisley spoke with several players' agents, each of whom had a different take on who was really running the club's contract negotiations. Krisley concludes, "[E]veryone involved in a deal with the Yankees always knows the best-laid plans of agents and executives can go astray in a New York minute if Big George doesn't care for the deal."

When Ng's contract with the Yankees expired after the 2001 World Series, it was not renewed. She did not publicly discuss why—perhaps four years with the Bronx Bombers were just enough. She did say, "After the season for two or three weeks I just got lost, got out of town and tried to clear my head for a little bit."[62] Ng was considering a job outside baseball when Dan Evans, then the general manager of the Los Angeles Dodgers, reached her just after Thanksgiving. He wasted no time in making her an offer.

Ng dove into seventy- and eighty-hour work weeks, initially concentrating on negotiations with players, before undertaking a reorganization of the Dodgers salary structure. She also managed the front office's daily operations, including budget and payroll, and tracked the player development system because Evans wanted her to come up with creative ways to add flexibility to the roster. She negotiated the contract with Paul Lo Duca and made the $11.2 million deal for negotiating rights with pitcher Kazuhisa Ishii.

Ng has said that she loves coming to work at the ballpark. She appreciates the game's bottom-line end to each day during the season, the comfort of its statistics. You win or lose, and you adjust, always aiming for improvements. "I'm interested in sports in general—what motivates people, how to get someone to perform at their absolute peak of consistency," she said. "Baseball is about respect. That's the unwritten code. You hit a home run and you don't gaze out at the fans [rather, most players don't]. You're supposed to trot down the line. You don't see anything like touchdown dances. It's the opposite of showing up the other guy. It's about humility."[63]

That is one reason she ducks the prime question that trails her. Will she be MLB's first female general manager? To understand her aspirations, one can look to her response to another question: When asked whom in sports she most admired, Ng's answer was Martina Navratilova, "because she changed the game of tennis and she did what she did for so long. She changed the way women athletes are perceived. . . . She made it OK for women to be the best they can be physically."[64] Kim Ng could similarly change the way women in MLB's front offices are perceived. According to a number of her colleagues, Ng is on the fast track. As Roland Hemond, a veteran front-office executive, claimed, "Kim Ng could be the Major Leagues' first female general manager—she's that good."[65] Jean Afterman, a lawyer who holds Ng's former job with the Yankees, has said she too is betting on Ng.

Afterman has claimed that the bar remains higher for front-office women while the men "skate by because they memorize the stats." Men are still presumed to know the game in a way that women do not. Yet women like Linda Alvarado and Kim Ng grew up with baseball and have the same passion for their roles in the game as their male colleagues. And women like Cristine Hurley and Elaine Weddington Steward speak the language of finance and business as well as any man. These women send the message that MLB is best served in today's competitive sports environment when it does not limit its consideration of potential top-level executives and owners to men only.

Some clubs have begun to understand this. Forbes.com in its 2003 survey of the issue, said, "Some owners who hire [women] are reaping the benefit of higher franchise values." The Cleveland Indians, for example, with more than 40 percent of its front-office personnel female, lead the Major Leagues in gender equity, according to Jayne Churchmack, the club's vice president of licensing and merchandising. Under Churchmack's leadership, the club's merchandising sales have been among the top five of the Major League teams since the mid-1990s. *Forbes* also lauded the Los Angeles Dodgers front office, with its "deep bench" of talented women: 21 percent of its executives, 44 percent of its managers, 56 percent of its supervisors, and 21 percent of its directors. During her first five years with the Dodgers, Cristine Hurley reduced non-baseball expenditures by 10 percent and oversaw the sale of the teae's Vero Beach, Florida, spring-training compound, which brought in $17.5 million. Meanwhile, Kris Rone, the executive vice president of business operations, doubled the marketing revenue from sponsors in her first four years with the club and increased ticket revenues by $18 million. *Forbes* reported that the Dodgers, which were then for sale, had increased 44 percent in value since Rupert Murdoch's purchase of the franchise from the O'Malley family in 1998. "If he sells the team," concluded *Forbes*, "he will owe this tidy profit in part to the bright female executives who helped boost the franchise's revenue from $94 million to $150 million."[66] When

Murdoch sold the club in January 2004 to Frank and Jamie McCourt, however, some of those "bright female executives" left. Despite the firing of her mentor, general manager Dan Evans, Kim Ng stayed on. She was even mentioned as his possible replacement, but the job went to Paul De Podesta, lately of Billy Beane's brain trust in Oakland. Ng then interviewed for an assistant GM position with the New York Mets but withdrew her name, saying, "When I came here, I wanted to be part of an effort that was going to bring a winning club back to Los Angeles . . . I still want to be here."[67] Stay tuned.

8 In the Press Box
Women in the Media

ONE SPRING EVENING DURING MY SENIOR YEAR in high school, I joined my parents at the dinner table and announced that I had decided to become a sportswriter. Enamored of the scent of freshly sharpened pencils, the possibilities in a fresh sheet of paper, and the beauty of the game played by young men in pinstripes up in the Bronx, I saw sports writing as the ideal career choice. My father was appalled and declared that no daughter of his was going into a locker room. Utterly innocent of locker room culture, I turned to my mother, who was still laughing. She said, "Are you crazy?"

It was 1960, and most people would have agreed. Several years earlier, a reporter named Gloria Swegman, who wanted to become a sportscaster, surveyed a few members of the New York chapter of the Baseball Writers Association of America (BWAA). They did not care for the idea. Vin Scully, for example, just starting his career with the Brooklyn Dodgers, found it "awkward. . . . Mighty awkward. . . . I mean you couldn't get in on the locker room confabs." Besides, Scully said, "Don't know if there is a woman's viewpoint to baseball. It's not as if you could describe the uniforms—silk and taffeta."[1]

Vin Scully's comment is significant in two ways. First, he identified the central issue raised whenever women set out to cover baseball. Access to the locker room, full of mostly naked men, has always made things "mighty awkward," both for the players, who consider the place their sanctuary, and for female sportswriters, who believe they belong there in order to do their job even as their gut instinct warns that they are, and always will be, outsiders. (Less understandable is why access to the press box and broadcasting booth, where men are decently clothed, was also off limits to women for so long.) Scully also raised a second intriguing point: Does a feminine viewpoint to baseball exist? If it does, what is it, and what does it signify?

These questions are best answered by the pioneering women who broke into the front lines of sportswriting: the beat writers who follow a ball club through the season, going on road trips, sitting day and night in the press box, and frequenting the locker room. Also helpful is a consideration of the women who interpret the game in other genres. "Sport offers ancient raptures," Thomas McGuane writes, "and its best writers are like guides in old cathedrals."[2] McGuane's words apply especially well to baseball, whose rich literary canon encompasses the historical, political, sociological, and satirical. Throughout much of baseball's history, however, the feminine point of view was rarely heard in this canon. That changed dramatically during the 1970s. Ever since, increasing numbers of women have been writing of their baseball raptures, guiding the fan to a deeper understanding of the game through their essays, fiction, memoirs, poems, and scholarly writing, as well as through the visual arts of film and photography.

Such latitude was not easily won. The birth of sportswriting about 150 years ago was symbiotic with baseball's rise in popularity. Coverage in the nation's daily newspapers quickly grew from announcements and sociable reports of early amateur games to analyses of professional games, news of popular players, and columns lamenting the current state of Organized Baseball. The fans' daily thirst for this information sold newspapers, while the game thrived on publicity. By 1900, books, guides, and periodicals devoted to baseball were proliferating. All of these endeavors, however, were men's work. In a time when women were considered intrusive even as spectators, it was laughable to think that they had the insight and knowledge to write about baseball, and scandalous were they found lingering with ballplayers and sportswriters in hotel lobbies, saloons, and other unseemly hangouts. It is no surprise, then, that the press boxes of the nineteenth century were as closed to women as the pulpit of an ancient cathedral.

One of the earliest known women to challenge the profession of sports-writing was Ella Black.[3] During the troubled season of 1890, with fans abuzz over the upstart Players' League challenge to the National League and the American Association, Black published regular dispatches from Pittsburgh in the *Sporting Life*. Home of both the former league's established club, the Alleghenies, and the upstart Burghers, Pittsburgh was a workingman's town, sympathetic to labor.[4] Black favored the Players' League too, although the preference did not prejudice her sharp critiques of its strategies and decisions.

Writing in the form of a letter to the editor, Black gave readers a holistic view of Pittsburgh baseball. A typical column might offer an analysis of which clubs and league were prevailing, a discussion of various players' talent and performance, and a polemic on the hierarchy of local sportswriters. Black did not stop there: she also reported on the marital problems of the Players' League stalwart, John Montgomery Ward; critiqued the latest baseball fads among female fans; and wrote unblushingly about which players were most adored by women and when that adoration became objectionable. Her column was conversational and knowledgeable. "She had a great subversive writing style," said baseball historian Marc Fink. "Under the guise of playing the poor, dumb, subservient female, she delivered some very pithy and opinionated columns."[5] Tracking both Pittsburgh clubs' attendance throughout the season, she took issue when Alleghenies president, J. Palmer O'Neill, derided the Players' League opening day crowd as "composed of servant girls with aprons over their heads, women with babies in their arms and men wearing blouses." After challenging O'Neill for his lack of gallantry, she concludes, "When he cannot find any greater fault with the new club than the costumes of its visitors, he should stop for a minute to think of some of the transactions he figured in during the past winter."[6]

As she debated which league would prevail, Ella Black's byline itself became newsworthy to the readers of the *Sporting Life* that season. The headlines attending her early columns broadcast the fact that the author was a woman. March 5: "The Base Ball Situation Considered and Commented Upon From a Female Standpoint." April 12: "Only A Woman: But She Has Some Ideas About the Make-up of the Pittsburg clubs." April 26: "The First Game: As Viewed by One of the Weaker Sex." Some questioned whether a woman was capable of writing of baseball as knowledgeably as Black did—was she really a man, masquerading behind a feminine pen name? Baseball's ubiquitous patriarch, Henry Chadwick, said, "Well, I almost thought Ella Black was a man."[7] Black's response to such perceptions was not shy. "Everyone seems to think that all a woman knows how to do is to work around her home, talk dress and fashion," Black writes in May. "I only hope some day . . . to be able to force some of the brilliant (?) masculine members of humanity, who have seen fit to ridicule the idea of a woman writing base ball, to admit that I am competent to do it."[8] As for Chadwick's left-handed compliment, she writes, "I appreciated it highly because it was not the usually flattery given to a woman on account of her sex, but because he seemed to find some real merit in my work."[9] Such debates distracted Black from the business at hand, however. Rather than writing about baseball, she found herself defending her right to do so, a practice that would continue for nearly a hundred years.

Black claimed she was not a radical advocate of women's rights, yet she had strong feelings about the importance of women to Organized Baseball. In a time when the propriety of women even in the stands was arguable, Black supported Ladies' Day, reasoning that free admission would draw more women to the ballpark, which in turn would attract more men. Given the number of women who turned out that season at both Pittsburgh ballparks, she could argue, "There is one thing sure, and it is one that is recognized by both the local clubs, and that is that whichever one is a winner in the struggle so soon to commence that one will have to thank the ladies of Pittsburg and Allegheny for having done a great deal to land the victory on its side."[10] She herself longed to be fully a part of Pittsburgh's cadre of sportswriters, lamenting at one point that she was unable to join her male colleagues in an Opening Day carriage parade. Constrained from joining her male colleagues at the venues where insiders talked over the game, Black had to draw her material from informal conversations in the stands and on the street, and, admittedly, by eavesdropping. She also relied upon close observation and deduction. By August, having noticed that both clubs had begun housing their players at less expensive hotels, she concluded that both leagues were struggling financially.

Although the customs of her day prevented Ella Black from full membership in the sportswriting profession, her work is a valuable legacy to the game's feminine voice. As she reflected in May 1890, "I only wish that I was a man so that I might be able to do some interviewing, for I think

I might get some things that others miss. You know a woman's ideas are often different from those a man will have." By the 1891 season, the Players' League was defunct, and inexplicably Black's column no longer appeared in the *Sporting Life.*

PETTICOATS AND THE PRESS BOX

In the early 1900s, Trinidad, Colorado, was a boisterous mining town of some twenty thousand people with a lively case of baseball fever. As the *Trinidad Chronicle-News* sporting editor observed, it was the sort of place "where the first word the babies say is 'Slide.'"[11] This editor had been just such a baby and was now a baseball-savvy young woman named Ina Eloise Young. During the 1908 season, Young covered local semi-pro games, where she also served as the official scorer. A scorer assigns putouts and assists and distinguishes a base hit from an error. One play may fall under a number of different rules, so it behooves the scorer to know well the official rulebook. The sight of a young woman with such responsibility agitated many a visiting team to Trinidad. Young said that in the beginning she was "driven almost to tears" by players' disputes over her decisions: "He usually takes it as a joke and when I hand my score book to him or answer his question intelligently he departs with a bewildered look that plainly says he believes that someone must have told me."[12]

Young learned to shrug off the confrontations. In an essay for *Baseball* magazine, she wrote with enthusiasm of her career, claiming that she understood the game better than many men. The *Chronicle-News* apparently agreed, sending "its clever little sporting writer" East to cover the Detroit-Chicago World Series of 1908. Young's observations—she writes that the third game "lacked the snap and the pitching features" of the previous game; that Detroit "scored first and [Ty] Cobb broke into the limelight at once"[13]—were noted by the *Chicago Tribune,* which praised her for reporting "fluently and intelligently of the crucial baseball situation, not only as it appeals to Colorado but to the world at large."[14] At the end of Series, Young was elected an honorary member of the Sporting Writers Association.

As did Ella Black, Young reported on the feminine aspects of baseball, giving readers a glimpse of life among the players' wives in the stands during the World Series: Ty Cobb's wife was "the aristocrat of the bunch . . . pretty and bridey," while Joe Tinker's wife was a "tiny scrap of a woman . . . who sheds tears when he strikes out." Whether Young wrote of these things on her own or at her editor's behest, her comments surely influenced how her work was presented:

- *Baseball* magazine, editor's note: "As Sporting Editor of the Chronicle-News, Trinidad, Colorado, Miss Young enjoys the distinction of being the only woman in the world engaged in such work."[15]
- *Trinidad Chronicle-News,* headline: "Enjoy Dresses and Hats As Well As Worlds' Series Games: Characteristic of Her Sex, Miss Young Notes How Wives of Champion Ball Players Dress"[16]

Such headlines portended two difficulties for female baseball writers: First, fans and readers were encouraged to see women not as bona fide reporters but as curiosities incapable of grasping the game's deeper intricacies. Young herself complained, "I am regarded somewhat as a freak when I meet old ball players."[17] Second, a female sportswriter setting out to report on the Players' League or the World Series usually ended up becoming part of the story, which tended to undermine her credibility and slant her stories from sports toward human interest and fashion. Trinidad's grandstand was filled with women in white dresses, and Young expressed hope of discovering her successor among them. But the ensuing decades saw the ever more popular game welcome only token female broadcasters and reporters, such as golf star Helen Dettweiler, who in 1938 joined the General Mills team of baseball announcers with a roving assignment to do parts of various Major League ball games.

From the barnstorming women's clubs and the All-American Girls Baseball League, we know that the Depression and World War II had a liberalizing effect upon the roles women were allowed to take on in Organized Baseball. These years also saw a small number of women enter the press box. Just out of Los Angeles High School in 1937, Jeane Hofmann began covering Pacific Coast League games for the *Hollywood Citizen-News.* (At age seventeen, she became the first woman to sit in the press box at the Los Angeles Angels' Wrigley Field.) By 1942, she was writing features on Bob Feller and Sam Chapman, interviewing Yankees manager Joe McCarthy, and covering spring training in Florida for the *Philadelphia Evening Bulletin.* During the regular season, she published three-column sports cartoons and reported on games from the Shibe Park press box before moving to New York. With the men away at war, her regular column in the *New*

York Journal-American kept baseball's home fires burning. "From the Feminine Viewpoint" tended to gossip in a city where café society and the management and players of the resident and visiting teams mingled: "Al Simmons, the Red Sox' post-deb starter, was all dressed up the other night, headed for the Ziegfeld Follies. Our Commodore Hotel operator, Keyhole Kate, reports Al even stopped to have his shoes and teeth polished. . . . G'wan, Al, all the chorus girls are 4-Fs these days."[18] Hofmann also wrote of fashion, which in 1943 served to brighten the readers' day against the grim news from the battlefronts:

> The ball players are all affecting the same type of garb this spring. . . . The overcoat is grey-tan with a slouch brim hat. . . . Yankee Stadium is blossoming out in new spring apparel. . . . There are two luscious shades of green for the grandstand seats, apple green, lower seats, and dark green, upper. . . . Branch Rickey, who dreamed up the timely red-white-'n-blue motif for the Ebbets Field renovating, dropped everything the day before the grand opening to run over and check up on the report that the aisles were still a glaring green. Rickey, who personally decreed the big "V" on the stadium rotunda, would likely have taken a hand at the painting job himself in order to get things done, if the rain hadn't given all concerned a day's grace.

Hofmann's style was lighthearted and breezy. In an account of the rebuffs suffered when she crashed the Yankee Stadium press box, she relied upon humor to carry the message of her "commando raid" on "Ye Forbidden Palace," writing of the president of the New York Baseball Writers Association "staggering to his feet, shrieking: 'A WOMAN!'"[19]

Hofmann's colleagues noticed her good looks. She was headlined as a "Comely Blonde Reporter"[20] and described by the press as a "tall, willowy blonde" whose "favorite athletes are ball players, and she believes they make excellent husbands."[21] She sometimes unwittingly participated in her trivialization, smiling for a photograph that was eventually published with the caption "Visiting the Giants' training camp last spring, Jeane Hofmann marveled at the muscle of Johnny Mize, while interviewing the big first baseman and Manager Mel Ott (left) on the bench."[22] Hofmann was not alone in being trivialized this way. During the 1946 season, writer Betty Peebles covered the Erie (New York–Penn) Sailors for her column, "A Woman's Angle on Baseball." The Sailors manager, Steve Mizerak, apparently developed a crush on her and took to calling Peebles on the intercom he had installed between the dugout and the press box. "I quit speaking to him," she said. "He was always asking me out. He would look up at me from the dugout during the game, when all the players could see him. I called him 'Miserable Mizerak.'"[23] Hofmann's and Peebles' treatment as marginal figures illustrates another problem female sportswriters faced. It was generally thought that men turned to sportswriting because they could not make it as athletes. Women who wanted to work as sportswriters were perceived as being interested not so much in the job but in finding a boyfriend or a husband and thus were considered fair game sexually.

Although the distractions of novelty and gender bias endured into the latter decades of the twentieth century, a North Carolinian demonstrated that it was not impossible for a woman to succeed in sportswriting. Mary Garber got her break in 1944 when, with the men at war, her editor at the *Twin City Sentinel* (later the *Winston-Salem Sentinel*) moved her from the society beat to sports. The following spring, Garber covered the Winston-Salem Cardinals of the Carolina League. Garber reminisces here about the beginning of her forty-two-year career in sports writing:

> Minor league baseball was a big deal at the time I was covering it. Everyone in town went to the games. The Cardinals manager, Pappy Smith, said he was told in spring training there would be a lady here, and he didn't believe it. That first year, most of the players were fifteen or sixteen years old, too young to be drafted. It was just like covering a high-school team. They used to ask for a lift in my car so they wouldn't have to ride the bus. The scouts I sat with sort of took me into their fraternity, and I learned a whole lot of baseball from them. In the fall of '45, they held a Hot Stove League meeting in High Point. The fellow I rode over with dumped me once we got there. There was nothing but men, and I didn't see a soul I knew. Then George Ferrell—he was a scout and a former ballplayer—reached out and pulled me into the circle of men, and said, "This is Mary Garber, she's my friend."[24] He did a wonderful thing. And from then on, I was one of them. I sat in the press box from the beginning—mind you, this was the minor leagues; it wouldn't have been possible in Major League Baseball.[25]

It was impossible because the Baseball Writers Association of America (BWAA) controlled access to Major League press boxes, where the men smoked cigars, swore, and enjoyed their own society. With clubs offering free food and beer, alcoholic excess was common. Garber was barred for years from membership in the Southern Conference Sportswriters Association and the Atlantic Coast Conference Sportswriters Association, although the latter organization eventually let her in, and she later served as a board member and president.

Garber did not enter the locker room until the thirty-first year of her career, which did not bother her at all. Locker rooms were grubby, smelly, and inconvenient. "If I needed to talk to a player, I sent some little boy into the locker room to ask for 'Jimmy,' and 'Jimmy' came out and we talked," she said. When a new player joined the Cardinals, his picture was taken on the field while Garber interviewed him. "By the time we were done, everyone was hot and sweaty, and the men would disappear into the locker room to wash up. They'd throw me a wet towel."

Garber was able to persevere without locker-room access because the *Sentinel* was an evening paper. Without the tight postgame deadline of a morning paper, her need for timely locker-room quotes was not urgent. She went on to cover every high-school, collegiate, and professional sport that the *Sentinel* followed, and, although she retired in 1986, she continued going into the office a couple of days each week. Because she grew up locally and was well known in town, she may have been more accepted than a stranger might have been. Garber said she never tried to become one of the boys. Asked why she stayed with sports for forty-two years, Garber replied, "The people in sports, why they were just fascinating. They loved what they were doing. Sportswriting was loads of fun."

A WOMAN'S WORK

The years immediately after World War II are often cited as a lost Eden of traditional values, with Mom home where she belonged, in an idealized suburban split-level. For many women, this was myth. After experiencing the independence of the Depression and the war years, they found the 1950s a time of frustrated ambition. When eighteen-year-old Dorothy Jane Zander enrolled at Fenn College in Cleveland in 1946, she had been writing stories for nine years and planned a career in journalism. As part of Fenn's work-study program, she got a job as copy "boy" for the *Cleveland News*. The newspaper world enchanted her; soon she was writing "sports shorts." For inspiration, she looked to Doris O'Donnell. O'Donnell "became my role model," Dorothy recalls in *A Woman's Work*. "She had made it to the exalted level of news reporter despite the usual relegation of women to lifestyle reporting no matter what their particular interests were."[26] At Fenn, Dorothy's developing writing and editorial talents were noticed by her history instructor, Harold Seymour, after he hired her to type his lectures. She quickly learned of his dissertation-in-progress on baseball history. The scholarship had to be impeccable, as Seymour had had difficulty persuading the history department of Cornell University that the subject was worthy of academic study. Seymour's "The Rise of Baseball to 1890" was completed and accepted by Cornell in 1957. By then, Dorothy Zander had become his wife. The dissertation was the first of its kind, and Seymour continued to expand the research accumulated to publish a trilogy of baseball history for Oxford University Press. *Baseball: The Early Years* appeared in 1960, *Baseball: The Golden Age* in 1971, and *Baseball: The People's Game* in 1991. The opus made Seymour's reputation as the game's preeminent historian. Meanwhile, at her husband's urging, Dorothy abandoned her dream of a career in journalism for teaching in order to help with his research during summer vacation. As the work progressed, she moved from assistant to undertaking much of the research and organization of the material, and editing and revising Harold's writing. (She always remembered editor J. G. Taylor Spink's shock in 1949 when she entered his all-male newsroom at the *Sporting News* to do research.) She began producing outlines so detailed that "Seymour," as she called him, could write directly from them, "often copying the very words I used in preparing the material."[27] Forty years would pass before she told the full truth of her role in creating what has been termed the "trilogy that forms the foundation of every serious baseball library."[28]

If she did not have a husband embarked upon a life's work of baseball research, a woman of the 1950s found little opportunity to write about baseball. Gloria Swegman, who had a master's degree in journalism from Columbia University and five years' reporting experience with the *Washington Post* and the Associated Press, captures the mood the times in "Baseball's Unfair to Women," an account of her quest to become a sportscaster. In addition to Vin Scully, who found the idea "mighty awkward," other New York media personalities responded negatively as well. Bert Lee Jr. said, "It's just that listening audiences just don't accept a woman sports broadcaster. . . . The same as we fellows don't accept a woman pilot on a DC-6, a woman engineer on a locomotive, or a woman president of the United States." Marty Glickman said, "I think women would make good sportscasters for sports in which women excel. . . . Let them report tennis, golf, and swimming . . . but football games, prizefighting, or baseball . . . No!" Said Connie Desmond, "I see no reason why a girl couldn't come in for an inning or so if they know baseball well. . . . If pretty enough, she could sit next to me."[29]

Women who did get to cover baseball continued to be trotted out as novelties. The role model of Dorothy Zander Seymour's college years, Doris O'Donnell, enjoyed a career as an award-winning investigative reporter that would span fifty-three years. When the *Cleveland News* assigned her to baseball in 1957, however, she ran into trouble. O'Donnell recalled, "I had this great editor at the *News*, Nat Howard, who liked to come up with flashy stories for 'summer' reading. He said, 'Hey, how about traveling with the Indians?'"[30] O'Donnell joined the Cleveland Indians on their eastern road trip in May. O'Donnell was a knowledgeable fan whose family was close to the McGillicudys—Connie Mack's clan. (She says she grew up playing baseball in the street "with these wonderful autographed balls Mack brought whenever the Athletics came to Cleveland.")

The *News*, however, announced her assignment as this: "Leaving batting averages and statistics to the contingent of all-male sports reporters, Miss O'Donnell will present the woman's view and behind-the-scenes glimpses of the athletes."[31] The ballplayers and the "all-male reporters" who covered them were not interested in offering such "behind-the-scenes glimpses." In 1957, Major League press boxes were still posted with this sign: "No Women or Children." A colleague O'Donnell considered a friend was especially vehement. "In my generation," O'Donnell said, "they didn't want girls anywhere near sports writing because of the proximity to the showers—there was no lounge to interview the players. Beyond that, it was clear the men—the players and the writers—wanted their privacy, for drinking, going to the racetrack, fooling around, whatever, without me around." She resorted to writing "the light, frivolous stuff," a series of profiles of the Indians' twenty-year-old bonus baby, Kenneth Kuhn, manager Kerby Farrell, and umpire Bill Summers.

O'Donnell is blessed with a hearty sense of humor, which came in handy. She was admitted to the press boxes in Washington, D.C., and Baltimore, where she sat with Roger Maris, who was recovering from an injury. When the two of them applauded a good play—a cardinal sin in the press box—they were ordered out. One night in the capital, a few players invited her up to the rooftop of the Shoreham Hotel. And did she have a flashlight to bring along?

A flashlight, I wondered. We took the elevator to the roof and—how can I put this nicely?—watched people copulating. I said, "How the hell am I going to write *this* story?" In Baltimore, two young pitchers said, "Come on, we're going to buy some stuff for our wives," and I thought, *Oh, we'll go shopping.* But they were so young, kids born on a farm, and ended up buying crazy stuff, like a box with a penis that jumped out . . . I wanted to take the group to an art museum, and [manager Kerby Farrell] said, "This ain't no Ladies Aid Society."

In "Stags Keep Doris Out Of Yank Press Box," O'Donnell explored the silliness of her exclusion from the Yankee Stadium press box by demystifying the place. "A press box," she writes, "is nothing more than makeshift, weather-worn tables for typewriters and Western Union equipment, and folding chairs. There is nothing plush about it. Usually it is crowded and untidy."[32] At eighty-one, O'Donnell still remembered the response to her presence. "I was just going to do some feature stories, and all of a sudden I became the news."[33] In "No Wonder Indians Look Better," the *New York Post*'s Jerry Mitchell itemized O'Donnell's wardrobe for the road trip, down to her underwear, describing her as "young, darkhaired, brown-eyed and exceedingly pretty. She has a fashion-model figure."[34] Although Mitchell admitted that O'Donnell had won converts to the idea of female sportswriters, access to the press box for such women remained problematic into the 1960s. When President Richard M. Nixon decided to attend a game at Robert F. Kennedy Stadium in 1969, even a respected White House correspondent like Helen Thomas of United Press International had to seek the president's help in order to join her colleagues in the press box.

The 1970s proved the breakthrough decade for women both in beat reporting and in other forms of baseball literature. Charline Gibson, the wife of the St. Louis Cardinals ace Bob Gibson, was actually invited to coauthor a book for baseball "widows" who wanted to share their husbands' and sons' interest. *A Wife's Guide to Baseball* is a polite, thorough explanation of the game. It also includes a four-page digression about the racism festering in baseball, which the Gibsons, who are African American, had witnessed up close and personal. "Baseball," Charline Gibson wrote, "is highly contradictory. A white third baseman never hesitates before throwing to a black first baseman. It is only when the uniforms come off that race ever becomes an issue."[35] Twenty-three years after Jackie Robinson broke the MLB color line, Gibson challenged the unwarranted publicity given to black and white players rooming together and the lack of opportunity for blacks in baseball when their playing days were done. "Perhaps by the time you read this page a black manager will have been appointed in the major leagues, or a black front-office executive will have been hired," she writes in 1970. "I hope so, for that will mean that another bar is down."[36] Given the tradition that a proper baseball wife must avoid controversy, Charline Gibson's stand took courage.

Writing about the male-dominated world of baseball was one thing, but what of the prejudice toward women in the broadcasting booth? Would fans accept a woman *talking* baseball? As Red Barber once argued, "the feminine voice just doesn't connote what people expect in the broadcasting of sports events."[37] Those expectations involved timbre (could a woman's voice resonate in the familiar way?) and expertise, for it was still thought that women lacked that innate understanding of sports— what feminist Donna Lupiano calls testicular knowledge. In 1971, a Bay Area publicist named Wendie Regalia felt the time was right to find out. Regalia's knowledge of the game began years earlier when her young son began peppering her with questions: "Why does Stan Musial wiggle at the plate and what are the 17 ways a pitcher can balk?" While looking for the answers, she fell in love with the game. When she learned that San Francisco Giants announcer Russ Hodges planned to retire, she called the station manager at KSFO-Radio and asked, "What's wrong with me? I know as much about baseball as any man. And I've done radio talk shows before."[38] Hired to do a portion of the pregame shows that season, Regalia declared she was "not going to be Howard Cosell in skirts," and promised a fresh style. "I'm not going to stand around, asking somebody how his pulled groin muscle is, that's for sure. I plan to ask solid questions." Regalia expected to draw more women to Candlestick Park, demonstrating once again that women saw themselves as having unique baseball sensibilities. Other women followed Regalia into broadcasting: In 1976, Anita Martini became the first woman to broadcast a National League game; the following year, Mary Shane, joined the Chicago White Sox play-by-play team.

FOR GOD'S SAKE, DON'T WRITE ABOUT THE GAME

As the 1970s wore on, more and more women were given baseball beats. Sports editors liked this "new" angle, although they were not always certain what it might be. In 1973, *Boston Herald* reporter Laura White was vaguely told, "Go out to Fenway Park and give me your impressions. A woman's view of the game." White reported on the sense of intimidation she felt when she approached the press box. "Sure, one or two other women have crossed the sacred threshold of the Kenmore Sq. coliseum," she mused. "But it's still considered hallowed ground."[39] A few years later, the *Herald* recruited another woman, Marie Brenner, who was working as a freelance writer in Europe. According to Brenner, the editor said, "'I want you to come home and cover the Boston Red Sox.' And I said, 'There's one problem. I've never been to a Major League baseball game.' A pause. 'Well, you'll have a fresh eye. We'll run you on page 1 of the sports section.' It wasn't that they wanted me to do the women's point of view toward baseball," Brenner explained. "They just wanted a skirt."[40] Despite her misgivings, Brenner took on the assignment and found the players accommodating "to this wacky writer who showed up for Opening Day at Fenway in high heels, a blazer, and pearls." Like Ella Black and Ina Eloise Young, such women were pressured to write primarily about the female experience at the ballpark rather than what was happening on the field. Brenner said she was told, "For God's sake, don't write about the game."[41]

> So out of a woeful ignorance of the game and because as a writer I have always been fascinated by personality, I began writing about the ball players as people. I noticed there were only two blacks on the Red Sox in 1979—George Scott and Jim Rice—and as I looked around at Fenway, I noticed few black fans. So I wrote a piece entitled "Why are there no black fans at Fenway?"

In this, Brenner was ahead of the times; it was not until 2002 that Howard Bryant published a full-length treatise on the subject: *Shut Out: A Story of Race and Baseball in Boston.* Women's fresh approaches to baseball were, in fact, proving beneficial. By 1976, journalist Daniel Rapoport pronounced female sportswriters "one of the hottest properties in journalism."[42] Male athletes did not seem as nervous about revealing their sensitivities to a woman, according to Rapoport—the *Washington Star*'s Lynn Rosellini had broken "new ground in sportswriting with a revealing series on homosexual athletes, a subject her male colleagues had studiously avoided" and the *New York Post*'s Sheila Moran found her gender advantageous when she covered baseball's most curious trade of 1973, the wife-swap by New York Yankees Mike Kekich and Fritz Peterson. Rapoport concluded that "[b]oth the men and the women talked more openly with her than with male reporters."

ACCESS TO THE LOCKER ROOM

For female beat writers, however, the issue of locker-room access still simmered, and it boiled over during the 1977 World Series. While her male colleagues interviewed Reggie Jackson and his teammates in the Yankees clubhouse after each game, *Sports Illustrated*'s Melissa Ludtke had to wait outside until the players emerged. Ludtke argued that because she was denied equal access, she was missing quotations, interviews, and deadlines, but the Yankees held firm: the players wanted their privacy. Her employer joined Ludtke in filing a federal lawsuit, charging MLB with sexual discrimination. Judge Constance Baker agreed, and told the Yankees to work out another way to protect the players' privacy. Baker suggested they wear towels.

The issue of locker-room access may have been adjudicated, but it was not fully settled. The Yankees complied with Baker's order by giving all reporters, male and female, a mere ten minutes to interview players in the locker room before leaving for 30 minutes to allow the players to shower. "You never heard such hollering," Ludtke wrote. "Suddenly it dawned on them that they were unable to do their job. . . . It really opened their eyes to what we'd been dealing with." MLB quickly returned to court, arguing that Judge Baker's order had turned Yankee Stadium's locker rooms into a three-ring circus. Then, on March 9, 1979, Commissioner Bowie Kuhn announced a resolution: each club would be free to set their own policy. For Ludtke, that begged the real issue—*why* women needed locker-room access, and she took MLB to task for its part in the circus:

> Baseball has succeeded brilliantly in making equal access appear as a moral and not a political problem, and as sexy, but not the sexist issue that it is. I, and others like me, were presented as women who wanted nothing more than to wander aimlessly around a locker room, to stare endlessly at naked athletes and to invade the privacy of individuals whose privacy had already been disrupted for years by our male colleagues.[43]

What Ludtke sought was equal, consistent access to all Major League locker rooms for male and female sportswriters, a position the BWAA now supported. She feared the complication of varying policies would prompt editors to resist giving women a beat, undoing the hard-won progress of recent years. Kuhn's edict also confounded female sportswriters as they moved from club to club. The following incident occurred during the 1984 World Series: Just after Game 2, with the San Diego

Padres celebrating their win over the Detroit Tigers, security personnel pushed the *Hartford Courant*'s Claire Smith out of the clubhouse while the players swore at her. Smith stood outside, wondering how she was going to file her story on time. Steve Garvey responded to her plight, went outside, and said to Smith, "You've got a job to do. I'll stand here until you have whatever you need."[44] The incident became a story in itself, which embarrassed Smith, a quiet, dignified woman. When Peter Ueberroth, new on the job as commissioner, heard about it, he made sure Smith got access for the following game. The following spring, he instructed both leagues to give full and equal access to female reporters.

Claire Smith went on to become a national baseball writer for the *New York Times*, although she never lost the sense of being an outsider. Smith, an African American, equated being a woman in the locker room with being black in America, given that both groups shared the sense of being intruders in a white man's world. This commonality explains why many of the female sportswriters mentioned here feel an affinity with the black players they encountered. Marie Brenner recalled the encouragement she received from Jim Rice of the Boston Red Sox: "You've been getting more and more uptight, just like us. Well, don't let us do that to you. The guys'll get used to you."[45] "Black athletes tend to know what prejudice feels like. . . . They empathized with us. And sometimes, they rescued us," recalls Susan Fornoff.[46] Alison Gordon, who covered the Toronto Blue Jays from 1979 to 1983, writes, "More often than not, the ones I liked and respected most were black players and it galled me to see how they were treated."[47]

Susan Fornoff was just getting out of college when she was sent on her first assignment to help cover the Baltimore Orioles. It was 1979, and she quickly saw that the Orioles manager, Earl Weaver, was distinctly unhappy about the idea. "I think they should have to bring a note from their fathers," he told the press.[48] Fornoff used humor to diffuse the situation, presenting Weaver with her father's blessing: "With quivering pen, I hereby give my daughter Susan permission to enter the Oriole locker room, mainly because I know that even if I don't she'll find a way to get in there anyway. . . . Yours in gentlemanly spirit, Bill Fornoff."[49] Once in the locker room, however, figuring out how to fit in preyed on the minds of many female sportswriters. Many devoted an inordinate amount of attention to the image they presented. By 1985, Susan Fornoff had won the Oakland

A's beat at the *Sacramento Bee,* but she still fretted over her appearance. "I did not so much as want my toes to show through a pair of sandals. If I thought I looked a little too 'butch,' I was sure to put on some lipstick, just as I was certain to replace a skirt with pants if 'party girl' might appear to be the message."[50]

The concerns of female sportswriters went beyond dress and makeup into ethics. How should they handle the long-standing tradition of sportswriters' informal postgame drinks with players, coaches, and managers? A woman who joined in risked accusations of romantic or sexual involvement with her sources. How much fraternizing was permissible with the players on your beat? On one evening, Fornoff ended up at the Hot Rod Café, dancing with pitchers Bob Welch and Dave Stewart. She acknowledged that dancing with players—she got Welch for the rock numbers and Stew for the funk numbers—went against the ethical guidelines of the Association of Women in Sports Media (AWSE), which she cofounded in 1987. She justified the fraternizing because it helped her to dig for more than the players' usual routine responses during group interviews. "[Others] probably thought I got answers because I'm female, but I think I got answers because I had gotten to know Welch personally and he had gotten to know me."[51] Male sportswriters, however, resented her advantage, and Fornoff heard about it. Some women writers dated men in baseball. If they did date, how much of the information they gathered was publishable? Fornoff admitted she dated Dave Stewart, but only after she left the A's day-to-day beat. In her memoir, she discusses their relationship. Other female sportswriters did not date but complained of having to "act like nuns."[52] Claire Smith was one who preferred clear boundaries. Covering Billy Martin's New York Yankees during the 1980s was a ride on the wild side, but Smith tended to avoid the late night hangouts where Martin so often ran into trouble, with sportswriters as eager witnesses. Because she did not consider bars and nightclubs part of her beat, Smith missed some of those stories.

Many ballplayers are convinced that a female reporter is in the locker room to view their naked bodies, the popular term being "pecker-checker."[53] The players respond in various ways. If a woman walked into the locker room, Reggie Jackson made sure to remove his towel, according to Fornoff, who in her memoir devotes an entire chapter (entitled "I Never Peeked!") to defending her premise that female sportswriters Do Not Look. Most reporters carry a small notebook, but women in the locker room often carry a large-sized one to screen their view. They make a habit of locking eye contact, and of always looking up, rather than down. Yet the stigma of sexual attractiveness and availability has lingered. Michele Himmelberg, a cofounder of AWSM, recalled arguing with a born-again Christian ballplayer, "Look, I'm not an immoral person because I'm in the locker room. I'm just doing my job." Alison Gordon remembered the ballplayer who told her that his teammates had offered him $500 to have sex with her, and offered her $200 of it. As her "baseball epitaph," Gordon cherished this memory of Earl Weaver: At a postgame party during the 1979 World Series, "He hailed me warmly, the latest gin and tonic gripped firmly in his hand, and dragged me across the room to meet his wife. 'Marianna, this is Alison,' he announced, in his gravelly voice. 'She ain't no pecker checker, she's okay.'"[54]

Although their number was increasing, female sportswriters found that their male colleagues were sometimes more resistant to their presence in the press box than the ball players were to their presence in the locker room. Jerome Holtzman had covered baseball in Chicago since 1957 and enjoyed smoking his Churchills in Wrigley Field's enclosed press box. He lamented the arrival of women. "Some of the women didn't like the cigar smoke, they complained, there was a big argument, and I did have to give 'em up," Holtzman said.[55] "They said, 'If you want to smoke, you have to sit four rows up'—that was way high up in the back, and I always sat in the front. Comiskey Field was different—it was open air, though I'm sure there were complaints there, too." Aside from the trouble over the cigars, however, Holtzman said, "It seemed to work out fine with women there—some are good writers." What he did not like was the rush into the clubhouse after a game:

> I had put women on a high pedestal, and I don't think they even realized how they looked, rushing around and competing, to me. I remember walking into the clubhouse after a Toronto game with Alison Gordon, whom I liked. Once she was in, the White Sox players started acting like little kids—it was embarrassing. She looked at me with a silent appeal, as if I should do something, but why? Why put everyone in that position? But did I come to terms with it? I had no choice.

In 1987, Michele Himmelberg, Kristin Huckshorn of the *San Jose Mercury News,* and Susan Fornoff of the *Sacramento Bee* founded the

Association for Women in Sports Media (or AWSM, as in *awesome*). Sixty women showed up at the first convention in 1988. Since then, AWSM has grown into an organization dedicated to the day when gender in the profession is no longer an issue. To that end, it offers a forum for addressing the complex issues its eight hundred members face, a job bank in print and broadcast journalism and public relations, a fund for scholarships and internships, and a clearinghouse for sexual harassment and pay inequity complaints. Its code of ethics offers members clear guidelines: Give players time to dress and don't linger near the showers; verify with the public relations director you'll be there; use courtesy, common sense, and discretion; and learn to laugh off the inevitable. "What I didn't know was how much fun AWSM was going to be," said Himmelberg. "That we'd have such a good time. Thank God, we can have a sense of humor and share the awful common experiences."[56]

Part of the excitement of beat writing is the travel, and at the Major League level, you travel in style. But the appeal of traveling with the team can pale for women—Susan Fornoff compared it to taking a field trip with high school boys accompanied by three kegs of beer. Many women leave the field by their midthirties. "The glamour and fun of sports writing—the travel—is also the downfall of it," explained Himmelberg, who felt a growing tension between the demands of work and family and ultimately moved to the business section of the *Orange County Register*. She recalled that very few of the women she knew in sportswriting were mothers. Even Claire Smith eventually left her coveted baseball beat at the *New York Times* to spend more time with her son. Honored in 2000 with the AWSM Pioneer Award, Smith offered this advice to its members: "Don't ever forget when you're building your career to leave time to build your life."[57] Susan Fornoff said she could not imagine sustaining a marriage while a beat writer, yet even she, single and childless, tired after five seasons of "hotel bars that served as the family living room." The *Sacramento Bee*'s Nancy Cooney concluded, "Men don't leave [sportswriting]. They do it all their lives and are thrilled to do it. But women get to a certain level and say, 'What's next?'"[58]

The 1990s saw the expansion of cable networks into sports, and ESPNews, Fox Sports Net, and CNN/SI began to open up sportscasting opportunities for women. In 1991, fewer than fifty women were employed in such jobs; a decade later, 127 were in the field.

Suzyn Waldman was at the forefront. Waldman had received her education in baseball as a girl at Fenway Park in the company of her grandfather. Years later, after a career in musical theater, she was at a ballpark, speaking with some Red Sox players while she waited to sing the national anthem. Sportscaster Wes Parker was standing nearby and asked Waldman whether she had considered a career in the field. Waldman recalled the encounter:

> I had never met [Parker] before, and never saw him again, but he changed my life. His comment got me thinking about the way sports were being covered and how the humanity of the game was getting lost. Little kids didn't feel the same about sports as I did growing up, and there were no women in sports broadcasting with the exception of some ex–beauty queens. I thought maybe I could do something about this. I was a performer. I knew sports as well as any man; I'd been on TV and on radio. How hard could it be?[59]

Waldman made a tape and presented it to WFAN, the nation's first all-sports radio station. After her debut in 1987, however, the first response she heard was the station owner's bellow: "Get that smart-mouthed broad with the Boston accent off my air." Demoted to the overnight shift, she did live sports updates every fifteen minutes, which turned out to be excellent training. She was assigned the New York Yankees' beat because, as she put it, all the men wanted to cover the World Champion Mets. For nearly fifteen years, Waldman reported on the games, interviewed the players, "did everything." Along the way, she found out just how hard the job could be for a woman: she was spat on, yelled at, and ignored. During the 2003 World Series, a photographer was standing nearby as Waldman conducted an interview. He heard someone yell, "Hey, Suzyn, show us your tits"—this directed at a woman who has fought and survived breast cancer. There have been death threats. "Imagine wanting to kill someone for talking baseball," Waldman told *People* magazine. "But you can't let people stop you."[60] She broke through the resistance a game, a season, at a time. Waldman was covering the 1989 World Series when the Loma Prieta earthquake hit. With hers the only telephone line still working in Candlestick Park, Waldman's reporting that day and through the ensuing crisis won her an International Radio Award. In 1996, she became the first woman to do regular play-by-play; that season she was named the New York Sportscaster of the Year by the National Sportscasters and Sportswriters Association. In 2002, she moved to the Yankees

Entertainment & Sports Network (YES) to do play-by-play as well as pregame and postgame shows. Along the way, she has shared the mike with Rick Cerone, Tim McCarver, Jim Kaat, and John Sterling, among others. "I never really wanted to do play-by-play, but the executives pushed it," she said. "The female voice at the moment is a hard sell." Even so, Waldman understands the importance of timbre in the voice of a female sportscaster. "I had a whole other career as an actress, with voice training," she explained. "You need a voice that commands—I always remember that line from *Death of a Salesman*—'attention must be paid.'"[61] In 2005, WCBS Radio named Waldman the first full-time color commentator in MLB history.

Waldman has become known for her thoroughness. As one female fan observed, "She is superlative at color commentary . . . all the kinds of things that an overeducated fan like me craves but rarely ever gets." Said a male fan, "I thought her reporting was lights out the best I'd heard anywhere anytime over a consistent basis. She seemed to have the ear of the players."[62] It seems to Waldman, who is single, that she is "always at the ballpark" or traveling with the club. This proximity supports her approach to the game: "It's *why* did he throw that pitch? I'm a reporter at heart. Every time I'm on the air, I try to tell people what's behind what they see." Most challenging is conveying to listeners the entire picture of what is happening on the field. "Most of us of a certain age grew up with little transistor radios under our pillows, and to hear those beautiful voices from far away—why, that's your childhood. Which brings to mind Vin Scully. "I don't think anybody's going to be Scully," said Waldman. "They don't write and they don't speak that way anymore. I still remember when Steve Finley hit the last ball of the [Dodgers'] regular season [in 2004] and Scully said something to the effect, 'It's up in the air and wherever it lands the Dodgers are going to the playoffs.' To be able to think like that! I was stunned."

Given its visual medium, it is not surprising, however, that female sportscasters are subject to the old game of sexual objectification. When Lisa Guerrero, an anchor on Fox Sports Net, learned she was a contender in Playboy.com's sexiest sportscaster poll of 2001, she expressed horror. How could a woman expect to be taken seriously in her job if she was subject to such inappropriate attention? Yet Guerrero chose to sit in on a discussion about women in sportscasting on Fox-TV's "The Best Damn Sports Show" dressed in a short skirt and spike heels. Tossing her tawny hair, she concluded, "Looking good gets you in the door; after that, you better know your stuff."[63] Although some female sportscasters railed at Playboy.com's poll, Angie Arlati, who played center field for the Silver Bullets before going to work for Fox Sports Net, took a different view. "If Alex Rodriguez and Derek Jeter were put in a poll to choose the sexiest major league baseball player, do you think they would say, 'Why can't you respect me for the shortstop that I am?'" reasoned Arlati. "Just because somebody votes for me as the sexiest sportscaster—now I no longer know my stuff? It's as absurd as saying, 'Because he's sexy, he doesn't know how to hit that well.'"[64] Guerrero's style and Arlati's words indicate their willingness to express and even exploit their femininity and their personal style in their careers in the sports media. Like Mary Garber, they wear dresses, but they do not blend in. In doing so, they follow the practice of the baseball players who play like pros yet understand that sexual objectification is one more American pastime.

Early in his career, Vin Scully expressed doubt that a feminine view in baseball existed. Curious as to how the past fifty years had affected his opinion, I contacted Scully. At 6:30 on a May evening in 2002, he was doing much the same as when Gloria Swegman interviewed him in 1950: preparing to broadcast another Dodgers game, this time from the West Coast. Revisiting his comments of that time—that a woman's presence in the locker room would be "mighty awkward" and what could she describe anyway, the uniforms as being "silk and taffeta?"—Scully rummaged through his memory. Thinking "fabric," he remarked that the Dodgers wore uniforms of satin during a World War II material shortage. "But that comment about taffeta—I doubt I even knew the term in those days." Scully tried a pun: "Maybe she fabricated that quote?" Then he turned serious. "But fifty years ago, there was no way for women to go into the locker room. I think the players today are more respectful; they remember to cover up, and I don't think it's a problem any more. Times change."[65]

As for his old doubt that a feminine viewpoint to baseball existed, Scully said, "The point I was probably trying to make was this: A home run, a line drive to right, a double play—I don't see a female or a male perspective on those things. You're just calling the plays." Without checking the byline, who can tell whether the writer is male or female? (Mary Garber once challenged a panel of sports editors to determine the gender of the authors of a collection of articles; they could not, for the days when female writers were part of their stories are over.) Scully's point is that reporting or broadcasting a ball game has nothing to do with gender. With luck, anyone possessing the proper knowledge, talent, and interest can do it successfully, though the Scullys among us remain as rare as a World Series championship in Boston.

Women were proving capable of working alongside men in Organized Baseball's press boxes and broadcasting booths, but what of participating in the game's literary canon—the novels, biographies, essays, poems, and films that go beyond reporting what happens within those nine innings to explore a rich variety of the social, political, and cultural issues concerning Americans. In a 1994 review of Ken Burns's television series *Baseball,* Susan J. Berkson argued, "Ken Burns calls baseball a metaphor for democracy. He's wrong. It is a metaphor for sexism. The great theme is that it's a boy's game; women have been shut out again and again."[66] For a writer, however, being "shut out" offers valuable material, for our most compelling stories involve the struggle for what has been denied. For more than a century, women had been the perennial outsiders to baseball. By the 1990s, that sense of exclusion was inspiring an increasing number of female writers.

Women turned to fiction. Barbara Gregorich wrote a novel about the first female major leaguer, *She's on First.* Some women used their background in sportswriting to write mysteries—Alison Gordon's *Dead Pull Hitter* and *Night Game* and Diane K. Shah's *High Heel Blue*—while Jane Leavy published the novel *Squeeze Play.*

Anthologies were published. Elinor Nauen's *Diamonds Are a Girls' Best Friend: Women Writers on Baseball* captures the sense of longing with which many women view the game; Ron Rapoport's *A Kind of Grace: A Treasury of Sportswriting by Women* reveals the battles fought and refought for acceptance in the press box and the locker room; and Susan Fox Rogers's *Sportsdykes* recounts the homophobia directed at female athletes.

Biographies and histories authored by women appear regularly. Barbara Gregorich's *Women at Play: The Story of Women in Baseball* and Susan E. Johnson's tribute to the AAGBL, *When Women Played Hardball,* were well received. Black baseball history is covered in Patricia McKissack's *Black Diamond: The Story of the Negro Baseball Leagues* (cowritten with her son, it won the Coretta Scott King Honor Book Award) and in Leslie Heaphy's *The Negro Leagues, 1869–1890.*

Memoirs began to appear: Following Alison Gordon's *Foul Ball! Five*

Years in the American League, Susan Fornoff published *Lady in the Locker Room: Uncovering the Oakland Athletics.* Jane Gross, Marie Brenner, Melissa Ludtke Lincoln, and others have published reflections about their sportswriting careers in various newspapers and magazines. In *You've Got to Have Balls to Make It in This League,* Pam Postema recounts her thirteen seasons as a minor league umpire; historian Doris Kearns Goodwin views her Brooklyn childhood through baseball in *Wait Till Next Year;* and Arlene Howard recollects her life as a baseball wife in *Elston and Me: The Story of the First Black Yankee.* These memoirs serve to inspire and guide future generations of women in avoiding the difficulties experienced by the pioneers.

In this regard, one of the most instructive is *A Woman's Work: Writing Baseball History with Harold Seymour.* In 2004, Dorothy Seymour, who married Roy Mills after Harold's death, published an account of her collaboration with her first husband. She thought her book would be the story of a man and the woman who helped his career, but, writes Dorothy Jane Mills "my editor at McFarland asked me to write instead about my own experiences as the first woman to write baseball history. So the book reflects my own career as a writer and the way I fit my writing into the work I was doing with Dr. Seymour."[67] Dorothy Mills writes with grace about Seymour's appropriation of her work. As her husband sank into depression and later Alzheimer's disease through the 1980s, she worked to complete the third book of the trilogy virtually on her own. As *The People's Game* approached publication, she pressed him to properly acknowledge her part in the project; Seymour refused. In essence, Dorothy Seymour was a collaborator and ultimately the uncredited co-author, of her husband's highly regarded work.

The dictionary definition of the term "plagiarism" involves the theft of another's published words or ideas. What Harold Seymour used as his own were his wife's unpublished ideas and words. Baseball historian Steven P. Gietschier examined the seventy-one boxes of materials used in the trilogy's preparation (housed as the Harold and Dorothy Seymour Collection at Cornell University's Kroch Library) before writing the foreword to *A Woman's Work.* Gietschier put it this way: "Seymour's crime went beyond plagiarism. It was part of a . . . relationship that required that he denigrate anything Dorothy accomplished as unimportant and insignificant. When she did do something of value, write his books, he simply could not accept it. . . . What he stole was not just her words; it was her personhood."[68] *A Woman's Work* stands as a testament to how things were between men and women not so long ago. Although her case is extreme, Dorothy Seymour was one of many women who ignored their own goals and worked without proper recognition.

Women have now entered the field of scholarly baseball research paved by the Seymours. After becoming the first woman to write a dissertation on the game as a PhD candidate at the University of Notre Dame in 1976, Cordelia Candelaria published *Seeking the Perfect Game: Baseball in American Literature,* in which she points out, "One of the chronic deficiencies of baseball fiction is its male chauvinism—that is, its uncritical chronicling of the onesided male-centeredness of the sports world."[69] Later came Janet Bruce's *The Kansas City Monarchs—Champions of Baseball,* and Justine Siegal's thesis "A Sociological Analysis of the Current Subculture of Women's Baseball."

Candelaria went on to become a professor of English at Arizona State University, where her class English 494: Baseball Fiction has drawn many an unsuspecting undergraduate hopeful of a snap course. Charlie Vascellaro was one such student. Over a couple of beers at a local bar, Vascellaro looked through Candelaria's syllabus. "It became immediately apparent that this was going to be a very intense class with a heavy work load," Vascellaro said.[70] "The vocabulary that she used even in the first getting-to-know-you lecture was daunting."

English 494 changed the course of Vascellaro's life. With Candelaria's encouragement, he began to write about baseball. "Cordelia was instrumental in my being hired to coordinate ASU's Diamonds in the Desert International Baseball Conference, recommending me as a guest lecturer and mediator in her classroom, and for teaching positions, and recommending me to potential employers. We're also just plain friends. There were times in my life," he went on, "when I questioned my intense enthusiasm for baseball and the writing that chronicles the sport. I wondered if I was spending a disproportionate amount of time on this stuff. Cordelia's treatment of the subject matter made me realize that I was OK and that baseball and its fiction were topics worthy of serious inquiry. As far as gender is concerned, I suppose I was surprised to meet a woman whose passion for the subject ran so deep. . . . I had not encountered a woman who was as on top of the writing about baseball, fiction and in some cases, nonfiction, as Cordelia. Now it seems quite natural to simply think of her as an expert in her field regardless of gender."

Women also began to make baseball films of consequence. In different ways, these films can be seen as works of reconciliation. Producer-director Penny Marshall had trouble convincing the film industry's financiers that people would pay to see a story about the All-American Girls Baseball League, but her 1992 movie *A League of Their Own* scored as the best-selling baseball movie of all time. Marshall reconciles baseball's masculine tradition with the truth that women also play the game. Aviva Kempner's documentary *The Life and Times of Hank Greenberg* won critical acclaim when it appeared in 2000. Kempner—who grew up believing that Greenberg was integral to the Jewish High Holy days her family observed, so often was his name invoked in temple—made her film an homage to her baseball-loving father's memory. Vanalyne Green's video *A Spy in the House That Ruth Built*, discussed in chapter 1, is a further effort to reconcile women's disparate feelings toward the game. Green speaks of being lost in her own private world while making the film, haunted by "the constant voice of obsession, willing me to make peace, somehow." Her conflicts with her attraction to the ballplayers, her desire for professionalism as a journalist, and her sense of being an intruder begin to resolve as she makes a connection between the pressures she feels as an artist—to get it right, to not fail, to produce day after day—and the pressure the players feel on the diamond. In one scene, Green is shown slicing into the red seams of a baseball, then dismantling it down to its threads. It is a metaphor for her deconstruction of both the game and her feelings for it. In *Spy*, we see one woman's attempt to rearrange and resolve, through baseball, the conflicted pieces of her life—her family, her childhood, her relations with men. In the end, Green accepts the game's ambiguities—she's "home," a safe place of female solace, albeit shadowed by the fear of man as intruder. For Green, baseball is "like a metaphor for life—that you are alone and have to do something. . . . I identified with that—no matter about gender there, it just seemed beautiful and poetic."

Epilogue

Into the Future

IN THE BEGINNING, IT SEEMED REASONABLE to organize this manuscript into nine chapters. Our subject is the game's women, however, and I came to believe that the ninth chapter of this book could not be written until we see a female player or umpire in Major League Baseball, or a viable women's league. So an epilogue must suffice, with reflections on the status quo in the early twenty-first century and what the future may bring. Thus far, the stories told here demonstrate the strength and depth of women's ties to baseball. These stories also show that in several areas of the game, the old prejudices and biases against women are lessening. There has never been a better time to be a woman in baseball.

As fans, women have shown an abiding interest and affection for the game for more than a century. They have proven to be just as loyal, knowledgeable, and crazy as their male counterparts. The Baseball Reliquary, the Southern California–based populist Hall of Fame, recognizes this in its annual Hilda Chester Award, given to a notable fan of the game. The 2003 Award went to songwriter Doris Roberts, whose credits include the popular tune "Meet the Mets." How fitting that such a woman would be recognized—throughout baseball history, female spectators have carried the game's music in their hearts and minds. Lest we forget this, "Take Me Out to the Ball Game," the hit song of 1908 in celebration of Katie

Casey, serves to remind us during seventh inning stretch at ballparks across the country.

In 1999, MLB undertook an Initiative on Women and Baseball, a market study of female fans, and found that they made up 46 percent of its fan base. Two years later, however, when MLB launched a $250 million advertising campaign to attract young fans, television consultant Neal Pilson told the press, "Baseball has to differentiate itself from the other sports. The grandfather, father, son connection is a good way to do it."[1] What about the grandmother, mother, daughter connection? MLB's ongoing market studies showed that during the 2002 season, women favored televised baseball games over other major sports by a two-to-one margin. "We agreed with the findings," said Robert Alvarado, the Anaheim Angels director of marketing since 2000.[2] "And we realized we had been sending a pretty homogeneous message targeted at the core baseball fan, whether male or female. But we knew we were missing markets—women, kids, Hispanics." While some clubs might have said "Hey, let's do female night or professional women's night," Alvarado thought that "gratuitous and contrived." Instead, the Angels made a fundamental shift in their marketing strategy. The club's print advertisements are now seen both in newspaper sports sections and in local parenting and family magazines. Radio spots are now heard both on sports stations and the "easy-listening" stations that women favor. And television ads are not just "hard-core baseball" anymore, according to Alvarado. "We show them not just as players but as human beings because women want to know the story behind the player." At the ballpark, ticket packages to the Left Field Family Pavilion have become more affordable as has the merchandise in the Team Store. No surprise, then, that women comprise 40 to 50 percent of the Angels fans in the stands and purchase the same percentage of season tickets.

During the writing of this book, the question arose and was debated as to whether the subject of Baseball Annies warranted an entire chapter. The answer was *yes,* for two reasons: Women become groupies, in part, because they are unwelcome to take part in their culture's centers of fame and power. For women, baseball's message from Little League to the Show was historically one of exclusion. If you want to send the message to the next generation of girls that you need not have sex with a ballplayer (or umpire, coach, or sportswriter) to get close to the game, then make all aspects of baseball more available to them.

Even so, Baseball Annies will always be with us to some degree—their role has been ingrained in civilization dating to antiquity. There are, however, inherent risks, and the chapter on Baseball Annies serves a reminder of these costs. Such women are morally accountable for the consequences of their aggressions: the damage done to players' marriages, families, and careers; the hazards of the sexually transmitted diseases they may pick up or carry; and their own self-esteem. The story of Baseball Annies is presented here, then, as a cautionary tale.

More than three decades have passed since Charline Gibson called for more diversity in MLB's front offices. The top positions in baseball still go mainly to white men. (And it still helps to have the right bloodline. Wendy Selig-Prieb's advancement in 1998 to President and Chief Executive Officer of the Eilwaukee Brewers came when her father, Bud Selig, was named the Commissioner of Baseball.) Despite the fact that the 2002 season saw only two minority general mangers and no women, Bud Selig said, "I'm proud of what we've done and comfortable where we are with minority hiring at all levels. We've matured to a point with minority hiring that we don't have to talk about it all the time. The clubs have followed the [interviewing] memorandum to a T. I have no complaints."[3] Richard Lapchick's Center for the Study of Sport in Society, which has tracked the issue since 1990, offers a different view. The Center's 2003 Racial and Gender Report Card gave MLB an overall D in gender hiring practices. Fewer than 30 percent of the subject employees at the team vice president and senior administration levels were women. Lapchick reported an overall decline since 2001 of both women and people of color among those who run MLB.

It is unsurprising, then, that female front-office executives find themselves in a sometimes inhospitable climate. In October 2003, for example, Juri Morioka's $3.4 million lawsuit against MLB alleged that "she was subjected to racial slurs and then fired after she complained. . . . She said the hostilities were evident while she worked for a year as an administrative assistant in baseball's broadcasting department."[4] One month later, Kim Ng, the highest ranking Asian American in MLB, was relaxing in a Phoenix hotel bar after a general managers' meeting when she was confronted by Bill Singer, the newly hired special assistant to the New York Mets general manager. According to press reports, Singer interrogated Ng as to why she was there and mocked her Chinese heritage. Ng shrugged it off, but the Mets did not; despite his apology, Singer was let go. The front office may be where women have come farthest in Organized Baseball, but much more needs to be done in the cause of gender equity.

In the field of baseball history, female baseball researchers are on the increase. At annual baseball conferences such as the Cooperstown Symposium on American Culture and Baseball, the Nine Spring Training Conference, and SABR's national conventions, women like Kristin M. Anderson of Augsburg College, Roberta Newman of New York University, and young scholars like Lisa Alexander and Trish Vignola gather to present research papers, enjoy field research at the ball park, and renew acquaintances and friendships. Here the network of women in baseball can be expected to strengthen and grow, given time and the best spirit of feminism—mutual support and encouragement.

The Association of Women in Sports Media (AWSM) has yet to achieve its goal of making itself obsolete because women in the game's press boxes still contend with gender bias and harassment. Yet female sportswriters are gaining recognition. When Sally Jenkins of the *Washington Post* was named the Associated Press Sports Editors best sports columnist of 2001, she became the first woman in history to win the coveted award in the 250,000-plus circulation newspaper category. (Christine Brennan of *USA Today* was also a finalist.) "I hope what it means is that people no longer discern a difference between male and female sports writing," said Jenkins.[5] Such bylines on the sports page are daily reminders of the balance being brought to baseball's literary canon by female authors. When Jane Leavy's biography *Sandy Koufax: A Lefty's Legacy* appeared in 2002, nothing was made of the author's gender. What mattered was that the book was worth reading. As Hank Aaron put it, "This book is as good as Koufax."[6] Also growing more familiar in baseball is the feminine voice. For the 2004 season, the San Francisco Giants public-address announcer Renel Brooks-Moon also handled a number of pregame shows for Fox Sports Net Bay Area. In San Francisco, at least, the next generation of fans is likely to grow up believing that the feminine voice has a place at the ballpark.

What does it mean that women are now involved in so many aspects of the game? For one, it reflects the ideal that all Americans deserve a fair chance to compete. This is good for the country and good for the game. As Carolyn Heilbrun writes, "The sexes require one another for civilization; walls must be climbed together."[7] Heilbrun believes, and I agree, that only when women fully participate in society, with all individuals, regardless of gender, free to go as far as their interest and talent takes them, can that culture be considered fully civilized. Organized Baseball, which for so long limited or excluded women from most aspects of the game, is still in a fairly early phase of civilizing. We must remember that the social mandates and federal legislation supporting gender equity have existed for a mere thirty years; only since the 1970s has an appreciable number of women been able to begin to find their way into positions of influence in Organized Baseball.

Heilbrun's comment also raises the old question of whether encouraging women to come to the ballpark would serve as a civilizing influence on the game. The question is best not generalized. Women, it turns out, are not more civilized than men, in the stands or anywhere else in baseball. The game has seen the demure female fan as well as Hilda Chester; owners with the social conscience of Linda Alvarado as well as one with the bigotry of Marge Schott; and female beat writers who will not sit at a hotel bar with the ballplayers they cover as well as those who date the players. Women, then, do not necessarily bring a higher standard to baseball—they are not the game's moral guardians. What they do offer are differences in experience and perspective that complement the traditional male view. Baseball, we have seen, has feminine ties dating to antiquity. Contemporary women's passion for the game can be seen as part of its full and true history and represents its innate integrity. Shut women out, and Organized Baseball loses something of that wholeness. For the game to fully thrive and mature as an American institution, it must honor its feminine side. In this regard, a few issues must be addressed.

PLAYING THE GAME

At the amateur level, girls' and women's basketball, soccer, and softball are thriving, yet baseball is in its infancy. In 2004, a girl who dreams of playing competitive baseball is better off in Toronto, Canada, with its full array of team play, than in the United States. Phil Niekro recognized the problem when he managed the Colorado Silver Bullets over three seasons. Because most of his players had grown up with softball, they lacked in baseball fundamentals, and Niekro spoke of the need for high school and college baseball programs for women. A serious lobbying effort in favor of girls' baseball is particularly important because many Little League coaches do not want girls on their team and push them into softball and many high school coaches refuse girls of talent a tryout. The next time you hear of a girl going out for baseball, give her a hand—she needs it. She is the future of women's baseball. The amateur leagues forming around the country, thanks to people like Jim Glennie and Justine Siegal, are taking hold. The Amateur Athletic Union now includes women's baseball, with eleven leagues from New York to California (though not much in mid-America). And in 2004, USA Baseball announced the appointment of a general manager and steering committee to organize its first Women's National Team. Bob Hope (the organizer of the Silver Bullets), Jim Glennie, and Justine Siegal are on the committee. In August 2004, the team competed in the International Baseball Federation Women's World Cup at Edmonton, Canada, winning the gold medal with a 2–0 victory over Japan.

At the professional level, women's sports are still young. The oldest active professional women's sports organization, the Ladies Professional Golf Association, dates to 1950. Billie Jean King did not cofound the Women's Tennis Association until 1970. Today, women's sports must compete with one another as well as with major men's sports and junk sports for sponsorship dollars; media exposure in the newspapers, radio, and television; and fan affection. As I write this, the Women's United Soccer Association (WUSA) has just folded. With low TV ratings (the games were telecast on PAX-TV—*PAX-TV?*), a 20 percent drop in attendance over three seasons, and financial losses, the sponsors pulled out. The Women's National Basketball Association (WNBA) is also seeing smaller crowds and falling TV ratings. The WNBA continues to exist because the prosperous men's league, the NBA, supports it. (Recognize that these problems are not limited to women's sports. The National Hockey League's combined operating losses totaled nearly $300 million in 2003. With TV ratings and attendance dwindling, some NHL franchises are reportedly near bankruptcy.) Yet we must not give up on the idea of women's professional sports. Many of the difficulties described here were common to Organized Baseball's struggle to establish itself in the latter nineteenth century. Leagues and teams cropped up, flourished briefly, fought for market share with rivals, and faded from the scene. Women's sports are simply a century behind. To prosper, they need not just money but time and long-term commitment.

The question is how should women's baseball be organized? The Colorado Silver Bullets demonstrated that playing against men does not work. And given the plethora of sports currently being played in this country, it is doubtful that a women's league, like the AAGBL of the 1940s and

1950s, could effectively compete for fans, sponsorship dollars, and media attention. Perhaps the most viable program for women's pro baseball would involve two or four teams, well-sponsored and televised on a channel that people can easily find. These teams, drawing on the best of the girls coming through the amateur system, could tour the country, familiarizing people with the idea that women play baseball. The problem is who will sponsor them? We can rightly ask if the NBA supports women's basketball, why does not Major League Baseball follow suit. During her twenty years of umpiring in baseball, Theresa Cox has seen the amount of money that MLB spends in its pursuit of good young male players. "MLB can afford to support women's baseball," she said. "They throw money around all the time. I know of a coach who's paid $70,000 a year to work with fourteen-to-sixteen-year-old prospects, and here you have women who are adults who can't get sponsored?"[8]

Whenever women play competitive hardball, the talk eventually turns to whether a woman could make it in the Show. Essays, novels, and magazine covers have been devoted to the idea. Elinor Nauen, the editor of the anthology *Diamonds Are a Girl's Best Friend,* observed, "I used to say there'll be a Jacqueline Robinson, a female major-leaguer, but I'm less sure any more."[9] Like Nauen, I used to be more sanguine about the possibility. Here again, deep shifts in thinking are in order before we see a Jacqueline Robinson in a Major League uniform. The first change, involving our perceptions of women's true strength, is already underway. One of Title IX's profound effects is that, through competitive sports, girls are now growing up with a greater sense of their own physical power. Colette Dowling addresses this sea change in *The Frailty Myth,* arguing that only recently have studies on women's strength begun that are not gender-biased. "Eventually the study of motor development brought scientists to the astounding concept that males' greater physical skills were chiefly the result of learning and practice," Dowling wrote in 2000. "They were not a matter of 'superior' physiology."[10] As young women shed their individual frailty myths, many may well demonstrate the physical ability to play competitive hardball. One cannot predict, however, how long it will take the men who run the game to begin to accept that notion.

Young women are not only growing stronger, they are also taller than previous generations. In 2001, *USA Today Baseball Weekly* ran a photograph of Harmon Cillebrew, the power-hitting outfielder for the Minnesota Twins during the 1960s, flanked by two women from the U.S.

Professional Volleyball Dream Team.[11] Both women towered over Killebrew, who stood 6 feet, 195 pounds in his prime. The good news, then, is that many contemporary female athletes equal or surpass in size the male baseball players of earlier generations, and these women are training as never before. Furthermore, the size of ballparks is virtually unchanged—bases are still 90 feet apart, the mound remains 60 feet, 6 inches from home plate. (This point came up at Arizona State University's Diamonds in the Desert baseball conference in 1998: At a panel discussion about women's baseball, a young shortstop spoke of playing women's baseball at Scottsdale Stadium, the San Francisco Giants' spring training site. A woman who had played with the AAGBL wondered how she could make the throw from deep short to first. The younger woman did not understand the question; to her, such a throw was of no consequence. The answer lay in their stature and the younger woman's conditioning. The young shortstop was a powerful six footer; the AAGBL player was noticeably shorter and slighter.)

Male ballplayers, however, have also grown bigger than their boyhood heroes. Consequently, expectations have increased in players' ability to hit for power. Second base, traditionally where light hitting but strong fielders play, has usually been deemed the most likely position for a woman to break the gender line. But as Merritt Clifton, a self-described former "marginal pro prospect" has pointed out, in "1970 or 1980, no one even expected a second base player to hit home runs. Now it is expected—or at least hoped for with reasonable frequency."[12] Women tend to carry their strength in their hips and legs, and their upper-body strength does not lend itself to power hitting. Thus, the rise of power-hitting second basemen like Bret Boone, Jeff Kent, and Alfonso Soriano dims the prospects of a woman at that position.

Likelier is the possibility of a female left-handed spot reliever. Here the young woman who dreams of following Ila Borders into professional baseball may find the times on her side. Throughout Organized Baseball's history, scouts and front-office personnel have dreamed of signing the next big pitcher who consistently throws 90-plus-mile-an-hour fastballs. Such glamour pitchers have become increasingly expensive, which has left the less wealthy teams of MLB at a disadvantage—until the Oakland A's hired Billy Beane as their general manager in 1998. Despite the club's low payroll, the cerebral Beane has since fielded a perennial contender by going after the unwanted: players of unorthodox style and stature who do not fit the hallowed image of baseball hunk. His revolutionary approach is well documented in Michael Lewis's *Moneyball*.[13] According to Lewis, Beane seeks control pitchers, low in walks and high in strikeouts, who give up ground balls rather than fly balls and home runs. A pitcher who can do all that, despite a fastball in the low 80s, is welcome in Oakland. In light of Beane's success, the Boston Red Sox, the Toronto Blue Jays, and, most recently, the Los Angeles Dodgers, have hired Beane alumni who analyze in fresh ways player stats at drafting and trading times. Other clubs may well follow. I believe there are young women who could compete under these parameters. The question remains: which team will be first to give them the chance? A good possibility would be the Blue Jays, who are known for their favorable attitudes toward women's baseball. Given the club's proximity to the girls' and women's baseball leagues of Toronto, the Jays may well be the first to sign "Jacqueline Robinson."

BARRIERS TO CROSSING THE DIAMOND'S GENDER LINE

Off the field, women in baseball are hampered by other issues. One is a palpable discomfort with the label "feminist." Over time, negative connotations have attached to the term, much as happened with the old term "tomboy." Men may hear "feminist" and think "man-hater" or "lawsuit for equal rights," while many women reject the term's implications of "extremist" or "lesbian." During their careers, Bernice Gera, Christine Wren, Ila Borders, and Pam Postema all declared *I am not a feminist.* In doing so, they hurt their own cause. Pam Postema came to acknowledge this. From her earliest days of umpiring, Postema said she was asked if she was "another of those 'radical feminists.'" And she would reply that while she believed in equal rights, she was not interested in umpiring for "a cause." Postema realized the error of her position when she read a story about sixteen-year-old Ila Borders, who by 1991 was voicing similar opinions. "How could she not be a feminist?" Postema writes. "She should have said, 'Yes, I'm a feminist, but I also love baseball and I realize that the only reason I'm able to play on a boys' team is because of the strides made by other women.'"[14]

Feminism has everything to do with women's drive for a place within baseball. Feminism is what got them into the game. Early feminists supported women's right to exercise (including playing baseball), to attend baseball games, and to own property (such as baseball clubs). The feminists of the early 1900s were instrumental in gaining women the right to vote. Feminists of the 1970s fought for the passage of Title IX as well as anti-harassment and fair employment legislation; they prepared the many lawsuits that made those laws effective. True feminism benefits both genders by freeing people from stultifying roles determined by culture, rather than by natural interest and ability. Feminism must be reclaimed not as an angry radical fringe movement, but as the centrist ideal that women deserve a fair chance to compete on a level playing field. Moreover, feminists must do a better job of supporting others' choices and challenges. It is ironic that just as the new wave of feminism of the latter 1960s and 1970s was building, the women who might have benefited from dialogue with one another—umpires Bernice Gera, Christine Wren, and Pam Postema—failed to connect with one another. The underlying theme of feminism has always been about sisterhood, and with it, an acknowledgement of our shared humanity with men.

Women in baseball are making connections with one another as never before. We see this particularly in the field of umpiring. Discerning the need for female officials to complement women's amateur baseball, Justine Siegal organized the Women's Baseball League's Umpire Association. Its development program offers clinics and evaluations and lists job openings throughout North America. A number of its former students now officiate at the college level. Shanna Kook, one such graduate, later attended Jim Evans's umpiring school in Florida, where she got to know Ria Cortesio, one of her instructors—who better than Ria to teach a rookie how to cope with being the only female on the field? Cortesio had sought the job as instructor at umpire Theresa Cox's repeated urging. Cox also keeps in touch with umpire Pam Postema, luring her out of retirement twice to call games together. "I'm really connected to women in baseball," Cox said, "and I'm proud of that. . . . We've got to stand together."[15]

Advocates like the Women's Sports Foundation keep watch over instances of gender discrimination in youth baseball. After years of lobbying, the foundation announced that Little League has agreed to develop a "'blind draft' system that would prevent discrimination based on gender, race or any other inappropriate factor" for inclusion in its 2004 Operations Manual.[16] Dorothy Seymour Mills keeps in close touch with Justine Siegal. Mills, who claims she was always a fan of history rather than baseball, annually speaks at SABR's Seymour Conference in Cleveland. And Ila Borders regularly returns to Japan each summer to coach at the World Children's Baseball Fair. In 2003, she was named the best coach by both her colleagues and the children. In this way, she encourages the next generation of Japanese girls who want to play hardball.

Another continuing problem for women is the homophobia extant in Organized Baseball, whose discomfort at the idea of a female in the Show parallels its anxiety over that of an openly gay ballplayer. The issue of gay ballplayers cropped up again in December 2002, when the *New York Post* implied that author Jane Leavy agreed to keep secret Sandy Koufax's alleged sexual orientation in order to gain his cooperation for her biography about him. Both Leavy and Koufax vigorously refuted any such arrangement, and the outraged Koufax, an intensely private man, severed his long-standing ties with the Los Angeles Dodgers, who were owned at the time by Rupert Murdoch, whose holdings also included the *Post*.

Women who umpire or play baseball, as we have seen, are often presumed to be lesbian. Some are, and it is reasonable to think that some of them are talented enough to serve as players or umpires in Organized Baseball. I find it encouraging that American attitudes toward sexual orientation appear to be softening. Even the term "tomboy" is losing its old taint: In 2003, the *Atlantic Monthly's* "Language Police" added "tomboy" to its list of stereotypical terms to be avoided, which suggests that athletic, sports-minded girls and women are winning acceptance as a norm rather than being considered deviant. Yet Organized Baseball is probably lagging in reforming its thinking on the issue of homosexuality—what Jim Caple of ESPN.com calls "baseball's toughest 'out.'" Given the furor that an openly gay male ballplayer would currently face, it is unlikely that Organized Baseball is quite ready to accept a lesbian in the Show. (Witness Jackie Robinson, who was not necessarily the best black ballplayer of 1946, but was thought to possess the best "temperament"— a euphemism for the belief that Robinson was, along with his qualities of fortitude and self-control, sexually unthreatening because he was engaged to a black woman.) Should gay ballplayers begin to emerge from the locker-room closet—and I believe the day is coming—it will take time before Organized Baseball, dare we say, embraces the idea. Until then, a woman who aspires to the Show had better be certifiably straight, or stay deep in the closet.

With these issues in mind, my thoughts returned to Cooperstown. I had recently visited there in autumn, when the hopes and disappointments

of another season begin to ebb, leaving memory and the distant promise of spring. Snowfall would soon isolate the village from all but the most
intrepid visitors. I still saw Cooperstown as charming, beautiful, and, all
right, quaint, much like MLB's assiduously marketed image. I also had
come to see that despite the town's studied nostalgia, the staff at the Hall
of Fame and Museum has not frozen baseball in time. This is as it should
be, for baseball is mutable—that is why it survives. The museum is in a
constant state of change, as the staff revises and updates the exhibits to
reflect the constant flow of new information and new ways of thinking
about the game. As I write this, the Women in Baseball exhibit is undergoing another renewal.

Cooperstown has its shadows. One finds few people of color here, and
few who are poor. Cooperstown is home to the wealthy, and it can appear exclusionary quite without thinking about it. A friend of mine,
hurrying to the 2003 Hall of Fame Induction Week ceremonies for Gary
Carter and Eddie Murray, rounded a curve and was greeted by a large
Confederate flag waving from the flagpole of one of the town's homes.
He wondered how Murray, who is black, felt about that flag when he
arrived in town. That spring, Dale Petroskey, the president of the Hall
of Fame, had canceled plans to celebrate the fifteenth anniversary of the
film *Bull Durham*, one of the most popular baseball movies ever, because
two of its stars, Susan Sarandon and Tim Robbins, had spoken out against
the U.S. invasion of Iraq. Eric Enders, a former employee of the Hall of
Fame, took Petroskey to task. According to Enders, the Hall operates as
a highly conservative political bastion, espousing inclusiveness but demonstrating little of it, given that the first African American was not hired
there until 2001. Enders concludes, "Petroskey will clearly never be the
visionary executive the institution needs: someone who can not only
move the organization forward, but also cater to the concerns of the fans
rather than the politicians."[17] If such a climate reflects the true feelings
of Organized Baseball, then the idea of a female umpire or ballplayer
breaking the ultimate barrier, gender, loses some of its promise.

Baseball, however, is always about hope—just ask fans of the Boston Red
Sox and the Chicago Cubs. Just when you least expect it, baseball surprises
and even astounds us. We fans revel in the moment when the game's
conventional wisdom and statistical probabilities and pundits' predic-
tions are upended. Giants fans still thrill to the sound of the call of Bobby

Thomson's bottom-of-the-ninth home run to steal the 1951 pennant from the Brooklyn Dodgers. Pittsburgh Pirates fans still recall the rally culminating with Bill Mazerowski's home run to clinch the 1960 World Series. As the New York Mets rallied to win the 1986 World Series in the sixteenth inning, Steve Gietschier of the *Sporting News* turned to his young daughter. "Cherish this moment," he commanded. "It happens once in a lifetime—if you're lucky." Losing the 1986 Series was, of course, a heartbreaker for the Boston Red Sox, who had to wait another eighteen seasons for their victoraous moment. For weeks after the 2004 World Series finale, many a citizen of the Red Sox nation awoke each morning with a need to reconfirm that the events of October were not just a dream.

At our house, the magic arrived in October 2002, when, after their slowest start ever, the Anaheim Angels edged into the playoffs as the American League Wild Card. Sitting with family and friends in the nosebleed seats of Section 530 at Edison Field throughout the postseason games, I vacillated between cheering and writing. I had come to baseball first as a fan, and the Angels' come-from-behind wins were too thrilling, their uncelebrated players too game, their manager Mike Scioscia too classy not to indulge with the forty-five thousand other red-shirted, ThunderStix-clapping fans in screaming for the New York Yankees' blueblood, the Minnesota Twins' hide, and the felling of the San Francisco Giants. I was glad, then, not to be in the press box, where cheering is prohibited, no matter what heart-swelling heroics occur on the field. And when Darin Erstad, suddenly recalling his father's admonition to use both hands, gloved Kenny Lofton's fly ball for the last out of the World Series, the moment hung timeless amid the crowd's roar.

Then, all gender distinctions were far from this writer's consciousness. The middle-aged couple in the row just below us, season-ticket holders who had endured the team's misfortunes for years, gazed at one another in unabashed wonder; the young girl who had wept when the Angels fell behind 6–1 against the Yankees paraded with her rally monkeys draped around her shoulders, sharing the joy of two boys, their torsos smeared with Angels red, clear up through their blond brush cuts, who were highfiving strangers. In the Diamond Club, businessmen and businesswomen, who had not known David Eckstein from Darin Erstad, but now knew a good thing when they saw it, pocketed their cell phones to embrace the moment. The Anaheim Angels—the odds ran 50–1 against it in April—had won the World Series.

After the smoke from the fireworks lifted and the confetti settled on the infield, I read through the recent e-mails from baseball colleagues. "Just wanted to say how pleased I am that this is all happening for you guys," wrote Elinor Nauen, a transplanted Yankees fan from South Dakota. "I went to the first two games of the '87 World Series, so did get to share some of that mania that envelops a city [Minneapolis], but never really takes over New York—always too much else going on. Nothing is ever the only game in town here."[18]

"Now that the Angels have won, do you think we could get a little of that magic on the north side of Chicago?" asked Tim Wiles from the Hall of Fame Library.[19] (In support of the Cubs' hopes for the 2003 season, into the mail went two battered ThunderStix, but . . . alas.)

"Wouldn't it be great if you finished the book the same year the Angels won the World Series," encouraged the Writing Baseball editor of this book, Pete Peterson.[20]

"Mazel tov!" wrote Aviva Kempner, the creator of the documentary *The Life and Times of Hank Greenberg*. Kempner suggested that the Angels and women had much in common: "Just like women are the under-known fans and experts of baseball, so did the Angels rise. Whole premise of your book, no?"[21]

Kempner's analogy made sense. All season long, we had watched the team persevere in a relative haze of anonymity—last up on the sports shows each evening despite Erstad's body-slamming horizontal catches in center field, the diminutive Eckstein's gratifying on-base percentage, and the Angels' forty-three come-from-behind wins. Lacking a star of Barry Bonds's magnitude, the club played cerebral, fundamental baseball to the best of its ability. For their efforts, the Angels were deemed a curiosity, much as women have been viewed throughout most of baseball history. Every woman who challenges the odds by learning well the fundamentals of her particular role in baseball—Ila Borders, Ria Cortesio and Pam Postema, Linda Alvarado and Kim Ng, and Dorothy Seymour Mills come immediately to mind—chips away at the idea that they are mere curiosities.

Like the Angels, who were not thought to be remotely capable of winning the World Series, diminished expectations have too long applied to all women in baseball. The 2002 World Series showed some progress here. In San Francisco, Renel Brooks-Moon became the first female public-address announcer to work a World Series game. And when Bud Selig presented the club its first World Series trophy—a gaudy thing—there was Jackie Autry, who had been drawing upon her expertise as banker and former club owner to do pro bono work as honorary president of the American League. Beside Autry was Jeanne Zelasko, FOX-TV's sportscaster, who handled the interviews and introductions.

There remains, of course, the absence of a woman in the Show as player or umpire. Given the prejudices that linger in Organized Baseball as well as the rare combination of temperament, talent, luck, and timing required of her, the odds are formidable against a woman playing hardball anytime soon. We will know the odds are improving when female prospects are covered as a sports story rather than as a celebrity or news event. More likely is the possibility of a Major League umpire. Female referees have been working full seasons in the National Basketball Association since 1997, so why not in baseball? In 2004, Ria Cortesio and Shanna Kook were the only women in the system.

Yet we know that the odds in baseball are surmountable. Part of the game's genius is the absence of a running clock, granting us the coveted commodity of time, in which anything can happen before the last out is made. To paraphrase Yogi Berra, it ain't over till it's over. Just ask David Eckstein, the Angels 5'6 ½" shortstop—a walk-on in college and released on waivers by the Boston Red Sox before Anaheim claimed him. In a game dominated by the likes of shortstops Nomar Garciaparra, Derek Jeter, Alex Rodriguez (moved in 2004 to third base), and Miguel Tejada, it is Eckstein who wears the 2002 World Series ring. So it is with the women of this book. Their stories show that women have always found a way to involve themselves in the game they love best. I have come to find a sense of inevitability in this. After all, years after I had abandoned my own dreams of sportswriting, the idea for this book arrived, unbidden. So if the idea of a female major leaguer appears improbable, we cannot say it is impossible. In baseball, anything is possible.

You could look it up.

Chronology
Notes
Index

Chronology

1847: Mrs. Doolittle signs a score card as umpire for the Knickerbockers

1866: Vassar College students form the Abenakis and the Laurel Base Ball Clubs

1867: The Knickerbockers declare the last Thursday of every month to be Ladies Day; Cincinnati's Great Baseball Tournament attracts many female spectators

1869: Female club plays in Peterboro, New York

1875: Professional game between Blondes and Brunettes, Springfield, Illinois

1882: Elisha Green Williams begins a secret, nine-year career as the official scorer for the Chicago White Stockings

1883: The Young Ladies Baseball Club plays in Manhattan before taking to the road; two African American women's teams play, the Dolly Vardens, of Chester, Pennsylvania, and a Philadelphia team; several National League teams institute Ladies' Day

1890: Ella Black's columns appear in the *Sporting Life*

1893: The American Female Baseball Club plays a men's team in Cuba

1897: Lizzie Arlington pitches in one game for the Reading, Pennsylvania, minor league club

1903: The Boston Bloomer Girls play the first night game in Oklahoma Territory; a Brooklyn, New York, women's team is jailed in Fort Worth, Texas, for playing a men's team; co-ed teams play at Kearsage Village, Massachusetts

1904: The women of Flat Rock, Indiana, organize two ball clubs, the Marrieds and the Singles; Amanda Clement begins a five-year career as umpire of semi-pro games throughout the Upper Midwest

1907: Alta Weiss signs to pitch for the semi-pro Vermilion Independents

1908: Ina Eloise Young, sporting editor, *Trinidad (Colorado) News Chronicle,* serves as official scorer before going to Chicago to cover the World Series

1910: Barnard College adds baseball to its list of women's sports; the *Freeman* advertises the St. Louis Black Broncos, an African American female baseball club; Agnes Malley Havenor inherits the Triple-A Milwaukee Brewers from her husband

1911: Helene Hathaway Robison Britton becomes the first female owner of a Major League baseball club when she inherits the St. Louis Cardinals; Maud Nelson founds the Western Bloomer Girls

1917: Pearl Barrett plays first base for the Havana Red Sox

1918: Lizzie Murphy plays for the semi-pro Ed Carr's All-Stars out of Boston

1922: Olivia Taylor inherits controlling interest of the Indianapolis ABCs of the Negro National League

1925: The Philadelphia Bobbies barnstorm the Western United States and Japan

1926: Margaret Donahue, of the Chicago Cubs, becomes MLB's first female corporate secretary

1928: Margaret Gisolo stars on the Blanford Cubs, an American Legion Junior team

1929: The American Legion bans girls from its junior teams

1930: Lucille Thomas buys a minor league franchise in Wichita, Kansas, and moves it to Tulsa, Oklahoma

1931: Jackie Mitchell signs with the Class-A Chattanooga Lookouts and pitches in one game before Baseball Commissioner Kenesaw Mountain Landis voids the contract

1932: Florence Wolf Dreyfuss inherits the Pittsburgh Pirates

1933: Isabel Baxter plays a game for the Cleveland Giants of the Negro Leagues

1935: Babe Didrikson pitches in two exhibition games for the Philadelphia Athletics

1937: Jeane Hofmann is hired by the *Hollywood Citizen News* as a cartoonist and sports writer

1938: Helen Deitweiler is hired by General Mills as baseball announcer

1939: Little League Baseball is chartered, for boys only

1942: Jeane Hofmann is hired by the *Philadelphia Evening Bulletin* as cartoonist and sports writer

1943: The All-American Girls Baseball League (AAGBL) is founded

1945: Mary Garber covers the Winston-Salem Cardinals for the *Twin City Sentinel*, the beginning of her forty-two-year career in sports writing

1946: Edith Houghton is hired as a scout by the Philadelphia Phillies

1947: Toni Stone joins the semi-pro San Francisco Sea Lions

1948: Dorothy Zander and Harold Seymour begin their collaboration as baseball historians

1949: In Japan, a women's baseball league is organized

1952: Eleanor Engel signs a contract with the Harrisburg Senators, which is voided when Major League Baseball adopts a rule barring the signing of women

1953: Toni Stone signs with the Indianapolis Clowns, Negro American League

1954: Mamie "Peanut" Johnson and Connie Morgan sign with the Indianapolis Clowns when Stone jumps to the Kansas City Monarchs; the AAGBL ceases play

1957: Journalist Doris O'Donnell is assigned by the *Cleveland News* to cover a road trip with the Cleveland Indians

1967: Bernice Gera enters the Florida Baseball Umpire School

1969: Helen Thomas, UPI's White House correspondent, requests President Nixon's help to gain access to press box at John F. Kennedy Stadium

1970: Charline Gibson publishes *A Wife's Guide to Baseball*

1971: Nancy Miller begins two seasons of umpiring with the Indianapolis Clowns; Wendy Regalia joins the San Francisco Giants as broadcaster

1972: Bernice Gera umpires one game in the Class-A New York–Penn League before quitting; Congress enacts Title IX of the Education Acts

1973: The Pawtucket, Rhode Island, women's baseball league is organized; the New York Human Rights Commission orders the New York Mets and the New York Yankees to end free admission and the sale of discounted tickets to women

1974: Little League Baseball is ordered to admit girls

1975: American Legion Baseball elects to admit women; Christine Wren begins her umpiring career in the Northwest League

1976: Anita Martini becomes first woman to broadcast a National League game

1977: Christine Wren is promoted to the Class-A Midwest League; Pam Postema begins her umpiring career in the Gulf Coast League; Mary Shane is named to the Chicago White Sox four-person play-by-play team; Melissa Ludtke of *Sports Illustrated* files a lawsuit for equal access to the locker room; Patty Cox Hampton is named general manager of the Class-A Oklahoma City 89ers

1978: The Baseball Writers' Association of America votes unanimously that women be admitted into MLB clubhouses; Jean Yawkey heads a syndicate to purchase the Boston Red Sox

1979: Marie Brenner (Boston Red Sox), Susan Fornoff (Oakland A's), and Alison Gordon (Toronto Blue Jays) are hired as baseball writers

1980: Umpire Pam Postema is promoted to the Class-A Florida State League

1982: Umpire Pam Postema is promoted to the Double-A Texas League

1983: Umpire Pam Postema is promoted to the Triple-A Pacific Coast League

1984: Joan Kroc inherits the San Diego Padres; Marge Schott purchases a majority interest in the Cincinnati Reds

1985: Tracy Lewis becomes the first African American club president in Organized Baseball when she takes over the Savannah Cardinals

1987: Sportswriters Susan Fornoff, Michele Himmelberg, and Kristin Huckshorn found the Association of Women in Sports Media; Suzyn Waldman is the first sportscaster—man or woman—for WFAN, the first all-sports radio station

1988: *Bull Durham*, the first baseball movie with a female protagonist, is released; Darlene Mehrer founds the American Women's Baseball Association

1989: Cordelia Candelaria publishes *Seeking the Perfect Game: Baseball in American Literature*, based on her PhD dissertation; Vanalyne Green's videotape *A Spy in the House That Ruth Built* is released; Julie Croteau plays first base for St. Mary's College (NCAA, Division III)

1990: Elaine Weddington Steward joins the Boston Red Sox as general counsel and assistant general manager

1991: Linda Alvarado becomes the first Hispanic Major League owner when she purchases a minority interest in the Colorado Rockies

1992: Penny Marshall's film *A League of Their Own* is released; Jim Glennie founds the American Women's Baseball League

1993: Southern California College awards left-hander Ila Borders the first baseball scholarship for a woman; Elinor Nauen publishes the anthology *Diamonds Are a Girl's Best Friend: Women Writers on Baseball*

1994: Ila Borders becomes the first woman in history to win a men's collegiate game; the Colorado Silver Bullets play their inaugural season of professional baseball

1996: Suzyn Waldman joins the New York Yankees broadcasting team and is named the New York Sportscaster of the Year by the National Sportscasters and Sportswriters Association

1997: Ila Borders pitches for the St. Paul Saints; Kim Ng is named Director of Waivers and Player Recgrds for the American League

1998: Ila Borders, pitching for the Duluth-Superior Dukes, becomes the first woman to win a professional men's game; the New York Yankees hire Kim Ng as their assistant general manager; Wendy Selig-Prieb is named president and chief executive officer of the Milwaukee Brewers

1999: Ria Cortesio begins her umpiring career in the Pioneer League; Justine Siegal founds the Women's Baseball League; Ila Borders pitches for the Madison Black Wolf

2000: Aviva Kempner's documentary *The Life and Times of Hank Greenberg* is voted the best documentary of 2000 by the National Board of Review of Motion Pictures; Ila Borders retires

2001: Umpire Ria Cortesio is promoted to the Class-A Midwest League; the Los Angeles Dodgers hire Kim Ng as assistant general manager

2002: Umpire Ria Cortesio is promoted to the Class-A Florida State League; Evelyn Begley wins the Society for American Baseball Research's highest honor, the Bob Davids Award; Janet Marie Smith is hired as Vice President of Planning and Development by the Boston Red Sox, charged with evaluating options to renovate Fenway Park; Suzyn Waldman is hired to do play-by-play and to anchor pregame and postgame shows by the Yankees Entertainment & Sports Network

2003: Shanna Kook begins her umpiring career in the Pioneer League

2004: Dorothy Seymour Mills publishes *A Woman's Work*

Notes

1. IN THE BEGINNING

1. Lil Levant, telephone interview, September 15, 1994.

2. Rick White, "Diamonds Are . . ." *Atlanta Braves Yearbook, 1979,* 57, 58.

3. Edna Ferber, "Bush League Hero," 1912. Rpt. in *Diamonds Are a Girl's Best Friend,* ed. Elinor Nauen (Boston: Faber and Faber, 1994), 161.

4. Nauen, 123.

5. Nauen, 141.

6. Nauen, xii.

7. Eliot Asinof, keynote speaker, Nine Spring Training Conference, March 13, 2004, Tucson, Arizona.

8. Vanalyne Green, personal interview, June 27, 1994. *A Spy in the House That Ruth Built* (New York: Women Make Movies, 1989).

9. Doris Kearns Goodwin, "From Father, With Love," *Boston Globe,* October 6, 1986; *Wait till Next Year* (New York: Simon and Schuster), 13.

10. Emily Hancock, *The Girl Within* (New York: Fawcett Columbine, 1989), 8. See also Colette Dowling's *The Frailty Myth* (New York: Random House, 2000), which includes the comment: "Psychologists today see girls' self-esteem *peaking* at nine" (122).

11. Kimberly Rae Connor, letter to the author, June 26, 1992.

12. Pam Postema and Gene Wojciechowski, *You've Got to Have Balls to Make It in This League* (New York: Simon and Schuster, 1992), 255.

13. While the 1846 game is documented by a scorebook entry, continuing research demonstrates that organized games of early variants of baseball were played in Manhattan as early as 1823. (See "Baseball's Disputed Origin Is Traced Back, Back, Back," Edward Wong, *New York Times* July 8, 2001, which quotes baseball historian John Thorn as saying, "The [1823] article supported the theory that baseball gradually evolved from prototypes."). Furthermore, in baseball, statistics authenticate, and they have yet to be discovered for these earlier games.

14. "Early Games of Ball 2000 BC–1800 AD," National Baseball Hall of Fame and Museum.

15. Allen Guttmann, *Women's Sports: A History* (New York: Columbia University Press, 1991), 11.

16. Robert W. Henderson, *Ball, Bat and Bishop,* (New York: Rockport Press, 1947), 4.

17. Cordelia Candelaria, *Seeking the Perfect Game* (New York: Greenwood Press, 1989), 8.

18. Harold Peterson, *The Man Who Invented Baseball* (New York: Scribner's, 1973), 42–46.

19. Tom Heitz, personal interview, August 6, 1994.

20. Guttmann, 8.

21. Guttmann, 18.

22. Guttmann, 25.

23. Stephen G. Miller, *Arete: Greek Sports from Ancient Sources* (Berkeley: University of California Press, 1991), 102.

24. Peterson (24–25) traces baseball's lineage through stoolball, as does Candelaria (9–10).

25. Candelaria, 10; Henderson, 71.

26. Henderson, 72, also Guttmann, 77.

27. Jane Austen, *Northanger Abbey,* 1818 (rpt. New York: Penguin Books USA, 1995), 14–15.

28. Thanks to Roberta Newman for pointing out that Catherine's tomboy ways are a two-edged sword, and that *Northanger Abbey,* a spoof on gothic novels, suggests that Catherine would have done well to pay more attention to the business of being a woman.

29. All references to the term "tomboy" from *The Oxford English Dictionary,* 2d ed., vol. 17, 211.

30. The Leatherstocking Base Ball Club, *The Origins of Our National Pastime* (Cooperstown, N.Y.: 1992) and *Information for Spectators* (Cooperstown, N.Y.: 1992). As Guttmann points out, Native Americans greeted the Pilgrims with their own forms of stickball, "many of which were clearly courtship or fertility rituals," played by women (8).

31. Peterson, 18.

32. Elizabeth Wayland Barber, *Women's Work: The First 20,000 Years* (New York: W. W. Norton, 1994). John Noble Wilford, in his review of this book, highlights Barber's point that clothing represents power: *New York Times Book Review,* July 10, 1994, 12–13.

33. Jerome Holtzman, ed., *Fielder's Choice: An Anthology of Baseball Fiction* (New York: Harcourt Brace Jovanovich, 1979), 3.

34. *New York Clipper,* 1874, Alfred G. Spalding Baseball Collection, New York Public Library.

35. George Wright, *A Record of the Boston Base Ball Club* (Boston: 1874), Alfred G. Spalding Baseball Collection, New York Public Library.

36. John Montgomery Ward, *Base-Ball: How to Become a Player* (Philadelphia: Athletic Publishing, 1888. Rpt. Cleveland: Society for American Baseball Research, 1993), 9.

37. Ward, 21.

38. Carolyn G. Heilbrun, introduction to *Toward Recognition of Androgyny* (New York: W. W. Norton, 1982), xiii.

39. Kathleen E. McCrone, *Sport and the Physical Emancipation of English Women (1870–1914)* (London: Routledge, 1988), 192, 206.

40. Guttmann, 103. Guttmann points out that none of the teams of the late 1880s was able to tour successfully.

41. Harold Seymour, *Baseball: The People's Game* (New York: Oxford University Press, 1990), 475.

42. *Cincinnati Commercial,* September 28, 1869.

43. "A Lesson to Invalids," *Sporting Life,* April 26, 1890.

44. Tina Baker, personal interview, August 7, 1994.

45. Jessie Ravage, personal interview, August 7, 1994.

46. James R. Tootle, letter to the author, March 29, 2001.

47. Martha Sherwood, personal interview, August 7, 1994.

2. IN THE STANDS: FANS

1. Lyrics, Jack Norworth; Arrangement, Albert Von Tilzer, *Take Me Out to the Ball Game.*

2. Translated: "With kindest regards to Monsieur [Henry] Chadwick." The Alfred G. Spalding Baseball Collection, New York Public Library.

3. Lyrics, H. Angelo; Arrangement, James W. Porter, *The Base Ball Fever* (Philadelphia: Marsh and Bubna, 1867). Courtesy: Milton S. Eisenhower Library, Special Collections, The Johns Hopkins University.

4. Joel Zoss and John Bowman, *Diamonds in the Rough* (New York: Mac-Millan, 1989), 198.

5. Dorothy and Harold Seymour, *Baseball: The Early Years* (New York: Oxford University Press, 1960), 198.

6. Ella Black, "Sensational Rumors," *Sporting Life,* May 10, 1890, 10.

7. "Mysterious Disappearance of the Pet Blonde," *Cincinnati Commercial,* November 16, 1869. Thanks to Darryl Brock for the reference and the idea that the "pet blonde" hints of the ballpark as fashion show. "The pet blonde" appears in Brock's acclaimed novel, *If I Never Get Back:* "I used Maude in my novel—her name and general type, anyway—in connection with pitcher Asa Brainard" (letter from Brock to the author, undated).

8. "She Was Stuck on the Game," *Sporting Life,* April 18, c. 1886.

9. "Young Ladies Talk over Game," *New York Journal,* June 1882.

10. "Made It Three Straight," *New York Daily Tribune,* May 12, 1898.

11. Baseball historian Peter Morris of SABR argues that the free admission of women "was a common practice from the earliest efforts to collect admission at baseball games," citing the game of June 8, 1866, played by the Detroit Base Ball Club and the Washington Base Ball Club of Bay City, Michigan: men paid ten cents, women got in free. Morris argues, "I believe that free admission for women spectators continued to be the rule for many years ("First Ladies' Day," SABR-L, November 25, 1999).

12. Marshall K. McClelland, "Baseball's Pioneer," *Pacific Stars and Stripes*, 16.

13. Black, "Natural Gas Surprises," *Sporting Life*, May 8, 1890, 9.

14. Vance Garnett, "The Day Baseball Took a Beating," *Washington Post*, June 12, 2000, sec. B, p. 6.

15. Ella Black, "An Eastern View," *Sporting Life*, June 21, 1890, 8.

16. W.C.C., "Admit the Women Free," *Baseball*, August 1908, 42.

17. Henry Chadwick, "The Sin of Kicking," *Baseball*, November 1908, 20. As late as 1906, Chadwick still referred to baseball as an "amateur fraternity."

18. Ina Eloise Young, "Petticoats and the Press Box," *Baseball*, May 1908, 53.

19. Orel L. Geyer, "A Fair Fan," *Baseball*, October 1909, 71; Lulu Glaser, "The Lady Fan," *Baseball*, September 1909, 20.

20. E. W. Dunn, "Stella the Stellar Star," *Baseball*, September 1908, 58.

21. The St. Louis Browns' history with Ladies' Day illustrates the ups and downs of the tradition. As early as 1883, the Browns admitted women free to Ladies' Gala Day and handed out souvenir paper fans. Lloyd Rickart, the club secretary in the early 1900s, recalled a Ladies' Day from his era that landed the club "in trouble. Girls from a nearby high school came in droves and occupied all the seats to the exclusion of paying customers." (Letter to the editor, *Sporting News*, June 19, 1938).

22. Gerald Holland, "Mr. Rickey and the Game," *The Best American Sports Writing of the Century*, ed. David Halberstam (Boston: Houghton Mifflin, 1999), 228.

23. Richard Ben Cramer, *Joe DiMaggio: The Hero's Life* (New York: Simon and Schuster, 2000), 59.

24. Paul Debono, *The Indianapolis ABCs: History of a Premier Team in the Negro Leagues ABCs* (Jefferson, N.C.: McFarland, 1997), 55–56.

25. David Pietrusza, "Grace Coolidge—The First Lady of Baseball," *Elysian Fields Quarterly* 12, no. 2 (1993): 36–39. Information on Grace Coolidge also came from Maryann Hudson, "Decades of Bipartisan Support," *Los Angeles Times*, July 7, 1992, sec. C, p. 6.

26. Letter from Pietrusza to the author, February 4, 1994.

27. Margaret Truman, *Bess W. Truman* (New York: Macmillan, 1986), 427–28

28. Harry Shelland, "Fair Fans 'Crash' Ball Games, Cheer Plays," *Police Gazette*, July 11, 1931, 7, 15.

29. Charline Gibson and Michael Rich, *A Wife's Guide to Baseball* (New York: Viking, 1970), v.

30. Dan Daniel, "Mary, Lollie, Hilda—Loudest Fans in Stands," *Sporting News*, February 2, 1963, 1.

31. J. G. T. Spink, "Looping the Loops," *Sporting News*, April 23, 1943.

32. Spink.

33. Red Smith, "'Happy Birthday, Miss Ruby'—Yaz," *New York Times*, July 24, 1972.

34. Lil Levant, telephone interview, September 15, 1994.

35. Aviva Kempner, *The Life and Times of Hank Greenberg* (Washington, D.C.: Ciesla Foundation, 1998).

36. Oscar Kahan, "Gals Watch Baseball—and Enjoy It, Too—Video Survey Shows," *Sporting News,* December 7, 1963.

37. Betty Friedan, lecture, University of Southern California, January 13, 1993.

38. Eleanor McMenimen, "Yankee Fan," *Newark Sunday News,* March 30, 1969, 17.

39. Grace Lichtenstein, "They'd Rather Break a Date Than Miss a Game," *TV Guide,* March 6, 1976, 9.

40. Marcy Bachmann, "Back to the Old Ball Game," *Oakland Tribune,* October 7, 1975.

41. Bill Kirwin, personal interview, March 17, 2001; Magna Global USA, from Sam Walker, "Strike Averted, Baseball Teams Try to Woo Fans," *Wall Street Journal,* September 3, 2002.

42. Gerald Eskenazi, "In the Stands, Many Cheers Have a Higher Pitch," *New York Times* June 6, 1977, sec. C, p. 35.

43. Untitled clipping, February 24, 1979, Baseball Hall of Fame Library.

44. Anna Newton, telephone interview, June 25, 2003.

45. Vanalyne Green, "Mother Baseball." *Diamonds Are a Girl's Best Friend,* ed Elinor Nauen (Boston: Faber and Faber, 1992), 226.

46. "Guys and Gals Hit It Off at Baseball Games," *Baseball Weekly,* August 8, 2000.

47. Brittany and Phil Tennyson, personal interviews, March 13, 1993.

48. Levant, personal interview, June 25, 1994.

49. Aviva Kempner, telephone conversation, August 15, 2001.

50. Black, "Only a Woman," *Sporting Life,* April 12, 1890, 4.

51. Nancy Moran, "For Women, Home Is Where the Plate Is," *New York Times,* September 26, 1969, 6.

52. Diane Lesniewski, letter, "Baseball Has Plenty for the Female Fan," *USA Today/Baseball Weekly,* October 19, 1994, 27.

53. Debbi Dagavarian, "Yes, Costas Is Cute," SABR-L@apple.ease.lsoft.com. October 31, 2000.

54. Alicia Fombona, "Views of Pitcher Fernando Valenzuela," Letters to the editor, *Los Angeles Times,* July 13, 2001, sec. B, p. 14.

55. Green, 225.

56. The four-hour-and-three-minute game, played on May 17, 1979, ended with a record-breaking 97 total bases. When it was over, Pete Rose said, "What's everybody so excited about? Just another one-run ballgame." Courtesy Bill Deane, SABR, and Joseph J. Dittmar, *Baseball Records Registry* (Jefferson, N.C.: McFarland, 1997).

57. Stephanie Leathers, personal interview, June 27, 1994.

3. IN THE SHADOWS: BASEBALL ANNIES

1. Roberta Israeloff, "City Ball," *Diamonds Are a Girl's Best Friend,* ed. Elinor Nauen (Boston: Faber and Faber, 1994), 85.2. Jim Bouton, *Ball Four* (Briarcliff Manor, N.Y.: Stein and Day, 1981), 38.

3. Bouton, 218.

4. Pam Postema and Gene Wojciechowski, *You've Got to Have Balls to Make It in This League* (New York: Simon and Schuster, 1992), 215.

5. *The New Dickson Baseball Dictionary* cites the term "Baseball Annie" as "given prominence after the Phillies' Eddie Waitkus was shot without provocation on June 15, 1949. 'He sat up in bed and tolerantly described [his assailant] as a "Baseball Annie"'" (*Dickson* quotes Peter Tammony's *Time* magazine article of June 17, 1949).

6. Ron Shelton, *Bull Durham,* with Kevin Costner and Susan Sarandon, Rank/Orion/Mount, 1988.

7. Dana Kennedy, "Baseball Annies' Swing in Annual Racy Rite of Spring," *Arizona Republic,* April 2, 1992, sec. A, p. 2.

8. Dan Gutman, *Baseball Babylon* (New York: Penguin Books, 1992), 2.

9. "Mysterious Disappearance of the Pet Blonde," *Cincinnati Commercial,* November 16, 1869. Darryl Brock uses the motif of "the pet blonde" in his novel *If I Never Get Back.*

10. Jules Tygiel, *Past Time: Baseball as History* (New York: Oxford University Press, 2000), 19.

11. Ella Black, "Only a Woman," *Sporting Life,* April 12, 1890, 7.

12. David Pietrusza makes this point in *Judge and Jury: The Life and Times of Judge Kenesaw Mountain Landis* (South Bend, Ind.: Diamond Communications, 1998), 405. Johnson's motivation, however, was apparently not so much the fear of groupies as the fear of losing to blacks.

13. Pietrusza, 511n.

14. Review of *Papa Jack: Jack Johnson and the Era of White Hopes,* by Randy Roberts, *Journal of Sport History* 11, no. 2 (1984): 90.

15. R. Reese, "The Socio-Political Context of the Integration of Sport in America," *Journal of African American Men,* Spring 1999.

16. Review of *Black Hero in a White Land,* by Chris Mead, *Sports Illustrated,* September 16, 1985, 17.

17. Gene Wojciechowski, "Sam Lacy: Force Behind Integration of Baseball," *Chicago Tribune,* July 20, 1997, sec. C, p. 16.

18. Roger Kahn, *The Boys of Summer,* (New York: Harper and Row, 1972), 390.

19. Henry Aaron with Lonnie Wheeler, *I Had a Hammer* (New York: Harper-Collins Publishers, 1991), 89. Thanks to Charlie Vascellaro for the lead on the Aaron incident.

20. Kahn, *The Era: 1947–1957* (New York: Ticknor and Fields, 1993), 189.

21. Al Demaree, "Grandstand Girls," *Collier's,* January 3, 1929.

22. Jimmie Reese, personal interview, April 20, 1989.

23. Betty [pseudonym], "Baseball and Me: A Lifelong Romance," unpublished.

24. Kennedy.

25. Bouton, 218.

26. Betty, personal interview, May 13, 1992.

27. Shelton.

28. Carolyn G. Heilbrun, *Toward a Recognition of Androgyny* (New York: W. W. Norton, 1982), 4.

29. Anonymous, personal interview, March 7, 1992.

30. Susan Zeidler, "Gloria Steinem Focuses on Building the Next Generation of Feminists," *Orange County Register,* June 7, 1992, sec. G, p. 3.

31. Kennedy.

32. Steve Jacobson, "A Reminder: The Road Will Make a Bum of the Best of Them," *Newsday,* February 26, 1989, sec. III, p. 1.

33. Jacobson.

34. Bouton, 218.

35. Kennedy.

36. Patrick Goldstein, "An Outta-the-Ballpark Look at Baseball," *Los Angeles Times,* June 21, 1988, sec. VI, p. 1.

37. George Vecsey, "Sports of the Times: For Polonia, a New Leaf and Season," *New York Times,* April 13, 1990, sec. A, p. 23

38. Bouton, 284.

39. Gutman, 7.

40. David D. Shumacher, "Fielder's Choice," *Penthouse,* May 1989, 51.

41. Robyn Norwood, "Polonia Hopes to Give Angels a Quick Start," *Los Angeles Times,* March 3, 1992, sec. C, p. 1.

42. Susan Fornoff, *Lady in the Locker Room: Uncovering the Oakland Athletics* (Champaign, Ill.: Sagamore Publishing, 1993), 118.

43. I am indebted to Bill Kirwin and George Gmelch for suggesting the mutual insecurities of groupies and players.

44. George Gmelch, *Inside Pitch* (Washington, D.C.: Smithsonian Institution Press, 2001), 42.

45. Dianne Klein, "On the Road Again," *Los Angeles Times,* March 10, 1989, sec. IX, p. 1.

46. Phyllis Goldfarb, e-mail to author, August 12, 1999.

47. Demaree.

48. Gutman, 36.

49. Dick Young, "Young Ideas," *New York Daily News,* December 3, 1971, 101.

50. Bobbie Bouton and Nancy Marshall, *Home Games* (New York: St. Martin's/Marek, 1983), 141.

51. Bob Nightengale, "Learning from Love Lost," *USA Today Baseball Weekly,* April 14, 1999, 9.

52. Paul A. Nakonezny, Robert D. Schull, and Joseph Lee Rodgers, "The Effect of No-Fault Divorce Law on the Divorce Rate Across the Fifty States and

Its Relation to Income, Education, and Religiosity," *Journal of Marriage and the Family* 57 (1995): 477–88.

53. National Center for Health Statistics and U.S. Census Bureau.

54. Tom House, *The Jock's Itch: The Fast-Track Private World of the Professional Ballplayer* (Chicago: Contemporary Books, 1989), 126–27.

55. Julie Cart, "Sports Heroes, Social Villains," *Los Angeles Times,* February 2, 1992, sec. C, p. 3.

56. Tom Weir and Erik Brady, "In Sexual Assault Cases, Athletes Usually Walk, *USA Today,* December 21, 2003. <http://usatoday.com/sports/2003-12-22-athletes-assault-side_x.htm>.

57. Jeff Blair, "Future Uncertain for Perez," *Montreal Gazette,* September 26, 1995, sec. D, p. 10.

58. David Goldiner and Rafael Hermoso, "Young Met Rape Rap," *New York Daily News,* July 7, 1998, 38.

59. Rafael Hermoso, "Met Minors in Major Trouble," *New York Daily News,* July 5, 1998, 68.

60. Hermoso, "Harsh Reality Dampens Dreams," *New York Daily News,* July 6, 1998, 48.

61. Hermoso, "Met Minors in Major Trouble."

62. *Sixty Minutes,* CBS-TV, April 15, 2001.

63. John P. Carmichael, "The Barber Shop," *Chicago Daily News,* April 4, 1946.

64. "Girl Isn't Sorry She Shot Eddie," *New York Post,* June 16, 1949.

65. "Frank Yeutter, "Phils Star Gets Transfusions in Chicago Hospital," *Bulletin,* June 15, 1949.

66. "A Report to Felony Court," The Behavior Clinic. Rpt. in *The New York Baseball Reader,* by Charles Einstein (New York: Penguin, 1991), 130. Thanks to Phil Francis for this reference.

67. Ed Pollock, "Playing the Game," *Bulletin,* June 16, 1949.

68. Barry Levinson, *The Natural,* with Robert Redford, Robert Duvall, Glen Close, and Kim Basinger, AGM, 1984.

69. Harley Henry, "'Them Dodgers Is My Gallant Knights': Fiction as History in *The Natural,*" *Journal of Sport History* 19, no. 2 (1992): 121.

70. Shelton.

71. Rich Ashburn, "Waitkus Tragedy Recalled," April 22, 1975. National Baseball Hall of Fame Library.

72. John Theodore, *Baseball's Natural: The Story of Eddie Waitkus* (Carbondale: Southern Illinois University Press, 2002), 94.

73. *Playing the Field: Sports and Sex in America* (HBO-TV, 1999). Dan Klein, producer; narr. by Liev Schreiber.

4. FOR LOVE OF THE GAME: AMATEUR PLAYERS

1. Shirley Povich, who died June 4, 1998, was the father of television executive Maury Povich.

2. Jim Glennie, e-mail to the author, August 5, 1999.

3. Game between the Ocala Lightning and the Chicago Storm, Bethesda, Md., September 3, 1999.

4. Dorothy and Harold Seymour, *Baseball: The People's Game* (New York: Oxford University Press, 1990), 447. This history features an entire section devoted to women's baseball.

5. "Teams Made Up Mostly of Girls to Play Baseball at Forest Hills," *Boston Herald,* August 31, 1903.

6. John Egan, telephone interview, May 13, 1993.

7. Information regarding the game of softball from the Amateur Softball Association web site: <http://www.softball.org>.

8. Annie Dillard, *An American Childhood* (New York: HarperPerennial, 1988), 100.

9. *Junior Baseball Handbook of the American Legion, Official Rules and Guide for 1929 Competitions* (Indianapolis: National Americanism Commission, 1929), 3.

10. See Kent M. Krause, "From Americanism to Athleticism: A History of the American Legion Junior Baseball Program," (PhD diss., University of Nebraska, 1998), 260.

11. Jerry Izenberg, "The Girl Pitcher Who Took Puerto Rico by Storm," *New York Post,* May 27, 1983.

12. Carolyn Heilbrun, introduction to *Toward a Recognition of Androgyny* (New York: W. W. Norton, 1964), xiv.

13. "Achieving Success under Title IX," December 8, 1999, <http://www.ed.gov/pubs/TitleIX/part5.html>.

14. Michele McCormick, personal interview, August 8, 2000.

15. David Corr, "She Was First on Second for the Little League," *Vineyard (Mass.) Gazette,* September 3, 1986, 6. Corr's article refers to "Guys Are Playing with Dolls," which appeared April 24, 1974, in the *New York Daily News.*

16. "Title IX: A Sea Change in Gender Equity in Education," <http://www.ed.gov/pubs/TitleIX/part3.html>.

17. In the late 1960s, working women had few options other than teacher, secretary, airline stewardess, or nurse. Even those low-paid professions had barriers: In 1966, when the daughter of the president of the United States, Luci Baines Johnson, attempted to continue her studies at Georgetown University's School of Nursing after her marriage, she was turned down. The school did not admit married women as students. As late as 1970, state law forbade women, single or married, from attending the University of Virginia's prestigious College of Arts and Sciences.

18. Richard W. Riley, "Title IX: Twenty-Five Years of Progress," <http://www.ed.gov/pubs/TitleIX/part1.html>.

19. Figures on girls' athletic participation courtesy Women's Sports Foundation.

20. "Title IX: Twenty-Five Years of Progress—June 1997 Achieving Success under Title IX." <http://www.ed.gov/pubs/TitleIX/part5.html>.

21. Sue Lukasik, personal interview, September 5, 1999.

22. Joe Moschetti, telephone interview, July 15, 1999.

23. Ila Borders, personal interviews, February 9 and May 2, 1999; telephone interview March 9, 1999.

24. Barbie Ludovise, "Despite Taunts, She's Undaunted about Crossing These Borders," *Los Angeles Times,* February 5, 1993, sec. C, p. 7.

25. Rolland Esslinger, telephone interview, May 19, 1999.

26. Ludovise.

27. Steve Randall, telephone interview, June 4, 1999.

28. Miki Turner, "She won't be in a league of her own," *Orange County Register,* February 5, 1993, 1.

29. Martin Beck, "SCC Baseball Signs a Woman, Makes History," *Los Angeles Times,* February 5, 1993, sec. C, p. 1.

30. "Pitcher Takes Loss, Verbal Abuse," *Arizona Republic,* March 6, 1994, sec. D, p. 2.

31. Richard Dunn, "Charlie Phillips: SoCal College," *Newport Beach/Costa Mesa Daily Pilot,* May 20, 1999, sec. B, p. 1.

32. Letter to Ila Borders from Dusty Baker, February 24, 1994.

33. "Borders Has Come," *Nikkan Sports,* July 30, 1994.

34. Borders's record in her year at Whittier College reads: 17 games; 81 innings, 118 hits, 71 runs, 47 earned runs, 25 walks, 38 strikeouts, 5.22 ERA, 4 wins, and 5 losses.

35. Julie Barela, SABR national conference, June 27, 1999.

36. Justine Siegal, personal interview, September 4, 1999.

37. Jessica and Denise Nardone, personal interviews, September 4, 1999

38. Jim Glennie, personal interview, September 3, 1999.

39. Jim Glennie, e-mail to the author, October 31, 1999.

40. Brown to Darlene Mahrer, March 30, 1988.

41. Glennie is one of a number of entrepreneurs who finds women's amateur baseball exciting. In 1993, Mike Boyd, the brother of pitcher Dennis "Oil Can" Boyd, formed two teams in Los Angeles that lasted a year. In 1994, the men of the National Adult Baseball Association (NABA) decided to start a for-profit women's league. Leagues were organized in New York, Florida, Washington, and California; however, none lasted more than three years.

42. Justine Siegal, telephone interview, May 7, 2003

43. John Corbett, "'Just One of the Boys,'" (undated clipping, author's collection).

44. Glennie, personal interview, September 3, 1999.

5. FOR LOVE AND MONEY: PROFESSIONAL PLAYERS

1. "Coming! Coming!" *New York Clipper,* September 22, 1883.

2. "Blondes and Brunettes at Baseball." National Baseball Hall of Fame Library.

3. *New York Times,* September 23, 1883. National Baseball Hall of Fame Library.

4. Jean C. Robertson, "Women in Sports and What They Wore: 1880–1915" (thesis, State University of New York: Cooperstown, N.Y., 1978), 38.

5. "The League Clubs Keep out of the Rain but the Females Play," *New Orleans Daily Picayune,* January 5, 1885, 8.

6. *St. Louis Globe-Democrat,* April 11, 1886. Quoted also in Robertson, 32.

7. "A Disgraceful Move," *Sporting Life,* August 30, 1890, 9.

8. Oscar Ruhl, "The Ruhl Book," *Sporting News,* July 9, 1952. Before her debut in Reading, Lizzie Arlington played briefly for the Philadelphia Reserves, earning $100 a week, and for the New York Athletic Club.

9. "Bloomer Ball Tossers," *Cincinnati Enquirer,* July 20, 1903.

10. "Base Ball," *Jeffersonville (Ind.) News,* May 18, 1908.

11. Dick Reynolds, "Lizzie Murphy: Queen of Diamonds," *Old Rhode Island* 4, no. 3 (1994): 12. Murphy made baseball history on August 14, 1922. In a two-inning appearance for the American League All-Stars against the Boston Red Sox, she handled a grounder at first and went 0–1 at bat—the first woman to play, however briefly, Major League baseball. On September 7, 1936, Sonny Dunlap played a full game as right fielder for the Fayetteville (Arkansas-Missouri League) Bears, going 0 for 3, with no fielding chances.

12. Nettie Gans Spangler, diary, National Baseball Hall of Fame Library.

13. Nettie Gans Spangler, undated letter to the Baseball Hall of Fame.

14. Edith Houghton, telephone interview, January 16, 2004.

15. Carpenter reportedly "grinned" as he made the announcement of Houghton's signing as a scout. "Know I'm going to take a ride on this," he told the *Washington Post.* "But by gosh, I sure hope she comes in here with a real prospect someday. I'll have the laugh then." ("Phillies Sign Former Wave as a Scout," *Washington Post,* February 16, 1946.)

16. Barbara Gregorich, "In '30s, Women Got in the Game," *USA Today Baseball Weekly,* June 24–30, 1992, 34.

17. "This Woman *Did* Bat in the Major Leagues," *Albany Times Union,* July 31, 1985.

18. Toni Stone, telephone interview, August 17, 1992.

19. James A. Riley, "Lady at the Bat," *Diamond,* March/April 1994, 22.

20. "The Gal on Second Base." National Baseball Hall of Fame Library.

21. "Is Negro League Baseball Through?" *Our Sports.* National Baseball Hall of Fame Library.

22. The film *A League of Their Own* alludes to the league's segregation in a brief scene: a black woman retrieves a ball and throws a zinger over catcher Geena Davis's head. No words are exchanged, nor are they necessary; the look that passes between the two acknowledges the black woman's ability and segregation's denial of her freedom to be a part of the league.

23. Marjorie L. Pieper, "Chapter," 3. National Baseball Hall of Fame Library.

24. When the players' association was formed in the late 1980s, it adopted the current, and presumably final, name, the All-American Girls Baseball League.

25. Ron Berler, "Mama Was a Major-Leaguer," *Arizona Republic,* October 4, 1987, sec. F, p. 1.

26. Don H. Black, *Racine (Wis.) Belle,* March 22, 1950, 1.

27. Don H. Black, *Racine (Wis.) Belle,* April 18, 1950, 4.

28. Joanne Winter, personal interview, April 15, 1992.

29. Helen Hannah Campbell, memo to the author, undated, and personal interview, September 9, 1993.

30. Jack Finchen, "The 'Belles of the Ball Game' Were a Hit with their Fans." National Baseball Hall of Fame Library.

31. Susan Johnson, *When Women Played Hardball* (Seattle: Seal Press, 1994), 115.

32. *Sports and Sex in America: Playing the Field in America* (HBO-TV, 1999), Dan Klein, producer; narr. by Live Schreiber.

33. Berler.

34. Frederick C. Klein, "Women Take Swing at Hardball," *Wall Street Journal,* July 9, 1988.

35. Barbara Gregorich, *Women at Play: The Story of Women in Baseball* (New York: Harcourt Brace, 1993), 15.

36. Bulletin 639, June 24, 1952, to Club and League Presidents, from George S. Trautman.

37. Pat Jordan, "The Girls of Summer," *American Way,* June 1992, 38.

38. Berler.

39. "Japan Female Baseball League Formed," *Sankei Shimbum,* March 2, 1993.

40. Barbara Tiritilli, "Gal Makes Pitch for White Sox Job but She Encounters Cool Reception," *Chicago American,* September 11, 1965.

41. Roger O'Gara, "Gloria Jean's Tryout Proves Pretty Failure," *Sporting News,* September 7, 1971.

42. C. C. Johnson Spink, "We Believe," *Sporting News,* August 13, 1977.

43. Furman Bisher, "Girls of Summer: An All-Female Lineup for the Sun Sox?" *Sporting News,* October 1, 1984, 7.

44. Pete Williams, "Women Share Passion for Diamond," *Baseball Weekly,* March 16, 1994, 62.

45. Susan Fornoff, "Playing Hardball," *Sporting News,* May 30, 1994, 16.

46. Dave Kindred, "For Love, Not Money, *Sporting News,* December 5, 1994, 7.

47. Fornoff, 15

48. Leslie Petty, "'War Between the Sexes' or 'A League of Their Own.'" Diamonds in the Desert Baseball Conference, Arizona State University, March 1998.

49. Peterson, 18.

50. Brendan Lemon, "Letter from the Editor," *Out,* May 2001.

51. Jim Caple, "Baseball's Toughest 'Out,' ESPN.com <http://espn.go.com/page2/s/caple/010523.html>.

52. Gai Ingham Berlage, "The Colorado Bullets," *Baseball Research Journal* 27 (1998): 40.

53. Dave Kindred, *The Colorado Silver Bullets: For Love of the Game* (Atlanta: Longstreet Press, 1995), 47.

54. Phil Borders, telephone interview, June 18, 1999.

55. Ila Borders, personal interview, May 2, 1999.

56. In Game 2 of the 2001 American League Divisional Series, the Seattle Mariners left-hander, Jamie Moyer (6'0", 170 lbs.), started the must-win game. Moyer won easily, 5–1, but his velocity drew special attention. The *Los Angeles Times* noted that he never once hit 90 mph on the radar gun, and wondered at the 77-mph pitch that struck out slugger Jim Thome, and a 76-mph called third strike: "There were dozens of changeups and soft curves, pitches that barely broke the speed limit but seemed to break the Indians' spirit." Seattle's manager Lou Piniella explained, "[Moyer's] not a power pitcher, obviously, but there's different ways to skin a cat. And he does it the sly way." Moyer, virtually apologizing, said, "That's all I have to offer. . . . I can't reach back and throw 95 mph. So I feel like I have to use the abilities that I have and try to find ways to get people out." "Notes," *Los Angeles Times*, October 12, 2001, sec. D, p. 12.

57. Mike Veeck, telephone interview, July 13, 1999. During the late 1970s, Mike Veeck was hired by his father, Bill, who then owned the Chicago White Sox. The Veecks' dream of finding that woman was derailed by their errant genius for promotion when Mike came up with the idea of Disco Demolition Night in 1979. Over the radio, the invitation went out to fans to bring their old disco records on July 2 to Comiskey Park, to be destroyed in one grand bonfire between games of a doubleheader. But records are convenient missiles, and the evening culminated in a riot that became a part of baseball legend. Mike Veeck found out the hard way what happens to the game's unorthodox thinkers—he was out of Organized Baseball.

58. "Woman Breaks Gender-Barrier with Saints," *Dimension*, WCCO, St. Paul, May 8, 1997.

59. Pat Jordan, *A Nice Tuesday* (New York: Golden Books, 1999), 167.

60. Neal Karlen, *Slouching Toward Fargo* (New York: Avon Books, 1999, 290.

61. Karlen, 299.

62. Karlen, 301.

63. Karlen, 311.

64. Mike Wallace, *Sixty Minutes*, "A League of Her Own," October 4, 1998, WCBS-TV.

65. Steve Shirley, personal interview, June 8, 1999.

66. "Ila Borders Gives Herself the Hook, Retires, *Los Angeles Times*, July 1, 2000 sec. D, p.10.

67. A. Bartlett Giamatti, *Take Time for Paradise* (New York: Simon and Schuster, 1989), 82.

68. Annie Leibovitz and Susan Sontag, *Women* (New York: Random House, 1999), 18.

6. BEHIND THE PLATE: UMPIRES

1. Although a number of umpires have not had their contracts renewed for various reasons, only one, Richard "Dick" Higham has ever been expelled, for colluding with gamblers in 1882. For a discussion of the Higham case, see Larry R. Gerlach and Harold V. Higham, "Dick Higham: An Umpire at the Bar of History," *National Pastime*, no. 20 (Cleveland: SABR Publications, 2000), 20–32.

2. The New York Knickerbockers' game books are part of a collection of Henry Chadwick's papers, housed in the A. G. Spalding Baseball Collection, the New York Public Library.

3. Mark Alvarez, "Baseball's First Lady Ump," undated monograph. Thanks to Mark Alvarez for the background on early umpires.

4. During the late 1800s, the role of umpire was hardly a profession. The National League did not hire its first paid umpire until 1876; by 1878, home teams were paying $5 per game for the job of umpiring. The first umpire training school opened in 1935. Source: MLB.com.

5. "Pioneer Woman Umpire," *Denver Post*, October 21, 1905

6. "Pioneer Woman Umpire.

7. "She Can Umpire: There Are No Kicks Because Players Are Gallant," *Enquirer*, September 8, 1905.

8. Will Chamberlain, "Queen of the Diamond," c. 1905. National Baseball Hall of Fame Library.

9. "Pioneer."

10. "She Can Umpire."

11. Joe McCarron, "Woman-Ump Gimmick Given Fast Heave-Ho in Frick Edict," *Sporting News*, August 31, 1960, 37.

12. "And Now . . . The Rest of the Story," *Referee*, May 1979, 24.

13. "Lady Umpires?" *Columbus Citizen-Journal*, May 8, 1968.

14. Charles McCabe, "The Fearless Spectator," *San Francisco Chronicle*, c. 1969.

15. "Housewife Learning to Call 'Em Out at Home," *New York Times*, June 13, 1967.

16. Nora Ephron, "Women," *Esquire*, January 1973, 36, 40.

17. "Housewife."

18. Edward Doherty, administrator of the Umpire Development Committee, in a letter dated April 23, 1968, wrote that he told "this person [Gera] that . . . required height is 5'10", required weight approximately 170 pounds, required age between 21 and 35. . . . I do not feel that there has been any discrimination. . . . You may be sure that [the committee] has only one objective in mind—to better umpiring."

19. Blacks moved more quickly onto Organized Baseball's diamonds as players than as umpires. The first black minor league umpire was not hired until 1961, fifteen years after Jack Robinson broke the color line with the Montreal

Royals. Major League baseball did not see its first black umpire until 1966 and did not see its first Hispanic umpire until 1974.

20. William Travers, "No Lady Oomphires Need Apply," *Oneonta (N.Y.) Star,* October 25, 1969.

21. "And Now," 27.

22. Dave Anderson, "Woman Umpire Returns to Plates at Home, *New York Times,* June 26, 1972, 44; undated clipping, National Baseball Hall of Fame Library.

23. Ephron, 36.

24. Will Grimsley, "Bernice Leaves Dishes in Sink," April 23, 1972. National Baseball Hall of Fame Library.

25. Ephron, 40.

26. Herme Shore, "So Long, Bernice," *Seaford-Wantaugh (N.Y.) Observer,* October 26, 1978, 2.

27. Bill Heward with Dimtri V. Gat, *Some Are Called Clowns* (New York: Thomas Y. Crowell, 1974), 63.

28. Heward, 4.

29. Karen West, "Passion for Diamonds." National Baseball Hall of Fame Library.

30. "And Now . . .," 14.

31. Dwight Jensen, "Umpire Wren Makes Her Debut Look Routine," *Christian Science Monitor,* June 26, 1975, 12.

32. Gannett.

33. "Interview: Chris Wren," *Referee,* July/August 1977, 13.

34. One of Christine Wren's coworkers acknowledged her contribution to his career. In 1995, National League umpire Gerry Davis was asked by *Referee* magazine whether it was "an unusual or difficult experience" to work with her during the 1977 season in the Midwest League. He replied, "I've said a number of times that working with Christine made me a better umpire because I had to deal with many situations at an early time in my career. Many young umpires get so caught up in balls and strikes and safes and outs that they don't realize the importance of handling situations. Handling situations correctly separates a minor league umpire from a major league umpire." "Gerry Davis: Interview," *Referee,* May 1995, 74.

35. Gannett.

36. "The Female Official," *Referee,* June 1979, 9.

37. Julie Zeller Ware, personal interview, September 21, 1992.

38. Perry Barber, telephone interview, March 2, 2004.

39. Theresa Cox, telephone interview, March 23, 2004.

40. Pam Postema and Gene Wojciechowski, *You've Got to Have Balls to Make It in This League* (New York: Random House, 1992), 37–38.

41. Joe Biddle, "Umpiring Is No Ego Trip for Pam," June 23, 1979. National Baseball Hall of Fame Library.

42. Postema and Wojciechowski, 162.

43. Postema and Wojciechowski, 131–40.

44. Keenan, 45.

45. Keenan, 44.

46. Ira Berkow, "Sports of the Times," *New York Times,* March 22, 1988. Bob Knepper did not stop at criticizing Postema's right to be an umpire. In June 1988, *Sports Illustrated* quoted Knepper on the National Organization for Women. "NOW is such a blowhard organization. They are a bunch of lesbians. Their focus has nothing to do with women's rights. It had everything to do with women wanting to be men."

47. Berkow.

48. Mike Downey, "Knepper: Women Shouldn't Be at Home (Plate)," *Los Angeles Times,* March 16, 1988.

49. Postema, telephone interview, March 29, 2002.

50. Joe Garagiola, personal interview, March 6, 1992.

51. "Briefly Speaking," *Referee,* February 1993, 14.

52. Bart Wright, "Yer Out! And She Says So," *Greenville News,* July 10, 2003.

53. Anonymous, personal interview.

54. Dave Pallone with Alan Steinberg, *Behind the Mask: My Double Life in Baseball* (New York: Viking, 1990), 223. The noted anonymous sports historian adds, "Guys go nuts when they find out there are homosexuals in the Hall of Fame. As for current players, you don't mention names when it can mean someone's career." And Pallone corroborates this point: "[A]lthough I knew through rumors on the gay scene that there were quite a few gay major league players, we had no network or signaling system to identify each other on the field. Like me, other guys realized that revelation to the wrong people in the game could ruin their careers." At a time when a number of scandals had touched others in baseball, Pallone wondered, "How could they allow people who were guilty of breaking laws to continue their careers, but then turn around and force me out for being *innocent?* What was the message there—that baseball considered manslaughter [Cesar Cedeno], political corruption [George Steinbrenner's illegal campaign contribution], solicitation [pitcher Bryn Smith], and sex with a female minor [Luis Polonia] more acceptable than being gay?" (321).

55. Albert Kilchesty, "The Shrine of the Eternals: 2000 Electees," Monrovia, Cal.: Baseball Reliquary.

56. Jim Evans, personal interview, July 12, 2003.

57. Ria Cortesio, telephone interviews, March 30 and May 4, 2002. Cortesio's full name is Maria Cortesio Papageorgiou.

58. Ria Cortesio, e-mail, June 15, 2002.

59. Kary Booher, "Just Like One of the Guys," Jacksonsun.com.

7. IN THE FRONT OFFICE: CLUB OWNERS AND EXECUTIVES

1. Nancy Mazmanian, personal interview, November 21, 2002.

2. *The New Dickson Baseball Dictionary* (New York: Harcourt Brace, 1999),

ed. Paul Dickson. Dickson traces the term "front office" to two 1948 newspaper articles and adds, "The term has a long history as an underworld term for police headquarters, an interrogation room, or the warden's office in a prison."

3. The owners of the Cleveland Spiders and the St. Louis Cardinals swapped franchises in 1899.

4. "My Experience as a Big League Owner," *Baseball,* February 1917, 13.

5. Ed Bang, "Cleveland Chat," July 3, 1915. National Baseball Hall of Fame Library.

6. "How Just One Word Kept Woman Magnate in Game," January 6, 1916. National Baseball Hall of Fame Library.

7. George Biggers, "Winning the Pennant in the American Association, *Baseball,* January 1914, 46.

8. Information about Olivia Taylor came from Jules Tygiel's *Past Time,* Paul Debono's *The Indianapolis ABCs,* and from Leslie Heaphy.

9. Debono, 95.

10. Debono, 98.

11. Debono, 101.

12. Letter to the author, Bill Ellis, July 18, 1992.

13. News clipping c. February 18, 1978. National Baseball Hall of Fame Library.

14. Allan Morris, "Mrs. Sandlin's Temporary Job of '31 Comes to End," July 20, 1968. National Baseball Hall of Fame Library.

15. Lawrence Hogan, James Overmyer, and James DiClerico, "Black Baseball as Black Comfortability," Cooperstown Symposium on Baseball, Cooperstown, New York, June 17, 1992, 5.

16. Gai Berlage, "Effa Manley," Cooperstown Symposium on Baseball, June 16, 1992, Cooperstown, New York.

17. Hogan, Overmyer, and DiClerico, 8. *(Baltimore Afro American,* February 10, 1940). For background information on Effa Manley, I relied upon the work of Hogan, DiClerico, and, in particular, Overmyer and Berlage.

18. John Holway, *SABR-L Digest,* August 18–20, 2000, no. 2000-288.

19. Hogan, 10. (Amiri Baraka, *The Autobiography of Leroi Jones* [New York: Freundlich, 1984], 33).

20. Hogan, 15. (Baraka, 34).

21. Thanks to George Gmelch for pointing this out.

22. "Directs Woman Fans," April 13, 1939, 33. National Baseball Hall of Fame Library.

23. Joe Falls, "Bengals' G.M.s Come and Go, Efficient Alice Outlasts 'Em All," *Detroit Free Press,* March 21, 1964.

24. Marvin West, "Bonnie's Business Manager Directs Knoxville's Office," April 6, 1963. National Baseball Hall of Fame Library.

25. Dottie Enrico, "Breaking the Glass Ceiling," *Newsday,* March 17, 1994, sec. A, p. 92.

26. Charline Gibson and Michael Rich, *A Wife's Guide to Baseball* (New York: Viking Press, 1970), 19–20.

27. Background information for this section came from *The Baseball Encyclopedia* (New York: Macmillan Publishing, 1993), 9th ed.

28. Charlotte Lazarus Witkind, letter, *New York Times,* May 20, 1973.

29. "It's Still a Long Haul for Women in Baseball," *New York Times,* July 27, 1987.

30. Bill Koenig, "Boston Sports Loses a Gracious, Giving Friend," *USA Today Baseball Weekly,* March 4, 1992, 16.

31. Howard Bryant, e-mail to the author, January 14, 2004. Howard Bryant is the author of *Shut Out: A Story of Race and Baseball in Boston* (New York: Routledge, 2002).

32. Craig Muder, "Induction Weekend: Smith Reflects on Outstanding Career," *Utica (N.Y.) Observer-Dispatch,* July 26, 2002.

33. "A Woman's Prerogative," *Sporting News,* June 8, 1987, 26.

34. Tom Gallagher, review of *Field of Schemes: How the Great Stadium Swindle Turns Public Money into Private Profit,* by Joanna Cagan and Neil de Mause, www.zmag.org.

35. Mike Bass, *Marge Schott: Unleashed* (Champaign, Il.: Sagamore Publishing, 1993), 12.

36. Paul Daugherty, "Schott Was Certainly Original," *USA Today Sports Weekly* March 10–16, 2004, 11.

37. Dave Kindred, "Still Not Owning Up," *Sporting News,* December 14, 1992, 5.

38. "Schott's Statements on Race Fuel Concern," *Los Angeles Times,* November 21, 1992, sec. C, p. 6.

39. "Schott's Statements."

40. Anne Mudgett, telephone interview, May 10, 1993.

41. Dottie Enrico, "Breaking the Grass Ceiling," *Newsday,* March 27, 1994, sec. A, p. 92.

42. Bill Conlin, "Is Senior Circuit Fair to Women?" *Philadelphia Daily News,* August 4, 1986, 17.

43. Pat Jordan, "Jocks: The Only Baseball Boss Who's Young, Female and Black, Tracy Lewis Holds the Cards in Savannah," *People Weekly,* May 18, 1987, 108.

44. Jordan, 108.

45. Information on the Savannah franchise came from "Savannah Baseball Milestones," <http:/www.savannahmorningnews.com/features/playball/stats/milestones.html>, November 12, 2002.

46. Stan Grossfeld, "Black Exec Does a Class A Job," *Chicago Tribune,* June 28, 1987, sec. 4, p. 2.

47. Marcus Holland, telephone interview, November 27, 2002.

48. "Oklahoma City's Patty Cox Baseball's Woman of the Year," *Baseball '78,* 48.

49. "It's Still Long Haul for Women in Baseball," *New York Times,* July 27, 1987, sec. C, p. 4.

50. Mindy Rich, personal interview, June 19, 1992.

51. William Plascencia, "A Hands-On Dream Builder," *Hispanic,* October 2002, 40.

52. Linda Alvarado, personal interviews, May 15 and July 17, 1994.

53. Al Lopez had broken new ground as the first Hispanic full-time manager in MLB. Those numbers rose in the 1970s, then declined in the 1980s and 1990s. By 1997, a study by Milton Jamail, of the University of Texas, showed that only one Hispanic executive was involved in ML personnel decisions: the New York Mets assistant general manager Omar Minaya. "Foul Play," *Hispanic,* Angel Rodriguez, April 1999, 54; e-mail from Elain Weddington Steward to the author, July 8, 2003.

54. E-mail from Elaine Weddington Steward to the author, July 8, 2003.

55. Janet Wiscombe, "Diamonds Are This Girl's Best Friend," *Los Angeles Times Magazine* July 14, 2002, 8.

56. Mike Steere, "This Is the Life," *Sports Illustrated Women* March/April, 2002, 94.

57. Jon Herskovitz, "Female Executive Helps to Shape Yankees," *Reuters,* e.library.

58. Peter Schmuck, "Baseball Inside," *Sporting News,* March 16, 1998.

59. Herskovitz.

60. Ken Davidoff, "Mendoza's Work Cut Out," *Bergen County (N.J.) Record,* February 18, 2001, sec. S, p. 13.

61. Michael Krisley, "Yanks Try to Save by ... Spending," *Sporting News,* February 7, 2000, 36.

62. Ben Platt, "Kim Ng Named Dodgers VP and Assistant VP," dodgers.com. December 5, 2001.

63. Wiscombe.

64. Wiscombe.

65. Roland Hemond, telephone interview with the author, April 24, 2002.

66. Cecily J. Fluke, "Female Execs Step Up to the Plate," Forbes.com, April 25, 2003.

67. *Los Angeles Times,* March 24, 2004, sec. D, p. 3.

8. IN THE PRESS BOX: WOMEN IN THE MEDIA

1. Gloria Swegman, "Baseball's Unfair to Women." National Baseball Hall of Fame Library.

2. Thomas McGuane, introduction to *The Best American Sports Writing 1992,* ed. Thomas McGuane (New York: Houghton Mifflin, 1992), xviii.

3. In *Baseball: The Early Years,* Dorothy and Harold Seymour mention a woman who reported on games between the Muffins and the Biscuits for a Cincinnati newspaper in 1868; and another woman, Mrs. Elisha Green Williams,

who served as official scorer for home games of the Chicago White Stockings from 1882–1891. Ella Black, writing in 1890, spoke of Irene Meredith, who wrote for a Cincinnati newspaper.

4. Thanks to Pete Peterson for background on the 1890 Pittsburgh Alleghenies and to Tim Wiles for pointing out that the terms "Burghers" and "Innocents" were unofficial nicknames.

5. Marc Fink, e-mail to author, March 12, 2002.

6. Ella Black, "Natural Gas Surprises," *Sporting Life,* May 8, 1890, 9.

7. Black, "An Eastern View," *Sporting Life,* June 21, 1890, 8.

8. Black, "Sensational Rumors," *Sporting Life,* May 18, 1890, 10.

9. Black, *Sporting Life,* April 19, 1890.

10. Ella Black, "A Woman's View," *Sporting Life,* March 5, 1890, 8.

11. Ina Eloise Young, "Petticoats and the Press Box" *Baseball,* May 1908, 54.

12. Young, 53.

13. Ina Eloise Young, *Chronicle-News,* October 15, 1908, 4.

14. "Miss Young Visits a 'Fellow' Sporting Writer," *Chicago Tribune,* October 11, 1908.

15. Young, "Petticoats," 53.

16. Young, *Chronicle-News,* October 15, 1908, 4.

17. Young, "Petticoats," 53.

18. Jeane Hofmann, "Bleachers Asking for Break—Home Plate in Center Field," *New York Journal-American,* April 29, 1943.

19. Jeane Hofmann, "No 'End' to Jokes, Girl Finds, in Yankee Stadium Press Box," *New York Journal-American,* December 3, 1942.

20. Associated Press dispatch, "Comely Blonde Reporter to Go South with Philadelphia Club," *Washington Post,* February 21, 1942, 19.

21. "The Feminine Touch," March 12, 1942. National Baseball Hall of Fame Library.

22. Hofmann, "No 'End.'"

23. Danny Robbins, "Morning Briefing," *Los Angeles Times,* June 23, 1992, sec. C, p. 2.

24. George Ferrell, the brother of Major Leaguer Wes Ferrell and Hall of Famer Rick, never made it to the show. He was a scout for many years.

25. Mary Garber, telephone interview, May 20, 2002.

26. Dorothy Jane Mills, *A Woman's Work* (Jefferson, N.C.: McFarland, 2004), 10.

27. Mills, "A Woman's Work," www.blueear.com, April 18, 2000.

28. Steven P. Gietschier, foreword to *A Woman's Work,* by Dorothy Jane Mills (Jefferson: N.C., McFarland, 2004), 1.

29. Swegman.

30. Doris O'Donnell, telephone interview, August 6, 2002.

31. "Doris O'Donnell to Cover Tribe," *Cleveland News,* May 14, 1957.

32. Doris O'Donnell, "Stags Keep Doris Out of Yank Press Box," *Cleveland News,* May 20, 1957.

33. From an interview with O'Donnell by Bill Nowlin, September 9, 2002.

34. Jerry Mitchell, "No Wonder Indians Look Better," *New York Post,* May 24, 1957.

35. Charline Gibson and Michael Rich, *A Wife's Guide to Baseball* (New York: Viking Press, 1970), 19.

36. Gibson and Rich, 20.

37. Wells Twombly, "A Woman's Place Is in Broadcast Booth," March 27, 1971. National Baseball Hall of Fame Library.

38. Twombly.

39. Laura White, "Maybe Dame Boston's Got Something to Dream About," *Boston Herald,* July 14, 1973, 21.

40. Marie Brenner, personal interview, November 26, 2003.

41. Marie Brenner, "Girls of Summer," *New York Times,* April 5, 1993, sec. A, p. 17.

42. Daniel Rapoport, "Help Wanted: Women Sportswriters," 1976. National Baseball Hall of Fame Library.

43. Melissa Ludtke Lincoln, "Locker Rooms: Equality With Integrity," *New York Times,* April 15, 1979.

44. Nichole Gantshar, "Claire Smith: An AWSM Pioneer," AWSM Newsletter, Fall 2000, 5.

45. Brenner, "Girls."

46. Susan Fornoff, *Lady in the Locker Room* (Champaign, Il.: Sagamore Publishing, 1993), 109.

47. Alison Gordon, *Foul Ball! Five Seasons in the American League* (New York: Dodd, Mead, 1985), 43.

48. Fornoff, 30.

49. Fornoff, 31.

50. Fornoff, 74–75.

51. Fornoff, 113.

52. Jane Gross, "Female Sportswriters Make Their Mark," *New York Times,* May 26, 1988, sec. D, p. 25: "'We have to act like nuns,' said [Julie] Cart. 'I don't like it but it's a reality.'"

53. Jim Bouton, *Strike Zone* (New York: Viking Press, 1994), 80.

54. Gordon, 137.

55. Jerome Holtzman, telephone interview, September 11, 2002.

56. Michele Himmelberg, personal interview, May 11, 2002.

57. Nichole Gantshar, "Claire Smith: An AUSM Pioneer," *AUSM Newsletter,* Fall 2000, 5.

58. Fornoff, 105.

59. Suzyn Waldman, "From Broadway to Broadcasting," http://www.GirlsCanDo.com.

60. Gallina Espinoza and Joseph V. Tirella, "Woman on First," *People,* October 8, 2001, 132.

61. Suzyn Waldman, telephone interview, February 16, 2005.

62. Comments taken from a survey conducted on SABR-L, 2005.

63. *The Best Damn Sports Show,* Fox Sports Net, KFOX-TV, Los Angeles, August 14, 2002.

64. Erin Harvego, "Women, Sports and Playboy.com," *AWSM,* April 2001, 3.

65. Vin Scully, telephone interview, May 14, 2002.

66. Susan J. Berkson, "America's Real Pastime—Sexism—Is Still Played," *USA Today Baseball Weekly,* October 12–18, 1994, 16.

67. Dorothy Jane Mills, *HSC Baseball History Newsletter,* 3, no. 1 (January 2, 2004), 2.

68. Steven P. Gietschier, e-mail to the author, March 30, 2004. When Sheldon Meyer, the editor of Oxford University Press who worked with the Seymours on the trilogy, learned the extent of Dorothy Seymour's contribution, he sent her a note, which reads in part, "My only great regret about the whole project was my failure to recognize the central role you played in the whole enterprise. It was mean and unfair for him to give you such short shrift. My only defense was that he was so plausible in his role of "author." But I still should have been aware what was going on. Leona [Capeless] and I still regret his last trip to deliver *The People's Game.* I apologize for my lack of perception at the time.

69. Cordelia Candelaria, *Seeking the Perfect Game* (Westport, Connecticut: Greenwood Press, 1989), 112.

70. Charlie Vascellaro, e-mail to the author, December 30, 2002.

EPILOGUE: INTO THE FUTURE

1. Michael McCarthy, "$250M Ad Campaign Aims to Hit Homer," *USA Today,* April 3, 2001, sec. B, p. 3.

2. Robert Alvarado, telephone interview, April 29, 2004.

3. Ross Newhan, "Angels Make Argument for Selig's Perfect Plan, *Los Angeles Times,* November 15, 2002, sec. D, p. 12.

4. "Baseball Notes," *Los Angeles Times,* October 17, 2003, sec. D, p. 11.

5. "Jenkins Named Top Columnist," *Association for Women in Sports Media,* Spring 2002, 1.

6. Jane Leavy, *Sandy Koufax: A Lefty's Legacy* (New York: HarperCollins, 2002), back cover.

7. Carolyn G. Heilbrun, *Toward a Recognition of Androgyny* (New York: W. W. Norton, 1993), 145.

8. Theresa Cox, telephone interview, March 23, 2004.

9. E-mail from Elinor Nauen to the author, October 29, 2002.

10. Colette Dowling, *The Frailty Myth* (New York: Random House, 2000), 61.1

11. "Inside Pitch," *USA Today Baseball Weekly,* July 12–17, 2001, 3.

12. Merritt Clifton, "Relative Skill," *SABR-L Digest,* June 7–8, 2001. SABR-L@apple.ease.lsoft.com.

13. Michael Lewis, *Moneyball: The Art of Winning an Unfair Game* (New York: W. W. Norton, 2003).

14. Pam Postema and Gene Wojciechowski, *You've Got to Have Balls to Make it in This League* (New York: Simon and Schuster, 1992), 247.

15. Cox, telephone interview, March 23, 2004.

16. Keryann Cook, "Victories," *Women's Sports Foundation*, Spring 2004, 14.

17. Eric Enders, "Petroskey Shames Hall," *Elysian Fields Quarterly* 20, no. 3 (2003), 5.

18. E-mail from Elinor Nauen to the author, October 25, 2002.

19. E-mail from Tim Wiles to the author, October 30, 2002.

20. E-mail from Pete Peterson to the author, October 30, 2002.

21. E-mail from Aviva Kempner to the author, October 28, 2002.

Index

AAGBL. *See* All-American Girls Baseball League

Aaron, Henry (Hank), 56, 120, 178, 219

Aaron, Tommie, 178

Abenakis Base Ball Club, 20, 233

Adams, Margo, 64–65, 67–69

African Americans, 212; Baseball Annies and male players, 53–57; black press, 110; colleges, 113; owners, 177–79, 236; sportswriting on racism, 201–2; umpires, 252–53n. 19. *See also* Negro Leagues

African American women, 5, 233–34; fans, 34–35; professional players, 103, 105, 109–13

Afterman, Gene, 188

After the Game (video), 62–63

Ainsmith, Eddie, 106

Alexander, Clifford, 177

Alexander, Lisa, 219

Alfonso, Carlos, 152

All-American Girls Baseball League (AAGBL), 39, 97, 112–14, 118–19, 168, 212, 234, 235, 250n. 24. *See also League of Their Own, A*

Allentown Red Sox, 140–41

Allred, Gloria, 155

Al Somers School for Umpiring, 141

Alvarado, Linda, 182–85, 188, 220, 236

Alvarado, Robert, 217

Amateur Athletic Union, 99, 221

amateur baseball, 5–6, 79–80, 96, 123, 220–21; historical context, 81–83

American Childhood, An (Dillard), 82

American culture, 11, 37–38, 47

American Female Baseball Club, 233

American League, 54, 106

American Legion Baseball, 82–83, 86, 234, 235

American Women's Baseball Association (AWBA), 97, 236

Anaheim Angels, 64, 161, 217, 228–30

Anderson, Kristin M., 219

anti-miscegenation laws, 54

Ardell, Dan, 3

Ardell, Jean, xiii

Arizona Fall League, 151

Arlati, Angie, 211

Arlington, Lizzie, 105, 233

Arlt, William, 22

Ashburn, Richie, 76

Asinof, Eliot, 9–10

Association of Women in Sports Media (AWSM), 207–8, 219, 236

Atlantic Coast Conference Sportswriters Association, 197–98

Atlantic League, 105, 150

Auburn Phillies, 143–44

Austen, Jane, 16–17, 240n. 28

Australia, 100

Autry, Jackie, 230

Babe Ruth Birthplace and Baseball Center, 5

Babe Ruth League, 96

baby boom, 39

Baker, Constance, 204

Baker, Dusty, 94

Baker, Tina "Sweetbread," 20–23, 24, 25

Baldwin, Jeri, 80, 98

Ball, Bat and Bishop (Henderson), 14

Ball Four (Bouton), 52, 60, 67

ballparks, 30, 181, 223; beauty of, 8–9, 178

Baltimore Orioles, 39, 165–66, 205

Barber, Perry, 149–50

Barber, Red, 202

Barela, Julie, 95

Barnard College, 233
barnstorming, 103, 105, 115
Barrett, Pearl, 234
Barrow, Edward Grant, 105
Barzun, Jacques, 5
baseball: Abner Doubleday creation myth,
    8, 12, 13, 26, 106; ancient origins, 13–
    20, 102; feminine lineage, 10, 13–17, 19;
    religious metaphors, 26, 44–45, 50, 136
base ball, as term, 16–17
Base-Ball: How to Become a Player (Ward),
    19
Baseball: The Early Years (Seymour), 199
Baseball: The Golden Age (Seymour), 199
Baseball: The People's Game (Seymour),
    199, 213, 260n. 68
Baseball Andies, 129
Baseball Annies, xiv, 7, 51–78, 131–32,
    217–18; African American ballplayers
    and, 53–57; code of silence, 57–61; di-
    vorce and, 70–72; domestic violence
    and, 69–70; hierarchy of, 60, 66; law-
    suits, 66–67; mutual comfort and, 68–
    69; personal stories, 58–61; recognition
    and, 63–64; self-esteem and, 61–63;
    sexual assault and, 72–74; sexually
    transmitted diseases and, 67–68; sexual
    misconduct charges, 65–66; spring
    training and, 59–60; terms for, 52–53,
    60; violence by, 75–76, 244n. 5
Baseball Babylon (Gutman), 53, 70
Baseball (Burns), 212
baseball commissioners, 177; Landis, 55–
    56, 83, 109, 167, 234
Baseball (magazine), 32, 33, 194, 195
Baseball Reliquary, 157, 216
*Baseball's Natural: The Story of Eddie
    Waitkus* (Theodore), 76–77
"Baseball's Unfair to Women" (Swegman),
    199
Baseball Weekly, 46, 49
Baseball Writers Association of America
    (BWAA), 190, 197, 236
Basho, Renee, 80–81
Bass, Rick, 175
battery, 105, 106
Baxter, Isabel, 234

Bean, Billy, 125
Beane, Billy, 189, 223–24
Begley, Evelyn, 5, 237
*Behind the Mask: My Double Life in Base-
    ball* (Pallone), 156, 254n. 54
Belinsky, Bo, 58
Benson, Joel, 42
Berkow, Ira, 154
Berlage, Gai Ingham, 125
Berra, Yogi, 85
"Betty" (Baseball Annie), 58–63
Biaggi, Mario, 143
Bill Allington's All-Stars, 118
Bill Kinnamon Specialized Umpiring
    Training Course, 146
Binghamton Triplets, 141
Bisher, Furman, 120–21
Black, Don H., 115–16
Black, Ella, 30, 31–32, 45, 54, 192–94, 203,
    233
black colleges, 113
*Black Diamond: The Story of the Negro
    Baseball Leagues* (McKissack), 212
Black Pelicans, 110
Bleacher Banter, 47, 49–50
Bleacher Bums, 50
Blondes and Brunettes, 233
bloomers, 18, 106
Blue Birds (Japan), 119
Bo: Pitching and Wooing (Belinsky), 58
Bobby Sox Softball, 86, 89
Bob Davids Award, 5, 237
Boggs, Debbie, 69
Boggs, Wade, 64, 67–69
Borders, Ila Jane, 26, 89–95, 100, 126–34,
    223, 224, 236; on Duluth-Superior
    Dukes, 129–33, 237; effects of profes-
    sional play on, 131–32; on Madison
    Black Wolf, 133–34; on St. Paul Saints,
    128–29; trips to Japan, 225–26; value of
    accomplishments, 134–35; women crit-
    ics of, 133; on Zion Pioneerzz, 134
Borders, Phil, 89, 90, 91, 126
Boston Bloomer Girls, 105, 233
Boston Herald, 202–3
Boston Red Sox, 39, 56, 185, 227
Bouton, Bobbi, 58, 71

Bouton, Jim, 52, 58, 60, 65, 67
Bowa, Larry, 153
Boyd, Mike, 248n. 41
Boys of Summer, The (Kahn), 56
Bragan, Jimmy, 151
Brennan, Christine, 219
Brenner, Marie, 203, 213, 236
Bresnahan, Roger, 163
Brewer, Theresa, 51
Britton, Helene Hathaway Robison, 162–64, 234
Brooklyn Dodgers, 37, 228
Brooks-Moon, Renel, 219, 229
Brown, Bobby, 153
Brown, Robert W., 97–98
Bruce, Janet, 214
Bryant, Howard, 203
Buffalo Bisons, xiii, 181–82
Bull Durham, 15, 53, 58, 63, 227, 236
Burke, Glenn, 125
Burke, Kitty, 109
Burke, Mike, 42
Burns, Ken, 212
Butler, Dick, 154
Byrne, Charles, 32, 104

cable networks, 208–11
Cactus League (Arizona), 42–43
Cadiz, Trixie, 33
Calautti, Lucy, 6
Callahan, Chad, 101
Cameron, Lucille, 55
Campanis, Al, 176
Campbell, Helen Hannah, 116
Campbell, Nolan, 143–44
Canada, 100
Candelaria, Cordelia, 14, 214, 236
Cape Cod League, 150
Caple, Jim, 125, 226
Caray, Harry, 43
Carey, Max, 114
Carney, Mary, 30
Carolina League, 197
Carpenter, Bob, 108, 249n. 15
Cartwright, Alexander J., 12, 18
Center for the Study of Sport in Society, 218

Central Ontario Girls Baseball League, 100
Chadwick, Henry, 32–33, 36, 54, 193
Chamberlain, Will, 139
chaperones, 116
Chapman, Sam, 195
Chappell, Don, 143
Charleston, Oscar, 165
Chattanooga Lookouts, 109, 166–67
Chester, Hilda ("Brooklyn Foghorn"), 37, 40, 220
Chicago Bloomer Girls, 105
Chicago Colleens, 113
Chicago Cubs, 8, 42–43, 47–48, 117, 194, 227; fans, 36–38, 43–45; front office, 49–50, 180–81
Chicago Defender, 110
Chicago Shirley, 52
Chicago Storm, 80
Chicago White Sox, 42, 44, 127, 202; internships, 185–86; tryouts, 119–20
Chicago White Stockings, 233
Christian School League of Southern California, 91
Churchmack, Jean, 188
Cimunic, Doug, 128, 130
Cincinnati Reds, 166, 175, 236
Cincinnati Redstockings, 18, 31–32, 53–54, 103
civil rights law, 87, 143
class issues, 33–34
Clemens, Roger, 186
Clement, Amanda, 81–82, 138–40, 233
Clement, Hank, 139
Cleveland Bears, 96
Cleveland Indians, 188, 200, 235
Clifton, Merritt, 223
clothing, xiv–xv, 18; bloomers, 18, 106; feminine image, 112, 114–16; male baseball players, 9–10; vintage games, 24
coaches, 96–97
Cobb, Ty, 194
Colavito, Rocky, 45
Collins, Dorothy, 114
Colorado Rockies, 43, 182–85, 236
Colorado Silver Bullets, 5, 26, 96, 100, 121–26, 211, 220, 221, 236
Columbus Citizen-Journal, 141–42

Comiskey Field, 207; Disco Demolition Night, 179, 251n. 57

Connor, Kimberly Rae, 11

Convention for Women's Rights (Seneca Falls), 18

Coolidge, Calvin, 35

Coolidge, Grace Goodhue, 35

Cooney, Nancy, 208

Cooper, James Fenimore, 13

Cooperstown, 12–13, 26–27, 98, 226–27

Cooperstown Symposium on American Culture and Baseball, 219

Coors Brewing Company, 121, 123, 124

Coors Field, 183

Coretta Scott King Honor Book Award, 212

Cortesio, Ria, xiii, 157–60, 225, 230, 237

Coste, Chris, 130

Cox, Theresa, 5, 150, 156, 160, 222, 225

Cramer, Richard Ben, 34

Crandall, Otis (Doc), 70

cranks, 29–30

cronyism, 162, 179–81

Croteau, Julie, 88–89, 93, 121

Dagavarian, Debbi, 46

Daisy-Clippers, 81

D'Angelo, Josephine "Jojo," 117

Daniel, Dan, 37

date rape, 72

Daugherty, Paul, 176

Davis, Gerry, 253n. 34

Dean, Paul "Daffy," 109

Debono, Paul, 34–35, 164–65

Deitweiler, Helen, 234

De La Cruz, Ruddi, 73

Demaree, Al, 57

De Podesta, Paul, 189

Desmond, Connie, 199–200

Detroit Tigers, 38, 194, 204–5

Dettweiler, Helen, 195

de Varona, Donna, 83

DeWitt, Chris, 131

Diamonds Are a Girl's Best Friend: Women Writers on Baseball (Nauen), 9, 212, 222, 236

Diamonds in the Desert baseball conference, 223

Diaz, Mike, 152

Dickson, Paul, 255n. 2

Didrikson, Mildred "Babe," 109, 234

DiMaggio, Joe, 37, 94

Disco Demolition Night, 179, 251n. 57

Dolly Vardens, 103, 233

domestic violence, 69–70

Donahue, Margaret, 166, 234

Doolittle, Mrs., 138, 233

Doubleday, Abner, 8, 12, 13, 26, 106

Doubleday Field, 8, 12, 98

Dowling, Colette, 135, 222

Downey, Mike, 154

Dreyfuss, Florence Wolf, 234

Driskoll, Melvin, 156–57

Duluth-Superior Dukes, 129–33, 237

Dunlap, Sonny, 249n. 11

Dunn, Jack, 165–66

Dunn, Jack, III, 166

Dunn, Mary, 165–66

Eagleton, Tom, 36

Ebbets, Charles H., 34

Ebbets Field, 37

Eckstein, David, 228, 229, 230

Ed Carr's Traveling All-Stars, 106, 234

Education Amendments of 1972, 87. See also Title IX

Edwards, Harry, 177

Egyptian tombs, 14

Eight Men Out (Asinof), 9–10

Ellis, Bill, 166

Elston and Me: The Story of the First Black Yankee (Howard), 213

Elysian Fields (Hoboken, New Jersey), 12

Emaneth, Lexie, 98

Emery, Jim, 147

Enders, Eric, 227

Engel, Eleanor, 235

Englewood Orioles, 86

English 494: Baseball Fiction (Candelaria), 214

Ephron, Nora, 144

Equal Employment Opportunity Commission (EEOC), 155

Erstad, Darin, 228, 229

Esom, Cecilia (Cece), 47, 49

Esslinger, Rolland, 90–91
Euripides, 16
Evans, Dan, 185–86, 187, 189
Evans, Jim, 157

"Fair Fans 'Crash' Ball Games, Cheer Plays" (Shelland), 36
fans, 8–9, 220; adult introduction to baseball, 47–50; African American women, 34–35; American culture and, 37–38, 47; attraction for male players, 31–34, 45–46; class issues, 33–34; cranks, 29–30; early ambivalence toward, 28–29; economic need for, 31, 33, 34; first ladies of baseball, 35–36; gender differences, 9–10; Hilda Chester Award, 216; inspired by players, 46–47; marketing to, 39, 41, 111, 217; outspoken, 45–46; percentage of women, 6, 33, 42, 181, 217; protection of women as concern, 29–33; teenagers, 45–47; television, 39; women as distraction, 30–31, 36; women in sports as, 41–42; women's movement (1960s) and, 39–40. See also Ladies' Day
Fargo-Moorhead Redhawks, 129, 130
farm system, 108–9
Federal League, 163
Feeney, Chub, 180
Feeney, Katy, 162, 180
feminine image of players, 112, 114–16
Feminine Mystique, The (Friedan), 39–40
feminism, xiv, 146, 224–25
Ferber, Edna, 9
fertility rites, 14–16
Fields, Wilma, 48–49
films, 4, 45, 215, 237. See also Bull Durham; League of Their Own, A
Fink, Marc, 192
Finley, Charlie, 41
first ladies of baseball, 35–36
Fisk, Carlton, 9
Fitz, Geri Lisa, 124
Florida State League, 120–21, 152
Fombona, Alicia, 46–47
Ford, Gerald, 86
Fornoff, Bill, 205

Fornoff, Susan, 68, 205–7, 208, 213, 236
Foster, La'Leta, 7
Foul Ball! Five Years in the American League (Gordon), 212–13
Fox Sports Net, 210
Frailty Myth, The (Dowling), 135, 222
Freeman, Harry H., 104
Freeman's Female Base Ball Club, 104
Frick, Ford, 141
Friedan, Betty, 39–40
front office, xv, 161–62, 166, 218, 229, 234, 255n. 2; cronyism in, 162, 179–81; Hispanic women in, 182–85; Los Angeles Dodgers, 187–89; minorities and, 176–77. See also owners

Gaea, 15
Galvin, Maureen, 141
game cards, 138
Garagiola, Audrie, 4
Garagiola, Joe, 4, 155
Garber, Mary, 197–98, 211, 234
Gardner, Pam, 185
Gardner, Tike, 80
Garvey, Steve, 74
Gehrig, Lou, 109
Geneva Rangers, 143
Gera, Bernice "Bernie," 11, 141–46, 152, 224, 225, 235, 252n. 18
Giamatti, A. Bartlett, 134, 153
Gibson, Bob, 40, 201
Gibson, Charline, 40, 201–2, 218, 235
Gietschier, Steven P., 213–14, 228, 260n. 64
Girl Within, The (Hancock), 10–11
Gisolo, Margaret, 83, 109, 234
Glaser, Lulu, 33
Glennie, Jim, 79–80, 96–101, 221, 236, 248n. 41
Glick, David, 131
Glickman, Marty, 199
Gmelch, George, 68
goddesses, 15
God's Country and Mine (Barzun), 5
Golden State Conference, 92–93
Goldfarb, Phyllis, 69–70
Gonzalez, Milton, 73, 74
Goodwin, Doris Kearns, 10, 213

Gordon, Alison, 207, 212, 236
Gottlieb, Ed, 168
Grace, Mark, 49
Grayson Stadium, 178
Great and Only Young Ladies Base Ball
    Club, 102–3
Great Baseball Tournament of September
    1867, 29, 233
Great Black Swamp Frogs, 24
Great Depression, 108–9, 110, 166, 195,
    198
Great Lakes Women's Baseball League, 98
Greek culture, 15–16
Green, Dallas, 180
Green, Edith Starrett, 87
Green, Vanalyne, 9, 10, 12, 42, 47, 215, 236
Greenberg, Hank, 38–39
Gregorich, Barbara, 212
Grimm, Charlie, 117
Gross, Jane, 213
Grubbs, Rosie, 121
Guerrero, Lisa, 210–11
Guillen, Pat, 93
Gutman, Dan, 53, 70
Guttmann, Allen, 14, 15, 240n. 30

Haller, Jodi, 93
Hall of Fame game, 153–54
Hamilton, Earl, 106
Hamman, Ed, 145
Hammerstein, Stella, 33–34
Hampton, Patty Palmer Cox, 180–81, 235
Hancock, Emily, 10–11
Harry Wendelstedt School for Umpires,
    137, 149, 157
Hartigan, Carmella, 49–50
Hartmayer, Doug, 144
Havenor, Agnes Malley, 234
Hawkins, Kimberly, 121
Hayden, Ron, 50
Heaphy, Leslie, 4–5, 212
Heilbrun, Carolyn G., 19, 63, 84, 219–20
Heitz, Tom, 14, 23–24
Hemond, Roland, 6, 188
Henderson, Robert W., 14, 16
Herman, Babe, 109
Hess, Max, Jr., 140–41

Heward, Bill, 145
Higgins, Scott, 158
Hilda Chester Award, 216
Himmelberg, Michele, 207–8, 236
Hines, Paul, 45
Hispanics, 182–85, 236, 257n. 53
Hodges, Russ, 202
Hofmann, Jeane, 195–97, 234
Hogan, Lawrence, 167
Holland, Marcus, 179
Holtzman, Jerome, 207
Holway, John, 169
*Home Games: Two Baseball Wives Speak
    Out* (Bouton and Marshall), 71
homophobia, 124–25, 155–56, 203, 226.
    See also lesbians
Hope, Bob, 120–21, 123, 125, 221
Hope, Major, 120–21
Hopkins, Lollie ("Hub's No. 1 Howler"),
    37
Hornsby, Rogers, 105
Houghton, Edith, 107–8, 234, 249n. 15
House, Tom, 71, 72
House of David teams, 109, 110
Howard, Arlene, 213
Howard, Nat, 200
Huckshorn, Kristin, 207, 236
Huggins, Miller, 163
Hurley, Christine, 185, 188

Indianapolis ABCs, 34–35, 164–65, 234
Indianapolis ABCs, The (Debono), 164–65
Indianapolis Clowns, 5, 79, 111–12, 145,
    235
Inside Pitch (Gmelch), 68
International Baseball Federation Women's
    World Cup, 221
International Women's Baseball Tourna-
    ment, 100
Israeloff, Roberta, 51
"Ivory Hunter" (Ravage), 25–26

Jackie Robinson Foundation Sports Man-
    agement scholarship, 185
Jackson, Jackie, 120
Jackson, Reggie, 177, 206
Jacobs, Paul Q., 182

January Party, 50
Japan, 94, 106–8, 119, 149, 225–26, 235
Jenkins, Sally, 219
Jeter, Derek, 45, 186, 211
Jewish ballplayers, 38
Jim Evans Academy of Professional Umpiring, 137, 156–57, 158
Jim Finley's National Sports Academy, 141
Jock's Itch, The: The Fast-Track Private World of the Professional Ballplayer (House), 71
Joe, You Coulda Made Us Proud (Pepitone), 58
Joe DiMaggio: The Hero's Life (Cramer), 34
Johnson, Jack, 54–55, 244n. 12
Johnson, Mamie "Peanut," 79, 112
Johnson, Susan E., 117, 212
Jones, Chipper, 71
Jones, Karin, 71
Jones, Tommy, 122
Jordan, Pat, 127–28
Judge and Jury: The Life and Times of Judge Kenesaw Mountain Landis (Pietrusza), 55–56
Jurges, Bill, 75
Justice, David, 186

Kahn, Roger, 56–57
Kamenshek, Dottie, 117
Kansas City Monarchs, 5, 112, 168, 235
Kansas City Monarchs Champions of Baseball (Bruce), 214
Kansas City Royals, 36, 41
Karlen, Neal, 129
Kekich, Mike, 203
Kempner, Aviva, 45, 215, 229, 237
Kilchesty, Albert, 157
Killebrew, Harmon, 222–23
Kind of Grace, A: A Treasury of Sportswriting by Women (Rapoport), 212
Kindred, Dave, 125–26, 177
King, Billie Jean, 221
Kirwin, Bill, 41
Knepper, Bob, xv, 154, 254n. 46
Knickerbocker Base Ball Club of New York, 12, 29, 138, 233
Knoblauch, Ray, 150
Kono, Shigeko, 119

Kook, Shanna, xiii, 160, 225, 230, 237
Koufax, Sandy, 226
Krafft-Ebbing, Richard, 20
Krisley, Michael, 186–87
Kroc, Joan, 154, 236
Kuhn, Bowie, 36, 204
Kuhn, Luisa, 36
Ku Klux Klan, 54, 164
Kurys, Sophie, 114, 116

Lacy, Sam, 56
Ladies' Day, 32, 34, 41, 166, 193, 233, 235, 241n. 11, 242n. 21; 1929 Cubs game, 36–37
Ladies Professional Golf Association, 221
Lady Diamonds, 24
Lady in the Locker Room: Uncovering the Oakland Athletics (Fornoff), 213
Landis, Kenesaw Mountain, 55–56, 83, 109, 167, 234
Lapchick, Richard, 218
Lasorda, Tommie, 180
Laurel Base Ball Club, 20, 233
lawsuits, 11, 85, 86, 216; locker room access, 204, 235; Title IX, 88–89, 225; umpires, 151, 155, 156
League of Their Own, A, 4, 13, 100, 113, 121, 236, 249n. 22. *See also* All-American Girls Baseball League
Leathers, Stephanie, 47
Leatherstocking Base Ball Club, 20–23
Leatherstocking Tales (Cooper), 13
Leavy, Jane, 212, 219, 226
Lee, Bert, Jr., 199
Legg, Phoebe, 7
Leibovitz, Annie, 135
Leisure, George S., Jr., 143
Lemon, Brendan, 124–25
lesbians, 20, 116–17, 124. *See also* homophobia
Levant, Jerry, 44
Levant, Lil, 8, 37–39, 43–45
Levant, Rhoda, 44
Levy, Frances, 166
Lewis, Michael, 224
Lewis, Thomas, 177–78
Lewis, Tracy, 177–79, 236

Lieberman, Gary, 146
Life and Times of Hank Greenberg, The (Kempner), 45, 215, 229, 237
Lincoln, Melissa Ludtke. *See* Ludtke, Melissa
literature, baseball, 191, 201; biographies and histories, 211–13; fiction, 214–15
Little League Baseball, 11, 89–90, 234; exclusion of girls, 83–86; hiding gender identity, 83–85; umpires, 5, 148
Littlewood, Mike, 134, 135
lobbyists, 6
locker room access, 190–91, 198, 204–5, 235
Lo Duca, Paul, 187
Lofton, Kenny, 228
Longfellow, Henry Wadsworth, 17
Loop Legal Women's Softball League, 47
Lopez, Al, 257n. 53
Los Angeles Dodgers, 187–89, 226
Louis, Joe, 55
Ludtke, Melissa (Lincoln), 204, 213, 235
Lukasik, Sue, 88–89
Lupiano, Donna, 202
Lyle, Marcenia. *See* Stone, Toni
lynching, 55

Mack, Connie, 117, 200
Madison Black Wolf, 133–34
Madison Square Garden, 108
Major League Baseball (MLB): Baseball Annies and, 53, 57, 69–70, 77; farm system, 108–9; first female assistant general manager, 185; Initiative on Women and Baseball, 217; integration of, 111, 113, 168–69; marketing, 39, 41; women in, 126–34; women's influence on, 223–24
Major League Baseball Radio, 99
Malamud, Bernard, 76
managers, 163, 176, 178, 181, 185; Yankees, 186–89
Manhattan Athletic Club, 102–3, 125
Manley, Abe, 167, 169
Manley, Effa, 167–69
Mann Act, 54–55
Mantle, Mickey, 51–52

Man Who Invented Baseball, The (Peterson), 14
Marge Schott: Unleashed (Bass), 175
Maris, Roger, 200
Marshall, Nancy, 71
Marshall, Penny, 4, 13, 236
Martin, Billy, 2
Martinez, Pedro, 127
Martini, Anita, 202, 235
Maude, the pet blonde, 53–54, 241n. 7
Mayer, Bernadette, 9
Mazmanian, Nancy, 161
McCabe, Charles, 142
McCarthy, Joe, 195
McCormick, Michele, 85
McCourt, Frank, 189
McCourt, Jamie, 189
McCrone, Kathleen E., 19
McGraw, John J., 1–2
McGuane, Thomas, 191
McKissack, Patricia, 212
McNamara, Vincent M., 142
McSherry, John, 150, 157, 177
"Medical and Scientific Debate on Women's Sports, The" (McCrone), 19
Mediterranean Baseball League, 125
Medwick, Joe "Ducky," 109
Mehrer, Darlene, 97–98, 236
memorabilia, 13
Mendenhall, Rebecka, 60
Mercer, George "Winnie," 32
Merhige, Phyllis, 162
Michigan Stars, 79, 96, 98
Midwest League, 147–48
military teams, 108
Miller, Cheryl, 88
Miller, Ernestine, 5
Miller, Nancy, 145, 235
Mills, Dorothy Seymour, 213–14, 223, 235. *See also* Seymour, Dorothy
Mills, Roy, 213
Mills Commission, 106
Milwaukee Brewers, 234
Minaya, Omar, 257n. 53
Minnesota Twins, 6
minorities: front office and, 176–77. *See also* African Americans; Hispanics

minor leagues, 11–12, 68, 120, 137, 181. *See also individual teams*
Mitchell, Jackie, 109, 234
Mitchell, Jerry, 201
Mitchem, Shannon, 123
Mizerak, Steve, 196–97
Moneyball (Lewis), 224
Monsky, Robin, 177
Montreal Royals, 168
Moran, Sheila, 203
Morgan, Connie, 112, 235
Morioka, Juri, 218
Morris, Carolyn, 114
Morris, Peter, 241n. 11
Moschetti, Joe, 89, 90
Moss, Barry, 128
Mota, Manny, 184
Moyer, Jamie, 251n. 56
Mullane, Tony, 31–32
Murdoch, Rupert, 188–89, 226
Murphy, Margaret, 166
Murphy, Mary, 166
Murray, Bill, 127
Muskegon Lassies, 116

Nardone, Denise, 96
Nardone, Jessica, 96
National Amateur Baseball Federation, 82
National Amateur Playground Association of the United States, 82
National Association of Baseball Leagues (NABL), 142–43
National Baseball Hall of Fame and Museum, 8, 12–14, 26; Women in Baseball exhibit, 26, 169, 227
National Baseball Hall of Fame Library, 4, 12, 14, 31, 113
National League, 163–64, 192
National Organization for Women, 88, 144, 254n. 46
National Women's Baseball Association, 98
Natural, The (Malamud), 58, 76
Nauen, Elinor, 9, 212, 222, 228–29, 236
Navratilova, Martina, 187

Negro Leagues, 5, 56; American, 109–11, 235; decline of, 111; National, 34–35, 163; owners, 167–69; professional teams, 105; white promoters in, 168
Negro Leagues, 1869–1890 (Heaphy), 212
Neil, Ray, 112
Nelson, Maud, 105, 106, 234
Newark Eagles, 167–69
Newcombe, Don, 169
New Jersey Nemesis, 87
Newman, Roberta, 5
New Orleans Creoles, 111
New Orleans Pelicans, 31
Newton, Anna, 42
New York Baseball Writers Association, 196
New York Bloomer Girls, 37, 108
New York Giants, 1–2, 30, 31, 33–35, 39
New York Human Rights Commission, 41, 235
New York Mets, 59, 65, 72–74, 144–45, 150, 228, 235
New York–Penn League, 143–44
New York State Human Rights Commission, 143
New York Yankees, 2, 109, 204, 235; assistant general manager, 186–89; fans, 39, 42
Ng, Kim, 185–89, 218, 236, 237
Nice Tuesday, A (Jordan), 128
Niekro, Phil, 121–22, 220
Nine Spring Training Conference, 219
Nissan Pearls, 119
Nixon, Richard M., 201
Northanger Abbey (Austen), 16–17, 240n. 28
Northern League, xiii, 121–22; Borders and, 127–34
Northern League All-Stars, 122
Northwest League, 146
Norworth, Jack, 28, 35
"No Wonder Indians Look Better" (Mitchell), 201

Oakland A's, 41, 59, 205–6, 223–24
O'Brien, Eileen "Moose," 20, 24
Ocala Lightning, 79, 80, 98
O'Donnell, Doris, 198, 200–201, 235
Oh, Sadaharu, 94

Ohio Village Muffins, 24
Oklahoma City 89ers, 180, 235
O'Neill, J. Palmer, 192
Osder, Elizabeth, 86
Ott, Mary ("St. Louis Screecher"), 37
Our Sports, 112
Overmeyer, James, 167
Owens, Bob, 131
owners, 161–62, 164–66, 234; African
    Americans, 177–79, 236; amateur base-
    ball, 80; Hispanic women, 182–85, 236;
    Negro Leagues, 164–65; through inher-
    itance, 162–63. *See also* front office
Oxford University Press, 199, 260n. 64

Pacific Coast League, 37, 152
Paige, Satchel, 167
Palermo, Pete, 66
Pallone, Dave, 124, 154, 155–56, 254n. 54
Pannozzo, Sharon, 185
Parker, Sonja "Wishbone," 20, 24
Parker, Wes, 209
Parkin, Cy, 139
Passaic Girls, 108
Payson, Joan, 183
Peebles, Betty, 196–97
Pepitone, Joe, 58
Perabo, Susan, 93
Percival, Troy, 126
Perry, Claudia, 4
Peters, Frank, 146
Peterson, Fritz, 203
Peterson, Harold, 14
Peterson, Pete, 229
Petroskey, Dale, 227
Petty, Leslie, 123
Philadelphia Bobbies, 106–8, 234
Philadelphia Phillies, 48, 108, 234
Philadelphia Strikers, 98
Phillips, Adolpho, 45
Phillips, Charlie, 93, 95
Phillips, Steve, 74
physical culture, 18–20
Pietrusza, David A., 35, 55
Pilot Field, 181
Pilson, Neal, 217
Piniella, Lou, 176, 251n. 56

pink notes, 60
pitchers, 126–28, 223. *See also* Borders, Ila
    Jane; *individual pitchers*
Pittsburgh Alleghenies, 192
Pittsburgh Courier, 110
Pittsburgh Pirates, 228
plagiarism, 213–14
Players' Association, 69–70, 77
Players' League, 192–94
Playing the Field: Sports and Sex in America
    (documentary), 77
Pollock, Syd, 111–12
Polonia, Luis, 66–67, 68, 72
Postema, Pam, xiii, xiv, xv, 5, 52, 137, 151–
    57, 235; autobiography, 11–12, 137–38,
    155, 213; feminism and, 224, 225; law-
    suit against MLB, 11, 155, 156; on re-
    quirements for women umpires, 137
Powell, Abner, 31
Power, Victor Pellot, 57
power hitting, 117, 223
press, black, 110
press box, 194–98, 200–201, 207, 219
Prieb, Wendy Selig, 218
Professional Baseball Umpires Course, 158
professional players, 221; African Amer-
    ican women, 103, 105, 109–13; early
    games, 102–3; exhibitions, 102–4; femi-
    nine image, 112, 114–16; international
    travel, 106–8; lesbians, 116–17; as scan-
    dalous, 104, 105. *See also* All-American
    Girls Baseball League; Borders, Ila
Professional Umpire Development Pro-
    gram, 151, 155, 157
promoters, Victorian era, 18–19
prostitution, 30, 54–55, 104
public-address announcers, 219
Puerto Rican players, 57

"Queen of the Diamond" (Chamberlain),
    139
Quinn, Bob, 176

Racial and Gender Report Card, 218
Racine Belles, 114, 115
radio broadcasts, 35, 99, 202
Randall, Steven, 92

rape, 72–74
Rapoport, Ron, 212
Ravage, Jessie "Outlaw," "Jackrabbit," 20, 22–26
Rawlings award, 180
Red Sox (Japan), 119
Reese, Jimmie, 57
Reese, R., 55
Referee, 146, 148, 155
Regalia, Wendie, 202, 235
religion, patriarchal, 63
religious metaphors, 26, 44–45, 50, 136
Rich, Mindy, xiii, 181–82
Rich, Robert E., Jr., 181
Richardson, Dot, 85
Rickart, Lloyd, 242n. 21
Rickey, Branch, 34, 56, 169, 196
Rike, Eleanor, 166–67
Riley, James A., 111
Riley, Richard W., 87
"Rise of Baseball to 1890, The" (Seymour), 199
Rivera, Mariano, 186
Rizzuto, Phil, 127
Robbins, Tim, 227
Roberts, Doris, 216
Roberts, Morganna, 40–41
Roberts, Ruth, 51
Robinson, Jackie, 9, 56, 86, 113, 168–69, 201, 226
Robinson, Rachel, 9
Robison, Frank deHaas, 162
Robison, M. Stanley, 162–63
Rockford Peaches, 117
Rodgers, Debbie, 121
Rodriguez, Alex, 211
Rogers, Susan Fox, 212
Rone, Kris, 188
Rookie Development program, 74
Roosevelt, Franklin Delano, 37
Rosario, Vicente, 72–73
Rose, Pete, 40, 70, 243n. 56
Rosellini, Lynn, 203
Rosie the Riveter, 39
rounders, 12
Ruffler, Kevin, 152
Ruth, Babe, 57, 67, 108, 109, 165

Sabo, Tim, 176
Samonds, Shereen, 122
San Diego Padres, 204–5, 236
Sandlin, Davis (Sandy), 167
Sandy Koufax: A Lefty's Legacy (Leavy), 219
San Francisco Giants, 219, 227–28
San Francisco Sea Lions, 110, 235
Sarandon, Susan, 53, 227
Saskatchewan Major Baseball League, 94–95
Satriano, Gina, 121
Savannah Cardinals, 178, 236
Schlachweiler, Rudie, 9
Schott, Marge Unnewehr, 175–77, 178, 183, 220, 236
Schroeder, Dottie, 117
Schueler, Carey, 126
Schueler, Ron, 126
Scioscia, Mike, 228
scorers, 194, 233
Scott, Marty, 128
scouts, 26, 108, 126, 234
"Scribes and Mike Men" (Ravage), 25–26
Scully, Vin, 64, 190–91, 199, 210, 211–12
Seattle Mariners, 251n. 56
Seattle Pilots, 67
second basemen, 223
security staff, 60
See, Larry, 130
Seeking the Perfect Game: Baseball in American Literature (Candelaria), 14, 214, 236
Sekiura, Shinichi, 119
self-esteem, 10–11, 61–63, 239n. 8
Selig, Bud, 218, 229
Selig-Prieb, Wendy, 218, 237
Sells, Ken, 114, 116
seventh-inning stretch, 43, 217
sexual deviance, 19–20
sexuality, baseball terms, 77. *See also* Baseball Annies
sexually transmitted diseases, 67–68
Seymour, Dorothy, 12, 20, 29, 81, 198–200, 235, 260n. 64. *See also* Mills, Dorothy Seymour
Seymour, Harold, 12, 20, 29, 81, 198–99, 235; plagiarism, 213–14

Shah, Diane K., 212
Shane, Mary, 202, 235
Shantz, Bobby, 127
Shaughnessy Playoffs, 114
Shelland, Harry, 36
Sherwood, Martha, 23, 24
She's on First (Gregorich), 212
Shirley, Steve, 132
Shrine of the Eternals, 157
Shut Out: A Story of Race and Baseball in Boston (Bryant), 203
Siegal, Justine, 96, 98–100, 214, 221, 225, 237
Singer, Bill, 218
"Sin of Kicking, The" (Chadwick), 32–33
Sioux Falls Canaries, 130
Sixty Minutes, 130
Smith, Claire, 205, 208
Smith, Janet Marie, 6, 7
Smith, Red, 37
Society for American Baseball Research (SABR), 4–5, 42, 46, 95, 149, 219, 225, 237
"Sociological Analysis of the Current Sub-culture of Women's Baseball, A" (Siegal), 214
softball, 82, 88, 95, 108
Solomon, Jack, 37
Solomon, Lilyan, 37–39
Some Are Called Clowns (Heward), 145
Somers, Al, 152
songs: "The Base Ball Fever," 29; "I Love Mickey," 51; "Meet the Mets," 216; "Take Me Out to the Ball Game," 25, 28–29, 32, 33, 43, 50, 216–17
Sontag, Susan, 135
South Atlantic League, 178
South Bend Blue Sox, 117
Southern California College, 92–93
Southern California College Vanguards, xiii, 92–93
Southern Conference Sportswriters Association, 197
Southern League, 151
Spalding, Albert G., 12
Spangler, Nettie Gans, 106–7
Sparks, Terry, 80

Spartan women, 15–16
Spelius, George, 158
Spink, C. C. Johnson, 120
Spink, J. G. Taylor, 199
sponsorship, 98, 125, 221–22
Sporting Life, 30, 104, 192, 233
Sporting News, 37, 120, 141, 176, 177, 186
Sporting Writers Association, 194
sportscasting, 199–202, 235; cable networks, 208–9. *See also* sportswriting
Sportsdykes (Rogers), 212
Sports Illustrated, 133, 204
Sportsman's Park, 31, 34
sportswriting, 18, 25, 219, 236; Baseball Annies and, 57; beat reporting, 191, 202–3; birth of, 191–92; locker room access, 190–91, 198, 204–5, 235; new approaches, 203; organizations, 197–98; pioneers, 192–94, 257–58n. 3; press box, 194–98, 207; on racism, 201–2; trivialization of, 196–97; on women as distraction, 30–31. *See also* sportscasting
Spy in the House That Ruth Built, A (Green), 10, 215, 236
"Stags Keep Doris Out Of Yank Press Box" (O'Donnell), 201
Star Bloomer Girls, 105
Steinbrenner, George, 186–87
Steinem, Gloria, 64
Steinhagen, Ruth Ann, 75–77
Steward, Elaine Weddington, 185, 188, 236
stick and ball games, 12, 13–16, 81, 240n. 30
sticks and stones games, 14
St. Louis Black Broncos, 233–34
St. Louis Browns, 34, 242n. 21
St. Louis Cardinals, 234
Stone, Toni, 5, 109–13, 235
stoolball, 12, 16
St. Paul Saints, 127–28, 129
Strawberry, Darryl, 74–75, 127
Street, Gabby, 110
Strike, George, 175
Strom, Brent, 152
Suarez, Anthony, 73, 74
Sun Sox, 120–21, 122
Supreme Court, 88, 162

Sure-Pops, 81
Swegman, Gloria, 190, 211

Take Our Daughters to Work Day, 64
Take Time for Paradise (Giamatti), 134
taking the field, as term, 23
Tavarez, Natividad, 73, 74
Tavris, Carol, 9
Taylor, Ben, 164, 165
Taylor, Charles Isham (C. I.), 34–35, 164
Taylor, Olivia, 164–65, 234
Tenille, Toni, 9
Tennyson, Brittany, 43
Tennyson, Phil, 43
Terry, Donna, 84
testicular knowledge, 202
Theodore, John, 76–77
Thomas, Helen, 201, 235
Thomas, Lucille, 234
Thomson, Bobby, 227–28
Thorn, John, 239n. 13
Tiritilli, Barbara, 119–20
Title IX, 23, 41, 86–91, 120, 159, 222, 225, 235
Tokyo Stars, 119
tomboys, 5, 10–11, 17, 19–20, 226
Tootle, James R., 24
toppers, 105
Toronto Blue Jays, 134, 224
Tousent, Jose Brea, 73, 74
town ball, 12, 17, 20–24
Trezza, Betty, 114
Truman, Bess, 36
Truman, Margaret, 36
tryouts, 119–20

Ueberroth, Peter, 97, 153, 177, 205
umpires, xiv, xv, 5, 230, 237; African American, 252–53n. 19; early days, 138–40; gay male, 155–56; harassment of, 137, 140, 142, 148; lawsuits, 151, 156; minor leagues, 11–12, 137; physical demands on, 136–37, 147, 159, 252n. 18; promotion, 147; requirements for success, 137; in youth and amateur baseball, 148–51. *See also* Gera, Bernice; Postema, Pam; Wren, Christine

USA Baseball, 221
USA Today Baseball Weekly, 100–101, 222

Vahanian, Tilla, 41–42
Valentine, Harry, 180
Valenzuela, Fernando, 46–47
Valli, Violet, 75
Vander Meer, Johnny, 166
Vargo, Ed, 156
varsity sports, 86
Vascellaro, Charlie, 214–15
Vassar College, 20, 35, 81, 233
Veeck, Mike, 127 28, 129, 131; Disco Demolition Night, 179, 251n. 57
Veeck, Rebecca, 129
Veeck, William L. "Bill," Jr., 42, 120, 127, 166, 179, 251n. 57
Victorian Baseball Association, 100
Victorian era, 17–19
Vignola, Trish, 219
Vintage Base Ball Association, 24
vintage games/variants of baseball, 20 24, 136, 239n. 13

Wagner, Rick, 132
Waitkus, Eddie, 75–77
Wait till Next Year (Goodwin), 10, 213
Waldman, Suzyn, 209–10, 236, 237
Walker, Moses Fleetwood, 54
Walker, Welday, 54
Wallace, Mike, 130
Wambsganss, Bill, 35
Ward, John Montgomery, 19, 192
Ware, Julie Zeller, 5, 148–49
Washington Metropolitan Women's Baseball League (WMBL), 5, 79, 96
Washington Senators, 11, 32, 35, 41
Weaver, Earl, 205, 207
Weil, Sidney, 166
Weiss, Alta, 233
Weiss, George, 56–57, 166
Welke, Tim, 152
Wells, David, 186
When Women Played Hardball (Johnson), 117, 213
White, Bill, 182
White, Laura, 202–3

Whittier Christian High School, 91–92
Whittier Christian Junior High School, 90–91
"Why I Love Baseball" (Tavris), 9
Wife's Guide to Baseball, A (Gibson), 40, 201–2, 235
Wiles, Tim, 229
Williams, Ann, 122–23
Williams, Elisha Green, 233
Wilpon, Fred, 73
Winston-Salem Cardinals, 197
Winter, Joanne, 114, 116
Wojciechowski, Gene, 155
Woman's Work, A: Writing Baseball History with Harold Seymour (Mills), 198, 213, 237
Women (Leibovitz and Sontag), 135

Women at Play: The Story of Women in Baseball (Gregorich), 212
Women in Baseball Committee (SABR), 4–5
Women in Baseball exhibit, 26, 169, 227
women in sports, 41–42
Women's Baseball League, Inc., 96
Women's Baseball League (WBL), 96, 98–99, 237
Women's Baseball League's Umpire Association, 225
women's colleges, 81
women's leagues, 221–22
women's movement, 17–19, 39–40, 144, 146
Women's National Basketball Association (WNBA), 221
Women's National Team, 221

women's sports, origins, 14–16
Women's Sports Foundation, 86, 225
Women's Suffrage Base-ball Club, 20
Women's Tennis Association, 221
Women's United Soccer Association (WUSA), 221
World Children's Baseball Fair, 94, 226
World Series: 1908, 49, 194; 1920, 35; 1924, 35; 1945, 38; 1951, 228; 1960, 228; 1973, 59; 1984, 204–5; 1986, 228; 1987, 229; 1989, 209; 1990, 175; 1993, 106; 2002, 229–30; front office and, 161; Negro Leagues, 1946, 168
World War I, 163
World War II, 39, 113–14, 168, 195
Wren, Christine, 147–48, 152, 224, 225, 235, 253n. 34
Wright, Charlene, 87
Wrigley, Philip K., 97, 114–15, 168
Wrigley Field, 43–45, 47–48
Wrigleyville Tap, 50

Yankee Stadium, 37, 196
Yawkey, Jean, 236
Yawkey, Tom, 56
Young, Dick, 70
Young, Ina Eloise, 33, 194–95, 203, 233
Young Ladies Base Ball Club, 104, 125, 233
youth leagues, 82–83, 100–101; umpires, 148–49. *See also* Little League
You've Got to Have Balls to Make It in This League (Postema), 11–12, 137–38, 213

Zander, Dorothy Jane. *See* Mills, Dorothy Seymour; Seymour, Dorothy
Zelasko, Jeanne, 229

Jean Hastings Ardell is a freelance writer whose work has appeared in *The Cooperstown Symposium on Baseball and American Culture: 2003–2004* anthology, *Diamonds Are a Girl's Best Friend: Women Writers on Baseball* (edited by Elinor Nauen), *Growing Up with Baseball: How We Loved and Played the Game* (edited by Gary Land), *Elysian Fields Quarterly*, the *Los Angeles Times*, the *Sporting News*, and *Nine: A Journal of Baseball History and Culture*. Her paper "Left-hander Ila Borders: Crossing Baseball's Gender Line from Little League to the Northern League" earned the 1999 SABR/*USA Today Baseball Weekly* Award for Research. She lives with her husband, Daniel Ardell, in Corona del Mar, California, and roots for the Los Angeles Angels of Anaheim.

Other Books in the Writing Baseball Series